The Family
Legal Advisor

The Family

Legal Advisor

A Clear, Reliable
and Up-to-date Guide
to Your Rights
and Remedies Under the Law

Edited by
ALICE K. HELM, LL.B., J.D.

Assisted by:
Allen H. Brill
Kenneth Birnbaum

Foreword by

Theodore R. Kupferman, LL.B.,
Justice, Supreme Court, Appellate Division

Bobley Publishing   WOODBURY, NEW YORK 11797

Designed by: HAROLD FRANKLIN
Illustrations by: ARIE HAAS

Library of Congress Catalogue Card Number:
73-93374

MANUFACTURED IN THE UNITED STATES OF AMERICA.

About This Book

The primary goal of *The Family Legal Advisor* is to give you an understanding of the law as it touches the daily life of an average family. As tenant or landlord, borrower or lender, parent or child, as the maker of a will or the holder of an insurance policy, as the owner of a car or a pet—sooner or later, you are likely to encounter questions of law. It is in these circumstances that you will find it especially helpful to have this book at hand, for it will enable you to discuss your problems intelligently with your lawyer, who is of course your ultimate legal advisor.

Although the law is complex, differing sharply in its details from state to state, general rules do govern your legal rights and responsibilities. In this book you will learn about such common concerns as your civil rights, the extent of a minor's responsibility for accidents or misbehavior, and how to make a will, as well as more unusual matters like the law of libel and slander, and what you should do if you are arrested. The book explains your rights vis-à-vis the United States government, either as a citizen or as an alien. It explains your Social Security and Medicare rights, and your doctor's legal responsibilities. In many cases, *The Family Legal Advisor* will also tell you about major exceptions to prevailing law; in other cases, tables provide a state-by-state catalogue of laws on marriage, divorce, and wills.

Secondarily, but still importantly, *The Family Legal Advisor* hopes to entertain as well as instruct. Although laws are written and enacted by legislatures, their validity is established in the courts, which must consider the law not in the abstract but in relation to the particular behavior of particular people. To clarify legal points, the book cites hundreds of cases, each of them a small drama of people in conflict. Some of the cases are touching or exciting; a number of them are even comic. Portions of court decisions are quoted to demonstrate the reasoning behind them, and thus to make the law vital and meaningful to you.

Legal terms are explained in this book as they occur in text. To help you still further, however, a Dictionary of Legal Terms appears at the end of the book, as does an index which enables you to quickly locate the information you seek.

Table of Contents

objects destroyed by fire — Can a pledged article be withheld? — When a pledged article is sold — Is notice of sale necessary? — Observe your redemption date — Gambling debts.

Dogs—Why your dog should be licensed—Damages for an unlicensed dog—If a dog is killed negligently—Dog enticement—Cows on the highway—When a hired animal causes injury—Horseback riding at one's risk—The normal hazards of sports—Animals that may be destroyed—Cruelty to animals is punishable—What cruelty means—Unusual treatment is not always cruel—Trespassing domestic animals—Killing an animal nuisance—When wild animals cause injury—Wild animals in the national parks—An accident despite reasonable care—Handlers must be skilled—Photographs of an animal—Care by a veterinarian—Nuisances—What about pets in an apartment?—Charitable trusts for pets.

Using the wrong name in a lawsuit—Names and voting—How the law views middle names—Incorrect middle initial—Omitting a middle initial on a check—Error in a title or degree—Is "Mrs." part of a name?—Junior and Senior-parts of a name? Abbreviations—Is a misspelled name valid at law?—Nicknames—Fraud and change of name—Changing your name by court process.

How to protect your security—Must the landlord oust trespassers?—Should rent be paid in advance?—When rent is due—If no date is set—Refund in eviction cases—Accidental destruction of premises—Your duty to pay promptly—Who must make repairs?—TV antennas and air conditioners—Control of rented premises—Is a landlord liable for injuries?—A landlord's agreement to make limited repairs—May you withhold rent?—How to end a lease early—When rent ends—How the landlord's acceptance is proved—Oral agreement to end lease—What holdover tenancy means—When notice is not adequate—Restriction on landlord—Rent control and holdovers—Subletting and assignment—Subletting against landlord's wishes—How a landlord waives the subletting restriction—Taking in roomers—License or lease?—The tenant's obligations after eviction—Rent control and statutory tenancy.

When there is a minor misrepresentation—An innocent misrepresentation may be damaging—Reinstating a policy—An important exception—The difference between brokers and agents—Whose agent is he?—When the broker is the company's agent—Who can be the beneficiary—What is an insurable interest in life insurance?—Can business associates insure each other?—Study your policy—Double indemnity—What accidental death means—Suicide—If you pay your premium late—How soon the company is liable—When a lapsed policy still has value—Can creditors claim your insurance?—Ordinary or whole life insurance—Term insurance—Endowment insurance—Property damage-automobiles—Car damaged by unknown cause—When a car is used as a public conveyance—Automobile collision and casualty insurance—No-fault insurance—Accident insurance—What is total disability?—Benefits while under a physician's care—"Continuously confined within the house"—Fire insurance—Two kinds of fires—When a "friendly fire" causes damage—If you drop an object into a fire—Fire as a proximate cause of damage—Extended coverage with a fire insurance policy—Theft—Robbery is not "trickery" —Theft and the unlawful use of an automobile—Burglary insurance—Credit insurance—Fidelity insurance or indemnity bond—State unemployment insurance—Liability insurance—Casualty insurance—Essential facts about Social Security—Disability provisions—Relatives who can collect benefits—Friend's compensation

Foreword

    The Family Legal Advisor was prepared by several lawyers of varying backgrounds. The amalgam of their work expands and brings up to date the original edition revised by me, and gives the reader the benefit of several points of view.

    When I became a judge, I could not, as a matter of law or ethics, continue with this book. I then asked my sister, Alice Kupferman Helm, a distinguished lawyer in her own right, to commence this revision. The publisher also had the benefit of the assistance of Allen H. Brill, Esq., and of Kenneth Birnbaum, Esq., of the New York bar.

THEODORE R. KUPFERMAN
Justice, Supreme Court
Appellate Division
First Department, New York

CHAPTER 1

The Law of Marriage

Although the institution of marriage may be considered a holy union, it is governed by numerous rules established by the state. Unless you are aware of them and conform, in the eyes of the civil authorities you will not have a legal relationship. Inasmuch as so many rights are dependent upon its being a valid relationship, it is extremely important that you know your state's regulations.

The state has the welfare of its citizens in mind, and under the Constitution may make rules governing that welfare. It prescribes, among other things, conditions concerning the marriage of blood relatives, the minimum ages for marriage, and requirements concerning the physical and mental health of the parties.

Miscegenation laws

For many years, some states have regulated marriage between persons of different races. These laws are called miscegenation laws. However, the United States Supreme Court has ruled that these laws are unconstitutional. Among the states that had such laws were Alabama, Arkansas, Delaware, Florida, Georgia, Kentucky, Louisiana, Mississippi, Missouri, North Carolina, Oklahoma, South Carolina, Tennessee, Texas, Virginia, and West Virginia. Maryland also had one, but repealed it in 1967.

In 1958, two residents of Virginia, a black woman and a white man named Loving, were married in nearby Washington, D.C., and then returned to Virginia to live. They were charged by the state with violating the state's law banning interracial marriages. They pleaded guilty and their sentences were suspended on the condition that they leave Virginia, and not return for 25 years. They went to the District of Columbia to live, but in 1963 they challenged the judgment and sentence, claiming it was unconstitutional. The case went all the way to the United States Supreme Court. That Court decided that though marriage is a social relationship subject to the state's police power, the state's power to regulate is not unlimited. The restriction, by the state, of the freedom to marry solely because of racial classifications violates the meaning of the equal protection clause of the United States Constitution. Marriage, said the Court, is one of the basic civil rights of man, and the Constitution requires that the freedom of choice to marry not be restricted by racial discrimination. The freedom to marry outside your race is a matter of individual choice and cannot be infringed upon by the state.

Marrying a relative

The reason behind the prohibition of the marriage of near relatives is that harmful physical and mental characteristics are much more likely to appear in the offspring of such close blood relations. Thus, though it is a well-recognized rule of law that a marriage which is valid where it is entered into is valid everywhere, an exception is the refusal of some states to recognize the marriage of persons with prohibited degrees of relationship. Relatives as near as sister and brother or aunt and nephew cannot marry in any state. The attempted marriage of a man and woman of closer relationship than first cousins is incest, a crime. In some states this prohibition is extended to include first cousins and first cousins once removed (that is, where one party is a grandchild and the other a great-grandchild of a common ancestor). In a number of states, second cousins may not marry if they are great-grandchildren of a common ancestor.

In an interesting case in New York, a girl named Eva married her father's half-brother, Albert Simms. They signed an antenuptial agreement under which Simms undertook to bequeath $25,000 to Eva (see Chapters 10 and 11 on wills).

The marriage, performed according to the canons of the Jewish faith, was thereafter annulled on the ground of incest. Subsequently Simms died, and the question before the court was whether the antenuptial agreement was valid and enforceable.

The Domestic Relations Law of the State of New York provides that a marriage between an uncle and niece is incestuous and void. It says nothing about "half blood." However, in prohibiting a marriage between a brother and sister, it covers both the whole and half blood. This leads to the conclusion that half blood in relation to uncle and niece is not interdicted. The agreement, in any event, was held valid because even if in New York the marriage might be considered incestuous, in other jurisdictions it would not be.

Alabama law formerly prohibited a man marrying the widow of his uncle. This had its origins in the Old Testament concepts of marital rules.

In an old case in Alabama, the widow of a Dr. Watkins asked to be appointed administratrix of her husband's estate. Years before, when she had become the widow of an uncle of Dr. Watkins, she and the doctor had gone from Alabama to another state to be married and then returned to Alabama, where they lived until the doctor's death.

The penalty for violating this law was imprisonment. By this law the marriage of Dr. Watkins and the widow of his uncle was not a marriage. It was incest, punishable by law. Before the widow's application for her appointment as administratrix was decided, she died, saved thus from the ignominy of possible proceedings branding her a criminal.

A marriage between a man and woman too closely related brought similar censure in a New York court. A 47-year-old woman and her 18-year-old nephew were married in Italy. After the marriage they migrated to New York, where some years later she asked the courts for support from her youthful husband. The court refused to recognize the relationship as a marriage or to grant the relief sought by the woman. Perhaps if the marriage had not also been invalid in Italy, the result might have been different.

Keeping in mind that some states have different interpretations of what a "cousin" is, a consideration of state marriage laws follows:

State	First cousins	First cousins once removed	Second cousins
Alabama	Permitted	Permitted	Permitted
Alaska	Prohibited	,,	,,
Arizona	,,	,,	,,
Arkansas	,,	,,	,,
California	Permitted	,,	,,
Colorado	,,	,,	,,
Connecticut	,,	,,	,,
Delaware	Prohibited	,,	,,
District of Columbia	Permitted	,,	,,
Florida	,,	,,	,,
Georgia	,,	,,	,,
Hawaii	,,	,,	,,
Idaho	Prohibited	,,	,,
Illinois	,,	,,	,,
Indiana	,,	Prohibited	,,
Iowa	,,	Permitted	,,
Kansas	,,	,,	,,
Kentucky	,,	Prohibited	,,
Louisiana	,,	Permitted	,,
Maine	Permitted	,,	,,
Maryland	,,	,,	,,
Massachusetts	,,	,,	,,
Michigan	Prohibited	,,	,,
Minnesota	,,	Prohibited	,,
Mississippi	,,	Permitted	,,
Missouri	,,	,,	,,
Montana	,,	,,	,,
Nebraska	,,	,,	,,

State	First cousins	First cousins once removed	Second cousins
Nevada	Prohibited	Prohibited	Permitted
New Hampshire	,,	Permitted	,,
New Jersey	Permitted	,,	,,
New Mexico	,,	,,	,,
New York	,,	,,	,,
North Carolina	,,	,,	,,
North Dakota	Prohibited	,,	,,
Ohio	,,	Prohibited	,,
Oklahoma	,,	Permitted	,,
Oregon	,,	,,	,,
Pennsylvania	,,	,,	,,
Puerto Rico*	Prohibited*	,,	,,
Rhode Island	Permitted	,,	,,
South Carolina	,,	,,	,,
South Dakota	Prohibited	,,	,,
Tennessee	Permitted	,,	,,
Texas	,,	,,	,,
Utah	Prohibited	,,	,,
Vermont	Permitted	,,	,,
Virginia	,,	,,	,,
Virgin Islands	Prohibited	Prohibited	Prohibited
Washington	,,	,,	Permitted
West Virginia	,,	Permitted	,,
Wisconsin**	,,**	Prohibited	,,
Wyoming	,,	Permitted	,,

*Puerto Rico—Court can waive impediment under certain conditions.
**Wisconsin—Permits first cousins to marry where the female is older than 55. Obviously this is based on the unlikelihood of conception after that age.

The age of consent

The law fixes the earliest date at which you can marry. Ordinarily, if either the man or woman has not reached that age, there is no marriage. However, with the consent of the parents, marriage is in most instances permitted at an earlier age. The following are the earliest ages at which a couple may marry in the various states, both with the consent of the parents of the girl and boy, and without that consent.

The age of consent

State	Minimum age with parental consent		Minimum age without parental consent	
	Man	Woman	Man	Woman
Alabama	17	14	21	18
Alaska	18	16	19	18
Arizona	18	16	21	18
Arkansas	18	16	21	18
California	None stated		21	18
Colorado	16*	16*	21	18
Connecticut	16*	16*	21	21
Delaware	18	16	19	19
District of Columbia	18	16	21	18
Florida	18	16	21	21
Georgia	18	16	19	19
Hawaii	17	15	18	16
Idaho	18	16	21	18
Illinois	18	16	21	18
Indiana	18	16	21	18
Iowa	18	16	21	18
Kansas	14	12	21	18
Kentucky	18	16	18	18
Louisiana	18*	16*	21	21
Maine	16	16	20	18
Maryland	18	16	21	18
Massachusetts	18	16	21	18
Michigan	18	16	21	18
Minnesota	18	16	21	18
Mississippi	17*	15*	21	18
Missouri	15*	15*	21	18
Montana	None stated		19	19
Nebraska	18	16	21	21
Nevada	18*	16*	21	18
New Hampshire	20* **	18* **	20	18
New Jersey	18*	16*	21	18
New Mexico	18*	16*	21	18
New York	16	14	21	18
North Carolina	16	16	18	18
North Dakota	18	15	21	18
Ohio	18	16	21	21
Oklahoma	18*	15*	21	18
Oregon	18	15	21	18

State	Minimum age with parental consent		Minimum age without parental consent	
	Man	Woman	Man	Woman
Pennsylvania	16*	16*	21	21
Puerto Rico	None stated		21	21
Rhode Island	18*	16*	21	21
South Carolina	16	14	18	18
South Dakota	18	16	21	21
Tennessee	16*	16*	21	21
Texas	16	14	19	18
Utah	16	14	21	18
Vermont	18*	16*	21	21
Virginia	18	16	21	21
Virgin Islands	16	14	21	18
Washington	17*	17*	21	21
West Virginia	18	16	21	21
Wisconsin	18	16	21	18
Wyoming	18	16	21	21

*Lower ages if court approval is obtained.
**Not below 14 for male and 13 female.

Marriage licenses

Since the state must consent to the marriage, in most states you must get a license for your marriage. In the states in which a common-law marriage is binding and legal (see page 20), statutes providing for a marriage license are merely directions. Failure to obtain a license will not affect the legality of the marriage, although it may result in a penalty for the person performing the marriage.

However, in states with laws such as those of Nebraska, which expressly state that a marriage without a license is invalid and illegal, a license is necessary and without it you will not be married.

An Alabama law directed the parties to a marriage to obtain a license but did not state, like the Nebraska law, that a marriage without a license is illegal and is no marriage. In that state, a child 15 years old forged her father's signature to a parental consent to her marriage and with that forged consent obtained a license. The court said that, unless the law clearly stated that a license was necessary for a legal and binding marriage and that without such a license the marriage was void, the marriage without a valid license was binding.

Medical certificates may be required

Since the state is concerned about the health and welfare of its citizens and prospective citizens, medical certificates or sworn statements of freedom from venereal disease (serological tests) are required of applicants for marriage licenses in many states. Moreover, in certain instances there is provision for a waiting period between the time the license application is filed and the license issued. In many instances, a court can modify the waiting time, especially for servicemen.

State	Affidavit or medical certificate	Minimum waiting period
Alabama	Required	None
Alaska	,,	3 days (waivable)
Arizona	,,	None
Arkansas	Required, but waivable	3 days
California	,, ,, ,,	None
Colorado	Required	,,
Connecticut	Required, but waivable	4 days (waivable)
Delaware	,, ,, ,,	1 day for residents 4 days for nonresidents
District of Columbia	,, ,, ,,	4 days (waivable)
Florida	Required	3 days
Georgia	,,	3 days except where both over 21 or female pregnant

State	Affidavit or medical certificate	Minimum waiting period
Hawaii	Required, but waivable	None
Idaho	,, ,, ,,	,,
Illinois	Required	,,
Indiana	Required, but waivable	3 days
Iowa	Required	3 days
Kansas	,,	3 days (waivable)
Kentucky	Required, but waivable	3 days
Louisiana	Required	None*
Maine	,,	5 days
Maryland	Not required	2 days (waivable for servicemen)
Massachusetts	Required	3 days (waivable)
Michigan	,,	,, ,, ,,
Minnesota	Not required	5 days
Mississippi	Required	3 days
Missouri	,,	3 days (waivable)
Montana	,,	5 days (waivable)
Nebraska	Required, but waivable	5 days
Nevada	Not required	None
New Hampshire	Required	5 days (waivable)
New Jersey	,,	3 days (waivable)
New Mexico	,,	,, ,, ,,
New York	,,	10 days after serological test and 24 hours after issuance of marriage license
North Carolina	,,	None
North Dakota	,,	,,
Ohio	,,	5 days
Oklahoma	,,	None (3 days if below age and no parental consent)
Oregon	,,	7 days (waivable)
Pennsylvania	,,	3 days
Puerto Rico	,,	None
Rhode Island	,,	None (5 days for female nonresidents)
South Carolina	Not required	1 day
South Dakota	Required	None
Tennessee	,,	3 days, unless both over 21
Texas	,,	None
Utah	,,	,,
Vermont	,,	None**
Virginia	,,	None
Virgin Islands	Not required	License application must be posted 8 days (waivable)
Washington	Required	3 days
West Virginia	,,	,, ,,
Wisconsin	,,	5 days
Wyoming	,,	None

*Marriage must be delayed for 3 days after issuance of marriage license.
**Marriage must be delayed for 5 days after issuance of marriage license, except for military personnel or by order of court.

Ceremonial marriages

Most people are joined in wedlock by a marriage ceremony, although other types of marriages, such as common-law, contract, and proxy marriages, are possible. The clergyman or other official who is empowered to perform your marriage ceremony is usually named in the laws of the state. Generally the ceremony can be performed by court and city officials and by properly ordained clergymen, priests, rabbis, or other religious authorities.

What is a common-law marriage?

When a man and a woman agree that they are husband and wife, live together in this relationship, and represent it as a marriage to their friends and the public generally, they are parties to a common-law marriage. Such an agreement is a legal marriage in some states, but in most it receives no recognition by the law.

States where common-law marriages are either valid or recognized

Alabama–   may be contracted within the state and are considered proper marriages.

Arizona–   may not be contracted within the state but are recognized if valid in the state where entered into; the same is true for Arkansas, Delaware, Maryland, Michigan, Minnesota, Missouri, Nebraska, New Mexico, North Carolina, Oregon, Tennessee, Virginia, Virgin Islands, Washington, and West Virginia.

California–   valid if entered into prior to 1895. Thereafter, if entered into in another state where valid, will be recognized.

Colorado–   valid.

District of Columbia–   valid.

Florida–   valid if entered into prior to January 1968.

Georgia–   valid.

Idaho–   valid.

Indiana–   valid if entered into prior to January 1958.

Iowa–   valid.

Michigan– valid if entered into prior to January 1957.

Minnesota– valid if entered into prior to April 26, 1941.

Mississippi– valid if entered into prior to April 5, 1956.

Missouri– valid if entered into prior to March 31, 1921.

Montana– valid.

Nebraska– valid if entered into prior to 1923.

New Jersey– valid if entered into prior to December 1, 1939.

New York– valid if entered into prior to April 29, 1933.

Ohio– valid.

Pennsylvania– valid.

Rhode Island– valid.

South Carolina– valid.

South Dakota– valid if entered into prior to July 1, 1959.

Texas– valid.

Common-law marriages are not recognized in New Hampshire, but out-of-state common-law marriages may possibly be recognized when the parties become permanent residents of the state.

Kansas recognizes them, but the parties are guilty of a misdemeanor. They are not generally recognized as valid in Kentucky but are considered so for recovery and distribution under certain sections of the Kentucky Workmen's Compensation Law; Kentucky also recognizes valid marriages of other states.

Improper ceremony In any state where a common-law marriage is binding, if, for some reason, the marriage ceremony is not performed by a proper official, the omission will not cause the marriage to be illegal. This ruling was established in a famous case decided by the United States Supreme Court. William Mowry in 1844 went from Pittsburgh, Pennsylvania, to the Saginaw Valley in Michigan. There he fell in love with an Indian girl. They were married. Later his wife died and Mowry returned to Pittsburgh.

The law in Michigan, where Mowry and the Indian girl had been married, was that the ceremony must be performed by an ordained minister or a justice of the peace. Long afterward it was discovered that the man who married them was neither a clergyman nor a justice of the peace. With this disclosure arose the question of whether or not Mowry and his Indian bride had been legally married. The court held that whatever might have been the form of the ceremony, or whether there had been any ceremony at all, made no difference. Since the two had agreed to be husband and wife and after that had lived together as husband and wife, there was a legal marriage.

Years after this incident, another case of the same character came before the Supreme Court. In 1865, James Travers, who was living in the District of Columbia, married a West Virginia girl at Alexandria, Virginia. After the marriage they went to New Jersey to live. The girl was an orphan and only seventeen. Four or five years after the marriage she learned that the man who had performed the ceremony was not a minister but merely a friend of her husband. The Court pointed out that in any state where a common-law marriage is valid, the marriage is binding and legal and the parties are husband and wife irrespective of statutes requiring that the marriage be solemnized by a magistrate or clergyman, a license issued, or that the ceremony be performed before witnesses.

State boundaries and marriage

The failure to follow the directions contained in statutes relating to marriage licenses and ceremonies has no effect on the validity of the marriage in states recognizing common-law marriages.

The laws that determine whether a marriage is binding or not are those of the state where the marriage ceremony takes place. If it is legal in the state where it is performed, it is legal everywhere, except when it is void by express provisions of statutes forbidding marriages such as those between persons closely related.

This ruling, that a marriage valid where contracted is valid everywhere, was declared to be the law many years ago in Massachusetts, and it is still the law. In that state a black man married a white woman. The Massachusetts law at the time forbade marriages between persons of the White and the Negro races. This was, however, not the law in Rhode

Island. When this couple learned of the Massachusetts prohibition of their marriage, they went to Rhode Island, were married there, and then returned as husband and wife to their home in Massachusetts.

When a marriage, said the Massachusetts court in this case, takes place in a state where it is allowed by law, that marriage is good everywhere. If this were not the law, you could dissolve the marriage merely by stepping across a state boundary into another state where the marriage is forbidden.

In another instance, a couple traveled from Delaware to New York, went through the wedding ceremony in that state before a notary public, and lived in New York for the next ten years. During three years of the ten that they were in New York, common-law marriages were legal in that state. Later they returned to Delaware, where common-law marriages are not binding.

A few years later, when the wife brought an action for divorce in Delaware, her husband's defense was that they were not married, as the ceremony before a notary public was not a marriage and as common-law marriages were not binding in Delaware, where the divorce action had been brought.

Here again the court held that since their marriage was a binding one in New York, where they had lived as husband and wife, they were still married, following the principle that a marriage good in the state where it is made is good everywhere.

Marriage in a foreign country

Another case involved a man and woman who were married in Germany in a ceremony that they believed was performed by an official authorized by German law. Thereafter they lived together as husband and wife in Germany, Austria, and later in St. Paul, Minnesota.

At the death of her husband, the woman asked to be appointed administratrix of his estate. Then it appeared for the first time that the ceremony had not been performed by an official authorized under German law, although, in spite of that fact, under German law it was a true marriage.

Brushing aside the question of whether or not the marriage in Germany would be a valid marriage in Minnesota, the court said that since the marriage was valid by the law of the place where it occurred, it was legal everywhere. If the law of any state where the marriage might be questioned should govern its validity, then the marriage might be valid in one state and no marriage in another.

Of course, the prohibition on degrees of relationship, discussed earlier, might be regarded as an exception to this rule.

Contract marriages

The Domestic Relations Law of New York State, although it outlaws common-law marriages consummated after April 1933, provides for marriage by a written contract, after the acquisition of a marriage license, if both parties are over 21. (With the change in the right to vote, 18 may be the more appropriate age.) This contract is signed by the man, the woman, and two witnesses. The residence of the groom, the bride, and the two witnesses are set down, together with the date and place of marriage and the future residence of the married couple. This agreement is acknowledged before a judge of a court of record in a form similar to that needed for recording a deed of real property.

Contract marriages are also recognized in Arkansas, Missouri, Montana, and South Carolina.

Contract-of-marriage form

A form of this civil contract of marriage could be:

This agreement made this *10th* day of *January, 1958*, by and between *Jane Brown*, residing at *Albany, New York*, and *George Smith*, residing at *Albany, New Yok*.

Witnesseth, that the said parties have this day mutually and each for himself and herself willingly agreed to become and do hereby declare themselves lawfully united in marriage in accordance with the provisions of the Domestic Relations Law of the State of New York and that on and after the date hereof each for himself and herself undertakes to assume all the obligations attendant upon the relationship of husband and wife and to be controlled in all respects by law in the same manner and to the same extent as if the marriage of such parties had been officially solemnized by a clergyman, minister, priest, rabbi or public official.

That this contract of marriage has been executed on the above date at *Albany, New York*.

That the witnesses to such marriage are *John Greene*, residing at *Albany, New York*, and *Charles Grant*, residing at *Albany, New York*, and that the undersigned will reside at *Albany, New York*.

Witnesses: (Husband) *George Smith*
Charles Grant   (Wife) *Jane Brown*
John Greene

State of New York
County of *Albany*

On this *10th* day of *January, 1958,* before me a Justice of a Court of Record of the State of New York personally appeared *Jane Brown* and *George Smith* and *Charles Grant* and *John Greene* to me personally known and known to me to be the persons described in and who executed the foregoing instrument and they duly and severally acknowledged that they executed the same for the uses and purposes therein mentioned.

David Warner
Justice of the Supreme Court of the
State of New York

Proxy marriages The conditions created by World War II and subsequent conflicts turned the spotlight squarely on the question of whether one can marry by proxy; that is, does a marriage, to be legal, require the presence of both the man and the woman at the ceremony?

The legislature in Minnesota, in 1945, authorized such marriages until six months after World War II. The Attorney General of Kansas has declared that marriages by proxy are binding marriages in that state. They are valid in Puerto Rico. The Attorney General of New Mexico has said they are valid, but advises the parties to arrange for a regular ceremony to be performed as soon thereafter as possible. In Nebraska, if both parties are members of a religious sect that recognizes proxy marriages and the ceremony is conducted in accordance with the customs of the sect, the proxy marriage is presumably valid. These marriages have frequently occurred in Oklahoma with no adverse effects. In Texas a marriage per-

formed by proxy because the couple are separated by military service is legal.

However, in 32 states marriages by proxy are expressly forbidden by statute.

If you are married in this manner in a foreign country where such a marriage is legal, our courts have repeatedly held the marriage is legal in this country.

Proxy marriage held to be a common-law marriage

During World War II, Margaret was living at Palm Beach, Florida. She had promised Jerry, who was in the armed forces, that she would marry him as soon as her divorce from her husband permitted her to do so. The divorce became final and she was free to marry. In the meantime Jerry had been transferred overseas and was in Scotland.

Under these conditions the two agreed by letter they would be married by proxy, as such a marriage was legal under the laws of Florida. An application for a marriage license was forwarded to Jerry in Scotland. This he filled out and returned to Florida. The application was filed and the license issued. The ceremony was then performed by a county judge, with a friend of Jerry, acting with his authorization, as proxy for the groom.

Some months later Jerry died in Europe, never having returned to this country. The question arose whether Margaret was entitled as his wife to his insurance. The Federal court in Florida said the marriage was legal and binding and Margaret the lawful widow.

However, in Florida, common-law marriages are legal. The marriage between the bride at Palm Beach and the groom in Scotland was legal in that state as a common-law marriage. Whether the proxy marriage would have been legal if common-law marriages were not accepted in the state where the ceremony was performed was not decided.

This proxy marriage held valid

In New York State, where proxy marriages are not valid and where common-law marriages are now no longer legal, another case arose involving a young soldier named Raymond. He was with the armed forces outside the country and his fianceé was living in the District of Columbia. His brother acted as his proxy, and the ceremony was performed by a justice of the United States District Court in Washington, D.C. It should be pointed out that, ordinarily, United States judges have no power to perform a marriage ceremony inasmuch as that is a state function, but in the District of Columbia, the local judges are Federal.

After Raymond was discharged from the army, he and his wife lived together for some months. Then he deserted her and refused to support either his wife or their child. The laws of the District of Columbia do not require both the man and the woman to be present either for the issuance of the marriage license or for the marriage ceremony itself. Nor do they provide that either of the parties may be absent. Nothing in this regard is set out in the statutes.

In the action brought by the wife in New York, the court held that the marriage was binding and that the husband was responsible for the support of his wife and child because all the statutory requirements of the District of Columbia had been met and the proxy marriage ceremony later affirmed and accepted by the husband.

The performance of a marriage ceremony in the absence of either the groom or the bride is as old as history, but new in this country. As an institution, it has not yet stood the test of time, and you should not, unless it is absolutely necessary, adopt this method for a marriage until its validity is better settled and more seasoned by time and use; your lawyer can better advise you on the law of your jurisdiction.

How to make property settlements before marriage

Your wife or husband, when you marry, acquires an interest in any property you have. In many states, a widow has a dower right, a life interest in one-third of all the real property her husband owned during their marriage; the husband has a curtesy right, a life interest in the real property owned by his wife at the time of her death. Further, when either husband or wife dies, the law in most states provides that the other has an interest in the estate of the one who has died no matter what the will of the deceased may provide.

This interest which the law gives to the husband or wife in the property of the other when they marry is often a source of trouble, not only at the death of either of them, but sometimes in the conduct of everyday business affairs.

To avoid this inconvenience, you can enter into a contract or agreement with the man or woman you are planning to marry, before the marriage, which will dispose of these rights in each other's property for all time and leave you free to do with your property after your marriage as you wish. Such instruments are sometimes called prenuptial or antenuptial agreements.

A representative agreement of this sort, made before a marriage, provided that the property of the husband—if he should die first and there were no children—should belong to his wife. When the husband died, the widow assumed that the property was hers. Her husband's relatives claimed the ownership in spite of the agreement. The court said that an agreement such as this was favored by the courts and would be enforced. The courts have held similar agreements legal and enforceable whenever they were fair and equitable in their terms and entered into in good faith. There is always the problem, however, of a court deciding that the agreement has the effect of a testamentary disposition or will and, therefore, must comply with the applicable state law on wills. Any such agreement should be prepared by a lawyer.

Form for property settlement before marriage

A form of such an agreement could be:

Whereas *James Lennox* and *Mary Powers* are about to enter into a contract of marriage, and whereas *James Lennox* is the owner of certain real estate and personal property at this date, and *Mary Powers* is also the owner of certain real estate and personal property at this date, and whereas *James Lennox* and *Mary Powers* may at any time be desirous of disposing of said real estate divested of the curtesy, dower, or other claims of the said *James Lennox* and *Mary Powers,* either by deed or will: now, therefore, in consideration of said *James Lennox* and *Mary Powers* consummating the said contract of marriage, said *James Lennox* and *Mary Powers* hereby agree to waive and release and do hereby waive and release and forever quit claim and renounce all dower, curtesy, and other interest in and to the said real estate and personal property that said *James Lennox* and *Mary Powers* may now have or hereafter acquire by any means whatever. The intention being hereby to leave the absolute disposal of said real estate and other property now owned or hereafter acquired by either of them, unless taken in their joint names, so that at the death of the said *James Lennox* and *Mary Powers,* all of the property of the said *James Lennox* and *Mary Powers,* real, personal, and mixed, shall descend to his or her lawful heirs, released and divested of all claims of dower, curtesy, or other interest that the said *James Lennox* and *Mary Powers* might have as widow or widower. And in consideration of the consummation of said marriage, said *James Lennox* and *Mary Powers* hereby release, cancel, and waive all claims to all property of said *James Lennox* and *Mary Powers* to which they might be entitled as wife or widow, husband or widower.

Such an agreement, of course, should be properly signed, witnessed, and notarized. Your lawyer will consider with you the other aspects of such an agreement, which does not in itself settle your estate but merely leaves you free to dispose of it by will or otherwise.

Engagement ring

An engagement ring is considered to be in the nature of a pledge for the contract of marriage. Subject to local statutes, the general rule is that if the man breaches the pledge, the girl can keep the ring. However, if she breaks the engagement, she is required, upon demand, to return the ring, on the theory that it constituted a conditional gift. Occasionally one finds an interesting variation on this situation.

A married man sued for the return of a valuable diamond engagement ring, or, in the alternative, for its asserted value of $60,000. He had been living apart from his wife, and they contemplated a divorce. He had given the ring to another woman upon the promise that she would marry him if and when he became free. Shortly after receipt of the ring, she told him that she had "second thoughts" about the matter and decided against the marriage. However, she retained her first thought about keeping the ring. The highest court in New York State held that she could keep the ring because, as long as he was married, it was against the public policy of the State of New York to enforce an arrangement that contemplated a divorce, and accordingly the condition was removed from the gift, and the girl could keep the ring.

For a variation of the foregoing, consider the situation in a New York case where a man arranged to have his girlfriend's apartment decorated. He had already paid a very substantial sum on account, with over $30,000 still to be paid, when he decided to marry someone else. The decorator sued him on the contract, but also sued the girl on the basis of unjust enrichment, asking that she also be responsible for paying the remaining amount due. She contended that it was a gift to her, and that she had no responsibility. However, she had been intimately involved in every step of the arrangements as to color, style, etc., and so the court held that she was also liable to the decorator, who had done his job and had no interest in this almost domestic tableau.

Breach of promise to marry

When you agree to marry, the two of you by this act of agreeing make a contract in the eyes of the law. Here, as with any other contract, the refusal of either person to carry out the agreement to marry is a breach of contract for which damages can be recovered. Lawsuits for breach of marriage promise, by the way, are almost always brought by the woman.

In California, Mansell promised Anna he would marry her as soon as his affairs were straightened out. The promise continued for two years. Always the straightening out of his affairs was his excuse for the postponement of the marriage.

Finally Anna sued him and the case was decided in her favor. Here the court declared not only that the promise of each one to the other made a contract, but that the failure of Mansell to agree to, or set, a definite date for the marriage did not excuse him from carrying out his obligation. Further, even if no date were set, it was implied in the marriage agreement that the ceremony was to take place within a reasonable time.

In recent years, actions for damages for breach of promise to marry have come to be looked upon with disfavor by many courts and the public at large. Too often in the past, unscrupulous women have constructed agreements to marry with only their own hopes and wishful thinking as building materials.

Now laws forbidding or modifying actions for breach of promise to marry exist in Alabama, California, Colorado, Florida, Indiana, Maine, Maryland (unless there is a pregnancy), Massachusetts, Michigan, Nevada, New Hampshire, New Jersey, New York, Pennsylvania, and Wyoming. In Illinois, such a law was held unconstitutional in 1946, and thereafter a law limiting damages and restricting the action was enacted. In Tennessee, if there is no written evidence of the contract it must be proved by two disinterested witnesses.

When the statute abolishing suits for breach of promise to marry was passed in New York State, its highest court carefully considered the effect of the statute. It declared that the marriage state ought not to be lightly entered into, since it involves the most profound interests of human life.

"From such a standpoint we view the marriage engagement as a period of probation, so to speak, for both parties—their opportunity for finding one another out; and if that probation results in developing incompatibility of tastes and temperament, coldness, suspicion and incurable repugnance of one to the other, . . . duty requires that the match be broken off." This statement clearly explains why laws are enacted to ban breach of promise suits.

While the right to sue for breach of promise has been abolished in some states, as well as a suit for fraud or misrepresentation for a false promise to marry, there may still be an action for deceit in inducing and entering into a marriage that is void because the deceitful party is already married.

Alienation of affections

The laws abolishing actions for breach of the marriage promise have generally also abolished actions for the alienation of the affections of either party to the marriage through the influence of some third person. The definition of alienation of affections given by the courts is: "The robbing of husband or wife of the conjugal affection, society, fellowship and comfort which inhere in the normal marriage relation."

However, in an Iowa case a recovery was allowed. A husband undertook the management of a farm for his mother's sister. With the increase of his affection for his aunt came a decrease in his love for his wife, ending in the breaking up of their home. The wife brought suit against the aunt, and it was established in court that the latter had actively sought to gain her nephew's love. The aunt was obliged to pay a money judgment to the injured woman.

Interspousal immunity

A recent case involving the law of the Virgin Islands raised the interesting question of the doctrine of interspousal immunity. Under the old common law, a husband and wife were considered to have a single legal existence, and therefore one could not bring an action against the other for damage because you could not sue yourself. This doctrine has been eroded or abrogated in many states. The consideration of the rights of husband and wife may be explored further in Chapter 5 on Father and Husband and in Chapter 6 on Wife and Mother.

In the Virgin Islands case, the wife sued her husband, a former governor of the Virgin Islands, seeking damages for falsely representing to her that he loved her when actually he had married her for convenience in order to secure and retain "high public office." He had failed to disclose his intent to terminate the marriage after he had completed his term of office. The wife's complaint was dismissed on the ground that the doctrine of interspousal immunity still had validity in the Virgin Islands. The wife had contended that the Married Women's Act eliminated this disability. The Married Women's Act has been adopted in many states of the United States to eliminate certain civil inequities in the status of a married woman. However, the court stated that removal of this disability applied only to a wife's disability and not to mutual disabilities.

Another aspect of the husband-wife relationship is the general rule that one spouse cannot be required, without the consent of the other, to disclose a confidential communication made by one to the other during marriage. In other words, a wife cannot testify against her husband or vice versa. Exceptions have been made to this rule, such as where one of the spouses takes some criminal action against the other (assault, for example), or where the spouse making the confidential communication tried to force silence by fear, thus indicating that reliance was not on the marital relationship but rather on force. Of course, if the communication is made in the presence of third parties, then it is obviously not confidential, and so there is no restriction.

In an interesting case in New York, which leads us to the next chapter on Divorce, a husband sued his wife for divorce on the ground of her adultery. He testified to a conversation in which she admitted the relationship with another man. She objected to the testimony on the ground that it was a confidential communication between husband and wife. The testimony was allowed. The theory of the disqualification of such testimony and the general incompetency for one spouse to testify against the other is based on the desire to maintain the marital relationship and not to interfere with the affection, confidence, and loyalty engendered by such a relationship. Obviously, here we had an entirely different situation.

CHAPTER 2

Divorce

Since the state has a special interest in creating the marital relationship, it also provides for its severance. Each jurisdiction sets up its own grounds for divorce and separation (separation is discussed in the next chapter).

Two kinds of divorce are provided by law. One is an absolute divorce that dissolves the marriage and releases both husband and wife from the obligation of marriage, except for the husband's duty to support his wife and any children. (In this context, it is interesting to note that the state of Florida has ruled that, as of July 1, 1972, such proceedings in that state will no longer be referred to as "divorce," but rather as "dissolution of marriage.") The second type of "divorce" is a separation by the court, a separation "from bed and board," with a determination of the amount to be paid by the husband for the support of the wife.

This is an area about which there has been a great deal of controversy through the years. Many critics have felt that the variety of divorce rules has led to divorce shopping, and that only those couples with money could take advantage of divorce statutes.

As a result, a number of states have subscribed to the Uniform Divorce Recognition Act, an act that discourages migration in pursuit of divorce. These states, contrary to the usual practice of recognizing the legal actions of sister states, refuse to recognize out-of-state divorces obtained by their own citizens. They are Louisiana, Maine, Massachusetts, Montana, Nebraska, New Hampshire, New Jersey, North Dakota, Rhode Island, South Carolina, Washington, and Wisconsin.

New York has a provision, which many think unenforceable, declaring that if you get a divorce outside the state, but have lived in New York 12 months before and returned within 18 months after, it is evidence that you were domiciled in New York at the time of the out-of-state divorce.

Because of the stringency of some divorce statutes, critics have alleged that fraud is common in the procurement of many divorces. In 1966, the State of New York, where adultery was the only ground, broadened the basis for divorce. A divorce may now be obtained on the grounds of cruel and inhuman treatment, either physical or mental; abandonment for one year or more; confinement in prison for three years or more; adultery; and separation for one year pursuant to a court decree of separation or a written agreement between the parties, filed with the County Clerk.

A famous case interpreting the changed New York law involved Jackie Gleason. Prior to 1966, his wife obtained a separation decree. Under the new law, Jackie Gleason sued for a divorce based on their living apart for the required period of time, pursuant to the separation decree with which he had complied. The wife objected, contending that it was unfair to allow the new law to be retroactive, especially where it affects the rights of the nonguilty party (here the wife) who obtained the separation decree under the old law. The court decided that the legislative purpose of the new law was to make irrelevant the concept of guilt or innocence. It is the fact of separation pursuant to a decree or written agreement, the terms of which have been complied with, that determines the situation, and the divorce was permitted.

Court decisions in the various states differ in their interpretations of the meaning of the grounds for divorce. The facts of adultery for which a wife may be granted a divorce in New York may not sustain a similar decree elsewhere. The judicial interpretations of cruelty as a cause for divorce are especially diverse and range from incompatibility and mental stress to brutal treatment actually endangering the life and health of the spouse.

Further, grounds that in one state may sustain an absolute divorce may, in other states, be causes for annulment or merely for separation from bed and board.

The causes for which an absolute divorce are granted in the different states are listed on the following pages. Later in this chapter you will find explained just what these causes may mean according to the law.

Grounds for divorce

Alabama– Impotency; adultery; abandonment; conviction of felony and imprisonment; sodomy; habitual drunkenness or drug addiction; insanity; undisclosed pregnancy of wife by man other than husband at time of marriage; violent temper; physical violence; nonsupport and abandonment for two years.

Alaska– Impotency; adultery; conviction of felony; desertion; cruelty; habitual drunkenness or drug addiction; neglect; insanity; nonsupport; incompatibility.

Arizona– Adultery; impotency; conviction of felony; desertion; cruelty; nonsupport for one year; undisclosed conviction of crime prior to marriage; undisclosed pregnancy of wife by man other than husband at time of marriage; failure to cohabit; habitual drunkenness.

Arkansas– Impotency; desertion for one year; either party having husband or wife living at time of marriage; conviction of felony; habitual drunkenness for one year; adultery; failure to cohabit for three years; insanity; indignities; willful nonsupport.

California– Adultery; cruelty; desertion for one year; nonsupport for one year; drunkenness for one year; conviction of a felony; insanity.

Colorado– Impotency; adultery; desertion for one year; cruelty; nonsupport for one year; habitual drunkenness or drug addiction; conviction of felony; insanity; three-year separation.

Connecticut– Adultery; fraudulent contract of marriage; desertion for three years; seven years absence without being heard from; habitual drunkenness; cruelty; conviction of felony; insanity.

Delaware– Adultery; either party having husband or wife living at time of marriage (this is a ground only for the previous spouse); conviction of felony; cruelty; desertion for two years; habitual drunkenness; at suit of wife when under 16 years of age at time of marriage unless marriage is confirmed after that age; at suit of husband when under 18 years of age at time of marriage unless marriage is confirmed after that age; nonsupport; insanity; voluntary separation for three years.

District of Columbia– Adultery; desertion for one year; separation for one year; conviction of felony; one year after either party obtains bed-and-board divorce.

Florida– Until July 1, 1971—Husband and wife related within prohibited degree; impotency; adultery; cruelty; violent temper; habitual drunkenness or use of narcotics; desertion for one year; divorce obtained by spouse in another state or country; either party having husband or wife living at time of marriage. See analysis of new law at the end of this state listing.

Georgia– Husband and wife related within prohibited degree; insanity; impotency; force or fraud in securing marriage; undisclosed pregnancy of wife by man other than husband at time of marriage; adultery; desertion for one year; conviction of felony; habitual drunkenness; cruelty; insanity.

Hawaii– Adultery; desertion for six months; conviction of felony; cruelty; habitual drunkenness or use of drugs; insanity; nonsupport for 60 days; mental cruelty; separation for two years.

Idaho– Adultery; cruelty; desertion; nonsupport; habitual drunkenness; conviction of felony; insanity; failure to cohabit for five years.

Illinois– Impotency; either party having husband or wife living at time of marriage; adultery; desertion for one year; habitual drunkenness for two years; cruelty; conviction of a felony; communicating venereal disease; attempt by either spouse on life of other.

Indiana–   Adultery; impotency; desertion for two years; cruelty; habitual drunkenness; nonsupport; conviction of felony; insanity.

Iowa–   Adultery; desertion for two years; conviction of felony; habitual drunkenness; undisclosed pregnancy of wife by man other than husband at time of marriage; cruel and inhuman treatment endangering life of other.

Kansas–   Desertion for one year; adultery; cruelty; habitual drunkenness; nonsupport; conviction of felony; insanity.

Kentucky–   Impotency; separation for five years; desertion for one year; living in adultery; conviction of felony; loathsome disease; force or fraud in securing marriage; habitual drunkenness; cruelty; violent temper; undisclosed pregnancy of wife by man other than husband at time of marriage; willful neglect; unchastity of wife; insanity; joining by either spouse of religious sect prohibiting cohabitation.

Louisiana–   Adultery; conviction of felony; separation for two years; after one year of bed and board divorce if there has been habitual drunkenness or cruelty or public defamation or abandonment or attempt on life or nonsupport.

Maine–   Adultery; impotency; nonsupport; desertion for three years; habitual drunkenness or drug addiction; cruelty.

Maryland–   Impotency; insanity; adultery; desertion for 18 months; separation for 18 months; either party having husband or wife living at time of marriage; conviction of felony.

Massachusetts–   Adultery; impotency; desertion for three years; habitual drunkenness or drug addiction; cruelty; nonsupport; conviction of felony.

Michigan–   Adultery; impotency; conviction of felony; desertion for two years; habitual drunkenness; nonsupport; cruelty; divorce obtained out of the state by either spouse.

Minnesota–   Adultery; impotency; cruelty; conviction of felony; desertion for one year; habitual drunkenness for one year; insanity; separation for two years, or five years under limited divorce.

Mississippi–   Impotency; adultery; conviction of felony; desertion for one year; habitual drunkenness or drug addiction; cruelty; insanity; either party having husband or wife living at time of marriage; undisclosed pregnancy of wife by man other than husband at time of marriage; husband and wife related within prohibited degree.

Missouri– Impotency; either party having husband or wife living at time of marriage; adultery; desertion for one year; conviction of felony; habitual drunkenness for one year; cruelty; vagrancy of husband; attempt by either spouse on life of other; undisclosed pregnancy of wife by man other than husband at time of marriage; personal indignities.

Montana– Insanity; adultery; cruelty both physical and mental; desertion for one year; nonsupport for one year; habitual drunkenness for one year; conviction of felony.

Nebraska– Adultery; impotency; conviction of felony; desertion for two years; habitual drunkenness; nonsupport; cruelty; insanity.

Nevada– Impotency; adultery; desertion for one year; conviction of felony; habitual drunkenness; cruelty; nonsupport; insanity; separation for three years.

New Hampshire– Impotency; adultery; cruelty; conviction of felony; violent temper; nonsupport; habitual drunkenness for two years; separation; member of religious sect believing cohabitation unlawful and refusing to cohabit for six months; desertion; absence for two years and not heard from; wife out of state ten years; husband abroad intending to become foreign citizen.

New Jersey– Adultery; desertion for one year; cruelty; separation for 18 consecutive months; addiction or habitual drunkenness for one year; institutionalization for mental illness for two years; imprisonment for 18 months; deviate sexual conduct.

New Mexico– Desertion; adultery; impotency; undisclosed pregnancy of wife by man other than husband at time of marriage; cruelty; nonsupport; habitual drunkenness; conviction of felony; insanity; incompatibility.

New York– Adultery; cruel and inhuman treatment either physical or mental; abandonment for one year; confinement in prison for three years; separation for one year pursuant to court decree or judgment or pursuant to formal written agreement.

North Carolina– Adultery; impotency; undisclosed pregnancy of wife by man other than husband at time of marriage; separation for one year; sodomy; insanity.

North Dakota–	Adultery; cruelty; desertion for one year; nonsupport for one year; habitual drunkenness for one year; conviction of felony; insanity.
Ohio–	Either party having husband or wife living at time of marriage; desertion for one year; adultery; impotency; cruelty; fraudulent contract of marriage; nonsupport; habitual drunkenness; conviction of felony; divorce by either spouse outside state.
Oklahoma–	Either party having obtained a divorce outside of the state; desertion for one year; adultery; impotency; undisclosed pregnancy of wife by man other than husband at time of marriage; cruelty; fraudulent contract of marriage; habitual drunkenness; nonsupport; conviction of felony; insanity; incompatibility.
Oregon–	Impotency; adultery; conviction of felony; habitual drunkenness; desertion for one year; cruelty; insanity.
Pennsylvania–	Impotency; either party having husband or wife living at time of marriage; adultery; desertion for two years; cruelty; fraud, force, or duress in securing marriage contract; conviction of felony; related within prohibited degree; violent temper.
Puerto Rico–	Adultery; conviction of felony; drunkenness or use of drugs; cruelty; desertion for one year; impotency; spouse corrupts or prostitutes children; separation for three years; insanity.
Rhode Island–	Impotency; adultery; cruelty; desertion for five years; habitual drunkenness or drug addiction; neglect; conviction of felony; insanity; separation for ten years; nonsupport for one year; either party having husband or wife living at time of marriage; under age of consent; related within prohibited degree; gross misbehavior.
South Carolina–	Adultery; desertion for one year; habitual drunkenness; physical cruelty; habitual drug addiction.
South Dakota–	Adultery; cruelty; desertion for one year; nonsupport for one year; habitual drunkenness for one year; conviction of felony; insanity.
Tennessee–	Impotency; either party having husband or wife living at time of marriage; adultery; desertion for one year; conviction of felony; violent temper; unnatural behavior; habitual drunkennness; undisclosed pregnancy of wife by man other than husband at time of marriage; nonsupport; cruelty; willful neglect; wife's absence for two years.

Texas– Cruelty; adultery; desertion for three years; separation for seven years; conviction of felony; insanity.

Utah– Impotency; adultery; desertion for one year; habitual drunkenness; conviction of felony; cruelty; insanity; nonsupport; separation for three years under court decree.

Vermont– Adultery; conviction of felony; cruelty; desertion for three years; spouse absent for seven years and not heard of during that time; nonsupport; insanity; husband and wife living apart for three years.

Virginia– Adultery; impotency; conviction of felony; desertion for one year; undisclosed pregnancy of wife by man other than husband at time of marriage; wife having been a prostitute before marriage; sodomy; separation for two years.

Virgin Islands– Impotency; adultery; conviction of felony; desertion for one year; cruelty; insanity; drunkenness for one year; incompatibility of temperament.

Washington– Fraud in securing marriage; adultery; impotency; desertion for one year; cruelty; habitual drunkenness; nonsupport; conviction of felony; separation for two years; insanity; indignities; not of legal age.

West Virginia– Adultery; conviction of felony; desertion for one year; cruelty; attempt by one spouse on life of other; habitual drunkenness or drug addiction.

Wisconsin– Adultery; conviction of felony; desertion for one year; cruelty; habitual drunkenness; separation for five years; nonsupport; violent temper.

Wyoming– Adultery; impotency; conviction of felony; desertion for one year; habitual drunkenness; cruelty; nonsupport; vagrancy of husband; undisclosed pregnancy of wife by man other than husband at time of marriage; insanity; separation for two years; violent temper.

Recent Florida divorce law Effective July 1, 1971, Florida enacted a revolutionary new approach to the question of divorce called "dissolution of marriage." Two grounds are now set forth for the dissolution, either mental incompetence or "the marriage is irretrievably broken." The previous list of various grounds for divorce is eliminated, although the six-month-residence requirement before you obtain a divorce remains. The old defenses are eliminated, such as, in an adultery action, that the adultery was condoned, etc.

Either party may obtain alimony. If there has been adultery, it is taken into account in the question of whether there should be alimony, and in what amount. Where in the past—and as is usual in most states—all other things being equal, the mother usually gets custody of the child, the Florida statute specifically says that the father has equal rights with the mother with respect to custody, and the determination is as to what is in the best interest of the child.

When the allegation in the request for dissolution of a marriage is that the marriage is irretrievably broken, if there are minor children or if there is a denial of the allegation, the court may order a psychiatrist, a marriage counselor, or a clergyman to look into the question and may grant a three-month continuance before making a determination. The court also takes into account the best interest of the minor children.

New Jersey "no fault" divorce law

New Jersey has recently enacted a "no fault" divorce law. The "no fault" provision completely eliminates the necessity of proving either party's guilt in the breakup of the marriage. Rather, divorce proceedings may simply be enacted after 18 months of legal separation. In this respect, it is similar to the New York law whereby a divorce may be obtained one year after the filing of a written agreement of separation, provided that the parties involved have complied with the terms of the document. No attempt is made to determine who was responsible for the breakup of the marriage; the mere passage of time following separation is enough.

One mate at a time

Polygamy was recognized by certain religious groups in our early history; however, present law permits you but one wife or husband at a time. The application of this law in the vast majority of instances is simple.

It is not always simple, however, in a world where wars and revolutions are a frequent occurrence and every generation witnesses the mass migrations of thousands of persons, desperately fleeing for their lives.

An extraordinary situation, involving insoluble doubts, arose some years ago in New York. In May, 1913, Emanuel and Molly Hayden were married at Ekaterinoslav, in Russia. Two years later, at the outbreak of World War I, Emanuel was drafted into the Imperial Russian Army.

He was captured by the Germans at Branowitz, Minsk, made a prisoner of war, and held at Munster, in Westphalia. Before his capture he had written regularly to his wife but never received a reply. In the spring of 1916 a friend and fellow prisoner told him Molly had been murdered in a Russian pogrom. On the day of the Armistice, Emanuel escaped into Holland and there found employment as an attaché at the Russian Embassy.

A year later he migrated to the United States and made his home in New York City.

He had continued sending letters to his wife at the place where they had their home. In 1921, six years after his induction into the Russian Army, he heard through another source that both his wife and baby had been killed.

Convinced at last that this was the truth, he married a second time and a child was born. In 1923, he learned that Molly and their baby had escaped the pogrom at Ekaterinoslav and had fled to Kiev, and that his wife had made constant but unsuccessful efforts to find his whereabouts. He immediately forwarded her passage money for herself and the child. At the same time, by mutual agreement, he and his second wife separated. In the action which he later brought for an annulment of this second marriage, the court established the legitimacy of the child with a complete exoneration of the husband.

The tragedy of this family of Russian refugees would gain the sympathy of any court. They were guiltless victims of a world condition in no way of their making.

Cruelty and what it means

The definitions of "cruelty" as a cause for divorce are often so inadequate that they create confusion even in the minds of the courts. The line dividing cruelty that justifies a divorce or separation from the misunderstandings and disagreements to which every family is sometimes heir is not drawn with precision.

While cruelty inflicted by either one of a married couple is in most states a cause for divorce, it is not always clear what the legislatures have intended by that term. Cruelty in one instance is not cruelty in another. Physical abuse is more easy to determine. But the mental stresses of a mobile, automated society are not as easily gauged. One harsh and unkind act alone may not be cruel, but the same act, continued over weeks and months, can readily entitle its victim to freedom from the marriage. The cat's suffering was not less because its tail was cut off a little at a time.

Where the divorce is not contested, one finds that the courts are more lenient in accepting certain circumstances as constituting cruelty.

Rudeness is not cruelty

At one end of any catalog of the definitions of cruelty is an often mentioned Illinois case. For three years the husband had been not only

a drunkard but a notorious one. He had on occasions torn the dress from his wife, threatened to kill her, repeatedly struck and bruised her face and body, and barred the door of their home against her. The wife was given a divorce.

In another instance in that same state, a husband had failed to provide proper food and shelter. The court said the wife could manage well enough. "Mere austerities of temper, petulance of manners, rudeness of language and want of civil attentions, occasional sallies of passion, denials of little indulgences and particular accommodations, which do not threaten bodily harm, are not legal cruelty." This is generally the rule. You may seek consolation from the "Advice to the Lovelorn" column, but not in the courts.

What is mental cruelty? In a Florida case the husband, a doctor, became overfond of his nurse and receptionist. He subjected his wife to no physical cruelty, but her suffering over his affair was long and intense. In one instance she followed the automobile of her husband in the car of a friend and observed her husband and the other woman engaging in demonstrations of considerable affection. As a result, she was so sick in mind that she required treatment for hysteria.

The opinion of the court in this case discloses the other extreme cruelty recognized by the courts. "It is a matter of common knowledge that mental pain and suffering, that thing commonly called worry, is one of the major afflictions which result in the destruction of both mental and physical health. It affects every vital organ and probably results in more mental and physical wrecks than any other one affliction."

The wife was granted a divorce because of cruelty. In some states a divorce would have been denied, since physical violence and threats to health and life were lacking.

Physical impotency as a ground for divorce

The legal definition of impotency is: "Such incurable sexual incapacity of one of the parties at the time of marriage as prevents true and natural copulation. It is such deformity or weakness as prevents the consummation of marriage by sexual intercourse. It is not sterility nor barrenness, nor is it pregnancy by another at the time of marriage."

A recent decision states that not only must this condition exist at the time of the separation preceding the suit for a divorce or annulment of the marriage, but it must also have existed at the time of the marriage and be an incurable condition. The inability of either husband or wife to maintain normal sexual intercourse at the time of their marriage is cause in some jurisdictions for divorce or annulment. On the other hand, barrenness or sterility of which the victim is ignorant provides no ground for such an action.

The ability to become a parent is not, under the law, an essential element of the marriage contract. The ability to maintain normal and complete sexual intercourse is such a condition.

The courts draw a sharp distinction between the inability to procreate children and the inability to maintain sexual intercourse. Were mere sterility, in the absence of fraud, a cause for divorce, the consequences would be disastrous. Such conditions are common after men and women have passed the prime of life. Many marriages are childless.

Courts would inflict great injustice if they deprived a person with such a condition of the privileges of the marriage relationship. However, a fraudulent concealment of sterility known to its sufferer before marriage is ground for annulment or divorce if cohabitation (sexual intercourse) ceases immediately upon the discovery of the condition by the other spouse and court action is not delayed. Such a fraud destroys the marriage agreement itself. Fraud otherwise may be a basis for annulment or divorce.

What about fraud? A marriage contract, like any other contract, must represent an agreement between the parties.

In everyday business, if a seller leads you to believe you are buying a new product and then delivers a second-hand article and knows he is doing so, he is not selling you what you thought you were buying and the agreement is dissolved.

With marriage, too, when an essential condition is known to one party and concealed by him from the other, there is not a completed agreement between the parties. Such an act of concealment is fraud. If it is of enough importance, the courts will annul the marriage, or grant a divorce.

Epilepsy before marriage A typical case of fraud involved a woman who had suffered from attacks of epilepsy since childhood and married without telling her husband about her condition. He learned about it for the first time 12 years later, when it became necessary for him to place her in an institution for treatment. This act of concealment, according to the court, was a fraud that entitled the husband to a dissolution of the marriage. He had not married the woman he thought he was marrying but the one she knew he was marrying.

At one time, epilepsy was a bar to marriage in some states because it was considered a mental illness. In 1957, Pennsylvania, for example, lifted the restriction, making it unnecessary for epileptics to obtain special judicial permission for marriage. In signing the bill, the Governor said that research showed epilepsy no longer was considered a mental illness. However, it might still be considered as a possible basis for a fraud action, in some jurisdictions, to dissolve the marriage if the situation was such as set forth in the example.

No act of concealment By way of contrast, let us examine a similar case from which, however, the factor of concealment was missing. A wife, by reason of a physical deformity, was unable to maintain sexual intercourse. Unlike the epileptic girl, she did not know of her condition, never having indulged in sexual intercourse before her marriage. The court held there had been no fraud and under the laws of the state the marriage could not be annulled.

In another case, a young girl was committed to a hospital for the insane and there treated for three months. She was discharged as cured. Later she was again sent to the hospital for seven months and again discharged as cured. For eight years after that she lived a normal, healthy life, with no reason to think her mental illness would recur.

This girl got married. Three years later, in consequence of childbirth, she suffered another attack and was committed to a hospital by her husband. He refused to continue living with her, claiming the marriage was fraudulent and he was no longer liable for her support.

The court refused to set the marriage aside. The girl believed that she had been cured and honestly held that belief when she had married her husband. Insanity, epilepsy, and similar conditions must be known or believed to exist at the time of marriage if, by fraudulent concealment, they are to affect the validity of a marriage. No party to a marriage can be penalized for not disclosing facts outside his knowledge.

Undisclosed pregnancy at marriage—a fraud

A woman pregnant by a man other than the one she is marrying, if she fails to disclose her condition before the marriage, is responsible for a fraud for which her marriage may be either annulled or dissolved by a divorce.

A case of this sort occurred in New Jersey when an 18-year-old boy was for the first time sexually intimate with a girl a few months younger. Two weeks later she told the boy she was pregnant and that he was the father of her baby. In a week the two were married. Six months afterward the baby was born, a fine and healthy child, normal in every way but conceived, according to medical testimony, three months or more before the intimacy between the boy and the girl he had married.

On this evidence the court annulled the marriage, ruling that the wife was guilty of fraud.

Adulterous pregnancy in marriage

Although an undisclosed pregnancy with another man's child at the time of a marriage voids it or makes it voidable, any child born of lawfully married parents is presumed to be the child of both parents. In some states, however, this can be overcome by proof that the child is the offspring of an adulterous relationship. Still, in every instance, any effort to show the father of the child to be other than the husband of the mother is hedged about with legal safeguards for the protection of the child.

Mental deficiency

The extent to which insanity may be ground for the dissolution or annulment of a marriage is governed by the statutes of the state in which the parties reside. A below-par mentality is not insanity. The continuation of the marriage relation does not rest on the I. Q. rating of either party.

Whether a spouse is a moron or a potential Phi Beta Kappa is a question that does not concern the courts, nor is there any point between these extremes where the law prevents one from becoming a party to a marriage contract.

The necessity for court interference in some instances of mental incapacity, however, clearly appears in a Mississippi action brought on that ground to set aside a marriage.

Annulment on grounds of insanity

Parkinson, a fairly successful businessman, was engaged to be married. The engagement was broken by the girl. The shock and disappointment affected him mentally and he began suffering from delusions of grandeur, holding exalted ideas of his importance. He lost his business and became abnormally excitable and irresponsible. After a couple of years his family had him adjudged insane and confined to a hospital in Mississippi.

At that time he had considerable property. An aunt was appointed his guardian. At the hospital he was considered harmless and allowed to spend weekends at nearby towns. On one of these furloughs he met Eleanor Seay. During the next three months he visited her on these weekend trips. Finally he and Eleanor were married.

When Parkinson had first met this woman, his grandeur complexes had manifested themselves in extravagant statements of his wealth and the extent of his property holdings. Shortly after the ceremony she inaugurated a campaign to obtain control of his property. This ended with an action by the aunt, his guardian, followed by a decree annulling the marriage on the ground of Parkinson's insanity.

Insanity after marriage

A different situation is presented when insanity arises after the marriage. Of such conditions one court has said, summing up the opinions of many:

"No principle of justice or morality will justify the severance of marital ties for any such cause. The judgment and conscience revolt at the thought that such a terrible affliction should be deemed cause for separating the wife from the husband. Divorces are granted not because of misfortune but of fault."

This is the rule in some states, and each instance of this character must be governed by the laws of the state in which the parties live.

Generally in states which by statute allow divorce for post-marital insanity, several years must first elapse.

Adultery has different meanings

In every state adultery is a cause for divorce. There is, however, in some states a distinction made in the types of infidelity. A single act of adultery may not be grounds for divorce, but only habitual adultery or "living in adultery."

In one state, the evidence submitted in a divorce trial was that the husband had been repeatedly seen driving in the streets "with a common prostitute and an inmate of a Megowan Street bawdy house."

Further, the husband had often been at Megowan Street, spending his time and money with one or another of the occupants of these houses.

The statute in that state provides that the wife is entitled to a divorce if her husband "is living in adultery." The facts here show clearly the wife's right to a divorce, as her husband was obviously "living in adultery."

How adultery is proved

Less rigorous proof is demanded by the courts in establishing the occurrence of adultery in a divorce action than in a criminal case. An undefended action in New York showed that the husband had dined with a woman other than his wife; after dinner they had gone to a hotel and registered as "Mr. and Mrs." under an assumed name; they had been assigned to a suite of rooms for one day for which payment had been made in advance, and then had been escorted by the bellboy to the rooms. The boy had left, and the door had closed behind him. On these facts a divorce was granted the wife.

The law relating to the proof of adultery in a divorce action is thus outlined by one court: "It was not necessary to prove him guilty beyond a reasonable doubt but only to establish his adulterous relations with the other woman or women. Persons intending to commit adultery do not in advance proclaim it from the house tops or call in witnesses to the act. On the contrary they court seclusion and secrecy in its commission and hence it must usually be proved by the circumstances that generally attend its commission."

To this might be added a famous conclusion once made in a New York appellate court that: "In the words of an ancient text writer, 'Methinketh they go not to the upper chamber for the sake of saying a paternoster.' "

Circumstances that often are evidence in the proof of adultery in divorce actions are the entries in hotel registers of assumed names preceded by "Mr. and Mrs." in the handwriting of the husband who is accompanied by a woman other than his wife, and the conduct, dress, and environment that are usually associated with adulterous intercourse.

How failure to support is determined

The failure of a husband to support his wife, which is often a ground for divorce, is not the same as a mere failure to pay the amount his wife considers adequate. Important factors are how much the husband is able to contribute, the efforts he is making, and whether the wife is doing her part. The various states have requirements for the duration of nonsupport before it may be considered the ground for an action.

Extravagance and nonsupport

One wife's conception of support left a wide wake of unpaid bills. In a filthy home where her husband cooked his own meals, there were a dining room suite for $850, a front room suite for $750, curtains for $300, and expensive carpets and other furnishings, bringing the total to $3,000 for him to pay from his earnings of $10 to $13 a day as a cabinet maker, when he had employment. His wife's efforts were confined to cabarets and night clubs. Yet she left him, asserting he was not supporting her properly. A divorce was granted the husband, who based his suit on this desertion. The court rejected the wife's claim of nonsupport on the ground that a woman cannot demand more expenditures for support than her husband's income permits.

The desire for more money than the husband earns does not justify a divorce or a legal separation. This is well illustrated in the following case.

A girl of 18 had married a boy whose income was small when she married him and was still small five years later when she sought a divorce for his failure to support her. He owned a little farm, and she had for her own the money she received from the sale of milk, eggs, and butter. She earned a little more by washing clothes, making quilts, and tending a hot dog stand. She lived and dressed as well as the farmers' wives in the vicinity, and her husband was a typical farmer, neither lazy nor aggressive. The food they ate was the meat, poultry, and vegetables from their own farm.

The court denied this woman's suit. To justify a divorce, the court declared, the failure to support must be willful and intentional, or of such callous neglect and indifference as to be the equivalent of intentional failure.

When mates are incompatible

Incompatibility pure and simple is not a ground for divorce in most states. The instances where divorces are granted for incompatibility, whether under that name or some such name as mental cruelty, are relatively few. Suppose we look at one case in which the court thought a divorce justified.

In Seattle, Washington, a 23-year-old girl married a man of 53. There were no children. For ten years the couple lived in the man's family home, a big old building lacking modern conveniences and even the comfort and warmth of other homes in the neighborhood. The tastes of the two were different. Their methods of enjoyment were not the same. She liked art, the opera, concerts, and the theater; he was bored and irritated by them. Ultimately their differences became like giants, overshadowing every thought and action.

"Troubles," said the court, "which many couples are able to overcome, and to live harmoniously afterwards, assumed greater proportions through the added difficulty of attempting to mate 'January and May.' It is not only impossible for these parties to live together as husband and wife but it is to their interest and the interest of society that they be divorced."

Much more typical is the case that was tried in a Baltimore court. The wife, bringing suit, complained of the cruelty of the husband, and that he called her "nutty" and "feeble-minded."

The husband's side of the picture was brought out by his attorney when he cross-examined her concerning certain visits she made to her husband's drugstore.

"Didn't you go in that store and start a quarrel with him?" asked the attorney.

"I had reason to," was the response. "I had no money and the races were going on and I needed money."

"And you would go into his store and make demands on him and do it in a loud tone of voice?" persisted the attorney.

"Yes, and I had reason to."

"Whenever you wanted money you would go to the store and start a quarrel," suggested the attorney.

"Not especially in the store. I needed money and I was not going to spend my money any longer."

The conclusion of the court in relation to this situation, characteristic of legions of marriages, was that no matter how desirable a marriage might be as a moral principle, two people living unhappily together should not be forced by the state to continue such a condition. However, the law did not permit their divorce for such incompatibility. The legislature had unfortunately provided no solution for them. Today there is new thinking on the subject and new legislation either enacted or being considered.

What is desertion? The desertion of a husband or wife by the other party is (1) ceasing to live together and have sexual relations, (2) a refusal to renew such relationship, and (3) the voluntary separation by one of the parties without the consent of the other and without justification. (Desertion is not a failure to support.) In some states it is ground for divorce; in others, only for a legal separation. The law in many instances prescribes the period of time the desertion must continue in order to be a cause for divorce.

The wife in a Georgia case claimed she was entitled to a divorce for desertion since her husband had not supported her for six years and had lived apart from her for four years. She failed to obtain her divorce, as she did not show that her husband had been absent without her consent.

A couple married in Maryland had lived together for two years. The wife disappeared and her husband found her in Virginia. The next year she disappeared again, and again he brought her back. The following year she left a third time. When she telephoned him to come and get her he refused. On this refusal she claimed a divorce for desertion.

Refusing to free her from this marriage and to compel her husband to contribute a specific sum for her support, the court declared that her husband had not actually deserted her—this was merely her own interpretation of the incident.

When a wife avoids sexual relations

In an unusual case, a husband and wife lived together for six years and during that time she refused to maintain any sexual relations whatever with her husband. It transpired later, although she did not know it at the time, that the act was physically impossible for her to perform. The husband sought a divorce, basing on the conduct of his wife a claim that by refusing sexual intercourse she had deserted him.

"Desertion consists in a cessation of cohabitation, coupled with a determination in the mind of the offending person not to renew it. Intent is a controlling factor," said the court. "A mere refusal to permit marital intercourse standing by itself and accompanied by no other fact does not constitute desertion."

There must be intention to desert

It is the intention of the party whose conduct is in question that determines whether or not desertion has occurred. A husband inducted into the Navy told his wife, after he had entered the armed forces, that he would not live with her again if she were the "last woman on earth." She was granted a divorce. The absence of her husband in the nation's armed forces was, of course, not desertion, but his vehement declaration that he would not return disclosed his intention of abandonment and desertion.

Lack of consent

Further, the desertion must be made without the consent of the deserted party. If the husband and wife separated or ceased cohabitation by common consent, the legal intent to desert is not present, and a divorce cannot be granted on that ground.

The presumption from continued absence— Enoch Arden Law

When a married person disappears and his whereabouts is unknown for a long period of time, this poses a grave problem for the mate left at home. The statutes in various states make such a disappearance by either husband or wife presumptive proof of death. Unfortunately, such a solution to the problem can hardly be considered satisfactory.

"Enoch Arden," a narrative poem by Alfred Lord Tennyson, published in 1864, is the story of a shipwrecked sailor, lost in the South Seas, who finds, on his return, that his wife has another husband. To avoid complications, he keeps his return secret until his death.

The law in most states in relation to this situation is that any person absent for seven successive years without being heard of is presumed to be dead unless it is shown that he is alive. Irrespective of the statute and the presumption, the one who is absent is either alive or dead. If he is alive, all the presumptions of law from the Babylonian Code of Hammurabi to the statutes enacted by the latest United States Congress cannot make him dead.

Building the hoped-for happiness of a second marriage on a mere presumption is like building a house on shifting sands. Either way you court disaster.

The protection of a court decree

The folly of such a presumption was spotlighted in a southern state. Shortly after his marriage, Dan Evans left Mississippi and migrated to Arkansas. No one heard from him. Dan's sister wrote for information to the postmaster at the last place she knew Dan to have been. The reply was that Dan had been drowned. She gave this information to Ollie, his wife. Twenty years after Dan went away, during which time no one had seen him or heard of him, Ollie remarried.

Three children were born of the marriage. After another ten years—30 years after his disappearance—Dan came back to the little Mississippi town where he had once lived. In the meantime, Ollie's second husband had died. When she sought her second husband's life insurance her relatives-in-law, heirs of the deceased husband, produced Dan. The presumption of death from absence was a broken reed, and the court sustained the suit of her relatives-in-law.

As we have seen, the presumption of death from continued absence of the other party to the marriage is set aside by any proof that shows its falsity. When you have such a situation to meet, above all consult a lawyer and obtain a court decree disposing for once and all time of the former marriage and the obligations it imposes. This is the surest way to protect innocent children from the brand of illegitimacy, and their parents from the crime of bigamy.

Residence and domicile

Suits for divorce in the United States have always been actions involving three parties: the husband, the wife, and the state. The state guards the morals of its citizens and the marriage status is a *res*, or thing, over which the state has control. The state therefore has jurisdiction not only of the people involved but of the relationship. States have established what are called "domicile rules" for divorce.

Your domicile is that place where you have your true, fixed, and permanent home, your principal establishment to which, whenever you are absent, you intend to return. Domicile is distinguished from residence. A person can have many residences but only one domicile.

Many state statutes will use the word "residence" when they set out the jurisdictional requisites for a divorce action, but the word is generally construed to mean domicile. The parties to a divorce are not supposed to create an artificial domicile to facilitate a divorce.

Recently, a new bona fide arrival as a resident of Wisconsin challenged the constitutionality of a state law requiring that before an action for divorce may be commenced, one of the parties must be a "bona fide resident of this state for at least two years." A special three-judge Federal court held the residence requirement unconstitutional as being an unfair discrimination to a new bona fide resident. When the argument was made that to eliminate this requirement would make Wisconsin a "quickie divorce mill," the court stated that a jurisdiction which behaves in that manner is one where visitors get divorces, and that Wisconsin would still require that the law of domicile be followed. The question of discrimination against new residents has been considered in other situations, such as the right of a new resident to receive welfare without a waiting period, and the United States Supreme Court has struck down the waiting period in other such cases.

How long must you reside in the state?

The length of time a person seeking a divorce must have resided (be domiciled) within the state in which the action is brought varies in the different states. The time set forth is for general purposes and in many of the states it will vary with the grounds or depend on whether the parties were married there or lived together there or if the grounds for the divorce occurred there. Military service also may be important.

In Alabama the courts have no jurisdiction to grant a divorce if neither party is domiciled in the state. And the mere personal appearance by both parties does not confer jurisdiction. The plaintiff must have resided in Alabama for at least one year if the defendant is a nonresident. However, there is no specific time period of residence for a plaintiff where the court has jurisdiction of both parties and one party is domiciled in Alabama. Until a few years ago, Alabama, because it had no specific time requirement, was a haven for uncontested divorces for those who merely came to Alabama for the divorce.

In general, residence requirements are:

6 weeks– Idaho, Nevada, Virgin Islands

60 days– Arkansas, Wyoming

3 months– Utah

6 months– California, Florida, Georgia, Kansas, Maine, North Carolina, Oklahoma, Vermont

One year– Alaska, Arizona, Colorado (except where the grounds are adultery or cruelty), Connecticut, District of Columbia, Hawaii, Illinois, Indiana, Iowa, Kentucky, Louisiana (except where the grounds are adultery or conviction of a felony), Maryland, Michigan, Minnesota, Mississippi,

Missouri, Montana, Nebraska, New Hampshire, New Mexico, North Dakota, Ohio, Oregon, Pennsylvania, Puerto Rico, South Carolina, South Dakota, Tennessee, Texas, Virginia, Washington, West Virginia (except where the grounds are adultery).

Two years— Delaware (except where the grounds are adultery or bigamy), Massachusetts, New Jersey (except where the grounds are adultery), Rhode Island, Wisconsin.

In many cases there are exceptions: in Illinois, for instance, the time period is one year, but if the offense complained of was committed in Illinois, one party must have resided there for only six months. In Nebraska, the period is one year if the cause arose in the state and two years if it arose outside the state. There are also varying periods for specific grounds like insanity (Vermont, two years). In every situation, the facts and the applicable law should be checked by a local lawyer.

In New York, an action for divorce may be maintained only when the parties were married in the state and either party is a resident and has been for one year when the action commenced *or* both parties have lived in the state as husband and wife and either has been a resident for a year when the action is commenced *or* the cause for the divorce occurred in the state and either party has been a resident for a year *or* either party has been a resident for at least two years.

Unless there is proper residence in the state where the divorce is granted, it is worthless, and, what is worse, it leaves the parties to the marriage in ignorance of whether they are free and at liberty to remarry or whether the obligations of the marriage still exist. The difficulty lies in the inability to foretell where the courts in your case will determine your legal residence to be.

Such a situation arose in Massachusetts, where a wife sued for support, claiming her husband had deserted her. The court awarded her $20 a week. Two years later the husband went to Nevada; then, after living there for the six weeks prescribed by the Nevada statute, he sued his wife for divorce, was granted the decree, and returned to Massachusetts.

The next year the wife had him arrested for failing to pay her the $20 a week awarded her by the Massachusetts court. The conclusion of the court shows the uncertainty of divorces involving this feature of residence. "Here it is evident that neither husband nor wife was domiciled in Nevada." This is supplemented by a Massachusetts statute: "If an inhabitant of this commonwealth goes to another jurisdiction to obtain a divorce for a cause occurring here, while the parties reside here, or for a cause which would not authorize a divorce by the laws of this commonwealth, a divorce so obtained shall be of no force and effect in this commonwealth.''

Normally, in the United States, full faith and credit and what is called ''comity'' govern divorce decrees obtained in other states. Comity is a body of rules that states observe towards one another because of courtesy or mutual convenience. Full faith and credit is required by the United States Constitution, Article IV, to be given by each state to the ''public acts, records, and judicial proceedings of every other state.'' However, some decrees are obtained *ex parte,* that is, without the other party making an appearance. These divorce decrees can be considered initially valid, but inquiry can be made as to whether the sister-state court had jurisdiction of the action. This can sometimes result in the divorce being found deficient. Of course, participation by the other party either by personal appearance, appearance by an attorney, or by petition precludes that party from attacking the decree. A state need not accept the determination of another state court where the other state had no jurisdiction.

Divorce outside the state

In an opinion involving the confusion arising from contradictory state laws and decisions relative to divorce, Justice Jackson of the United States Supreme Court said: ''If there is one thing that the people are entitled to expect from their lawmakers, it is rules of law that will enable individuals to tell whether they are married and, if so, to whom. Today many people who have simply lived in more than one state do not know, and the most learned lawyer cannot advise them in confidence.''

Gertrude and Joseph Estin had lived their entire married life in New York. Then the wife brought a separation action in that state and was awarded alimony. Three months later the husband went to Nevada, where he brought an action for absolute divorce. In the Nevada suit, the husband was given a divorce and freed of the obligation imposed by the New York court of the payment of alimony.

When the wife sued in New York State to collect her alimony awarded by the courts in that state, the court held that the marriage had been dissolved by the Nevada divorce decree but that the obligation to pay the alimony according to the New York decision was still in force, although the marriage no longer existed. This decision was sustained by the Supreme Court.

Justice Douglas of that court dissented and said of the decision, ''The result in this situation is to make the divorce divisible—to give effect to the Nevada decree in so far as it affects the marital status and to make it ineffective on the issue of alimony.''

''The court,'' commented Justice Jackson on this New York decision in a later case before the Supreme Court, "reaches the Solomon-like conclusion that the Nevada decree is half good and half bad under the Full Faith and Credit Clause. I do not see the justice of inventing a compensating confusion in the device of a divisible divorce by which the parties are half bound and half free, and which permits the husband to have a wife who cannot become his widow and to leave a widow who was no longer his wife."

Under the confusion of the law as it now exists in relation to out-of-state divorces, you should consult with your lawyer to determine the practical effect and consequences of any change of residence you make. It may be that, with the more liberal approach to grounds for divorce in each state, there will be fewer attempts to leave the state for the purpose of seeking a divorce.

Divorce and bigamy

In the month of May, a man named Williams left his wife, with whom he had lived for 23 years in North Carolina, and went to Nevada for a divorce. His wife did not go with him and was never in Nevada.

The same month, Lillie Hendrix, who had lived with her husband for 20 years in the same North Carolina town, left him and also went to Nevada, where she was divorced. A few months later Lillie and Williams were married at Las Vegas and returned to North Carolina. Early the following year both were indicted for bigamy by a North Carolina grand jury, tried, convicted and sentenced to imprisonment. Neither had had a legal or actual residence or home in Nevada whereby the courts of that state had authority to grant a valid divorce.

Whether your divorce is legal or worthless depends on your domicile (residence) in the state where you bring your divorce action. This point cannot be overlooked. If you are seeking a divorce outside the state in which the two of you have lived as husband and wife, you must know how your own state will treat your removal and also know the residence requirements of the state where divorce is sought, and observe them scrupulously.

What about divorces in Nevada?

Judging by the decisions of the courts, it would appear to be the law in most states that where a husband and wife have appeared in a Nevada divorce action, the decree is binding on the parties. This principle permits, in effect, a divorce by consent where one spouse institutes the Nevada proceeding and the absent spouse authorizes a Nevada attorney to appear in the action.

A divorce decree will also be valid despite the claim that the plaintiff spouse was not a bona fide resident if such a claim was made in a divorce action and decided against the other spouse.

In general, contesting any issue in a divorce proceeding in any state will make the decision on that issue conclusive and prevent it from being raised in later litigation. Once you have made an appearance in a divorce suit you are bound by what is decided there.

What about Mexican decrees, Olé?

While sister-state decrees are entitled to full faith and credit under the Constitution, those of foreign countries are not. The question usually asked is, "Is it against the public policy of the state to accept the decree of the foreign jurisdiction, or should it be accepted on the ground of comity?" Mexico itself is also a republic made up of states and a Federal District, and it is important to know where in Mexico the divorce was granted, since it too has its more liberal jurisdictions.

The usual procedure in obtaining a Mexican divorce is that one party appears in person in a Mexican state court *with* a local lawyer and the other party appears *by* a Mexican lawyer. In New Jersey, New Mexico, and Ohio a divorce granted in this manner is invalid. In New York, prior to the liberalization of its divorce statute, thousands of New Yorkers went to Mexico for their divorces. The courts then said that although they might disagree with the residence laws established in a state like Chihuahua, Mexico (where Juarez is located, opposite El Paso, Texas), the decree would have to be accepted if the parties had complied with the rules. The New York courts were concerned with whether personal jurisdiction had been established over both parties. They knew there was no real intention to establish a domicile in Mexico, but they were willing to accept the decree if both parties complied with the local residence requirements and submitted to the jurisdiction of the Mexican Court. It was not against the public policy of New York to do so.

However, since September, 1967, with the expansion of the grounds for divorce in New York, questions have been raised about New York treatment of a Mexican divorce decree obtained by a New Yorker. You should consult with your attorney about the situation in any event.

In California, although the Mexican divorce may be invalid as against public policy, if the spouses both participated no complaints will be heard.

It is important to note that "quickie" jurisdiction is no longer accepted in Mexico, so it will not be the site of future such divorces. However, in the Caribbean area, Haiti and the Dominican Republic have adopted laws along the same lines. Extreme caution should be exercised in attempting to take advantage of such laws, with a lawyer being consulted as to the legal aspects.

Mail-order Mexican divorces

These are completely unacceptable. A mail-order divorce is one where neither party appears in court, although both submit to the jurisdiction of the court.

Alimony and counsel fee

Except in rare and unusual instances where she is clearly the wrongdoer, a wife is entitled to her husband's support. When a marriage is under the bombardment of a divorce action, that right to support still continues, but under such circumstances it is subject to the determination of the court.

The order of the court for the contribution by the husband of alimony for the support of his wife is enforced by the court by fine and imprisonment. Orders for the payment of alimony have the status of a judgment that, under the Constitution of the United States, entitles them to full faith and credit by other states, where they are collectible in the same manner as any other judgment for money.

No yardsticks can be used for the measuring of alimony. The amount depends on the income of the husband, the amount of his wealth, and also on the conduct or misconduct of the husband and wife leading to the divorce. The same features, in addition to the amount of legal work involved, govern the award of whatever counsel fee the husband is compelled to pay.

The language of the recent New York statute on alimony may be a guide to the current thinking on the subject: ''. . . the court may direct the husband to provide suitably for the support of the wife as, in the court's discretion, justice requires, having regard to the length of time of the marriage, the ability of the wife to be self-supporting, the circumstances of the case and of the respective parties.''

Support during a divorce suit

The alimony that replaces the support that a wife receives under ordinary circumstances still rests on the marriage relationship. No man is liable for the support of a woman who is not his wife. In a celebrated action in New York, a wife sued her husband for support, asking alimony pending the determination of the action. The husband insisted the woman neither was, nor ever had been, his wife. Each of them submitted sworn statements and letters in support of these contrary contentions.

A doctor swore he had attended both parties professionally; that the husband had told him that he and the woman with whom he was living were married but that ''for family reasons it was not thought proper to announce it.''

The husband, on the other hand, submitted letters from the woman that, according to the court, were "condemnatory of her." The question of whether or not there was a marriage was clearly in dispute. New York's highest court held that the wife was entitled to a temporary allowance for her support during the suit and her expenses in prosecuting it even if the marriage itself was questioned, so long as it was not clearly shown that the marriage was nonexistent.

Custody and support of children

The care of children of divorced parents is the duty of the court that decrees the divorce. The court is, in a sense, the guardian of the child. In its discretion it determines what the care and support shall be and from whom the child shall receive it. A general rule is that the best interest of the child is the prime consideration.

Younger children are ordinarily placed in the custody of the mother. In regard to the actual custody, the rights of either the father or the mother are subordinated by the courts to the best interests of the child, even to the extent that custody is sometimes given to persons other than the father or mother. Under such circumstances, ordinarily, near relatives are selected rather than strangers. The preference of a child who has attained the age of discretion will be accorded much weight by the court in determining the person to whom the custody of the child will be awarded.

In general, the liability of a father for the support of his minor children continues after a divorce or separation decree until the children come of age.

When parents are not qualified

A case illustrating the difficulties arising in awarding custody of a child of divorce involved a 13-year-old girl. "You went off and left me when I was little and now I am big enough to help myself," sobbed the child to her divorced mother seeking to retain custody of the child.

A divorce had been granted the mother for the father's "habitual drunkenness and cruel and inhuman treatment." The mother had been given the custody of the child with the provision that the father have her during the summer vacation. The father, explaining his failure to return the little girl to her mother, told the court that the child's bitter antagonism to the mother made him prefer the punishment of the court to the heart-breaking protests of the youngster.

The court nevertheless ordered that the child be given back to the mother. The following morning she went with her mother to her father's people for some of her clothes the father had left with them. Again she refused to go home with her mother. In the confusion she disappeared. Later in the day she was finally found at her father's home 30 miles away, to which she had walked and hitchhiked.

In this case, the court had a knotty problem to decide. One parent it considered unfit to raise the child—the other the child refused to live with. The custody of the child was finally awarded to the father's parents. Normally, however, the parents take precedence over grandparents.

In a case that aroused national interest, the Supreme Court of Iowa determined custody in a contest between the father and the maternal grandparents. The boy, Mark, was given into the temporary charge of the grandparents at the age of five, after the mother's death. They had provided "stable, dependable, conventional, middle-class background" for the boy, and there was no dispute as to their competence, except that they were 60 years old. The father had remarried and wanted to take the child to California. The father lived an "unconventional, arty, Bohemian" life; he was an agnostic and a political liberal and had no concern for formal religious training. The court stated it was not criticizing the father's way of life, and while not agreeing with it, determined that he had the right to choose his own way of life "within the boundaries which are not exceeded here." Nonetheless, custody was given to the grandparents because the court determined that for the child a stable relationship was better than "an intellectually stimulating" one.

Distribution of property

The distribution of property upon the setting aside of a marriage lies, like the custody of the children, in the discretion of the court. In community property jurisdictions, Arizona, California, Idaho, Louisiana, Nevada, New Mexico, Texas, Washington, and Puerto Rico, a wife is entitled to her share in the property that she and her husband have accumulated. "She is entitled to eat and live in as good a style as he is," as a typical decision puts it.

A western farmer, owning a 1,200-acre wheat ranch, a half interest in another tract worth approximately $43,000, and $10,000 in farm equipment, grain, and livestock, was sued by his wife for a divorce for cruelty she had endured for the twenty years of her married life.

Here the wife was given $2,500 in cash, a real estate mortgage for $7,500, a house and lot for her residence worth $3,000, and $75 a month for her own support besides an equal amount for the support of six minor children, to be reduced as each of the children came of age.

But no hard-and-fast rule can be given for how the property will be divided in other cases, or how much alimony will be awarded. As already indicated, this depends upon the court.

**Remarriage
after divorce**

Except when prohibited by statute, either of the parties to a divorce action is free to remarry upon the granting of a final decree of divorce. In some states, however, there are restrictions on remarriage by either party, prohibiting it for a specified time, or, in the case of the guilty party, absolutely. As a rule, when a marriage is contracted in violation of these restrictions within the state in which the divorce was granted, it is void. On the other hand, marriages solemnized outside the state before the expiration of the prohibitions against remarriage are in some states recognized as valid on the ground of full faith and credit to the act in the sister state.

CHAPTER 3

Separation and Annulment

States in which the power to grant judicial decree of separation is possessed by the courts, and the grounds on which they may grant these decrees, are given below. In some states, however, the only remedy available to a husband and wife seeking a release from their matrimonial contract is an absolute divorce or their own separation arrangements or agreement. In these states the courts have no power to grant separation decrees.

The grounds upon which a separation may be granted in the various states are as follows (their meaning has been explained, in general, in the chapter on divorce, but is always subject to local interpretation):

Alabama– The same grounds as for divorce, plus cruelty.

Alaska– No statutory grounds.

Arizona– The same grounds as for divorce, plus conduct of the husband making it unsafe for the wife to cohabit.

Arkansas– The same grounds as for divorce.

California– The same grounds as for divorce.

Colorado– The same grounds as for divorce, and also where spouse abandoned.

Connecticut– The same grounds as for divorce.

Delaware– Cruelty; adultery; desertion for two years; conviction of felony; habitual drunkenness; insanity of the husband; either partner having husband or wife living at the time of marriage.

District of Columbia– The same grounds as for divorce, plus cruelty.

Florida– The same grounds as for divorce.

Georgia– No statutory grounds, although private agreements are acceptable.

Hawaii– The same grounds as for divorce; period of separation not to exceed two years.

Idaho– No statutory grounds.

Illinois– Separate maintenance.

Indiana– Cruelty; adultery; desertion for six months; habitual drunkenness or drug addiction; nonsupport for six months.

Iowa– The same grounds as for divorce.

Kansas– The same grounds as for divorce.

Kentucky– The same grounds as for divorce, plus other causes the court may deem sufficient.

Louisiana– Cruelty; adultery; desertion; conviction of felony; habitual drunkenness; public defamation of spouse; attempt on life of spouse; fugitive from justice.

Maine– Desertion for one year; separation for one year.

Maryland– Cruelty; desertion; abandonment; excessively vicious conduct.

Massachusetts– Desertion; nonsupport; separation.

Michigan– Cruelty; desertion for two years; nonsupport.

Minnesota– No statutory grounds, but allowed by court construction.

Mississippi– No statutory grounds.

Missouri– Desertion; nonsupport.

Montana– The same grounds as for divorce.

Nebraska– Cruelty; desertion for two years; nonsupport.

Nevada– The same grounds as for divorce, plus desertion for 90 days.

New Hampshire– The same grounds as for divorce.

New Jersey– The same grounds as for divorce.

New Mexico– Separation.

New York– Cruelty; desertion; nonsupport; adultery; unsafe conduct for cohabitation; confinement to prison for three or more years after the marriage.

North Carolina— Cruelty; desertion; habitual drunkenness; violent temper; barring spouse from home.

North Dakota— The same grounds as for divorce.

Ohio— No statutory grounds.

Oklahoma— The same grounds as for divorce.

Oregon— Cruelty; adultery; desertion; conviction of felony; habitual drunkenness; nonsupport for six months.

Pennsylvania— Cruelty; adultery; desertion; violent temper; barring spouse from home. Separation allowed only for wife.

Puerto Rico— No statutory grounds.

Rhode Island— The same grounds as for divorce.

South Carolina— No statutory grounds but allowed by court construction.

South Dakota— The same grounds as for divorce.

Tennessee— Cruelty; nonsupport; desertion; violent temper; barring spouse from home.

Texas— No statutory grounds.

Utah— Desertion; nonsupport; separation.

Vermont— The same grounds as for divorce.

Virginia— Cruelty; desertion; violent temper.

Virgin Islands— The same grounds as for divorce.

Washington— Separate maintenance. The wife must show that the husband abandoned her without cause or that she was compelled to live apart from him because of conduct on his part that, in law, constituted abandonment, and that having ability to support her, he neglected to do so.

West Virginia— Separation abolished.

Wisconsin–   The same grounds as for divorce.

Wyoming–   The same grounds as for divorce.

Divorce or separation?   Sometimes a plaintiff who brings suit for divorce finds that the ground on which the suit is based is sufficient only for a separation.

One case that occurred in Kentucky concerned a husband who was a confirmed drunkard, wasted his property, and treated his wife cruelly, endangering her life and health. He would go on weekend sprees, come home, effect a reconciliation, and then go on another spree. This happened again and again, and finally his wife brought suit for divorce.

These sprees did not constitute drunkenness within the meaning of the statute and hence, the court pointed out, did not permit the wife an absolute divorce, but they did entitle her to a separation from her husband and to support.

Before the change in New York divorce law, when adultery was the only ground, a court decree separating a husband and wife was granted for cruel and inhuman treatment. The wife maintained an intimate association with a man other than her husband, widely displaying her affection in such places as automobiles and the apartment house vestibule. Her conduct was notorious. The evidence showed clearly that her friendship for the man had long since passed the "casual, platonic and sisterlike" character she claimed for it. But there was no evidence of actual adultery. The only aid and comfort the husband found was a court decree of separation for three years on the ground of cruel and inhuman treatment and a release during that time from his obligation to support his wife.

The law decides   In the laws of South Carolina there was no provision for an absolute divorce prior to 1948. The statutes did, however, provide for a separation of the parties to a marriage "from bed and board" for cruel or barbarous treatment that endangered the life of the other party to the marriage, or such indignities as rendered the victim's life intolerable. In that state a wife stuck an ice pick a couple of inches into her husband's side, poured scalding water over him, shot at him with a pistol, and put his clothes in the back yard. The court found that this man had ample grievance against his wife—it justified a separation, but the parties had to stay married.

These limited divorces or separations from bed and board do not provide more than the parties themselves can arrange by contract if the agreement is made after they have separated. We shall consider the details of such an agreement or contract in the following pages.

**When
to make separation
agreements**

Don't make an out-of-court agreement for separation from your wife or husband before the actual separation occurs. The agreement must not be a contract to break up a home. This the courts in some instances say is illegal. But if the home is already broken up, you can arrange by this method the details of your future relationship.

In most instances these agreements have survived the onslaughts of litigation between spouses that often follow the execution of such agreements. Sometimes they have not. The law, however, has generally maintained that if you and your wife or husband are actually separated and you no longer live together as husband and wife, any agreement that you make with each other that is fair and that provides for the support of the wife is legal and binding.

**Why an agreement
may be unenforceable**

In Illinois, a husband and wife made a separation agreement by which the wife received $3,000 and the household furniture, and in return released her husband from any further obligation to support her. The court decided this agreement was illegal. It held that the husband could not escape his obligation to support his wife by trading secondhand furniture for a release without the consent of the third party to the marriage, the state.

The duty to support cannot always be avoided by a lump-sum payment. When the money is spent, you may be required to supply support. That is only one reason why consultation with your attorney is necessary for preparation of any separation agreement.

**Form
for separation
agreement**

A simple separation agreement for persons who have already separated runs as follows:

This agreement made and entered into this *10th* day of *February, 1958,* by and between *Charles Graham,* party of the first part, and *Dorothy Graham,* party of the second part, witnesseth:

Whereas the parties are living separate and apart and it is desirous that a settlement of property rights be had, it is mutually agreed as follows:

That the party of the first part will pay to the party of the second part upon the execution of this agreement the sum of *Ten thousand ($10,000.00) Dollars* and the further sum of *One hundred ($100.00) Dollars* per month from the date of this agreement, payable in advance until the death of the party of the second part, said payments to be deposited in the *First National Bank, New York City,* each month to the credit of the party of the second part.

It is further agreed and understood that the estate of the party of the first part shall be holden for said monthly payments until the death of the party of the second part.

The party of the first part agrees to pay to *Charles Haskins,* the attorney for the party of the second part, the sum of $500.00 in full compensation for his services in representing the party of the second part.

The party of the second part does hereby waive, renounce and relinquish all right of inheritance to the property of the party of the first part, and the party of the first part does hereby waive all right of inheritance to the property of the party of the second part.

It is mutually agreed and understood that at the time of the execution of this agreement the parties hereto have actually separated and that this agreement is entered into after actual separation.

This agreement shall bind the heirs, executors and assigns of the parties to the same.

In witness whereof the parties hereto have hereunto set their hands this *10th* day of *February, 1958.*

Charles Graham
Dorothy Graham

State of New York }
County of New York } *ss:*

On this *10th* day of *February, 1958,* before me personally and severally came the within named Charles Graham and Dorothy Graham, his wife, severally known to me and to me known to be the persons described in and who severally executed the within instrument and severally acknowledged that they severally executed the same for the uses and purposes therein named.

Charles Dennis
Notary Public

It should be noted that this agreement does not provide for children, household effects, or other property, and is intended only for illustration and so that you will understand what is involved when you consult your lawyer. Tax consequences must also be considered.

Annulment and its grounds

The annulment of a marriage is not a divorce. A divorce dissolves the marriage. After a divorce there is no longer a marriage. An annulment merely confirms that a marriage never existed. Neither party may assert any of the rights or assume any of the obligations of a divorced person. The law considers them as never having been married. The grounds in some states for the annulment of a marriage are the same as for divorce in other states.

The role played by these different grounds in disposing of a marriage varies with the different state laws. Essentially, the ground for the dissolution of a marriage by an annulment is a fraud inflicted on the other by one of the parties to the marriage contract. This element of fraud, the misrepresentation by one party to the other of a material fact, is the major factor in the voiding of the marriage contract by annulment, as it is in voiding of any other contract. This was discussed earlier.

However, the misrepresentation must be of a material fact. It must be made with the intent of inducing the other party to enter into a marriage contract which he would not have done if the true facts had been known.

False representations of previous virginity, intention to have children, intention to perform a religious ceremony, wealth, social position and earnings, as well as concealment of prior divorce or marriage or conviction of crime, are among the grounds for which an annulment may be sought, although a false representation as to some of these, such as wealth and social position alone, may not be sufficient basis.

The following are the state laws on annulment:

Alabama– Insanity; fraud; bigamy; incest; miscegenation (probably still true despite the Supreme Court decision).

Alaska– No statutory grounds.

Arizona– Any existing impediment.

Arkansas– Incapacity to consent; fraud; force.

California– Incapacity to consent; impotency; spouse alive; unsound mind; fraud; force.

Colorado– Incapacity to consent; fraud; a dare; impotency.

Connecticut– Incest; consanguinity; offense against chastity.

Delaware– Impotency; consanguinity; spouse alive; insanity; fraud; force.

District of Columbia–	Consanguinity; bigamy; insanity; incapacity to consent; fraud.
Florida–	No statutory grounds.
Georgia–	Incapacity to consent. An annulment cannot be granted on a ground that is also a ground for divorce, or where there are children.
Hawaii–	Consanguinity; incapacity to consent; force; fraud; Hansen's (leprosy) or other loathsome disease; bigamy; lunacy; impotency.
Idaho–	Incapacity to consent; bigamy; unsound mind; fraud; force; impotency.
Illinois–	No statutory grounds, but equitable relief will be granted on grounds of fraud or consanguinity.
Indiana–	Fraud; incapacity to consent.
Iowa–	Impotency; bigamy; insanity; consanguinity.
Kansas–	Bigamy; impotency; fraud.
Kentucky–	Force; fraud; incapacity to consent.
Louisiana–	Mistake; incapacity to consent; bigamy; consanguinity.
Maine–	Insanity; bigamy; consanguinity.
Maryland–	Bigamy; consanguinity.
Massachusetts–	Bigamy.
Michigan–	Incapacity to consent.
Minnesota–	Incapacity to consent.
Mississippi–	Bigamy; incapacity to consent; pregnant at the time of marriage; impotency; insanity; force; fraud; invalid license; incest; miscegenation.
Missouri–	Duress; fraud; incapacity to consent.
Montana–	Incapacity to consent; bigamy; unsound mind; fraud; force; impotency.

Nebraska— Consanguinity; incapacity to consent; fraud; force; insanity; impotency.

Nevada— Fraud; incapacity to consent.

New Hampshire— Incapacity to consent.

New Jersey— Bigamy; consanguinity; impotency; fraud; incapacity to consent.

New Mexico— Incapacity to consent.

New York— Bigamy; consanguinity; incapacity to consent; impotency; force; fraud; insanity.

North Carolina— Incapacity to consent.

North Dakota— Incapacity to consent; bigamy; insanity; incest; fraud; force; impotency.

Ohio— Incapacity to consent; bigamy; insanity; fraud; force; marriage never consummated.

Oklahoma— Incapacity to consent.

Oregon— Force; fraud; incapacity to consent.

Pennsylvania— Insanity; consanguinity.

Puerto Rico— Force; bigamy; incapacity to consent; impotency; insanity; consanguinity.

Rhode Island— No statutory grounds. The remedy is divorce.

South Carolina— Incapacity to consent.

South Dakota— Incapacity to consent; bigamy; insanity; fraud; force; impotency.

Tennessee— Incapacity to consent; force; the same grounds as for divorce or separation.

Texas— Impotency and other impediments.

Utah— Force; fraud; incapacity to consent.

Vermont— Incapacity to consent; insanity; force; fraud; impotency.

Virginia–	Bigamy; consanguinity; incapacity to consent; epilepsy; miscegenation.
Virgin Islands–	Impotency; insanity; force; fraud; incapacity to consent.
Washington–	Consanguinity. Where there is force, fraud, or incapacity to consent, divorce is the exclusive remedy.
West Virginia–	Bigamy; consanguinity; insanity; epilepsy; venereal disease; impotency; incapacity to consent; conviction of infamous crime; wife pregnant at time of marriage or a prostitute; husband licentious; miscegenation.
Wisconsin–	Impotency; consanguinity; bigamy; force; fraud; incapacity to consent.
Wyoming–	Incapacity to consent; force; fraud; impotency.

Marriage by force

In Chicago, some years ago, Margaret Eustice asked a man whom she had known for some time to drive with her in her automobile to a place in the Chicago suburbs, where she was going on an errand. O'Brien accepted her invitation. The two drove gaily toward the outskirts of the city. Soon a big limousine was following. When they stopped for the errand, two men stepped from the other car, tied O'Brien with a rope and set him on the back seat of the limousine.

Next they took him to the residence of a justice of the peace, where Margaret had already arranged the preliminaries for the wedding, and witnesses were waiting. O'Brien was kept in the car while the justice conducted the ceremony through to the pronouncement that they were husband and wife. On their return to the city O'Brien seized the emergency brake, jumped from the car, and fled to a policeman.

In the annulment suit brought later by O'Brien, the court said that this was no marriage. Where consent to a marriage is obtained, as it was here, by force, there is no marriage.

Two husbands at one time

More frequently, however, marriages are annulled for false statements made to get the consent of the other party to the marriage. At Ventura, California, Harold and Ruth Goff were married. She had told him she was a widow and he believed this statement until he learned, about three years after their marriage, that her husband from a previous marriage was still alive and she had not been divorced. Legally, she lacked the ability to wed, and her marriage to Goff was annulled.

When delay is fatal

Conditions for which you can have your marriage annulled cannot be held in reserve like an ammunition stockpile, for use at some future time. If you plan to seek an annulment of your marriage, do it at once. When you discover the grounds for which you can ask for that remedy, it is not wise to wait. Your delay may be a forgiveness of the fraud and you will be compelled to go on with your marriage, with the door for escape closed.

Take the case of a man and a woman who were married in Rhode Island. She did not tell her husband at the time of the marriage that she was suffering from the consequences of a venereal disease. They lived together more than a year, until the woman was forced to enter a Providence hospital for mental diseases. A week later her husband took her from the hospital. Then, for the first time, he learned that the mental condition with which she was afflicted was the consequence of a venereal disease. Nevertheless he lived with her for more than a year, and it was not until eight years later that he sought to have the marriage annulled.

The court refused to disturb their relationship. "The realization that he was to be burdened with an incurably insane wife seems to have been the motivating cause. He waived whatever right he may have had the day on which he first learned of his wife's blood condition or within a reasonable time thereafter, to have his marriage declared null and void for fraudulent concealment."

Certain aspects of annulment are also discussed in the chapter on divorce, which you should consult. As in all these situations, the facts and circumstances of each individual case are important and you cannot rely on generalization as a solution, but should consult your attorney as to the application of the law to your facts.

CHAPTER 4

Children

Childhood or infancy, in law, ends when the child becomes 18 years old, or 21, or whatever other age is set by law. It begins, however, with the life of the child when he is still unborn. By the law of some states a child, for most purposes, is fully as much a person in the nine months before his birth as he is after his birth and his introduction to the family.

That an unborn child has, in many instances, the same rights as one already born is a rule of considerable importance where legacies are concerned. This is well illustrated in the case of a trust fund left by a man named Roswell Colt. At his death, the income from the fund was to be divided among those of his children who survived him. He died on May 1. On November 17, six and a half months after her father's death, a daughter was born.

This child, at the time of her father's death, said the court, was as fully a person as some months later when she made her debut into a world of milk bottles and bassinets. She was entitled to the same rights and consideration and to the same share in that trust income as his other children.

Another incident of this sort occurred when an action was brought under the New Jersey Workmen's Compensation Act on behalf of an infant. The act provided for payment of compensation for death by accident to the surviving children of the deceased. A child born two weeks after the father had been killed was held by the court as much entitled to these benefits as it would have been, born two weeks or more earlier.

Can an unborn child bring suit?

The rule that an unborn child has the legal rights of a child after its birth has exception, however. In some states, actions cannot be brought by children for injuries suffered by them before they were born, unless the statutes specifically provide for such actions. Such states follow the old common law, which holds that an unborn child has no existence apart from its mother.

A typical case of this sort took place in New Jersey. A child sued for injuries from a physician's treatment of its mother six weeks before birth, where, as a consequence of an X-ray examination, the child developed into an idiot. The highest court in New Jersey refused to recognize the child's right to sue. California, on the other hand, would have decided this case differently, as its statutes permit suits of this kind. New York, without a statute, has permitted such a suit, and other states also permit it.

Now that abortion laws are being liberalized, the arguments about the rights of unborn children are becoming even more noteworthy.

**Obligations
of children
and responsibility
to them**

Children participate in our complex society as much as or more than adults these days. The percentage of youths in our population is rising and their economic power is enormous. We will first consider what obligations are owed to children and how they are protected, and then we will discuss what their responsibilities are toward others.

When childhood ends

The date when the minority of an infant ends is established by law and occurs at different ages in different states and under different circumstances. The age when a boy or girl may make a contract, a valid marriage, when he or she can make a will, all are set by law with different ages prescribed for the performance of different acts and deeds. For most legal purposes, but not all, a person becomes an adult at 21. A recent amendment to the United States Constitution lowered the voting age from 21 to 18 years, and many states have lowered the age of maturity from 21 to 18 years. New Jersey has just recently done this.

The life of a child before becoming of age is under the care of the father or other head of the family. The head of the family has this obligation and responsibility, which is offset by a right to whatever wages the child may earn.

**A father's right
to his
child's earnings**

Courts have held that a father is entitled to the earnings of his children until they become of age or until they are emancipated—"on their own." In case of the father's death, the mother is entitled to the earnings of their minor children. When they are no longer supported by their father but earn their own livelihood, children keep whatever wages they receive.

**The child who
earns his own living**

When a child is earning his or her own living, or when the father compels the child to support himself, the courts hold that there is no principle of law that will continue a father's right to receive the earnings of the child's labor.

**When the mother
is the head
of the family**

A boy employed by a Connecticut manufacturer died from injuries received in the course of his employment. The mother asked for compensation under the Workmen's Compensation Act of that state.

Long before, the father had deserted his wife and children. The five children had contributed to the support of their mother for three years. The only money she had had for the maintenance of the home had been their earnings. The award of this compensation was opposed by the state, which contended that as the father was living it should be made to him.

The father, the court held, was disqualified. He had been replaced by the mother of the children as the head of the family and she, not the father, was entitled to the compensation award that represented the boy's wages. "The obligations of a minor to his parents," said the court, "are obedience, subjection, and his earnings, if any, while those of the parent are protection, education, and support."

Contracts of children–are they legal?

The courts consistently extend to children protection from exploitation by their elders. One phase of this protection is the rule that no child or minor is liable for any obligations under a contract. Minors cannot ordinarily be made to pay for anything they buy except such things as are necessary to their health and welfare.

Their contracts are considered voidable at the option of the infant. But an adult cannot avoid a contract with an infant. An infant can compel another party to fulfill his contract.

A minor over 18 who owns his own business and who enters into contracts in connection therewith is bound by them if the contracts are reasonable. This is a special situation.

The consequences of the rule that minors don't have to honor their contracts places on the shoulders of those dealing with youngsters the burden of knowing whether or not they are dealing with minors. Children may misrepresent their ages, but this doesn't change their protection. Children are great mail-order devotees, but being minors they can't be made to pay for the merchandise.

However, if a minor disaffirms a contract he must return the value he has received and he is responsible for depreciation.

A disaffirmance has repercussions

Recently, an honor graduate from a law school in Arizona was almost deprived of the opportunity to practice law because, as a minor, he had disaffirmed a contract involving a substantial sum of money. A committee of the bar association felt that this showed a lack of moral character on the part of the graduate that rendered him unfit to become a member of the bar. The matter was appealed to the court, and the decision was to permit admission to the bar since the disaffirmance had been legal.

This case points up the fact that you never know what problems may ensue even from an accepted and legal course of action.

How a child's liability for bills is limited

A minor, says the law, must pay for his "meat, drink, apparel, necessary physic and other such necessaries, and likewise for his good teaching or instruction." Beyond that a child's obligations cease unless after he becomes of age he wishes to pay them. Don't overlook this immunity of minors from any debts except for necessaries. On the death of her father, Doris had agreed with an undertaker in Philadelphia to pay his funeral expenses. Before doing so, she consulted her guardian, the Provident Trust Company, and received its approval. Yet, although the undertaker had earned his money, the court refused her permission to make the payment to him as she had promised.

Real property

When a child is involved in a contract concerning real property, he cannot disaffirm the contract until he reaches majority. If he has given the property away while still an infant, he can, upon reaching majority, get it back.

Can payments be made to children?

In general, debts due a minor, other than wages, should not be paid to the child. Giving the child the money does not pay the debt. Even after the child takes the money, you still owe the debt. When a California insurance company gave a 15-year-old boy the money for a loss they had insured, instead of paying his guardian, the child had the money but the debt of the company had not been paid. The company had neglected the rule of law that a child is not bound by a contract. The court obliged the company to pay the debt over again to the boy's guardian.

This principle of law is to protect children not only from others but also from themselves. "It is a well-settled principle of law," say the courts, "that one deals with infants at his peril."

Injuries to trespassing children

An action brought against the Alabama Power Company showed that an eight-year-old child had trespassed on the company's property, run into a high-voltage wire, and been instantly killed. The conclusion of the court was harsh, but the rule that the wrongdoer cannot complain applies to children as it does to mature men and women. "It must be borne in mind that under our authorities a child may be a trespasser just as well as an adult."

The law of attractive nuisances

The laws in a number of states, however, make the exception that even though children may technically be trespassers, when conditions are such that children are naturally attracted into unsuspected dangers that the owner or person in charge should have foreseen, a liability for any injury to the child exists. The reason often is that this attractiveness is the equivalent of an implied invitation to the child, and the one responsible for the attractiveness is liable for the consequences.

An attractive nuisance exists when an artificial condition is maintained where children are likely to be, where the condition involves an unreasonable risk to such children, where the children don't realize the risks, and when the condition could be remedied without causing the owner too much trouble as compared to the risks to the children.

Some examples of attractive nuisances

Artificial bodies of water are hazards if they have unusual features. A raft in a pond where there is a sudden and hidden drop-off in depth can be an attractive nuisance, as can a large pile of debris near the shore of a canal. An abandoned excavation with debris of a razed residential building in a city was found to be one when a child was injured by a rusty nail on a hidden and loose plank. A junk yard near a public street was found to be one when a child was injured on broken glass from a wrecked car. Another attractive nuisance was a rotting wharf whose holes were covered by piles of sand; it was near a public road frequented by small children. A somewhat unusual example of an attractive nuisance is a mailbox with a spout used to receive mail at curbs from passing vehicles. A five-year-old climbed onto one that wasn't anchored in order to talk into the spout, and was injured. The government was found to be liable.

What is emancipation?

It can be reaching the age of 18 or 21, being married, or earning one's own living. It means independence, freedom from parental control.

When an infant daughter marries an infant husband it is his obligation to support her, and her father is relieved of that responsibility.

Being under 18 or 21 and emancipated, however, doesn't mean that the defense of infancy cannot be used. An emancipated minor can still avoid his contracts.

When is infancy not a barrier?

An infant can have life insurance coverage and be responsible for the premiums; an infant can deal with a credit union and be held responsible for the shares.

A child's liability for injuring someone

While children are not liable for the things they buy, except necessaries, or for any money owed by virtue of a contract, they may be liable for damages they inflict on others. Such obligations do not spring from contract but are torts, or civil wrongs. An infant of tender years may be liable for any tort he is capable of committing. Where malice is necessary, the child must be old enough to have the intent that is legally required for malice. Where negligence is involved, the child is held to the standard of a child of similar age and experience. Some courts say, however, that children under seven years of age are presumed to be incapable of negligence.

A five-year-old was accused of deliberately pulling a chair out from beneath an adult, who was injured. The court found that the child could possibly have the necessary intent. In another case, a four-year-old was accused of negligently pushing and shoving an adult so she fell and was injured. The court held that since a four-year-old was incapable of contributory negligence, he would be incapable of primary negligence.

What about parents' liability?

Usually a parent is not liable for the tort of his child except where the child is an agent or employee; where he entrusts the child with a dangerous instrument; where he knows of any dangerous propensities of the child and doesn't try to protect others from him; or where the parent ratifies the tort of his child—that is, he knows of a wrong the child has done but does nothing to help put things right.

In recent years, there has been support for legislation to make the parents responsible to innocent third parties for the wrongs committed by their children.

More about a child's age

This can be important both in determining whether a child can contribute to an accident to himself and in deciding whether he is old enough to be responsible for an injury to someone else. It is especially important when a crime has been committed.

Children under seven years are usually considered incapable of having the capacity to contribute to a personal injury, although in New York the age is four, and some courts have put the age as low as three. Up to about the age of 14, there is usually a presumption that children are not capable of contributing to their own injuries. However, their intelligence, schooling, and general knowledge are taken into consideration in deciding their maturity and the degree of care required of them in avoiding personal injury. Children must meet a standard just as adults do, and the standard is what can reasonably be expected of the ordinary child of like age, intellectual and physical development, and education or experience under the same or similar circumstances. In Louisiana, a normal child of 12 is presumed to be capable of contributory negligence.

After 14, there is no presumption in favor of the child and the child has no shield against his own negligence.

Can a child sue his parents?

Usually an unemancipated child cannot sue his parents in tort for negligence that causes him injury. However, if there has been a willful tort, that is another matter. A child can sue other members of the family for simple negligence.

In a recent case in the highest court of New York, the old idea that parents and children could not sue one another was abandoned.

The plaintiff sued her 16-year-old son for negligence. She was a passenger in a car owned by her and operated by him. The insurance company representing her son interposed the defense of interfamily immunity. It was argued that this rule of immunity should be continued as it would help prevent fraud. The court held that inasmuch as one could sue a child who has reached the legal age of majority, one should also be able to sue a minor child.

A child can sue his parents on a contract.

Auto accidents of children

Automobile insurance rates are very high for youthful drivers. This is because of the higher incidence of accidents involving young people.

Your son and daughter are liable for payment of the damages arising from their careless automobile driving. When the car they own is driven by someone other than themselves, however, it is often a difficult question to determine. When a minor lets someone else drive his car, any liability he assumes arises from a contract—the driver of the car is his agent, and minors cannot make contracts.

Mildred Scott was 17. Her father had given her an automobile as a birthday present. Dan Brooks was driving this car on a Louisiana highway with Mildred's permission. She herself was in the back seat when Dan hit another auto. As owner of the car, Mildred was sued for the damages. The court held here that a minor is only liable for his or her personal offenses. Since the collision was not Mildred's act and she could not thus be liable, her father was not liable either. Liability merely for ownership is applied by statute in a number of states.

In some states the minor owner of the car would be liable for damage caused by someone else operating it with his consent if in the same situation an adult owner would be liable.

Is a minor liable for fraud?

While a child is not liable under a contract, he may not benefit from his fraudulent acts. The law that a boy or girl cannot be held to a contract to pay for what he or she buys unless it is a necessary is carefully watched by the courts.

Sometimes courts are called upon to protect older and more experienced persons and shield them from frauds perpetrated by legally irresponsible minors. A boy 17 years old, driving an automobile, hit another car driven by a mature man. This driver asked the boy merely to pay the damages caused by his carelessness. The boy settled the claim by signing a memorandum, "I agree to pay for the doctor's and hospital bills in the sum of $75 at the rate of $2.50 a week." In addition he agreed to pay $500 "for actual property damage." In return the owner of the car agreed he would make no further claims against the youngster.

When the boy was 21, he had paid $240. Then he sued the man he injured for the money he had already paid, on the ground that he was a minor when he had paid it. The court decided against the boy. Although when under 21 the boy was not responsible for contract obligations, it was not proper for him to use this protection for the commission of a fraud in stalling an action for damages caused by an accident that was his responsibility.

In another case, a 19-year-old Creek Indian borrowed $125 from a land company and gave as security a deed of 40 acres of land. Having spent the money, the Indian brought suit to set aside the deed because he was a minor and incapable of executing it.

"Infants have no privilege to cheat men" was the laconic comment of the judge, deciding against the boy. Before the deed could be canceled, the borrowed money had to be repaid.

A child's responsibility for his parent's support

The economic burden of the family does not always rest on the shoulders of the parents. The law at times places on children the care of parents who are helpless, lest they become a public charge.

The support of parents by their children is a subject that has many interesting legal sides to it. A Pennsylvania woman filed a claim against her father-in-law's estate for "board, lodging, nursing and similar services at $5 a week for 72 weeks." She had rendered these services while the old man was living with her and her husband in the house that the father had given his son, her husband.

The food the father had eaten had been from his son, said the court, adding that because it was prepared by the son's wife did not take it out of the rule that when a father or mother comes to live with his or her son, the law implies no promise on the part of the parent to pay for board and lodging and kindred services.

In most of the states, the legislatures have enacted statutes concerning the responsibilities of parents for their children's support, sometimes only until majority. These laws are implemented with penalties for the enforcement of obedience. In most states, too, parents are under legal obligation to support children who are of age if they are impoverished and liable to become a public charge. Some statutes apply this liability also to grandparents, grandchildren, sisters, and brothers.

In Illinois, children are severally liable for the support of their parents if they are in need of such support and likely to become a public charge. When there are two or more children the court may assess the proportionate ability of each to contribute to such support.

Criminal acts

Many states have statutes that punish parents or others for contributing to the neglect or delinquency of children. The state statute enumerates which adult is responsible, the age the child has to be in order to be covered, and what makes for criminal behavior.

Ages for children's criminal acts

Usually, minors under seven years are not considered criminally responsible; up to the age of 15, they are called juvenile delinquents; between ages 16 and 19, children who break the law are juvenile offenders. When a 15-year-old commits a homicide, he may be treated as an adult criminal.

The Gault case

The United States Supreme Court handed down a landmark decision in a case involving a 15-year-old Arizona boy, Gerald Gault. The decision established that youths accused of juvenile delinquency are entitled to most of the constitutional rights of adult criminal suspects.

Gerald had been accused of making lewd and offensive phone calls.

If an adult had been punished for that offense in Arizona, he would have received a $50 fine and two months in jail. Gerald had a hearing before a regular trial judge sitting as a juvenile court judge, and he was committed to an industrial school for six years, that is, until 21.

The Gault decision applies to juveniles facing delinquency charges who may be confined to a state institution. The juvenile is given the right to remain silent, the right to have an attorney, the right to have full and adequate notice of the misconduct with which he is charged, the right to see the witnesses who will testify against him, and the right to have defense counsel cross-examine witnesses.

You should consult an attorney immediately upon receiving word that your child has been apprehended by a law enforcement authority. He will know how your state's juvenile court system operates and how best to proceed in light of the Gault case.

Federal offenses

The United States Attorney General, through local United States Attorneys, handles cases involving Federal offenses where the defendant is under 18 years. The majority of cases coming under the Federal Juvenile Delinquency Act seem to concern interstate car thefts.

Illegitimate children—who has custody?

The custody of an illegitimate child is usually determined in court proceedings. A writ is directed to whomever has the custody of the child, ordering the child brought before the court. Then the court determines the person or persons into whose care the child should be placed. The mother is of course entitled to the first consideration, subject, however, to the interests and welfare of the child. Second in consideration is the father.

When the care of the child is given the father, state statutes often prescribe the conditions he must meet. By a law of Georgia, the mother is entitled to the custody of her child "unless the father shall legitimate him." The courts invariably maintain that the welfare and happiness of the child is the paramount consideration in a proceeding for his custody.

The harshness and unfairness of this rule has in some instances been set aside by the sympathy of the courts. Some have ruled that the father of an illegitimate child too young to care for itself is under the nonstatutory obligation to support it, which may be enforced in an action brought by the child through its next friend. The state stands *in loco parentis* (in place of the parents) to see to it that the child is supported, and can pursue the father (if proved so to be) of the illegitimate child.

Rights of an illegitimate child

A suit was brought on behalf of illegitimate children for the wrongful death of their mother with whom they had lived and by whom they were supported. The Louisiana court decided that the right of a surviving child to sue did not include an illegitimate child and dismissed the case. The United States Supreme Court reversed this determination on the basis that to deny this right to an illegitimate child would be discrimination in violation of the equal protection clause of the Fourteenth Amendment to the United States Constitution. In a similar case, a Texas mother was denied the right to sue by a Louisiana court for the death of her illegitimate son in an automobile accident in Louisiana. She would have been allowed to sue if the accident occurred in Texas, because the Texas law did not make this distinction. The United States Supreme Court again reversed to put an illegitimate child on a par with a legitimate child for this purpose.

However, a recent United States Supreme Court decision, upholding the right of Louisiana to deny to illegitimate children the same right as legitimate children to inherit from their fathers, appears to cloud the issue as to whether a law that discriminates against illegitimates is unconstitutional. The opinion, upholding the Louisiana court's award of an entire estate to the brothers and sisters of a decedent over his illegitimate child, stated that the Constitution reserved to the states the power to "protect and strengthen family life as well as to regulate the disposition of property."

Adoption–how to adopt a child

The procedure for the adoption of children follows substantially the same pattern in every state. You may adopt an alien under fourteen who can qualify as a non-quota immigrant. See Chapter 8 on Aliens. You may also adopt an adult.

A petition is made to the court by those seeking the adoption. With this petition is submitted the consent of the parents and those who have custody of the child. Where the child may have arrived at an age set by the statutes for doing so, the child's consent must also be included.

You need the consent of the parents

The Louisiana laws, like those of other states in general, have a provision in relation to adoption that if the child concerned has a parent or parents or guardian, their full consent shall be obtained. Effie Harper and Willie Jackson, nine and ten years old respectively, were in the care of the Children's Home Society in Louisiana. They were adopted by Percy Owles and his wife. The adoption papers were signed by the superintendent of the Children's Society and by Percy and Mrs. Owles. Twenty years later, when Mrs. Owles died, there arose the question of their inheritance from her estate. The natural mothers of both children were living at the time of their adoption and alive at the death of Mrs. Owles.

In both instances the adoption proceedings had failed to include the consent of the mother of either child. The only consent to their adoption had been that of the superintendent of the Children's Society, and the adoption did not stand up in court.

An interesting case in the Family Court of New York City involved a section of the New York State Domestic Relations Law, heretofore rarely used, which defines the circumstances when parental consent is required.

The mother had a record of arrests on prostitution, robbery, and narcotics charges. The father, a narcotics addict, was in prison, but in any event his consent was not necessary because the child had been born out of wedlock.

The mother objected to the adoption, and the court held that her consent was unnecessary, since she had been deprived of custody due to neglect.

Other requirements

There may also be a required waiting period prior to adoption, during which time the adopting parents care for the child, in order to avoid a later objection to the child after the adoption has occurred.

In some states the adopting parents must be residents of the state in which the adoption proceedings are instituted.

The character and social conditions of the adopting parents must of necessity be judged by the court to be suitable, largely from the facts peculiar to each case. The only restrictions are those created by the way the court may interpret the meaning of the word "suitable" in its relation to their financial ability, character, or environment. They must be desirable parents, capable of giving the child a secure and decent home. The law, however, does contemplate that the adopting parents shall be of suitable age. For example, a man twenty-one years old would not be permitted to adopt a woman twenty years old. The mere fact that one has reached an advanced age does not make it impossible for him to adopt a child. Everything depends on the specific facts of who intends to adopt whom.

Some states have religious restrictions for adoptions. In New York, the state constitution provides that when a child is put up for adoption, the child's religion should be matched with that of the foster parents "when practicable." This means that, if all other things are equal, custody will be granted to those of the same religious persuasion, although religious interests will not predominate.

Recently a deaf-mute couple in California were deprived of their two-year-old foster son because the court decided they could not provide a normal home for him. The decision was appealed and the appellate court found that, since the couple had another older child who was normal and happy, there was no reason not to allow them to rear the boy also.

During the past century, an essential change has slowly been taking place in family relationships. One feature of this change is the inclination of courts to base their decisions in adoption proceedings less on the natural rights of the parents to their children and more on the interests of the child and society as a whole. In fact, recently even single women have been permitted to adopt children. In California, the State Department of Social Welfare modified its prohibition against placing children with unmarried persons. Usually children with peculiar problems limiting their adoptability by families are considered for adoption by singles. In Oregon a mature bachelor has been allowed to adopt a child. The Department of Welfare of the District of Columbia is also now permitting adoption by single persons, and private social agencies are seriously considering a change in that direction.

In adoption proceedings, be scrupulously careful to follow the statute of the state in which the proceedings are brought and the provisions governing the transfer of the relationship of the child from its natural parents to those who are being substituted. Adoption is no fundamental right such as marriage. This method for changing the parents of a child is created by statute. The natural parent of a child born out of wedlock may later change her mind about her consent to adoption and seek to set it aside.

Failing to obey the statutes

Failure to follow the laws of a state in regard to adoption may, many years later, have serious consequences. Thinking of a child as your own is not enough. Anna, born in Sweden, came to the home of her aunt, Mrs. Carl Brandl, in Kansas, when she was seven years old. For more than fifteen years she was treated as one of the family. When she left Sweden, that country had no adoption procedure and no such proceedings were taken here on her behalf.

Upon the death of her aunt, the settlement of the estate required a determination of her relationship to Mrs. Brandl. The court required that any claim Anna might have for a share of her aunt's estate must be supported by proof of her legal adoption. She was denied the share she sought. There had been no compliance by her aunt with the adoption statute of Kansas.

When adoption decrees become final

The adoption decree of a child had been made by a Michigan court on the last day of July and the consent of the parents properly executed and filed. Under the laws of Michigan and many other states, an adoption decree does not become final and binding until a stated period of time after it has been made. During that time the decree may be changed or modified by the court.

During the ninety-day period provided by the Michigan statute, the child's mother, apparently regretting the loss of her daughter, gave notice of her withdrawal of her consent. The court decided that not only was the mother entitled to withdraw her consent but that, "When the statutory provisions regulating the adoption of children cannot be complied with, the adoption will fail."

Why an adoption decree may be revoked

The decree of the court by which the foster father and mother supplant the natural parents of the child may be revoked or set aside for fraud, such as occurred in one instance where the adopting father was mentally unsound and misrepresented his condition to the court by a statement that he was of a sound and healthy mentality.

Except where the adoption decree is set aside for fraud or misrepresentation of the parties to the proceedings, it possesses the same permanency and finality as any other judgment of a court.

Abrogation of adoption

An adoption can be canceled by mutual consent of all concerned in the procedure, by the court on behalf of the child when the foster parents have been cruel or have refused to support the child, or, in very extreme cases, by the court on behalf of the foster parents for bad behavior by the foster child.

Can an adopted child inherit?

Adoption proceedings create an irrevocable relationship between the child and its foster parents. The child does not, however, become a "child of the blood" of its foster parents, unless the statutes of the state expressly provide this in relation to inheritance from relatives of the foster parents.

In all states, however, an adopted child is the legal heir of the foster parents and will inherit the property owned by them at their demise in the absence of contrary provision by will. The rule as to "blood" relationship only extends to property of relatives of the deceased foster parents. Unless the state has a statute permitting it, this rule may prevent the adopted child from representing the foster parent as would a natural child for purposes of inheritance.

Elizabeth was adopted by Will Warr. After the death of Mr. Warr, his sister, Isabel, also died, leaving an estate. Had Warr survived his sister, he would have been entitled to her entire estate. The problem before the court was whether Elizabeth inherited the share in Isabel's estate that would have been her foster father's had he lived.

The inheritance by adopted children from their adoptive parents being governed entirely by the laws of each state, the court, following the state statute, ruled that the property of the deceased, who had died without making a will, should descend to kindred by the blood.

The laws of many states have abolished this discrimination against adopted as contrasted with natural children.

The law of guardian and ward

A guardian has the care and management of the property and rights of another person who for some cause, as infancy or unsound mind, is not capable of caring for himself or administering his own affairs. The natural guardian of a child is its father, or, if the father is deceased or has abandoned the child, then the mother.

The mother is the natural guardian of an illegitimate child. In cases of divorce, the determination of the guardian is made by the court in the award of the custody of the child. Where a child is of tender years the mother is more frequently entrusted with guardianship.

This guardianship of a child, however, is subject at all times during the minority of the child to the control of the court. The guardian may be removed and replaced by another at any time when, in the opinion of the court, circumstances and the welfare of the child demand such a change.

In most of the states, a child older than fourteen has the right to select his own guardian, subject to the approval of the court.

Upon his appointment, the guardian is notified and must signify his acceptance before assuming the obligations of his trust. This acceptance may be assumed, however, by his performance of his guardianship duties, although in some of the states acceptance must be made within a specified time.

Upon acceptance, the guardian must execute the statutory oath and file with the court a bond as security for the faithful performance of his duties, unless he had been excused from so doing by the court.

Rights and duties of a guardian

A guardian, other than one who is a parent of the child, is not entitled to the child's earnings, nor does he have any personal liability for his ward's support. The maintenance of the ward is solely from the property the guardian holds in trust for him. Its disbursement is subject to the approval of the court by which the guardian was appointed.

The religious instruction of the child is within the control of the court. It may require the guardian to continue the child in the religious faith of the parents, or refuse to permit the guardian to change the child from that faith.

The proper education of the ward is the obligation of the guardian also.

Where the ward has been accepted as a member of the guardian's own family, it is a general rule that the guardian is entitled to compensation in a reasonable amount—determined by the court—for the support of the ward.

The guardian's compensation

The compensation of the guardian for the services rendered in the care and custody of the ward and his property is in most states governed by statutes. These allow the guardian either a commission on the amount of his receipts and disbursements of the property of his ward, or a reasonable allowance that is determined by the court.

A guardian ad litem

This is a guardian appointed by a court on behalf of an infant to prosecute or defend any suit to which the infant may be a party. Not every state requires that the court appoint a guardian ad litem. Suits by infants are brought also by the infant's next friend, usually a parent acting on his or her behalf.

When guardianship ends

The marriage of a male ward usually terminates the guardianship. Insofar as the property of the ward is concerned, however, the guardianship usually is continued until the ward attains his majority.

When the ward is a girl, upon her marriage the guardianship usually terminates as to her person and, in some states, her property.

Otherwise, guardianship generally ends when the ward reaches the age of twenty-one.

Upon the termination of the relationship of guardian and ward, it becomes the duty of the guardian to account for all receipts and disbursements from any trust fund in his control. Pursuant to the direction of the court, he must turn over whatever property of the trust still remains in his possession.

It is possible that a trust as set up in a will or in a deed of trust may by its terms continue beyond the age of twenty-one. However, this can apply only to the property of the ward and involves a relationship that is different from guardian and ward and instead concerns a trustee and a beneficiary of the trust. You may wish to set up a trust fund for your children to gain tax benefits and to be sure of proper estate management. Your lawyer will be able to advise you.

CHAPTER 5

Father
and Husband

From time immemorial the legal rule has been that the father and husband is the head of the house. This principle, which in bygone days frequently had crude and even savage applications, has been softened by the greater warmth and informality of present-day family relationships, but it still exists. In everyday life and law, occasions often arise when this fundamental rule becomes of vital importance.

A famous lawyer of this country, James Kent, said of the relationship of a father and his children, "A father's house is always open to his children; and whether they are married or unmarried it is still to them a refuge from evil and a consolation in distress. Natural affection consecrates and establishes this asylum. The father is even under legal obligation to maintain his children and grandchildren, if he be competent and they unable to maintain themselves; it is nature's provision to assist, maintain, and counsel a child." Written more than 125 years ago, this is still a basic statement of the law of this country.

Take the matter of a child's religious instruction, for example. Many times the court's permission is sought to change the religion of a child. In general, however, they will rule that the child shall be brought up in the religion of the father, who has the right to direct and regulate the child's religious education.

The recent movement for the rights of women, which has challenged the traditional positions of husband and wife, has raised legal as well as social questions. While we may expect to see movements for changes in laws that favor the husband, comparatively few such changes have been made.

Can a father chase away his daughter's suitor?

In cases involving the marriage of a child, the father's rights are often brought to the fore. In California, Emory Smith was a suitor of Mildred Kiger. His presence in the home was more than unwelcome to her father, who in one incident pushed Smith to the street door, with a "Get out and stay out."

Later, Mildred Kiger and Emory Smith were married secretly. Next came an action for alienation of affection by Smith against his father-in-law. The expulsion of Smith from Kiger's home was part of the evidence at the trial. The court commented that it was settled law that a father had the right to forbid a prospective suitor to call on his daughter; further, that he was under no obligation to permit anyone of whom he did not approve to enter his home.

Can a child sue his father for injuries?

The old rule that allowed a parent to be completely immune from civil liability for any injury he caused to his child has been abandoned in very few states, although some states have suspended the immunity in cases involving grievous injuries to the child, or in cases where the parent had a responsibility to a group of people including his child and the suit was obviously not designed merely to recover from an insurer.

A recent decision demonstrates how courts have tended to adhere to the old rule of immunity. A four-year-old boy was shopping with his father in a department store. He pulled away from his father and ran to an escalator. He fell down the escalator and was injured seriously. The court would not allow a suit to be brought on behalf of the son against his father. The judge in the case said: "It is impossible to imagine even the most devoted and intelligent parent . . . not being guilty of some occasional act resulting in injuries (to this child). And the threat of a civil suit by the injured child against a parent already horrified and remorseful from the consequences of his own negligence is utterly repugnant."

Nonetheless, the State of New York recently abandoned the old rule of immunity, and a child there may now sue its parents. It would seem, furthermore, that more states will come to adopt this view. See Chapter 4 on Children.

All states, of course, still do have criminal statutes that punish parents for any serious harm that they intentionally inflict on their children.

Your obligation to support your family

The burden of the family support is placed by law on the shoulders of the husband and father.

Most states have criminal statutes that punish the failure of a father to support his child. These laws were enacted to prevent a child from becoming a public charge. However, they may be invoked only when the father is able to support the child and does not do so. In such a situation, most states allow the child, or a person acting on his behalf, to sue the father for support. If a son or daughter over 21 is incapable of self-support, the father is also liable for the upkeep of that child.

In a typical case, a father was brought into court charged with failure to support his child. There was no evidence that he could support the child, and he had never provided for either the child or his wife, who had always lived with her parents. Accordingly, the court decided in his favor.

Illegitimate child

In cases coming from Illinois, the United States Supreme Court recently ruled that unwed fathers cannot be denied custody of their illegitimate children without at least being given an opportunity to prove that they would be fit parents.

A Chicago man had lived off and on with a woman for some 18 years, and three children were the product of this union. The mother died, and the state denied the father custody because he was not considered the parent under the law of Illinois. The children automatically became wards of the state. The father contended that he was denied due process of law because he was not given the opportunity at a hearing to show his qualifications, and he also contended that he was denied equal protection of the law because an unwed mother would be recognized, where an unwed father would not. Of course, a prerequisite in such cases would be to establish the parental relationship. This obviously is more difficult for an unwed father than for an unwed mother.

In a way this case is similar to another recent United States Supreme Court decision coming out of Idaho and discussed in the next chapter, where a law preferring men to women as administrators of the estates of deceased persons was struck down on the ground of sex discrimination. It seems readily apparent that men and women are being recognized on an equal status basis, and old ideas about denying rights because of sex are falling by the wayside.

The duty of a stepfather

The majority of states do not require that a stepfather support his stepchild. However, he does acquire that responsibility if he voluntarily takes the child into his family and assumes the duty of support for it. If he does not legally adopt the child, his responsibility is terminated when his tie to the family ends by the death of or by separation from the mother.

Workmen's compensation cases

The fact that a father has an obligation to support his children—their status as his dependents—is often of importance in workmen's compensation cases, as the following incident illustrates.

A workman's two children were cared for by an Indiana children's home after their father had suffered injuries from which he ultimately died. Under the Workmen's Compensation Act of that state, an award depended on whether or not there were dependents, and on the liability of the injured man for their support.

These children, the court held, were dependents even though in the care of a charitable institution. The father had a duty to maintain his minor children that was imposed upon him by law at their birth. The fact that he was temporarily unable to support them did not change their status as dependents.

From this obligation of a father for the support of his children stems his right to their earnings.

What support a father must provide

Generally speaking, the father's obligation for the support of his wife and children is confined to necessaries alone. "Necessaries," say the courts, is a relative term. It must be defined anew in each instance. Necessaries are defined generally as items or services reasonably appropriate for the support of a wife and child. What is "reasonably appropriate" depends upon the needs of the family and the means of the father.

The general position of courts historically was that a college education, though quite worthwhile to a child, was not a requirement. Recently, several jurisdictions have declared that it is a necessity and have ordered fathers to pay for the higher education of their children. The reasoning of these opinions is exemplified by a recent decision which noted that "not calling a college education a necessity may have been justified in former times when the needs of the family, and of society and government, were less exacting than they are today. But we are living in an age of keen competition. The importance of a college education is being more and more recognized in matters of commerce and government. The college graduate is being more and more preferred over those who are not so fortunate. No parent should subject a worthy child to disadvantages if he has the financial capacity."

When a child drives the family car

The advent of the family automobile has enlarged the range of liability of the father for the wrongdoing of his children. There is disagreement among different states regarding the broadness of this range. In many states, the rule is that when a father allows any member of his immediate family to drive, all negligence by the driver is imputed to the father. This rule only applies to a child who was using the car for the purpose for which his father lent it to him. An equal number of states have the **rule** which states that when a father lets his child drive his car, the child is not acting as the agent of the father. They do not hold the father liable for the negligence of the child.

Use of automobiles by minors

In some states the danger from the use of automobiles by minors has been made the subject of special statutes. Typical of these is the one in Idaho stating that the owner of a motor vehicle who causes or knowingly permits a minor under the age of 16 years to drive such a vehicle upon a highway, and any person who gives or furnishes a motor vehicle to such a minor, are liable with the minor for any damage caused by his negligence in driving the car.

Liability here of the father is limited to the negligence of youngsters under the specific age of 16. When the minor is over that age, the father's responsibility is limited to accidents that occur when the boy or girl is acting for him as his agent.

Your responsibility for your child's acts

As a general rule, parents are not responsible for wrongs committed by their children unless the wrongdoing is done with their knowledge and consent.

In Maryland, Margaret, a housemaid, brought suit against her employers. On their order, she had sprinkled gasoline on portions of the lawn infested with weeds. Their small son had touched a lighted match to the gasoline, which flared up, injuring the maid. Following the principle that a parent is not responsible for the wrongful acts of his minor child, the court could not grant any damages.

Parents are liable, however, if a child has a habit of any particular type of mischief. Then, according to the courts, the knowledge of the father and his failure to restrain or supervise the child becomes the equivalent of a consent, and the father is liable for damages. In this respect the law of liability for malicious children is similar to the law with respect to animals.

A father is also liable for the damage that his child does if the father was negligent in allowing the child to use some object or implement. If a father gave his eight-year-old child a loaded gun, for example, and it accidentally went off while the child was playing with it, the father would be responsible for any damage or injury that resulted.

Must you pay your wife's debts?

We have emphasized that there is an unquestionable obligation on a husband and father to furnish his family with the necessaries of living. When he fails to meet that obligation, his wife can buy the necessaries on his credit and he must pay the person who furnishes them.

This right that the law gives the wife to buy such goods on the credit of her husband has at times been somewhat overextended by women. What an extravagant wife may consider necessary does not always seem so in the opinion of the courts.

A husband is liable for all items that he has given his wife authority to purchase, on the theory that she is acting as his agent. Whatever goods are bought as necessaries must be bought by the wife on the husband's credit. Again, what may be deemed a "necessary" expense of the wife may depend on the customary standard of living that husband and wife have maintained.

The answers that courts have given to the question of whether a husband is excused from his obligation to provide necessaries for a wife who has independent means have shown a great inconsistency. Some states still require him to support her, while others excuse him from that responsibility.

When the husband's obligation ends

This obligation on the part of the husband for the furnishing of necessaries to his wife ends when the wife leaves the husband or refuses to live with him any longer, or when, for justifiable reasons, such as her adulterous behavior, he refuses to continue living with her. Some states have also enacted legislation that absolves the husband of the support obligation if the parties separate as a result of mutual consent.

The mere fact that the husband has published or given notice that he will not be responsible for goods furnished to his wife will not of itself relieve him from that liability. However, merchants furnishing such goods will be compelled by this notice to show that the husband's liability to them is for necessaries that he has failed to furnish his wife. Such a notice does not affect the husband's obligation to pay if he has wrongfully caused the separation.

The debts of a divorced wife

The rule that a husband's liability for his divorced wife's necessaries extends only to the amount a court decrees has sometimes led to legal entanglements, as in the following case. A husband and wife in New York had been separated by a divorce decree. The husband, under this decree, paid his wife a fixed weekly sum until she died. The executor of her estate refused to pay a bill for medical services furnished her after the divorce, claiming it was a charge against her husband. The court held, however, it was not an obligation the husband was bound to pay, and the charge was against the estate of the wife.

A husband is not liable for debts his wife incurs on her own credit—say, a fur coat she buys on her own account when he has specifically denied her one—nor for debts she owed before their marriage. A husband is not responsible for the services of a physician rendered his wife when she was living with an earlier husband, or before marriage.

Can a wife take her husband's funds? Although a wife is entitled to support, this right does not permit her to appropriate her husband's possessions without his approval. In one case, for example, a wife desired to leave her husband and set up her own home.

When he refused to give her funds for this purpose, she withdrew the entire balance of their joint bank account.

The court held that even though she might have spent this money for necessaries which the husband was legally responsible for providing, she still had no right to help herself to his bank account without his consent.

Joint bank accounts are normally presumed to be half owned by each spouse. However, courts have declared that if there is evidence that one spouse or the other placed all the funds in the account, then the money belongs to that party, unless the depositor expressed a different intention.

Joint ownership may not be desirable

Joint ownership with a right of survivorship may be helpful for a residence that the wife would continue to live in should her husband die. It also may make sense where the property the couple have is not large and they each want the other to have it all on the prior death of one of them. However, when one person purchases property with his or her funds and takes title in joint names with right of survivorship, for tax purposes this may be considered a gift, and the value of the gift depends on the state law as to the interest acquired by the joint owner receiving it as a gift.

Where a bank account is concerned, the gift does not take place until the money is withdrawn by the noncontributing joint owner. For estate-tax purposes, the value of all of the jointly owned property is included in the estate of the first one to die, unless the survivor can show what portion he or she contributed to the purchase price.

A man's responsibility for the conduct of his home

Despite the fact that the prerogatives of the husband and father have been modified from what they were in the past, since he still holds the position of head of the house he bears primary responsibility for the conduct of his home and its occupants.

A husband and wife were indicted in Georgia for having whiskey in their possession. Officers found a liquor cache behind the false back of a bookcase.

The house belonged to the wife, and the husband disclaimed any liability. He neither rented nor owned the property.

"As long as the husband and wife are living together," said the judge, "the husband is the head of the family and the house occupied by them may properly be denominated as his house although the wife pays the rent and supports the husband."

An incident that illustrates the rule of law that a husband determines the occupants of his house arose when a man who owned an apartment building brought a suit to put out of the building his wife's granddaughter, who lived there, and a discharged handyman, who slept in the basement.

The man had ordered both to leave, but on his wife's advice they had refused to obey his request. The court held that this man, as master of the household, was acting within his rights. With the obligation to support, maintain, and protect his family, he also had the right to exclude intruders and unwanted visitors from his home despite the whims of his wife.

The situation may change if the husband and wife have marital difficulties. If the husband owns the house, he would still enjoy the same position, as head of the household, that he assumed when the couple were married. He will only be forced to relinquish this position if the wife gains the house in the property settlement.

If the house is owned by the wife, however, many states will give the wife the right to prevent her husband from residing in it.

A newly married Delaware couple moved into an apartment in a building that the wife owned. After two years, during which time the husband paid for improvements in the property around the building, they quarreled and the wife left the premises. The court rejected the argument of the wife that she left him because she feared for her safety, but still ruled "that a wife who leaves her husband without his having given her lawful cause to do so may (still) evict him from possession of all real estate owned by her as her sole property."

When husband and wife own property

The law provides for a convenient arrangement between a husband and wife so that all or any part of the property they own together is owned not only by both but by the survivor when either dies.

Under such a plan, deposits are made in a bank by a husband and wife in the name of both. This fund has a unity of ownership by both husband and wife, and either can make withdrawals.

At the death of either, the deposit in the bank belongs to the one who survives.

Usually banks give a name to a joint bank account which includes the term, "or to the survivor," and carries the right of the survivor to the remaining balance on the death of the other joint tenant.

One real-life case involved the ownership of a bank deposit in the name of both the husband and the wife. The checks were signed by either. When the husband died, he was survived not only by his widow but also by a son and daughter. The man left no will. The problem was to determine the ownership of the fund in the bank, and the court's solution was to hold the widow the owner of the entire balance.

An interest in real property held in the name of both husband and wife is sometimes known in legal terminology as a "tenancy by the entirety." There are also joint tenancies and tenancies in common.

If the parties each have an undivided interest in the whole, but the survivor does not take the whole interest on the death of the other, it is a tenancy in common. If it is a joint tenancy or a tenancy by the entirety, then the survivor takes the whole interest.

In most jurisdictions, a joint tenancy or tenancy by the entirety cannot be conveyed or mortgaged by only one of the parties; the consent of both is needed.

At common law, the husband was considered the "entity" in a tenancy by the entirety and he could sell it if he so wished, but if his wife survived him, she got it back. Now that women are emancipated, the husband's right to act freely with such property has been curtailed.

The large majority of states allow husbands and wives to contract with each other for all goods and services, except those involving essential aspects of the marital relationship. A husband could not enter into an enforceable contract with his wife to pay for her sexual services. Other types of agreements are allowed, although courts do look closely at any transfers of property between husbands and wives when they are challenged.

The law of community property

Eight states have a system known as community property, which was a part of their legal system from the beginning or was introduced at a relatively early date. Under this system, property acquired by one or both during their marriage, other than by gift or inheritance, is treated in a manner similar to partnership property.

The community property system exists in Arizona, California, Idaho, Louisiana, New Mexico, Nevada, Texas, and Washington.

The husband is generally the manager of the community property and may sell or mortgage it. However, in some of these states, that part of it earned by the wife may be managed by her although it is still part of the community property. When either dies, such property is divided in most of the community property states; in some of these states, the survivor takes all such community property. When the marriage is dissolved by divorce, the property may be equally divided, or in some of those states, the proportion for each spouse will depend on the cause of the divorce.

How a husband becomes his wife's agent

That a husband may be the agent for his wife, and the wife may be the agent of the husband, is a familiar principle of law. This agency of the husband does not arise, however, merely by virtue of the marriage relationship. The agency must be created in the same manner as any other agency between those not so related. According to the law, in cases involving agency, an authority to the agent must be shown to bind the principal party, or there must have been acquiescence in the assertion of authority by the agent or ratification of his act. In general, however, the intimacy and confidence in the relation of husband and wife greatly enhances the possibility of the existence of an agency.

In California, a wife shared in the fraudulent profits of her husband from the sale by him to his partner of a ten-acre tract of land. The fraud arose because he pretended to his partner that he had bought the land from a stranger for $300 an acre, when, actually, it was his own, for which he had paid $35 an acre. Under the law, the wife, who cooperated in the transaction, was equally liable with her husband.

An incident that took place in Massachusetts illustrates another aspect of the responsibility of a wife for her husband's acts as her agent. Anthony Cobuzzy wanted to purchase a house and lot owned by Frank and Mae Parks. Anthony paid $20 down, all he had at that time, and Mrs. Parks took this money. Parks gave him a receipt: "Received from Anthony Cobuzzy deposit of $20 to apply on sale of house at 448 Concord Turnpike, Arlington, Mass. Balance of $1,980 to be paid 30 days from date. Buyer will forfeit deposit if balance of $1,980 is not paid as agreed."

This receipt was signed by Parks with his wife's name at her request, as well as by him in his own name. When Cobuzzy offered the balance, the wife refused to accept it. A better offer had been made for the property, and to justify her refusal she denied she had been a party to the transaction. This excuse the court refused to recognize. It held that in the receipt of the deposit by Mrs. Parks, the execution at her request and in her presence of the memorandum by Parks, and the subsequent conduct of one for the other, each was acting not only in his or her individual capacity but also as agent for the other. Her commitment to Cobuzzy had to be maintained.

CHAPTER 6

Wife and Mother

Woman's role in society has moved from one of passive acceptance to active participation. Women are entering the ranks of professional and white-collar workers in increasing numbers. Marriage does not change many of the rights and privileges a woman enjoys when she is single. Her earnings are her own. The property she had before her marriage remains her own after she marries. The ancient legal doctrine holding that the members of the family are completely subject to the control and desires of the father and husband is quickly fading from our law.

One survival of the law of yesterday is the rule that substitutes the surname of the husband for the woman's maiden name. A famous incident on this point arose from the laws enacted against Confederate sympathizers during the Civil War. Verina S. Moore had before the Civil War taught school in North Carolina. With the money she had saved she bought stock of the Phoenix National Bank of New York City in 1854. Seven years later she married a Presbyterian minister named Chapman.

In 1864, her stock was seized by the Federal government on the complaint that the owner of the stock was a rebel and that the stock "had been bought and taken and was held and used for the purpose of aiding and abetting and promoting insurrection and rebellion."

The papers in this action, however, named "Ver. S. Moore" the owner of the stock. After the war was over, Verina Chapman sued the bank for her loss. Asserting that the name of a married woman after her marriage is no longer the name of her father but of her husband, the court decided the suit in Mrs. Chapman's favor.

Using a maiden name   In Texas, Helen B. McK'y protested against the foreclosure of a tax lien on her land. Before marrying Scot McK'y, she had bought this tract in her maiden name, Helen M. Ball. No taxes had ever been paid by her, and seven years after her marriage a tax suit was brought against "Helen M. Ball." When this suit was instituted there was no Helen M. Ball. The woman of that name who had bought this land seven years before was then Helen B. McK'y—unless she was sued under that, her correct name, the suit was a nullity. Her maiden name of Helen M. Ball, said the court, was not her name.

In a case that went all the way up to the Supreme Court, the validity of an Alabama law was upheld, prohibiting a married woman from using her maiden name on her driver's license. The state law required each driver to secure a license in his or her legal name. The highest court in Alabama ruled that the state had a legitimate interest in requiring women to assume their husband's names. The Alabama court further stated that anyone, including a married woman, could take court action to change his or her name, and therefore there was no valid objection to the requirement that the current legal married name be used.

In Michigan a wife must change her last name if her husband changes his.

Cases like these can be used to illustrate the point that you cannot generalize too much from one case. As you will see in Chapter 21 on Names, there are other cases that have decided the question of the name used in a lawsuit differently.

Restoration of maiden name

At common law, a person can assume any name that does not interfere with rights of others. Therefore, unless there is a statute to the contrary, a woman who has obtained a divorce may resume her maiden name even without permission in the divorce decree. The decree may also provide for restoration of the maiden name, even where there are children of the marriage.

If a husband uses force

Long ago, the English law maintained that since the husband was responsible for his wife's behavior and support, in return for assuming these obligations, he had the right to chastise her when it became necessary. He was the head of the house and the family, and the conduct of his wife was his responsibility. The rule today was well summed up by a court considering the case of a wife-beater: "The law does not recognize the right of a husband to use physical force to control the acts and will of his wife or to compel her to obey his wishes."

However, this rule is subject to exceptions. A husband is not justified in using physical force to make his wife do as he tells her to do, nor does her failure to contribute to the peace and harmony of the home constitute a ground for such activity on his part. But a boundary line has been placed by the courts to what a husband may be compelled to endure. Overindulgence is not shown by them to a woman when she provokes her husband by acts of physical violence against him. Misconduct on the part of the wife may be considered as in a measure palliating the offense of the husband in beating her.

A wife's residence

The determination of where a wife's home will be—not only the neighborhood but the house or apartment as well—is the husband's. The law is substantially the same as the Bible saying: "Whither thou goest, I will go; and where thou lodgest, I will lodge."

When a wife refuses to recognize and conform to this right of the husband by willfully leaving him without a just cause for so doing, she forfeits by such conduct her right to his support, to which she is otherwise entitled. However, in many instances she may decline to live in a residence of her husband's choice if it is considerably inferior to what he can readily afford.

A wife's right to leave her husband's residence

The statute of one state sums up the general law of the land: ''The husband is the head of the family. He may choose any reasonable place or mode of living and the wife must conform thereto.''

But this rule, it has been pointed out in the courts, means that the wife must live where the husband directs so long as the husband behaves himself. When he adopts and persists in a course of conduct that renders it impossible for her to live with him in safety and decency, this prerogative of the head of the family comes to an end.

Are relatives-in-law an excuse for leaving?

Many cases involving the rule of the wife's residence arise because relatives are living with the parties concerned. Here is a good example. A six-room house in Baltimore sheltered not only Adam and his wife Marie but also his mother, an old and penniless widow. Adam and Marie quarreled often over the presence of his mother in the house. Finally Marie declared, "Either that mother of yours leaves this place or I do."

"If that's the way you feel about it," Adam replied, "I suppose you'll have to go. I can't turn my mother out. I'm sorry, but she has no place to go and nothing to live on."

When this quarrel reached the courtroom, the judge said, "The husband has a right to determine the domicile of himself and his family. The wife is compelled to accept as her domicile the place so selected and maintained, and as long as the presence of relatives leaves her under no restraint and mistress of the domicile, this does not constitute abandonment and desertion unless he is financially in a position to provide and support a home for such relatives who are dependent on him."

The law thus laid down by that court is the law accepted generally throughout this country.

Can a wife choose her husband's residence?

A wife agreed to pay her husband $300 a month and he in turn agreed to give up his job and go with her wherever she directed him. Later he changed his mind. The wife, trying to enforce this agreement, took her case to court.

A husband, according to the court's decision here, is bound to support and live with his wife. She, on the other hand, must contribute to the combination her services and society, and follow him in his choice of domicile. Since the agreement here violated this fundamental rule, the court declared it invalid.

A wife's right to her earnings

The ancient idea that the man is the head of the house still casts its shadow on the wife's right to the money she earns. This money is his, except as the old common law has been changed by statute. It has been so changed in most states, and she owns her own property and is free to dispose of it in all states. By law, a husband has a right to his wife's services in the care of the family and maintenance of the home. On the other hand, he cannot force her to work for him if he has a business of his own, nor can he oblige her to work for others.

Discrimination against married women

Job discrimination against women, especially married women, has been successfully challenged in the courts. The United States Supreme Court in a recent case upheld a decision that an airline policy barring married women from jobs as stewardesses constitutes sex discrimination in violation of the 1964 Civil Rights Act. The Act bars sex bias in employment, unless discrimination is based on a bona fide occupational qualification reasonably necessary to the normal operation of a business.

Can a wife ask wages from her husband?

The employee of an insurance company was injured while engaged in his work and confined to bed for a month. His wife cared for him during his recovery. Later his wife claimed $80 under the Workmen's Compensation Act for four weeks' nursing and attendance. The court refused to recognize her claim because a husband is entitled to his wife's services.

In an unusual case that was tried in California, a wife was compelled, because of this same rule, to repay her husband the wages he had previously paid to her.

This woman had worked as nurse for the man she later married. She had told her patient before their marriage that if he would marry her all she would ask from him would be room and board for herself and her child and $80 a month. He married her. During the next three and a half years he paid her under this agreement approximately $3,500. Then she took her child and made her home elsewhere. He sued her for the money he had paid.

The court awarded him the $3,500 he had paid, saying, "It would operate disastrously upon domestic life and breed discord and mischief if a wife could contract with her husband for the payment of services to be rendered for him in his home."

Women's property right

In the 1830's, the first of several versions of the Married Women's Property Act was passed in each state, granting married women the right to contract, sue and be sued independently of their husbands, manage their own property, and work and retain their earnings.

Various vestiges of male dominance still exist, especially where property is concerned. In common-law states, like New York, a woman who works only inside the home never has an opportunity to acquire property and may only obtain an interest in property through a gift from her husband.

At his death, a woman in any common-law property state has a right of dower in her husband's estate. This interest, however, can be in real property only. Thus a New Jersey widow has "a right" to one-third of her husband's estate, but if the couple lived in an apartment, this may amount to nothing. Some states, like New York, by statute have ended dower right and given the wife an interest in the husband's estate of which he cannot deprive her and from which he cannot cut her off by his will. For a further discussion, see Chapter 10 on How to Make a Will and Chapter 11 on Death Without a Will.

In community property states, husband and wife have equal rights in property acquired during the marriage; however, the husband has control. In only two of the eight community property states, Texas and Washington, do the husband and wife have separate control over property acquired during the marriage.

Who owns a husband's gifts to his wife?

Aside from the common-law dower right and community property, a wife owns, to the exclusion of the heirs of her husband, whatever property he may from time to time have given her during their married life.

Clifford Perkins was a successful banker in the East. Whenever he bought securities, he divided them with his wife. He died in New York and his widow moved to California. His son Wallace, the child of a former marriage, survived him. When the widow died in California, Wallace, her stepson, claimed her entire estate, asserting it was the property of his father, of whom he was the only heir.

The laws of New York, where the husband was a resident at the time of his death, allowed the widow, in place of the old dower right, a share of her husband's estate irrespective of whether the estate was land or securities or cash. Consequently, under the settlement of the father's estate, the widow had received a specific sum of money. This was hers in addition to whatever gifts her husband had made her during his life.

The inheritance, as well as the gifts, the California court refused to disturb. These were hers, and her right to them was independent of any interest of her husband's heirs.

Her responsibility for her husband's savings

When the property a wife holds represents the earnings of her husband that he has entrusted to her care, the law is far different from what it is in the case of gifts. Savings from a husband's earnings must be carefully accounted for unless it can be proved they were gifts.

For six years a husband gave his wife all his wages. These were to be put aside for their old age. She survived him and claimed this accumulation of money to be her own property. The court disagreed. It held that such money was a trust fund in which the heirs of her husband's estate as well as herself were beneficiaries.

Does a wife have a right to her husband's earnings?

A woman does not have a right to her husband's earnings. Although she assists him in his business, even caring for the money that is the product of their joint labor, this does not make any part of his wages her property.

A Maine physician sought to recover from his wife's estate the money he had earned and given her for saving. She had taken charge of the business side of his work and saved the money he received, but in her own name and for herself.

This woman had had no money of her own except what she had taken of her husband's income. Her estate was $30,000. Half of this she had willed to her husband; the other half to charity.

By the decision of the court, the doctor was entitled to all this money.

How a wife becomes an agent for her husband

The same rules of law that govern the right of the husband to act as the agent for his wife apply to the wife in acting as the agent for her husband. The mere relationship of husband and wife does not itself create such an agency. There must be acquiescence on the part of the husband in her assertion of authority, or ratification of her act. For the agency to be effective, it should be provable that the acts of the wife are binding on the husband.

What a wife can buy as agent

The purchase of food for the home provides the most common example of the wife acting as agent for her husband. A celebrated case was decided on the opinion of the late Justice Cardozo in one laconic sentence: "The husband through his wife, who acted as his agent, bought a loaf of bread."

When a husband and wife are living together, his relation with the neighborhood shops that supply the everyday household needs are in almost every instance carried on through the agency of the wife.

The law permits the wife to purchase the necessaries for the family on her husband's credit. But there the law says she must stop. Such an agency as the purchase of necessaries can be terminated on notice to the seller, as can be the purchase of any other goods on his account. The notice is ineffectual in the purchase of "necessaries" if he has ceased to give her the support he is obliged to by law.

Why notice to terminate agency is important

In some instances, when misunderstandings and trouble occur between a husband and wife, failure to bear in mind the need of a notice to terminate a right that either party has had in acting as the other's agent leads to disastrous consequences for the principal party. This is particularly true where valuable property is concerned.

A bank in Pennsylvania rented a safe-deposit box to a man, and he put some bonds into it. Afterwards, his wife frequently used the box. Six months after it had been rented, she made a visit to it that naturally aroused no suspicion. A few days later the depositor went to his box and found the bonds were gone. After another day or so his wife was gone too. Aside from the depositor, no one but the wife had had access to the box.

Later, when the husband sued the bank for the loss of these bonds, the agency of his wife in the use of the box and her appropriation of its contents were set up by the bank as a defense.

"The relation of principal and agent does not arise from the marital relationship," said the court, absolving the bank from liability for the loss of the securities. "The relationship of agency cannot be inferred from the mere relationship of family ties, but such relationship is competent evidence when considered with other circumstances as tending to establish the facts of the agency."

The "other circumstances" in this case were, of course, the wife's continued access to the box and her use of it with her husband's consent.

Women administrating estates

In 1971, the United States Supreme Court struck down an Idaho law that prefers men over women in administering an estate where two persons are otherwise equal. Mrs. Sally Reid of Ada County, in Idaho, brought a suit against her husband, who was named as administrator of the estate of their 16-year-old adopted son. The couple were divorced in 1958. The state legislature repealed the law in 1971. The Idaho Supreme Court had previously ruled that where persons in the same category, here parents, applied for an administrator's authority a male preference existed. Chief Justice Burger said that "to give a mandatory preference to members of either sex over members of the other merely to accomplish the elimination of hearings on the merits is to make the very kind of arbitrary legislative choice forbidden by the equal protection clause."

A wife giving evidence

At common law and carried over to the law of many states and in the Federal courts, neither spouse could testify against the other in any proceeding. The theory behind this rule was to preserve the family relationship. Designed to protect and strengthen the marital bond, it encompasses only those statements that are "confidential," meaning that they are "induced by the relationship and prompted by the affection, loyalty and confidence engendered" thereby.

In New York and other states, by statute, not all communications between husband and wife are privileged from disclosure. Further, in many states the privilege can be waived. It is clear that these statutes were not designed to forbid inquiry into personal wrongs committed by one spouse against another.

In an old separation and support case in New York, the husband testified that his wife told him of her adulterous relationship with another man. The wife objected to the admissibility of this evidence. The court said that the privilege was never intended "to label as confidential a communication aimed at destroying the marital relation or stamp with a seal of confidence and protect from disclosure an unfounded charge of adultery or, more to the point, a declaration by a wife that she loves another man and has had improper relations with him."

Under the statutory law of New York today, a husband or wife is not competent to testify against the other in an adultery action, "except to prove the marriage, disprove the adultery, or disprove a defense after evidence has been introduced tending to prove such defense."

The statutory law also provides that a husband and wife shall not be required, or, "without consent of the other if living, allowed, to disclose a confidential communication made by one to the other during marriage."

Abortion, contraception, artificial insemination

Scholars from all over the world in the fields of law, medicine, theology, and the social sciences, and laymen from every class in society are debating the subject of abortion as never before. "Abortion" and "miscarriage" are considered equivalent terms. They mean termination of pregnancy.

The effects of a drug called "thalidomide," which caused pregnant women to deliver deformed children, made the issue of legal abortion a widely discussed topic. Many women who had taken the drug and who were fearful of having deformed children sought abortions in the United States. But until very recently, the states prohibited abortions unless the life of the mother was threatened by continuation of the pregnancy.

Typically, in the District of Columbia, abortions were forbidden unless necessary for the mother's life or health. In Virginia, an abortion was only allowed to save the life of the mother. In Maryland, an abortion was permitted when two doctors agreed it was necessary to secure the safety of the mother. This has allowed for some more liberal interpretations.

The states have all had criminal abortion statutes. Some of them, Puerto Rico and the Virgin Islands, referred to acts done with intent to produce an interruption of pregnancy with no legal justification. There were various other rules. Wisconsin had two statutes dealing with illegal or unjustified abortions. One made it a crime, of manslaughter, while the other made it only an offense against morality. The difference is that the Wisconsin courts did not view a child in the womb under four months as a human being. Performing an abortion on a woman only eight weeks pregnant was an offense against morality only.

The child in the womb

It is conceded that pregnancy cannot, as yet, be determined before six to eight days since the tests work only after implantation. The circumstances of pregnancy are that an ovum or female egg is fertilized by a male sperm, and then the egg travels through the Fallopian tube, enters the uterus, and attaches to or implants itself in the uterine wall, where it grows for a period of approximately nine months. The initial stage, before attachment, takes about six to eight days. At this stage the child is what is called the "ovum." From the eighth day to about the eighth week, it is called an "embryo," and thereafter a "fetus."

Right to life or invasion of privacy

Some critics of liberalized abortion laws claim that, historically, the unborn child was considered a person. Damages have been awarded for injury to an unborn child, as in Massachusetts, where, because of an accident to the mother, the child was born prematurely and died. Others say, however, that the right to determine when and whether to produce offspring is a private matter, and therefore the state abortion laws are an invasion of privacy. The right to privacy and the use of contraceptives is discussed in detail in the section on contraception.

Abortion reforms

The Scandinavian countries, Japan, and Great Britain are among those nations whose abortion policies are extremely liberal. Many American women who could afford the expense went abroad to have the operation that was prohibited in the United States. Many simply suffered illegal operations.

On January 22, 1973, the United States Supreme Court reached a historic decision by ruling, 7 to 2, that states cannot prohibit voluntary abortions during the first three months of pregnancy. In the same decision, the Supreme Court also ruled that in the last ten weeks of pregnancy, abortion may be prohibited unless the medical findings indicate that the life of the mother is endangered. However, there can be reasonable state regulations concerning the period between the first three months and the last 10 weeks of pregnancy. The Court also ruled that there can be no prohibition directed against out-of-state residents. This historic ruling affects the abortion laws in the great majority of states.

When a doctor refuses to perform an abortion

Is such a refusal medical malpractice? In New Jersey, a child was born blind, deaf, dumb, and mentally retarded after the mother had contracted German measles early in the pregnancy. The mother sued two physicians who had refused to perform an abortion. The court dismissed the suit, since the New Jersey law allowed abortion only when the life of the mother was threatened by continuation of the pregnancy.

A liberalizing trend

Numerous states, including Arkansas, California, Colorado, Delaware, Georgia, Kansas, New Mexico, North Carolina, Oregon, South Carolina, and Virginia, have adopted reform statutes. These laws generally permit abortions to protect the physical or mental health of the woman, in pregnancies caused by rape or incest, and when there is a possibility of deformity or mental defect in the child. Most of the states have time limits for legal abortions. Colorado was the first state, beginning in 1967, to pass abortion reforms.

The New York abortion-reform law became effective on July 1, 1970. The basic decision of whether a woman may have an abortion in New York, up to her 24th week of pregnancy, is now solely up to the woman and her physician. Persons from out of state are eligible.

When to have an abortion

In addition to the right to protect the physical health or life of the mother, the code would allow abortions when there is a risk that the continuation of the pregnancy would impair the mother's mental health; when there is substantial risk that continuation of the pregnancy would lead to a child born with grave physical or mental defects; or when the pregnancy is a result of rape or incest. Two licensed physicians would have to certify that the abortion is justified. It would be performed only in the early stages of pregnancy, in a licensed hospital. This code, of course, is a proposal only and has no legal effect.

If you are considering an abortion, check with your attorney to determine the law in your state—as well as with your doctor regarding the medical consequences—and do it soon. There is great controversy even in liberal jurisdictions as to whether abortion should be permitted late in pregnancy.

Birth control information

A contraceptive is a device to prevent pregnancy.

This was another subject that was not discussed publicly until recent years. It has also been an area liberalized after years of test cases. However, the states have a variety of laws dealing with the subject and many cities have ordinances governing the sale and/or the advertising of contraceptives.

Police power

Since as far back as 1873, birth control devices have been regulated. The articles themselves were considered obscene. Congress prevented their possession, gift, or sale in the District of Columbia and all other areas of Federal jurisdiction, until doctors were exempted from the provisions. But regulation of contraceptives and of the dissemination of birth control information has generally been considered to be within the police power of the state. It was exercised to preserve the public morals, public health, and safety.

In a New York case, a wife instituted a separation suit against her husband. She sought money for support. During the hearing she admitted that after the birth of their child she refused to have sexual relations with her husband until he agreed to use contraceptives. The court denied the wife support and held that her insistence on the husband's use of contraceptives was contrary to New York public policy and violated the marriage contract.

Then claims were made that the regulation violated freedom of religion, deprived the marital partners of their rights, or interfered with the free practice of the medical profession.

Contraceptives

The United States Supreme Court recently found unconstitutional a Massachusetts law which barred the sale or distribution of birth control devices to single people. It was held that the Constitutional guarantee of equal protection of the law was violated because married people were treated differently than unmarried persons. Back in 1965, the United States Supreme Court invalidated a Connecticut statute which prohibited the use of birth control devices on the ground that it was a matter of privacy in the marital relationship as to whether such items could be used, and that the state had no right to interfere. In this recent case involving Massachusetts law, the court overturned the conviction of a birth control crusader who gave an unmarried woman a package of vaginal foam, and held that unmarried persons have the same rights and could not be treated differently than married persons.

The Massachusetts law involved was a strong anticontraceptive statute, and some other states have similar restrictions, now invalid. Most states have no anticontraceptive law. A number of states repealed them after the 1965 Connecticut ruling. Some states, like New York, make it a crime to sell or distribute contraceptives to minors (in New York anyone under 16), and for those over minimum legal age sales or distribution may only be made by a licensed pharmacist or physician and may not be advertised. Some states prohibit vending machine sales. Statutes like these are not affected by this recent Supreme Court ruling. An organization called Planned Parenthood keeps statistics and up-to-date information on the subject.

State laws

In 18 states and the Virgin Islands there have been no statutes dealing with the dissemination of contraceptive devices. They are Alabama, Alaska, Florida, Georgia, Illinois, Kansas, New Hampshire, New Mexico, North Carolina, North Dakota, Oklahoma, Rhode Island, South Carolina, Tennessee, Texas, Vermont, Virginia, and West Virginia. However, North Dakota, Vermont, Virginia, and West Virginia did have statutes that prohibited the advertisement of matter concerning venereal disease or referring to persons from whom treatment might be obtained.

Sixteen states and Puerto Rico had statutes regulating the advertising or dissemination of contraceptives and regulating sale by vending machines. They are Arizona, California, Colorado, Hawaii, Indiana, Kentucky, Louisiana, Maine, Maryland, Michigan, Nevada, Pennsylvania, South Dakota, Utah, Washington, and Wyoming.

Eight states prohibited the general sale of contraceptives except for physicians or pharmacists. They are Arkansas, Delaware, Idaho, Iowa, Montana, Ohio, Oregon, and Wisconsin.

In Nebraska and Missouri, the statutes prohibited the sale of contraceptives, but publication of standard medical information containing explanations was permitted, as was the teaching in medical colleges.

In Minnesota, the law prohibits the sale of contraceptive devices although it allows physicians to prescribe articles for the cure or prevention of disease.

In Mississippi, the sale and manufacture of contraceptives are prohibited. But the state does sponsor voluntary birth control clinics.

In recent years the restrictive laws of many states, including New York, Connecticut, and Massachusetts, have either been successfully challenged as unconstitutional or changed by the state legislatures.

The fact that your state may not have a strict rule does not preclude the possibility of substantial regulation at your local level. Many cities do have ordinances governing the sale of such devices. This area of the law is in a state of flux, and you should consult your lawyer.

Connecticut

This state's statute was the strictest of all. It made it a crime for any person to use any drug or article to prevent conception. So it became the basis for continued litigation. The Connecticut courts denied all claims, telling the parties to abstain rather than use contraceptives to prevent pregnancy. One early case went to the United States Supreme Court, but the Court found that, since contraceptives were being sold in drugstores in Connecticut, the law was not being enforced, so there was no basis for suit.

Then came Mrs. G

The Planned Parenthood League of Connecticut decided to defy the Connecticut state law. They opened a clinic in New Haven with Mrs. G as executive director. She was arrested, as was the medical director, and they were both convicted as accessories under the statute for giving married persons information and medical advice on how to prevent conception and for prescribing contraceptive devices.

The case went to the United States Supreme Court in 1965. It was decided that Mrs. G and the League's doctor had the standing to assert the Constitutional rights of married people not parties to the case. The Court decided that the Connecticut statute forbidding the use of contraceptives was a violation of the right of marital privacy that is within the area of specific guarantees of the Bill of Rights. The marital relationship definitely lies within the zone of privacy created by several fundamental Constitutional guarantees.

Artificial insemination

This process is sometimes called therapeutic insemination and was presumably first performed in the United States after the Civil War. It is the introduction of semen into the vaginal area of the female by artificial means rather than through sexual intercourse. The semen can come from the husband or from a third-party donor.

Oklahoma landmark statute

Oklahoma was the first state to legalize human artificial insemination and to give protection to all parties involved, including legitimatizing the offspring of the procedure.

The statute provides that before the technique can be used both the husband and wife must give written consent to a physician. A county judge must witness the consent and the physician must attest to the consent. Papers are filed in the same manner as in an adoption proceeding. The child has whatever status and privileges would be accorded to children born as the result of natural conception.

A contrary California case

In California, a court found that a man whose wife gave birth to a child as a result of artificial insemination could not be prosecuted for failure to support the child.

After the birth of the child, the wife left the husband and consented to a divorce. Later she found that she needed child support, and when the husband refused, he was prosecuted by the county for failure to make support payments. The appellate court reversed, saying paternity had not been proved, and under the law no man could be convicted of a crime for not supporting someone else's child.

Rights of the children in other cases

In Illinois, a wife sued her husband for divorce. She claimed that their minor child was conceived by artificial insemination, that the donor was not her husband, and since the husband had never adopted the child he had no right to it. The court granted the divorce but found that the child was illegitimate, and so the husband had no interest in it. The child had not been represented in the proceedings to determine his legitimacy, so he was not bound by the judgment that determined him to be illegitimate. However, of course, the case is a matter of record and in later life he will have to meet the issue.

In New York, a happier solution was reached as far as the children were concerned. A wife obtained a separation agreement in the state that provided for her support and joint custody of the children. At that time

there was no question raised concerning their birth. Thereafter, she went to Nevada and obtained a divorce that incorporated the custody arrangements of the separation decree. Sometime later both spouses remarried. However, after the wife's second marriage, something happened and she refused to allow her first husband to see the children. She made the claim that the children were conceived by artificial insemination, and since the donor was not the husband he had no rights. The court was very much concerned about the children, saying that they should not be made pawns of an unhappy marriage nor be made bastards at this late date. Inasmuch as the mother had never raised the issue before, it would not be considered now. The father was allowed his custody and visitation rights.

As a general rule, where the parties are married, there is a presumption of legitimacy for their children.

In a recent California case, a woman with a husband and children, all Caucasians of fair complexion, produced a dark-haired, almost black child bearing a resemblance to a black man with whom the woman had been intimate. The black man was ordered, in a support action, to provide care for the child. On appeal, the court held that as long as the woman was cohabiting with the husband at the same time and he was not impotent, there was a presumption that the child was legitimate, thus eliminating a support requirement for the black man.

Artificial insemination is an area of the law that has many uncharted zones. It is certainly important, since there are many couples who cannot have children by any other means. If you are contemplating the procedure, you are strongly advised to confer with your physician and your lawyer before making any arrangements at all.

CHAPTER 7

Citizenship

"Citizenship in this nation is a part of a cooperative affair. Its citizenry is the country and the country is its citizenry." The Supreme Court of the United States made this comment in a recent case involving the loss of United States citizenship.

The Constitution provides that "all persons born or naturalized in the United States and subject to the jurisdiction thereof" are citizens. You can therefore acquire citizenship by birth or through a legal process established by the Congress, called naturalization. The words "nationality" and "citizenship" sometimes are used interchangeably.

Who are citizens at birth?

A person is a citizen at birth if he is born in the United States and subject to its laws, or is born outside the United States of parents who are citizens, at least one of whom has a residence in the United States or an outlying possession. Anyone who is born in an outlying possession in the United States of parents, one of whom is a citizen who has been in the United States or one of the outlying possessions of the United States for one year prior to the time of birth, or anyone born outside the United States of parents, one of whom is a citizen who, prior to the birth, was in the United States for periods totaling not less than ten years, is a citizen at birth.

There are also other specific provisions that grant citizenship in particular cases. Children born outside the country are given a certification of birth as citizens from a United States consulate, an office of the Department of State. Sometimes these certifications have been held insufficient, and the American parents must go to the Immigration and Naturalization Service to offer proof of the child's citizenship.

Wong Kim Ark's parents were Chinese aliens. He was born in California and lived there for 17 years. In the early 1900's he went to China for a visit, and when he was 22 he returned to the United States. He was refused permission to enter under the then Chinese Exclusion Act. He sued, and the case went to the Supreme Court. It was decided that:

> A child born in the United States of parents of Chinese descent who at the time of his birth are subjects of the Emperor of China but have a permanent residence and domicile in the United States and are there carrying on a business and are not employed in any diplomatic or official capacity under the Emperor of China, becomes at the time of his birth a citizen of the United States.

Wong was born in this country and therefore he was a citizen here.

Children born in the United States of alien parents

The rule that if you are born in the United States you are a citizen holds true even though your parents are aliens. There are two minor exceptions: children born to alien parents residing here while on duty for a foreign government ("within the realm of foreign ambassadors"), or while conducting a hostile occupation of the United States, do not become citizens by virtue of birth on our soil.

The courts have declared generally that a child of alien parents born on a vessel of American registry flying the American flag attains the same citizenship as its parents.

What if parents give up their citizenship?

Marie Elg, born in Brooklyn, New York, of Swedish parents, was taken by her parents to Sweden when she was four years old. When Marie was 15, her father resumed his allegiance to Sweden. Marie remained there until she was of age and then returned to the United States. Six years after she had returned, the Department of Labor advised her that she was illegally in this country and subject to deportation.

The decision of the Supreme Court was made on the opinion of Chief Justice Hughes, who concluded:

> The mere fact that Marie Elg may have acquired Swedish citizenship by virtue of the operation of Swedish law on the resumption of that citizenship by her parents does not compel the conclusion that she has lost her own citizenship acquired under our law. As at birth she became a citizen of the United States, that citizenship must be deemed to continue unless she has been deprived of it through the operation of a treaty or Congressional enactment or by her voluntary action.

Derived citizenship

If you hold citizenship only because your parents became citizens through naturalization—you were born in a foreign country—you have "derived" citizenship. If your parents then lose their citizenship through denaturalization or revocation of citizenship, you also lose your citizenship.

An adopted child

A child adopted by citizens may be naturalized before turning 18 on petition of the adoptive parents. The child must have been lawfully admitted to the United States for permanent residence, must have been younger than 16 when adopted, and must have lived in the United States with his adoptive parents for two years prior to the petition. If one of the adoptive parents is serving overseas, then the two-year-residence requirement is not necessary.

Two nationalities

Some people who are citizens of the United States at birth are also nationals of another country. This is so because some countries where parents are born consider their children to be nationals of the homeland; this was the case of Marie Elg. Such people are called "dual nationals," and Congress has legislated in regard to the conduct of adult dual nationals.

After reaching adulthood they must be careful lest they lose their United States citizenship. If you are a dual national older than 22 and you voluntarily seek benefits from the foreign country and reside within that country for a period in excess of three years, you must periodically take an oath of allegiance to the United States before an American diplomatic or consular officer. Of course if you are in a foreign country in service, to study, for your health, or on business, this does not apply. Also, if you are more than 60 years of age and have lived for at least 25 years in the United States, you need not worry about taking a regular oath while in the country of your other nationality.

What about the alien who marries the citizen?

Normally an alien must be a resident for five years before becoming eligible for naturalization. An alien married to a citizen becomes eligible in three years.

In Maryland, a war bride had difficulty in obtaining her citizenship papers. She had married a soldier in 1956 and come to the United States. In 1965, her husband returned to active duty and was killed in Vietnam in April, 1966. In January, 1966, she had applied for citizenship in Kansas, where her husband had been stationed, and had passed her citizenship test. However, the family moved to Maryland before she could take her oath, and three weeks before the ceremony her soldier husband was killed. Since she had applied for citizenship as the wife of a citizen, her affidavits only proved three years residence. With the death of her husband the widow was required to prove a five-year residency. Because of the unusual circumstances of her case an exception was made, and in 1968 the exception became law.

When the citizen is in overseas employment

Anyone married to a United States citizen who is an employee of the Federal Government or of an American commercial firm and is regularly stationed abroad, needs no prior residence in the United States before making an application for naturalization, if the applicant intends in good faith to become a citizen.

An Air Force captain, stationed during World War II in New Guinea, was married to a girl of Sydney, Australia. After the war the captain and his wife lived for two years in the United States. He was then ordered to Korea and his wife was granted permission to join him in that country.

When his wife applied for citizenship, the provision of the statute quoted above, that the applicant's spouse be "regularly stationed abroad," was cited by the Federal court as a basis for granting her petition.

Naturalization

Some people give up their citizenship, or it is in some way lost. We will discuss that later. More people want American citizenship, and if you are not born to it you may receive it through a procedure called "naturalization." Once you are a citizen of the United States you are also a citizen of the state in which you reside.

A court has said, "Admission to citizenship is, as it ought to be, jealously guarded and granted only to him worthy to become one in the great partnership which makes up the nation. The prime consideration always is the nation's welfare and not the applicant's, which is wholly secondary."

No one has the right to be naturalized. It is a gift. But no person shall be denied naturalization because of race, sex, or marital status. Compliance initially with the country's immigration laws is the first step in establishing eligibility for naturalization. Chapter 8 on Aliens discusses this in part.

Procedures

The Attorney General's office promotes instruction and training in citizenship responsibilities for applicants for naturalization through the public schools, Americanization schools, and others. But the formalities of filing a proper petition and the procedures up to the actual taking of the oath by the alien should be handled by an attorney. This is too important a step in anyone's life to take the chance of error. In one case a petition that did not contain the alien's correct name was deemed to be improper and the court would not allow it to be amended. A new petition was required.

An alien must have legally resided in the United States for five years in order to attain citizenship; he must have demonstrated good moral character and attachment to the principles of the Constitution, and be well disposed to the national order and happiness of the United States.

An alien shall file in the office of the clerk of a naturalization court, in duplicate, a sworn petition for citizenship signed by himself and verified by two witnesses. The petition must be in a form prescribed by the Attorney General of the United States. If an alien is too ill to file the petition in person, the clerk may designate another place. But the illness must be truly serious and disabling. The government wants to be sure all petitioners make personal appearances when they initiate this vital procedure.

An alien must have resided for six months in the district of the court where he has filed his petition. These courts can be state as well as Federal courts. The alien petitioner must also file affidavits from two witnesses who are citizens, stating that they have known the petitioner and that he was a resident in the district for six months and has a good moral character and attachment to the Constitution of the United States.

Can a minor file for citizenship?

No person under 18 years of age can file a petition for citizenship on his own. Another must do it for him. Individuals over 18 years of age can file their own petitions.

After the petition

The Immigration and Naturalization Service of the United States Department of Justice conducts an investigation and makes preliminary recommendations to the court. No petition is heard until at least 30 days have passed. Remember, once you file a petition with the clerk of the court, you cannot withdraw it without the permission of the Attorney General.

The hearing on the petition takes place in open court. The alien must produce two witnesses who know of his residences and who can testify as to his character. The petitioner must also demonstrate some understanding of the English language, and an ability to read, write, and speak words in ordinary usage. Two exceptions to this requirement are the alien who is physically unable to comply with the procedure and the alien who is over 50. The former may be naturalized if he is otherwise qualified. The latter can qualify if he has been in the United States for periods totaling at least 20 years by December 24, 1952.

The oath of allegiance

The alien who wishes to be naturalized must pledge that he will support the Constitution, that he will renounce all allegiance to any foreign state or person, that he will defend the Constitution and the laws of the United States, that he will bear true faith and allegiance to the Constitution, and that he will bear arms on behalf of the United States when required by law, or perform noncombatant services. If the petitioner satisfies the court that he is opposed to bearing arms or to performing noncombatant military service by reason of religious training and beliefs, then he need not take the oath on this point. However, he must agree to perform alternative service of importance to the national welfare under civilian direction.

The court's order

The court decides whether the alien should be naturalized, and an order is issued one way or the other. If a certificate is denied because of poor moral character or the like, the alien must wait as much as five years before applying again. If naturalization is permitted, the alien receives a certificate. This certificate may be canceled later by the United States, but a United States Attorney must file an affidavit alleging good cause, and all doubts in a cancellation on denaturalization are usually resolved in favor of the citizen. We will discuss denaturalization shortly.

Some failures can be remedied

The laws relating to the granting of citizenship are strictly observed. Oversights, omissions, mistakes, all doubts in relation to these applications are decided in favor of the government. However, a person who fails because of some lack that may be made up in time, like a knowledge of English or the workings of our government, may apply for another hearing when he is able to meet these requirements.

A name can be changed in connection with naturalization proceedings by the court order that admits an alien to citizenship.

Naturalization after service in the army

Special citizenship benefits have been provided for aliens who have served in the armed forces. Anyone who has served a total period of three years honorably in any of the branches of the forces or who has similar Reserve duty time may be granted naturalization while he is still in the service or within six months after his enlistment terminates. Service in the armed forces of the United States during World War I or II, the Korean conflict, or the Viet Nam conflict from February 28, 1961 on, can also bring citizenship, with no particular amount of such service being specified.

Good moral character

The law is clear that an alien must be of good moral character in order to be eligible for naturalization. But what actions are considered not moral? As regards adultery, the courts have not been uniform in resolution of the issue. In one case a man named Russo had been married for only two weeks when his wife returned to Israel. Thereafter he had sexual relations with various women, and, at the time of his naturalization hearing, there were paternity and support orders outstanding against him. He was adjudged not to be of good moral character.

In another case, which arose in Illinois, a man had come to the United States leaving his wife, by her own choice, in a Communist country. He started divorce proceedings in this country, but before they were concluded he started to live with another woman. Two months after the divorce he married the woman. Technically, under the law of Illinois, he was an adulterer. But the court hearing his petition for naturalization felt he should not be penalized by being denied citizenship. The judge said that under the social norms of the community he had not exhibited such a lack of moral character as to prevent his attaining citizenship.

Gamblers and addicts

Certain undesirable aliens such as gamblers and addicts would be denied naturalization as being not of good moral character. What about someone who has obtained a Mexican divorce that is not recognized in his state but who has remarried anyway? As a bigamist, he may not be considered to be of good moral character, but the overall circumstances would be considered.

An alien was convicted of murder in California and then was given an unconditional pardon by the Governor. Despite the pardon, the conviction for murder barred his naturalization. This was true in a similar case in Florida. Other courts, however, have granted naturalization after a pardon.

An alien who had disregarded parking regulations on 23 different occasions was not denied naturalization, as the court did not feel this meant that he was against good order.

Anarchists and others

If a petitioner participates in certain proscribed activities during ten years preceding the filing of the naturalization petition, his naturalization will be barred. An anarchist or anyone else involved in activities designed to promote violence and disorder would be barred from citizenship.

Generally, offenses committed prior to the five-year period of residence required for naturalization are not a bar to citizenship, but information and evidence concerning them are received by the court to help the judge decide whether, in fact, the petitioner has conformed to the statutory requirements during the five years. Again you must remember that naturalization is not a right, and the petitioner has the burden of proving he or she is eligible in all respects.

Bearing arms for the United States

This is part of the oath of allegiance to be taken by a petitioner. An English woman met all the qualifications for naturalization, but she would not swear to take up arms against England. It was her love for her former country and not her religious beliefs that caused her to act as she did. She was denied citizenship.

In a recent case, an avowed pacifist and atheist was granted citizenship despite the fact she would not swear to bear arms. The court accepted her proof that her atheism was not a mere personal code but was a religion, and therefore she could claim it exempted her from the oath.

Losing your citizenship

You can lose your citizenship through involuntary expatriation if you commit certain acts that the law deems sufficient to deprive you of your citizenship.

You can also lose your citizenship through denaturalization after a court proceeding that revokes or cancels the naturalization certificate you received. Renunciation and involuntary expatriation can affect citizens by birth as well as naturalized citizens. Denaturalization can only affect those who were naturalized.

Voluntary expatriation

You must have a voluntary wish to surrender or abandon your citizenship. You abandon it by performing, as the Supreme Court has said, some act that is inconsistent with undiluted allegiance. A minor cannot voluntarily expatriate himself. But when a member of the Fleet Reserve became a citizen of a foreign country, the courts held his act was inconsistent with his oath of allegiance to the United States and was so repugnant to his status as a member of the armed forces that termination of his retirement pay was warranted. If you voluntarily perform some act that the law states can cause loss of citizenship, you must accept the result.

**Expatriation
under duress**

You have the burden of proving that your act was not voluntary. But the courts are very sympathetic to pleas that you were coerced into acting as you did to result in your subsequent loss of citizenship. Coercion can include not only fear of bodily injury, but retaliation, imprisonment, fine, or economic deprivation.

The question of voluntary renunciation of citizenship became very important following World War II. After Pearl Harbor, all Japanese in the United States were forcibly removed from their homes and sent to various internment camps. This included not only Japanese aliens but native-born citizens of Japanese ancestry. In 1951, many thousands of Japanese who had renounced their American citizenship while in certain camps sought to have the renunciations rescinded. They claimed that the conditions of their resettlement and the tension and terror in the camps caused them to lose free will and to execute documents renouncing their citizenship.

The court, after hearing lengthy testimony and reviewing documents that recounted all of the terrible experiences connected with the uprooting of families and their miserable internment for some years, decided that many had, in fact, renounced under duress, and their citizenship was restored.

**Expatriation
and statelessness**

If United States citizenship is lost, and the person is not a dual national, statelessness may result. However, many such persons, although they are considered aliens, have numerous rights while in this country. Even aliens subject to deportation are protected by law.

Anyone whose citizenship is in dispute has access to law to vindicate his status and title to citizenship. If you are abroad, you can apply to the State Department for a certificate of identity to enable you to return to the United States to press your claim. If your claim is rejected by the administrative agency officials, you can bring suit for declaratory judgment to determine whether you are a citizen.

**Voting in a
foreign election**

Until a recent Supreme Court ruling, this was considered a form of voluntary expatriation by accepting the jurisdiction of the foreign country where the voting took place. In a 5–4 decision, the Supreme Court reversed the denial of a passport to a naturalized citizen, holding unconstitutional a statute that took away citizenship for voting in a foreign election.

A Mr. Afroyim was born in Poland and was naturalized in 1926. In 1950, he went to Israel and voted in an election there. In 1960, when he applied for renewal of his United States passport, the State Department refused it on the ground that he had lost his citizenship by voting in a foreign state. Mr. Afroyim sued, and the Supreme Court said,

"Citizenship is no light trifle to be jeopardized any moment Congress decides to do so under the name of its general or implied grants of power." Therefore, the Court declared this part of the Immigration and Nationality Act unconstitutional.

Serving in a foreign army

The big question seems to be whether the service was voluntary or whether it was performed under duress. If it was done voluntarily, then the provision in the law that citizenship will be lost will be upheld by the courts. Marks was a native-born American who served with Fidel Castro's army from 1958-1960. After he returned to the United States, he was told he had lost his United States citizenship by such service. His case went to the Supreme Court. The Court found that by 1958 it was clear that Castro was a Communist and Marks' service was voluntary. So he had clearly manifested a lack of allegiance to the United States and his citizenship was rightfully lost.

But in the matter of Joao Camara, it was certainly clear he had been forced to serve in a foreign army. Joao was born at Fall River, Massachusetts, where he lived until he was 12 years old. Then, in 1921, he was taken by his parents to the Azores. At 21 years of age he was drafted into the Portuguese army. Fearful lest he lose his American citizenship, he consulted the American consul, who told him he should get permission to return to this country and join the United States Army as an alternative. He had no money for the return trip, and, on his protest against serving in the Portuguese forces, he was told by the Portuguese officials that either he would serve as he had been ordered or he would go to a concentration camp.

Discharged from the army of Portugal in 1945, Joao found a place as a stowaway on an air transport plane and landed in Massachusetts. When his case came before the Federal court in this country, the judge said, "Camara had never forsworn his American citizenship; on the contrary, he had done what he could to assert it and to preserve it. His service as a draftee in the Portuguese army, with a concentration camp as the alternative, was under duress. As soon as he could arrange it, he returned to this country as a stowaway, which attests the intensity of his purpose to retain his American nationality."

An oath of allegiance to a foreign state

Taking such an oath is a ground for loss of citizenship. A boy was born of Polish parents in Buffalo, New York. When he was seven years old he was taken by his family to Poland. In 1926, at the age of 21, he entered the Polish military service, continuing to wear its uniform until 1929. During the following year he returned to this country.

His deportation was approved by the Federal court because he enlisted in the Polish army after he became 21 years of age and later took an oath of allegiance, thereby becoming expatriated.

Employment by a foreign government

The law states that such employment is a ground for expatriation if nationality in the foreign state is a prerequisite to such employment. Obviously this does present a problem of divided allegiance, and you would be wise to seek counsel before embarking on any such venture, lest you chance the loss of your most valued citizenship. The nature of the employment will, of course, be a consideration.

Treason, sedition, insurrection

These are grounds for expatriation of a person who had previously been granted citizenship through naturalization. However, being a member of the Communist Party has been held not to be sufficient ground for loss of citizenship unless it can be proved in denaturalization proceedings that when the naturalization oath was taken the petitioner lied, and, at that time, he was fully aware of and was in favor of the party's tenet of overthrowing by force and violence the government of the United States.

Denaturalization

When the government believes it has good cause, proceedings can be brought to revoke or cancel the naturalization of citizenship. This "good cause" is usually that the petitioner concealed a material fact or willfully misrepresented a fact at the time of naturalization. There is no time limit in which the government must start proceedings; they can be brought many years after naturalization. But the party must be given 60 days notice, and the courts are loath to cancel a certificate without very good cause.

The right to travel

Among the rights of citizenship is the right to travel. The Supreme Court has held that a statute indiscriminately restricting the right to travel abridges the liberty guaranteed by the Constitution. The chairman of the . Communist Party in the United States thus became entitled to a passport. "Freedom of movement is basic in our scheme of values," said the Court.

CHAPTER 8

Aliens

An alien is any person not a citizen or national of the United States. The entrance of an alien into this country is allowed only at the discretion of the Federal government. He may only come into this country if the Congress gives him a right to enter. However, when an alien rightfully becomes a citizen, Congress can no longer exclude him.

The statutes governing the right of entry of aliens into this country are changed from time to time by Congress. Interested persons—aliens and attorneys representing aliens—must check these statutes periodically in order to stay abreast of current immigration law. The law no longer singles out any race or nationality as ineligible for citizenship.

What papers must an alien file?

With a few exceptions, all aliens who enter the United States must obtain a visa issued by a United States consular officer before applying for admission. A visa does not guarantee admission. Admission applications are made to the Immigration and Naturalization Service. Among those exempt from the visa requirement are alien members of the United States Army and permanent resident aliens who are returning to this country after less than a year abroad.

It is no longer necessary that aliens who are eligible and desire citizenship file a declaration of intention to become a citizen (commonly known as the "first papers") prior to filing their actual petition for naturalization. This declaration of intention may be filed, however, by an alien who needs it for such purpose as securing employment.

Until an alien becomes a naturalized citizen, he must file his alien address report with the Immigration and Naturalization Service during January of each year. Official forms for this purpose are available in every post office. An alien must also report any change in address to the INS within ten days of the change. Aliens who fail to follow the report requirements are in danger of being deported.

An alien also has all the obligations of a citizen. For example, every alien who earned income in this country must file an income tax return with the United States government.

Classification of aliens

Aliens are classified either as immigrants or nonimmigrants. Nonimmigrants must have a foreign residence that they have no intention of abandoning. Immigrants are either quota or nonquota immigrants. Included among those the United States allows in as nonquota immigrants are aliens who are spouses of citizens, fiancés of citizens (if the marriage occurs within 90 days of entry), and parents of citizens over 21 years of age. Nonquota immigrants are admitted even if others of their classification would be barred.

An immigrant can remain in the United States indefinitely as a permanent resident alien. Nonimmigrant aliens must depart from the United States within the period of their admission or any authorized extension thereof. They are usually admitted only for six months beyond the time it would take for them to accomplish their stated reason for entering the country. Although a nonimmigrant alien can apply to change his status to that of a permanent resident alien, it is difficult to make this change.

The rights of aliens

In certain respects, aliens, particularly those ineligible to become citizens, are not invested with the freedom from restrictions enjoyed by citizens. Nevertheless, these restrictions are in no instance harsh and are of little moment except during the tense days of wartime. By and large, the noncitizen enjoys the same rights and privileges as a citizen. One exception is that many states and municipalities do not allow aliens to work for them.

An alien who is eligible for citizenship and has filed a declaration of intention to become a citizen may hold any real property. Other aliens can also hold real property against all except the government, but they must sell it within ten years of acquisition. In their possession of personal property, all aliens are as untrammeled in their holding as any citizen.

The draft status of aliens

Any male alien who would be eligible to be drafted if he were a citizen can be called for induction into military service. He may refuse induction on the ground of his alien status and still remain in the country. If he makes a reasoned choice to refuse induction, however, he is permanently barred from becoming a citizen.

However, the United States Supreme Court recently held that an alien who had once claimed a draft exemption on the ground of alienage could not thereby be debarred from citizenship when he was later drafted, but found to be physically unfit.

An alien of Argentine birth who could neither read nor write English was notified by his draft board to report for induction into the United States Army. He never appeared. His application for citizenship was later refused on the grounds that he had made himself ineligible by refusing to report for induction. A court ordered that he be granted citizenship, since his lack of comprehension of the language may have prevented him from understanding the induction notice. However, courts have not always been this lenient in such cases.

Can an alien sue?   In a court action by a mother for injuries suffered by her son that resulted in his death, the defense was that both mother and son were aliens, illegally in this country, and were not permitted to seek relief in our courts.

"If it be assumed that her son's entry was illegal," the court declared, "it could not possibly follow that by such illegal entry he was made an outlaw whose death anyone could compass without legal accountability."

A similar question arose during World War II when a suit was brought involving the transfer of real property by an Italian family. Commenting on the defense that the Italians were aliens, the court mentioned that the ancient law once excluded all alien enemies from the courts. This law, said the court, does not represent the American concept of humanity and justice. Little by little, the teeth of that old law have been pulled. Today the law forbids the use of the courts by aliens only when they are enemies who seek to hinder the prosecution of war or to lend aid to the enemy. Otherwise the courts of this country are as available for the aid and protection of aliens and the citizens of foreign countries as they are to our own residents and citizens.

How the entrance of aliens is limited   The entrance of an alien into the United States is only by permission of the Federal government. He has no right to come into this country except as the right is granted him by Congress, and, so long as a person is an alien, he may be excluded from the country at any time by an act of Congress. When citizenship has been granted him, this right of exclusion ends.

The statutes governing the right of entry of aliens into this country are changed from time to time by Congress. But the underlying principle, the right of the government to determine who shall and who shall not enter, remains fixed.

Our changing naturalization statutes   If you are not a citizen, you should, on account of the possibility of changes in the naturalization statutes, watch the laws passed by Congress in relation to citizenship and the admission and exclusion of aliens. No safe guide can be set up that may not be subject to modification. The fundamental rules for becoming a citizen will be found in Chapter 7 on Citizenship.

Why aliens are deported   The powers of the Commissioner of Immigration and Naturalization over the deportation of undesirable aliens are broad and comprehensive. Aliens who may be deported include mental and physical defectives, criminals,

polygamists, prostitutes, procurers, illiterates, and similar undesirable persons. Aliens engaging in subversive activities are likewise subject to deportation. A 1948 statute added to these groups still others: "Aliens who are anarchists, or aliens who the Attorney General knows or has reason to believe seek to enter the United States for the purpose of engaging in activities which will endanger the public safety of the United States."

An additional reason for deportation is the entry into this country of an alien, as a spouse or fiancé of a citizen, for a marriage that is merely an excuse for gaining entry. To obtain a deportation order, the government must normally demonstrate that the couple never lived together as husband and wife.

When our country is at war

In time of national emergency, unless the President issues a decree to the contrary, the rights of aliens, such as their right to travel abroad, are limited.

Some years ago, a British merchant vessel, the *Silverash*, docked at the port of New York. Police arrested three Chinese sailors charged with engaging in a riot on board ship in which one of the crew had been killed. While they were still being held by the police, the boat sailed without them.

Later these sailors were ordered excluded and deported. The deportation statute provides that when the United States is at war and the country from which the alien embarked is under enemy occupation, the alien may be deported to "an approximate country."

These sailors were shipped to India. In answer to the protest at the disposition and their detention by the New York police, the court pointed out that an alien brought into this country under arrest does not actually enter this country. "His case is like that of one who has stopped at the border and been kept there all the time."

Using a false passport

Felich, a smelter worker in Croatia, acquired an unexpired American passport. Felich had it visaed, purchased a passage ticket, and came to the United States. A statute relating to the use of false passports forbids "using for entry a permit not designed for use by the holder." On this ground, Felich was deported.

Length of residence and deportation

An Italian alien, who had been brought to this country by his parents when he was three years old, was convicted of traffic in narcotics. When confronted in the Leavenworth penitentiary with a deportation order, he replied, "I don't see how I can be deported after being here for so long a time." He appealed the deportation ruling. On the grounds that the man had been convicted of participating in narcotics traffic, and that he was an alien criminal, the order was sustained by the Federal court, and he was deported.

An alien can be deported, on legitimate grounds, until he becomes a citizen. It does not matter that he has been a resident alien for a long period of time. However, the government must prove its case by "clear, unequivocal, and convincing evidence."

Private immigration bills

You can ask your Congressman to introduce legislation on your behalf. Some bills seek to change the status of individuals, some to grant permanent residence in the United States, some to admit aliens otherwise inadmissible because of disease. Some bills seek to cancel deportation orders. Many bills are never considered because of the tremendous volume of Congressional legislation.

These are called private bills, because they are introduced for an individual and do not deal with general law to apply to all. They seldom pass the Congress to become law, as it is not easy to convince the legislators that an exception should be made.

Be aware also that a private bill introduced on behalf of a nonimmigrant alien to give him the status of an alien admitted for permanent residence provides evidence of the intent of the alien to leave his own country and change his nonimmigrant status. This may hurt his status in his native country without actually helping him here.

CHAPTER 9

Your Civil Rights

The constitutions of the United States and the various state governments, with their amendments, guarantee citizens of the United States an equal opportunity to enjoy life, liberty, and property. These guarantees include the right to own property, freedom of contract, equal protection of the law, and the right to vote without restriction by reason of sex, race, color, religion, or previous condition of servitude.

These civil rights provisions of the Federal and state constitutions exercise a wholesome influence by preventing enactment in the various states of legislation that might conflict with the democratic spirit of our nation. These legal safeguards are also used to protect citizens from the abuse of public officials.

There is a law of the United States that has often conflicted with state laws, but which secures a fundamental right enjoyed by all citizens. Any person who, by acts done under state laws, subjects another to the loss of "any rights, privileges, and immunities secured by the Constitution and laws" is liable in damages to the person injured. Such illegal acts, when performed by public officials, are described as committed "under color of law"—that is, with a local law to justify them when actually a Federal law prohibits them.

This Federal civil rights statute has often been invoked in keeping prison officials in check. A typical case involved a prisoner at an Illinois state penitentiary. He complained that he had been struck by a prison attendant with a blackjack, dragged to a sub-basement cellar, chained by his wrists for 18 hours and kept in solitary confinement for 92 days. For six of every seven days during that time, his diet consisted only of bread and water.

The essence of this case, said the court, was that under the civil rights statute the warden had failed to secure to this prisoner immunity from injury—a civil right—while the prisoner was in the custody of the prison officials. The court held that under the conditions outlined by the prisoner he was entitled to damages from the warden for the injuries he had suffered.

Conspiracy of state officials

An indictment by a Federal grand jury was handed down against Arkansas law enforcement officers for conspiracy. They had falsely charged citizens of Arkansas with violations of the law, put them in jail, and permitted them to communicate with no one. Victims were tried before a "kangaroo court." Fines were imposed and collected by the members of the conspiracy.

Approving the conviction of these officers, the Federal Circuit Court of Appeals held that this misuse of power was made possible only because the wrongdoers were clothed with the authority of state law. Their action was taken "under color of" state law and therefore was a violation of this constitutional and legislative provision of the Federal government.

Suing a Federal agent

The United States Court of Appeals has recently ruled that Federal agents can be sued for violation of Constitutional rights after an arrest or search. Narcotics agents had searched a Bronx apartment and arrested the occupant, who contended that unreasonable force was used in connection with the arrest and that his home had been entered without a warrant. He sued the agents for damages. The court held that Federal police officers have no immunity to protect them from damage suits charging violation of Constitutional rights while they are enforcing criminal statutes. However, it is a defense to any such action if the police can prove good faith and reasonable belief in the validity of the arrest and search and the necessity for carrying out the arrest and search in the way it was conducted. This Federal rule is quite similar to the general law in state jurisdictions with respect to mistaken arrest.

Trial by due process

Every prisoner is entitled to trial by due process of the law. Law enforcement officials must observe this rule without exception. In a Georgia county, late one night, the sheriff, a policeman, and a deputy sheriff went to the home of a 30-year-old Negro citizen with a warrant for his arrest. Apparently, the sheriff was nursing a grudge against the Negro and had threatened to "get" him. The official charge was the theft of an automobile tire. Handcuffed and taken by automobile to the court house, the prisoner was beaten with a blackjack by these three officers when he stepped from the car. Although their prisoner was knocked to the ground, the beating continued until he became unconscious. Dragged into the jail, he was thrown onto the floor and an ambulance called. Within an hour the man died.

These three men were indicted under the Federal statute that makes it a crime willfully to subject any person "under color of law" to the deprivation of any rights or privileges, or to different punishments, pains, or penalties by reason of race or color.

They were found guilty and their conviction was appealed to the Supreme Court. Strangely enough, the defense urged it was murder they had done, committed in the official conduct of their duties, not deprivation of Constitutional rights. The court held this defense not valid, and found them guilty.

"Those who decide to take law into their own hands," declared the Supreme Court, "and act as prosecutor, jury, judge, and executioner, plainly act to deprive a prisoner of the trial that due process of law guarantees him."

In 1970, the United States Supreme Court significantly expanded the coverage of Federal civil remedies available to victims of private discrimination, stating that the "color of law" provision was not necessary to obtain a Federal remedy. A car containing five Negroes was stopped on a highway in Mississippi during the height of the civil rights activity in July, 1966, by two white residents. Mistaking the driver for a civil rights worker, the two white men severely beat the Negroes, causing bodily and emotional harm. The lower court's finding that the defendants did not act under "color of law," and that therefore plaintiffs were barred from recovery, was reversed by the United States Supreme Court. Holding that the section of the Federal statute under which the action was brought, based on the Ku Klux Klan Act of 1971, could not have existed independently unless it were intended that a private action existed where there were racial overtones, Justice Stewart, writing for a unanimous Court, thus construed this section of the Federal statute as the only Federal remedy protecting civil rights generally against private racial discrimination.

Immunity of state officials

No one, not even the governor of a state, is immune from violations of the Constitution of the United States.

A husband and wife were charged with using the United States flag in advertising. Efforts for their arrest in New York State were unsuccessful, and application for their extradition was made by New York State to the Governor of Pennsylvania. The accused were arrested and returned to New York. Later they sued the Governor of Pennsylvania on the ground that he had "unlawfully and maliciously issued purported warrants" for their arrest in violation of their civil rights.

Pennsylvania at that time had a law that the governor of the state, if he acted on the advice of the Pennsylvania Department of State, should be in no way liable for his action. Immunity from violating civil rights secured by the Federal Constitution cannot be thus acquired, asserted the Federal Court. "To Federal statute and policy a conflicting state policy and law must yield." This Pennsylvania statute was held unconstitutional and void.

Property rights

The Fourteenth Amendment of the Constitution of the United States has been held to give all citizens of this country the same right to purchase, lease, sell, hold, and convey real estate.

The meaning of this constitutional guarantee has been expanded in a recent Supreme Court case involving the refusal by a realtor in St. Louis to sell property to a Negro family. The court cited an old law, still in force, that provides that every individual shall have an equal opportunity to purchase property. The opinion stated that this must be upheld if the Thirteenth Amendment, which prohibits slavery, is to be effective. The Court noted that the inability to purchase property is a "badge of slavery," and it therefore ruled that permitting a realtor to refuse to sell to a Negro family would thwart the purpose of the Constitution.

It is not yet clear whether this decision will mean that property owners will be prohibited in all cases from all discrimination in selling their property. The Federal "open housing" statute does specifically prohibit anyone from refusing to sell a home to any person because of his race, creed, color, or national origin, unless the seller owns less than three houses and does not use an agent for the sale. Refusal on other grounds, if they are reasonable, is not prohibited.

What about leasing?

A Negro family leased a house in a community in Virginia. Under the rules of the community, the owner of the house could also lease his share in a recreational club that was open to homeowners in the area. The corporation that operated the club barred the Negro family from leasing the membership in the club. The Supreme Court ruled that the play facilities were not private, but that membership in the club was an integral part of the lease to the house. Normally, any person who had a right to live in a house also had a right to join the club. Using the "badge of slavery" argument again, the Court said that to prevent someone from leasing because of his race, creed, color, or national origin is also not permitted.

Can you be denied access to public places?

Federal law does not permit most facilities open to the public to refuse to serve any person because of his race, color, creed, or national origin. Included among those facilities are public transportation, restaurants, theaters, stadiums and other places of entertainment, gas stations, stores, and all hotels or motels except those with less than six rooms with the proprietor in residence. Facilities that are not open to the general public, such as private clubs, may legally discriminate.

A YMCA in North Carolina that had no stated limit on the size of its membership refused to accept a Negro and claimed that it was a private club. In response to a suit by the Negro to gain admission to the YMCA, the court noted that there were no stated membership limits and that the YMCA did not operate as a private club. The opinion stated that, "The simplest and most compelling answer is that serving or offering to serve all members of the white population within a defined geographic area (as was done here) is certainly inconsistent with the nature of a truly private club.'' It was therefore ruled that the YMCA was a public facility and must accept the Negro as a member.

This Federal law does not cover bars, although it does cover soda fountains, and also does not prevent discrimination on the basis of sex. Women may still be excluded, unless local laws have been passed to end that practice. However, the courts have determined that women may not be discriminated against in public facilities. For a further consideration of the rights of females, see Chapter 6 on Wife and Mother.

It must be remembered that public facilities may still bar people for other reasons. A California racetrack removed an irate spectator who was intoxicated and was causing a disturbance because he thought that a race was fixed. In a suit for damages for this removal, the judge found for the racetrack, ruling that a public facility has the right to bar a patron on reasonable grounds.

Can people be prevented from voting?

Each state has a right to pass laws regarding voting qualifications. These laws will be upheld if they are based on sound principles. There are, however, certain specific restrictions on preventing people from voting in primaries or elections:

1. Literacy tests and other voting qualifications may be used only if they are applied fairly to all. The Federal government will step in if it feels that these tests are being applied in a manner that excludes a specific ethnic group.

2. The poll tax is now illegal. A state or city cannot require you to pay money in order to vote.

A state may invoke requirements that affect a particular group only if the requirements are necessary for the proper operation of an electoral system. Some Negroes in Alabama brought a suit because the state had changed many of their electoral districts. They saw this as a means of preventing them from voting. Their suit failed, since the decision was that these changes were necessary and that they were not made with the intention to dilute the voting strength of Negroes in Alabama.

Equal rights in schools

Ever since the famous *Brown v. Board of Education* case in the United States Supreme Court in 1954, it has been mandated that schools cannot be segregated. This case has been interpreted to mean that not only the student body but also the faculty and administration of all public schools may not be segregated. The case has also been interpreted to mean that schools must be integrated. This integration has been accomplished in many areas by busing children from their neighborhoods to schools in other neighborhoods. Busing has been held to be constitutional, and, in some cases, mandated in order to achieve desegregation.

Private schools may choose their students on the basis of color and creed. However, if the school receives public monies or is technically considered an operation of a public authority, it must either abolish its discriminatory policy or give up its public funds and affiliation.

Hair length   School regulations in some states provide that the hair length of students may not exceed certain limits prescribed by school officials.

Federal courts in Utah, Colorado, and Oklahoma sustained these rulings, but in New Mexico a Federal court held that students' rights had been violated by the school board. The U.S. Circuit Court of Appeals for the Tenth Circuit, which covers this whole western area, ruled in favor of the school boards and the right to expel or punish a student who would not comply. The United States Supreme Court recently refused to review this determination by the Federal Court of Appeals, which in effect means that those school boards may continue to set such standards.

Federal courts in Massachusetts, Pennsylvania, Wisconsin, Illinois, Indiana, Alabama, and other states have held that the First and Fourteenth Amendments to the Federal Constitution protect the civil rights of students. This has been interpreted to prevent public schools from excluding students on the basis of the length of their hair. In a recent Pennsylvania case, a school's regulations included acceptable hair length. The court pointed

out that such regulations extended beyond the school and invaded and regulated a student's private life, thus becoming an illegal restraint on freedom of experiences. The court therefore held that the school's reasons for enforcing haircut requirements had to be especially serious, which the court could not find in this case. A New York court, confronted with a similar school hair regulation, recently upheld the dismissal of a student who violated the hair code. The law in this area is not yet settled. However, if a special rational basis for the rule can be demonstrated, such as requiring a wrestling team member to avoid long hair, then the rule will be upheld.

In 1969, a case involving the rights of students to wear black armbands protesting the Vietnam war reached the United States Supreme Court, which ruled that this was a form of symbolic speech and entitled to First Amendment protections. The Court went on to say that students retain their rights to freedom of speech or expression even while in the schoolhouse, although this would not extend to disruptive behavior.

Equal rights in employment

A firm that is in an industry affecting commerce and that has 250 employees during at least 20 weeks of the year is prohibited from hiring or firing someone or imposing unfair working conditions because of the race, color, creed, national origin, or sex of the person. Likewise, a labor organization cannot exclude a person on any of those grounds, nor can it refuse to refer someone for employment or have an employer refuse to hire someone.

One exception to this law is for jobs in which religion or sex is an occupational qualification reasonably necessary to the normal operations of the particular business. It would be legal, for example, for a men's locker room to deny employment as an attendant to a woman, or for a Christian church to refuse to hire a Buddhist as its rector.

The Civil Rights Act of 1964, Title VII, has been amended by the Equal Employment Opportunity Act of 1972. There were a number of important changes made. The 1964 Act prohibited discrimination in employment on the basis of race, color, religion, sex or national origin, in industries where there were more than 25 employees. The 1972 Act extends coverage to those employers with 15 or more employees; to state and local governments, governmental agencies, and political subdivisions; and to public and private educational institutions except for those incorporated by religious organizations. Religious organizations can still have particular religious qualifications, but they cannot discriminate on any of the other bases. Labor unions with at least 15 members and state employment agencies are also covered. One new section of the Act is devoted entirely to non-discrimination in Federal government employment and in educational institutions. This provision has created a wave of interest in the area of sex discrimination.

If you believe that you have a claim of discrimination, you should immediately consult your lawyer, as there are time limits for bringing complaints. The remedies range from injunctions against further practice of discrimination to receiving back pay for the two years prior to the filing of your charge. So do not delay your consultation with counsel.

Use of the streets

Our civil rights principles have often sheltered religious sects from antagonisms expressed by other denominations. The long catalog of acquittals of members of Jehovah's Witnesses throughout the country testify to protection secured to a minority group against unjust persecution.

At Haverhill, Massachusetts, members of Jehovah's Witnesses distributed on the streets of the city the magazines of their organization, *The Watchtower* and *Consolation*.

Haverhill had a city ordinance that no persons except newsboys should stand in any street or way for the purpose of selling any article. Attacking this ordinance, the Federal court said that the use of the streets as places for the distribution of literature is sanctioned by ancient custom and is a part of the liberties of the people protected by the Fourteenth Amendment against state encroachment. The ordinance was held unconstitutional.

Right of privacy

Among the civil rights enjoyed generally is a right that has been termed by Justice Brandeis as "the right to be let alone." Under the New York law this right is embodied in a civil rights law forbidding the use of the picture or name of a person for commercial purposes except with the written consent of the person involved. In other states, the law forbids the exploitation of the private life of individuals, or episodes that have occurred in their experience, for commercial purposes without their consent. These laws are known generally as laws of the "right of privacy," although in some states the recognition of this principle is refused.

The Constitutional privilege of freedom of speech and press has been raised in connection with the much criticized majority report of the Federal Commission on Sex and Pornography, which states that there is no warrant for continued governmental interference with the full freedom of adults to read, obtain, or view whatever material they wish. The United States Supreme Court has recently upheld the right of a citizen to have obscene material in the privacy of his own home. However, the Court has also held that there is no comparable right to distribute or sell obscene material through the mails to willing adult recipients.

The question of an individual's right to be let alone against the state's right to regulate in the public interest will continue to be argued in the years to come.

Searches and seizures and fingerprinting

The Fourth Amendment to the United States Constitution, which by U.S. Supreme Court interpretation also applies to the states, reads as follows:

> "The right of the people to be secure in their persons, houses papers, and effects, against unreasonable searches and seizures, shall not be violated, and no Warrants shall issue, but upon probable cause, supported by Oath or affirmation, and particularly describing the place to be searched, and the persons or things to be seized."

It is for this reason that evidence obtained in the home of an accused person is suppressed and not permitted to be used against him at a criminal trial, unless there is adherence to the Constitutional requirements. See Chapter 25 on Criminal Law.

Recently, the United States Supreme Court held that the police could not make investigatory detentions for the purpose of fingerprinting suspects in the absence of probable cause to arrest. Fingerprinting does not involve as much interference with personal rights as other forms of invasion and search. Justice Brennan stated it as follows:

> Detentions for the sole purpose of obtaining fingerprints are no less subject to the constraints of the Fourth Amendment. It is arguable, however, that, because of the unique nature of the fingerprinting process, such detentions might, under narrowly defined circumstances, be found to comply with the Fourth Amendment even though there is no probable cause in the traditional sense. . . . Detention for fingerprinting may constitute a much less serious intrusion upon personal security than other types of police searches and detentions. Fingerprinting involves none of the probing into an individual's private life and thoughts that marks an interrogation or search. Nor can fingerprint detention be employed repeatedly to harass any individual, since the police need only one set of each person's prints. Furthermore, fingerprinting is an inherently more reliable and effective crime-solving tool than eyewitness identifications or confessions and is not subject to such abuses as the improper line-up and the "third degree." Finally, because there is no danger of destruction of

Loitering   fingerprints, the limited detention need not come unexpectedly or at an inconvenient time. For this same reason, the general requirement that the authorization of a judicial officer be obtained in advance of detention would seem not to admit of any exception in the fingerprinting context.

A local law recently declared unconstitutional by the United States Supreme Court provided that it was unlawful for three or more people to assemble (except at a public meeting of citizens) on sidewalks, street corners, or the mouths of alleys and parks "and there conduct themselves in a manner annoying to persons passing by." The law was held unconstitutionally vague because a violation "may entirely depend on whether a policeman is annoyed." This was said to be "an invitation to discriminatory enforcement" because a gathering of whatever individuals might be considered annoying for "their ideas, their life-style or their physical appearance" could be resented by others. Therefore, the Cincinnati ordinance involved was declared unconstitutional because it was so vague that citizens could not know in advance if their conduct was unlawful, and also because it infringed on the First Amendment's guarantee of free assembly.

CHAPTER 10

How To Make A Will

"Say not you know another entirely until you have divided an inheritance with him," said Johann Kaspar Lavater, an 18th-century writer.

You must always remember that the right to make a will and to dispose of your property as you wish at your death is given you by the state in which you reside. The conditions and limitations to this right are embodied in the statutes of your state and must be observed if your will is to be fully effective.

You must also remember that your financial condition may change through the years and that your family may grow larger or smaller. What may have been a proper disposition under a will made years ago may not now reflect your true circumstances or intent. No will, or a poorly drafted will (homemade), may also create "bad will," hard feelings, and legal rifts, and may dredge up unknown relatives.

A number of important terms, whose meanings you should know because they are often used in connection with wills, are defined below:

Administrator/Administratrix: the man or woman appointed by the Court who takes charge of the distribution of your property when there is no valid will or there is no executor provided for in the will.

Bequest: the gift, under a will, of personal property.

Codicil: a separately executed later addition or modification of a will.

Devise: the gift, under a will, of real property.

Executor/Executrix: the man or woman appointed in a will to carry out the terms of that will.

Legacy: a gift, by will, of property.

Legatee: the person to whom a legacy is given.

To probate: the act or process of proving a will in court.

Testator/Testatrix: the maker of a will.

Capacity to make a will

The right to provide by will for the disposition of one's property at death is withheld only from those who are not sufficiently sound of mind to apprehend and understand the ordinary affairs of life, which include the nature, extent, and character of their own property.

Use of drugs or intoxicants

A mere use of drugs or intoxicants is not in itself sufficient to prove that a person does not possess the capacity to make a will. A person is considered to be deprived of that capacity, however, if he uses drugs or intoxicants to such an extent that it can be determined as a fact that he lacks the mental capacity to comprehend the extent of his property and the purpose of his acts in making a will.

The effect of senility on a will's validity

It is a mistake to think that because a man is old and forgetful he is incapable of making a will that will prove acceptable to the courts despite the allegations of relatives that he was mentally incompetent when he made it.

A will was made by an 80-year-old man. After his death the will was contested, and it was pointed out in court that he had behaved peculiarly during the period in which he made it. Only at rare intervals, testimony established, would he show sufficient interest to reply to questions; at other times he said nothing. He often failed to recognize acquaintances. Some of them considered that he was "not normal."

"There was nothing in the evidence," said the court in asserting the will of the old man to be a valid one, "that showed more than old age and a weakness of intellect resulting therefrom, and this does not constitute mental incapacity to make a will unless the weakness amounts to imbecility."

The probate of the will of a Michigan man was objected to for this same mental incapacity. Eighteen months after he had made the will, the man had been placed in the psychopathic ward of a hospital, a victim of senile dementia. One physician testified the man was mentally incompetent when the will was made.

The conclusion in this case demonstrates the attitude of some courts toward claims of weakened mentality and incapacity. "The entire testimony shows the case of a man who, after working hard at his trade of blacksmith the greater part of his life, finally became old and had the usual infirmities of age, forgetfulness, untidiness, and who eighteen months after the will in question was executed was committed to an institution as a senile dementia patient. Such facts alone are not sufficient to set aside a will. Weakness of mind and forgetfulness are not sufficient to invalidate a will if it appears that the testator's mind was capable of attention and exertion when aroused and was not imposed upon. The weak have the same right as the prudent and the strong-minded to dispose of their property."

Recently, a very old and infirm man married his nurse, a much-married younger woman who had at one time been accused of murder. The man died soon afterward, leaving a considerable fortune to his widow. There was no proof that she had coerced him into the marriage or that he had died of causes other than age, so his family's objections to her collecting his estate were not sustained. If she had been found guilty of his murder, for example, she would not have been permitted to receive his estate.

A court will not lightly set aside the wishes of a testator set forth in the will, unless incapacity to make the will is clear.

Undue influence and how it is proved

Sometimes one person possesses so much influence over another that he is able to substitute his own private aims for the other's wishes. This problem is of particular interest to us in connection with wills. When the victim is driven far from the course that would be charted by his own reason and fairness, this influence is labeled ''undue'' and is condemned by the law.

To prove a case of undue influence upon the maker of a will, the following factors must generally be shown to be present: (1) a person unquestionably subject to such influence, (2) opportunity to exercise such influence and effect the wrongful purpose, and (3) a disposition to influence unduly for the purpose of procuring an improper favor.

A clear-cut case of undue influence

Amalia Feeley, injured in a railway accident, for six years preceding her death suffered from delusions. Under their influence she committed such acts as tearing a mattress into pieces to secure filling for her house mop, throwing rugs out of her home, using an axe to remove a door that displeased her.

For 20 years preceding her accident, she and her husband had lived peaceably together in Chicago in a three-family house, which they owned. Evidently concerned about her health, her relatives invited her to Wisconsin for treatment. Eight days after her arrival in Wisconsin she made a will, naming her sisters and mother her sole beneficiaries, with no provision whatever for her husband. At the same time she transferred the bank account in which were the savings of her husband and herself into a joint account with her sister.

When her husband came to Wisconsin to see her, he was ordered from the house by her relatives, and did not see his wife again until he attended her funeral four months later.

This will the court refused to accept, holding that it was the product of the influence of the mother and sisters on the weakened mind of the maker.

**When objections
are not valid**

A different story is told by a New Jersey case, where objections were raised on the ground of undue influence upon a father for the benefit of his daughter.

Morris Alper was an invalid for 16 or 17 years. During that time, his daughter Theresa cared for him and his property, collecting the rents, superintending repairs, and carrying on various tasks for her father that were necessary from time to time.

Two years before Morris died, speaking to some friends of this daughter, he said, "She is a very good girl. She has given her life for me. I am worried about her. The other girls are married. They have homes, children—they have families and Theresa hasn't. But I provided for her. I took care of her, so if I go, she won't have much worry."

When Morris died, 60 percent of his estate had been willed to seven children and grandchildren and the other 40 percent to Theresa. It was claimed that the will was the result of undue influence exercised by Theresa over her father.

"The will," said the court, "is neither unnatural nor unjust. This is not to suggest that a testator may not dispose of his estate unnaturally or unjustly, but in the instant case neither criticism may be leveled at his will. It is for him, and him alone, to weigh those circumstances and influences which, in his mind and consciousness, justify such fairness in bounty as he chooses to denote."

**Describe property
in a will accurately**

Beware of loose or incomplete wording in your will. Be specific and detailed in your legacies, particularly where they are valuable. For a valid gift of property under a will there must be a description of the property given sufficient for its identification. Otherwise the devise or bequest may be void.

**How charitable
bequests are limited**

When you make your will, be sure that you are familiar with the state laws about gifts by will to charities and charitable institutions. Also be sure about the validity of forms provided for bequests to charities and associations. The forms you find in magazines and brochures may not be accurate. You should consult with your lawyer about the appropriate form for any bequest to such groups.

Many states restrict such bequests both in the period of time that must elapse between the execution of the will and the death, and in the proportion of the total estate that can be thus bequeathed when there are surviving relatives.

The laws of California, for example, provide that, where there are near relatives, charitable bequests are valid only when the will has been executed at least 30 days before the death of its maker, and the charitable bequests cannot amount to more than one-third of the entire estate. Any excess over the total of one-third is void, and each charitable bequest is reduced pro rata.

Cy pres   If a trust, devise, or bequest for charity is or becomes illegal, impossible, or impracticable of fulfillment at the time it is intended to become effective, a court may order settlement *cy pres*—"as nearly as possible"—to fulfill the general charitable intention. But the testator must show an intention to devote the property to charity.

In a New York case, a legacy was left in trust for an Italian religious institution. But it could not be paid because the institution had been discontinued by the time of the testatrix's death. The court applied the cy pres doctrine, and the money was given to a cathedral that was also an object of the testatrix's bounty.

In another case, money was left to the Society for the Prevention of Cruelty to Children in Richmond, Virginia. However, the Society was not capable of taking a testamentary gift, so it was determined that the Children's Home Society of Virginia, being an organization operating in the same locality and furnishing the same sort of charitable aid, would receive the money.

Cy pres could not be applied in a Connecticut case. There the testator wanted to create a public charity for the benefit of aged, respectable, indigent men over 65 who had been residents of New London. The existing facilities, however, already exceeded the need at the time of the death of the testator. The court said that since the testator was so definite in his terms for the bequest, no enlargement of the class of beneficiaries could be made.

If you leave money for an educational purpose, cy pres cannot be applied to divert it to a religious purpose or for the sick. It is best for a testator to provide his own alternatives in the event a primary wish cannot be fulfilled.

As was said in the beginning, periodic review of your testament will solve many problems and save expensive litigation after your death. Many estates have been dissipated because of suits to clarify a testator's wishes.

Form of a will   The following is a very simple will. In most cases it should be more elaborate and involved, generally providing for setting up trust funds, giving bequests, and naming successor executors, legatees, etc. Your attorney will go over the details with you so that your testament genuinely reflects your wishes and your family circumstances:

I, Lewis Helm, residing in the City of Denver, State of Colorado, do hereby make, publish and declare this to be my last will and testament, hereby revoking any and all former wills and codicils by me at any time heretofore made.

First: I direct that all my just debts and funeral expenses be paid as soon after my death as may be practicable.

Second: I give and bequeath to my cousin James Marshall of Adams, Massachusetts, the sum of One Thousand Dollars.

Third: All the rest, residue and remainder of my estate, of whatever kind or nature it may be, of which I shall die seized or possessed or to which I may be entitled at the time of my death not otherwise effectively disposed of (including any property over which I have power of appointment) I direct my Executor, hereinafter named, to divide into two equal parts, which I give, devise and bequeath as follows:

A. to my beloved wife Alice, her heirs, executors, administrators and assigns, absolutely and forever, one of said parts but in no event less than $10,000;

B. to my son, David Helm, his heirs, executors, administrators and assigns, absolutely and forever, the second of said two parts.

Fourth: I name, constitute and appoint John Romer of Denver, Colorado, executor of this my last will and testament and direct that he be not required to give any bond as such executor.

In witness whereof I have hereunto signed my name this 15th day of December, 1971.

(Signed) Lewis Helm

Follow this with the attestation clause:

The foregoing instrument was subscribed, published and declared by Lewis Helm, the testator above named, as and for his last will and testament in our presence and in the presence of each other, and we at the same time and at his request and in his presence and in the presence of each other have hereunto subscribed our names as witnesses hereto this 15th day of December, 1971.

This attestation should be signed by three witnesses, with their addresses following their names in each instance, after the maker has duly declared this to be his last will and requested the three persons to sign as his official witnesses.

Rules for executing your will

Carefully follow the directions of the statutes of your state in executing your will. If you fail, it may be valid but it may not. The defects will be discovered when you are no longer here to correct them.

Always follow two major rules in the execution of a will: first, sign the will at the end; second, sign it preferably before three witnesses, always before two, and ask them to add their names to the attestation clause at the end, with their addresses.

The law requires three witnesses in Connecticut, Maine, Massachusetts, New Hampshire, South Carolina and Vermont. In the rest of the states, only two are needed. But should you happen to own real estate in any of the states requiring three witnesses and have but two witnesses to your will, the property there will go as though you had made no will. Also, you might some day move to one of those states.

None of the witnesses to a will can be a beneficiary, or have an interest under it. If they do, at best they will receive only what they would have received if there had been no will. Also, it may be a reason for invalidating the will.

Intent of the maker

It has long been the law that the courts will direct their efforts to carrying out the wishes of the maker of a will. Nevertheless, the document must conform to the law—it must be a will. A typical situation where the intent of the maker of the will controlled occurred in Massachusetts where the ink in a fountain pen used in the writing of the will became exhausted and the will was finished in lead pencil, and part of the will was on one sheet of paper and part on another.

"The will was not drawn with precision," said the court, "but as it was duly executed and as the intention can be ascertained it was effectual to pass her property."

Signatures of witnesses

Witnesses to a will in the District of Columbia signed their names before it had been signed by the maker. Because of this omission the validity of the will was disputed. The court held the will was good and refused to deny it probate "merely because the testator signed after the witnesses in the same transaction where the will was in all respects according to the provisions of the statute."

This suggestion, however, was added: "It is of course preferable as well as usual for the testator to sign first but we think the validity of the will should not depend upon who signs it first, provided of course all sign at substantially the same time and in each other's presence."

How signatures can vary

Courts may be liberal in recognizing wills as valid when the maker fails to comply strictly with the law that he must sign at the end of the will. However, it is dangerous to rely on a liberal construction and best to comply strictly with the law.

The will of a New York woman was prepared for her execution when she was too ill to undertake the physical task of signing her name. She asked her husband to sign her name, which he did in her presence.

This will was accepted by the New York court. "While the provisions of the law seem to contemplate that the testamentary instrument must be 'subscribed' at the end thereof by the testator in person, the common-law rule that performance of the physical act may be delegated to another is impliedly recognized."

Leniency was shown by the court in a Virginia will case where the signature was "M. Calvin Lafew—X" (his mark). The meaning of signature is not restricted to the written name. Where the testator puts his mark (X) to the instrument in the presence of the required number of witnesses, this is a sufficient signing within the meaning of the statute.

If you fail to follow the statute

The following will was offered for probate in California:

Knowing we all must depart from this life someday, I want all my debts paid. I want all my insurance put on my funeral. The home I am buying at 2125 West 29th Street, Los Angeles, I want Clifton Muldrow to have. If I have not finished paying for it I want him to finish paying it out. I want Clifton Muldrow to have part of my household goods and Wayman More part of the household goods. Clifton Muldrow must pay all of my debtors' bills if there be any, and all of my other debts. (*Witnesses*) Mrs. Bobbie Rodgers Rhodes, Alphonse E. Cain. (*Signed*) Wretha Jordan.

P.S. I want Clifton Muldrow to send my brother Wash. Fatheree $20.00, my brother Rice Fatheree $20.00, and my niece Ina Jenkins $20.00, if they are alive. Clifton Muldrow is to be executor of my estate without bond. Anyone contesting this will will be paid one dollar and one cent. Subscribed and sworn to before me, a notary public in and for the county of Los Angeles, state of California, this 11th day of November, 1945. Hazel A. Macbeth.

The court here excluded the portion of the will written after the signatures of the witnesses, because it did not follow the law of the state giving the requirements for the execution of such a document.

What are codicils?

When you make a will and later want to change some of the provisions, you may do so by making a codicil instead of rewriting the entire will. This codicil must be executed and witnessed in every detail exactly as in the making of the original will.

A good definition of this term, embodying legal requirements, is: "A codicil is a clause added to a will after its execution, the purpose of which is to alter, enlarge, or restrict the provisions of the will, or to explain, confirm, or republish it. It does not supersede the will as an after-made will would do, but is a part of it, to be considered with it as one entire instrument."

Modifying a will by codicil

The will of Charles Clark of St. Louis, Missouri, set up a trust in real estate. From the income of this trust there was to be paid each month an allowance to Clark's son "in such proportions as the trustee named may deem advisable." Five months after he had made this will, Clark provided in a codicil, "Whereas I am of the opinion that an annual income of $6,000 is amply sufficient for his support and maintenance and that a greater income would be harmful, this income is curtailed to that amount."

This modification by the codicil was accepted by the court. "Viewing the will and the codicil as one instrument," the court said, "the testator intended the subsequent clear plan and unequivocal direction in the codicil should govern. The explicit direction erased, took away, and left no room for the discretionary power given the trustee."

The court's statement clearly shows the purpose of a codicil and its effect. It is part of the original will, but changes the effect of the will to the extent indicated.

Effect of a faulty codicil

A resident of Philadelphia created by his will a trust fund for the benefit of an adopted 15-year-old daughter. The income from this trust fund of $50,000 was to be paid the daughter quarterly after she had become 21 years old, and when she became 35, the principal of the trust was to be paid to her.

When the daughter became 22, the maker of the will made a codicil saying, "I revoke the trust fund in favor of my daughter Mildred and substitute a lump sum of ——— dollars in cash." The space left by the testator for the amount was never filled in by him.

By this man's will, his widow was entitled to the bulk of his estate, less this bequest. She contended that the codicil canceled the trust and that the daughter received nothing. Allowing the amount of the principal of the trust fund as the amount intended to be filled in the blank space, the court made this explanation:

"The general scheme of the will is not to be overborne by modifying directions that are incomplete, ambiguous, or equivocal." The codicil did not "destroy or change the dispositions of the will further than is necessary to give effect to the provisions of the codicil. We cannot conceive that by one short, incomplete sentence the testator intended to strike down all he had so thoughtfully constructed in the will."

Where to keep your will

After its execution, the original of the will should be left with your lawyer or placed in a safe-deposit box with your other valuable papers. You might also give a copy to the executor named in your will. In some states there is provision for deposit of the will with the Court prior to death. Your lawyer will be familiar with this procedure.

Automatic cancellation of wills

The law in many of the states is that when a person marries and becomes the parent of a child or children, these occurrences revoke, to the extent that such spouse or child would inherit in the absence of a will, any will made before the marriage and birth of the children occurred. This, however, does not apply when a provision is made in the will for a surviving wife by a marriage subsequent to the execution of the will, or for children born subsequent to the execution of the will.

Two wills

If a testator leaves two executed wills, it is generally an open question as to which one controls. Where the language of the later will does not indicate that the prior will is revoked, and the provisions of the later instrument are not so inconsistent with the previous will, a New York court has stated that both documents can be probated together as a last will and testament. It is always best to revoke specifically all prior wills by either completely defacing them or by specifically referring to revocation in the later will. Never leave an ambiguous will, which can cause more confusion than comfort.

Signs of revocation of a will

Whether the maker of a will attempted to cancel the document after its execution is determined by three factors: (1) the intent of the maker, (2) the efforts made for cancellation, and (3) the statutes of the state in which the maker lives that relate to the revocation of wills.

A woman in the District of Columbia made a will that was found after her death with pencil cross marks over the face of the will itself. The first page was completely defaced. Three pencil lines were drawn through the attestation clause. The signatures of the witnesses were torn.

The statute of the District of Columbia, like that of many other states, declares that a will may be revoked by another will, a codicil, or "by burning, canceling, tearing or obliterating the same" by or under the instructions of the maker. The court accordingly held that the marks manifested an intention of the maker to revoke the will.

Incomplete revocation

The New York statute says that no will in writing shall be revoked except by some other will in writing, or some writing of the maker declaring such a revocation, which must be executed in the same manner as a will, "unless such will be burned, torn, canceled, obliterated or destroyed" with the intent to revoke it.

In one case in New York, the maker of a will made cross marks on the face of the document and, opposite, in the margin, wrote, "See codicil."

A proposed codicil was found among his papers that had been signed but never formally executed. Here the court decided the marks were insufficient to effect a revocation of the will since no codicil had been executed.

How to make a revocation unmistakable

In West Virginia, a man made a will naming his wife, who had been married twice before, as his sole beneficiary. Four years later he was divorced from her, and at his death she was living with her fifth husband.

During the last days of his married life with this woman, the man had at one time crumpled up his will and thrown it into the waste basket. His wife recovered the will.

According to his version of the incident, quoted in court, "In order to have her clear of him he gave her $1,000 and she promised to burn the will."

She didn't.

When he died she offered the will to the court for its acceptance in a "crinkled" and "crumpled" condition. The intent of the maker of the will became the major feature in the determination by the court of whether or not there had been a revocation. His statement quoted above showed clearly what he desired, and the court refused to recognize the will as valid.

When you wish to revoke your will, do it in a regular manner. Have your lawyer draw up another document, and sign it and execute it in

exactly the manner you would a will. Then there can be no mistake or misunderstanding of your intent, or any possibility that your wishes will remain unfulfilled.

Mutual wills

When two people, most frequently husband and wife, each make a separate will that is part of a mutual plan or compact for the distribution of their property at death, the transaction has the legal features of a contract.

   These wills have a phase that is peculiar to them and that is not a feature of ordinary wills executed by only one person. When a husband and wife execute mutual wills, each making the other the beneficiary with a proviso for disposition of the property at the death of the survivor, then the survivor, upon receiving the benefits under the will of the other, must carry out his part of the agreement. He is not allowed to revoke the will or to make disposition contrary to its provisions.

A contract for mutual wills must be clear

A mutual will agreement must be free of doubt and uncertainty as to its existence. The mere fact that wills appear to have been made under such a compact is not sufficient proof that such a compact existed. A contract of this sort might well be expressed in the wills themselves or in a separate agreement made and executed by those concerned.

An effort to enforce such an agreement was made in California in a case where the contents of two wills were practically identical. The same-ness in itself proved nothing. "The mere fact that the wills are reciprocal or contain similar or identical provisions or that they are executed at the same time and before the same witnesses is not of itself sufficient evidence of an agreement."

Attempt to evade a mutual will

Anthony and Amanda Myers, husband and wife, made their wills, each leaving everything to the other. At the death of the survivor, their property was to go to a Grace McGrew, who had lived with the couple since she had been a child, done the housework, and helped them in many ways.

Anthony died first. Then Amanda changed her mind in regard to Grace and in the presence of a friend threw into the stove the will she had executed under her agreement with her husband.

The provisions of the will she destroyed were part of a binding contract that she could not evade, the court declared. There was an agreement with her husband and he had performed his part. The court required the agreement to be carried out, since the wife had accepted its benefits.

When husband and wife die simultaneously in a common disaster

With air and high-speed automobile travel, it is not unusual for an accident to take the lives of both spouses. When this happens, sometimes there is no way to determine which one lived the longer and who, therefore, inherited the family property.

New York has adopted statutory provisions similar to the Uniform Simultaneous Death Act that disposes of property when there is no will and when there is insufficient evidence that the people involved have died other than simultaneously. What happens is that the property of each person will be disposed of as if he had been the one to survive. However, if there is a will, but no provision in it to take care of a simultaneous death situation, and if the disposition of the property depends on one surviving the other, the statute says that all the assets will be pooled and then equally divided amongst all properly designated beneficiaries.

Be aware of the fact that there is no presumption that a particular person survived because of an age difference, or sex, or even relative physical condition. So if you wish to avoid your state's statutory provisions on the subject or the lack of any statute, you should make provision in your will for the disposition of all property in the event that death comes to you and your spouse, or other family member with whom you share assets, at the same instant of time. Your lawyer can help you to decide how best to dispose of your estate in this eventuality.

Holographic wills

A holographic will is one written entirely in the handwriting of the maker and is valid only when it complies with the statutes of the state in which it is executed. The ordinary attestation clause and declaration before attesting witnesses may be omitted in most instances.

Will by a member of armed forces

In some states, active service in the armed forces is essential to the legality of a holographic will; in other states, it is not. The New York law, for example, says in substance that a holographic will, to be legal, must be entirely in his own handwriting and made by (1) a member of the armed forces in actual service during war or armed conflict in which the member of the armed services was involved, or (2) a person who is attached to armed services in armed conflict, or (3) a mariner while at sea; that it is valid for a year after his discharge, and in the case of a mariner for three years after the date of the will; thereupon it ceases to be recognized as a will unless he is unable at that time to make one in the ordinary form, and then it remains valid until one year after such person is capable of making a will.

In Alabama, holographic wills are not recognized, but if a will is written in the handwriting of the testator and is attested to by at least two witnesses, it is not considered a holographic will.

Where holographic wills are valid

State	Number of witnesses as to validity of writing and signature
Alaska	none
Arizona	none
Arkansas	three
California	none
Idaho	none
Iowa	must be executed as regular testament (two witnesses)
Kentucky	none
Louisiana	none
Maryland*	none
Mississippi	none
Montana	none
Nevada	none
New Jersey	must be executed as regular testament
New York*	none
North Carolina (1)	three
North Dakota	none

State	Number of witnesses as to validity of writing and signature
Oklahoma	none
Pennsylvania	none
Puerto Rico (2)	none
Rhode Island (3)	none
South Dakota	none
Tennessee	two
Texas (4)	none
Utah	none
Vermont	must be executed as regular testament
Virginia	two
Virgin Islands*	none
West Virginia	none
Wyoming	none

*In Maryland it is valid only if made outside the U.S. by a person serving in the United States Armed Forces, but it is not effective more than one year after his discharge if he then has the capacity to make a will.

In New York it is the same as above, for (1) a soldier or sailor in actual service while in actual combat, (2) a person accompanying the military in actual combat, or (3) a mariner at sea. For (3), the will is valid for three years from its date.

In the Virgin Islands it is the same as in Maryland.

1. In North Carolina not only must the testator's handwriting be proved by three witnesses, but the will must be found among his valuable papers or put into someone's safekeeping.

2. In Puerto Rico the testator must be of age, the date made must be clear, and the will must be probated within five years of the date of death.

3. Rhode Island recognizes it only for the soldier and sailor and the mariner at sea.

4. In Texas the testator must add an affidavit that the instrument is his last will and that he was 18 years of age at the time of its execution (or, if younger than 18, that he was married or in the armed forces or maritime service), and that he was of sound mind. Otherwise two witnesses are needed as to proof of the handwriting.

In Connecticut, Hawaii, Maine, and Washington, a holographic will made in a state where it is valid will be accepted.

An unusual holographic will

A holographic will was made by a man in the Marine Corps. It directed the disposition of his property and was signed by him as follows:

> My $1,000.00 policy is to be split 4 ways, one equal part to Magda, Anna, Lydia, & Ted. My $10,000.00 policy all to the folks with the proviso (where did I pick up that word?) that when and if something happens to them that the proceeds go to Teddy. Oh yeah—Ted can also have my watch and anything else I forgot. And not a bloody cent to Maggie. Have a good time with this stuff, folks, and don't feel too unhappy. I ain't. W.O., U.S.M.C.

This unique document proved acceptable to the court as the last will and testament of the deceased.

An unsigned will— why the court accepted it

Another holographic will, probated in California, where the law makes no provision that the maker must be in the military service, read:

> Compton, Calif., March 10th, 1947. I, Mrs. Estelle Gardener, 433 West Laurel Street, do give, devise and bequeath Mrs. Dorothy Mathews and Mrs. Eleatra Hyatt of Compton all of my belongings, should they outlive me, consisting of house, lot, all household furnishings, trunk and clothing now situated at 433 West Laurel Street, Compton, Calif. I hold possession and life tenancy of the property during my lifetime. My only last will and testament. Signed this 10th day of March, 1947. Compton, Calif., 433 West Laurel St.

The court held this a valid holographic will although unsigned. "An inspection of the document shows it to have been written with care and that it is a complete declaration of the desires of the testator." Normally, however, the probate law of California requires that a will entirely in the testator's writing be signed and dated by him.

A hole in a holographic will

Someone said there can be a hole in a holographic will. This is because the writer may have his own personal quirks, and they may not be explainable after his death. In a New York case, a will written by the testator in his own hand bequeathed the sum of "twenty five ($2,500) dollars" to a nephew. Did the uncle mean $25 or $2,500? In some states, when the written lettered amount disagrees with the numbers, the former prevails. In this case, however, the nephew received $2,500.

Wills by word-of-mouth

Wills passed by word-of-mouth are called oral or nuncupative wills and are recognized by law. However, the law does not favor them except where the makers are soldiers in active service or sailors at sea. They are in many cases permitted for civilians, but their validity is strictly held to the provisions of the statutes of the state in which the maker has his residence. As a general rule, these wills can be made only in a "last illness," although this phrase is subject to various interpretations by the courts of the different states.

During World War I, George Mallery, who was with the American army in France, declared to some of the men with whom he was associated, "If I should not come back, I want my father and mother and no one else but them, no matter what happens, to get all I have coming from the government, and I want to tell this to enough of you boys from around home so some of you will go back to tell what I want, in case I don't."

Mallery died in France, still in the army. Accepting this oral declaration as a will, the court remarked that since Mallery's statement of his wishes was made in substantially identical terms upon two occasions, each time to a single witness, it was a sufficient compliance with the statute.

In World War II, a similar will was "executed" by Stanley Knapp, who was captured by the Japanese on Mindanao and imprisoned on Amboina, where he died. Knapp told two of the men with him in the Japanese prison that "he wanted his mother to get everything he had, nothing to go to his father." This statement was accepted by a New York court as a nuncupative will, since it was made during active military duty and before two witnesses, as the statute requires.

Typical restrictions on oral wills

The law in Idaho carries a further restriction—that a nuncupative will, to be accepted as a will, must be proved within six months after the testamentary words are spoken.

It is a vital essential under the Kansas law in the making of a nuncupative will that the maker declare the statement is intended as his will. The mere statement of wishes not declared as a will does not suffice. A patient in a Kansas hospital told a hospital nurse, the day before he died, the disposition he wished made of his property. The court refused to accept this statement as a will because he did not call upon those present, at the time of orally declaring his will, to bear witness that it was his will.

These are the state laws on oral wills

Alabama– Valid when made by soldiers on active duty or sailors at sea. For civilians, personal property bequeathed can be only $500 or less in value, and the will must be made during the testator's last illness at his residence or where he has resided for ten days or more, or when he becomes fatally ill and dies elsewhere. Testator must have asked persons present to bear witness that such was his will.

Arizona– Valid when property does not exceed $50 in value and the will is made in the last illness. Unlimited in amount when three witnesses testify that the testator declared to someone the statement was his will, and the substance of the testimony is written down within six days of the making of the will.

Alaska– May be made by mariner at sea or a soldier in military service, as at common law to dispose of personal property only. If oral, the words must be reduced to writing within 30 days and must be proved within six months.

Arkansas– When the Probate Code was enacted in 1949, provisions for oral wills were eliminated.

California– Valid when property does not exceed $1,000 and the will is spoken before two witnesses, one of whom is asked by the testator to witness the statement as his will. Testator, at the time of his declaration, must be in military service and in peril of death or must expect it from injury received on the day of making the will. The verbal statement of the deceased must be written down within 30 days after the making and filed for probate within six months.

Colorado– Does not recognize them.

Connecticut– Invalid.

Delaware– Valid for personal property not exceeding $200 when acknowledged by the testator during his last illness before two witnesses. It must be written down within three days and attested by signatures of witnesses. Valid only if the testator dies within three days of making the will or subsequently becomes incapable of making one. It must be probated 30 days after the testator's death.

District of Columbia– Valid only for servicemen on active duty or mariners at sea during last sickness. Valid only for personal property disposal. Must be acknowledged before two witnesses and written down within ten days.

Florida– Valid only for personal property when acknowledged before three witnesses, made during last illness, and written down within six days. Must be proved within three months.

Georgia– Valid only if made during last illness and must be proved by oaths of two witnesses, written down within 30 days, and probated within six months.

Hawaii– No provisions on this type of will.

Idaho– Valid when written down within 30 days of its declaration, and probated not less than 14 days after death and not more than six months after oral testament.

Illinois– Not valid.

Indiana– Valid for personal property not exceeding $1,000, except that soldiers on active service or mariners at sea may dispose of $10,000.

Iowa– Does not recognize them.

Kansas– Valid for personal property when made in last sickness if acknowledged and declared as the final will before two witnesses and written down within 30 days.

Kentucky– Valid only for soldiers on active duty or sailors at sea, when made within ten days before death in the presence of two witnesses, and reduced to writing within 60 days after making.

Louisiana– Can be made by public act or privately. To be done publicly, it must be received by a notary public with three persons dwelling in the place where the will is executed as witnesses or by five nonresidents. The testament must be written by the notary and signed by the testator and all witnesses. Privately, it must be written by the testator himself or anyone else from his dictation, in the presence of five witnesses residing in the place where executed or seven nonresidents; or the testator can declare to the five or the seven that the paper written out of their presence is his will. It must be read to all and signed by the testator and witnesses. If it is done in the country rather than the city, there can be three witnesses in residence or five nonresidents.

Maine– Valid for personal property of soldiers on active duty or sailors at sea. For civilians, valid for personal property not exceeding $100 unless three witnesses present. Must be made in the deceased's last illness at home or at the place where he resided for ten days before the making. If words not written down within six days, must be proved in court within six months.

Maryland– Valid for the personal property of soldiers on active duty or sailors at sea if there are witnesses.

Massachusetts– Valid for the personal property of soldiers on active duty or sailors at sea.

Michigan– Valid for soldiers on active duty or sailors on their ships, for personal property when acknowledged before two witnesses. For others, valid up to $300 when proved by two witnesses.

Minnesota– Valid for the personal property of a soldier on active service or a mariner at sea if acknowledged before two witnesses and reduced to writing within 30 days and probated within six months after oral testament.

Mississippi– Valid only if made during last illness at the residence where lived for ten days prior. If property exceeds $100 in value, the will must be acknowledged by the testator before two persons he asks to act as witnesses. Probate must wait 14 days to allow for notice to kin but must be accomplished within six months unless testament reduced to writing within six days after spoken.

Missouri– Valid for personal property of not more than $500 in value. It must be made in the last illness of testator, acknowledged before two witnesses, and proved within six months after death and written down within 30 days of the making of the will.

Montana–   Valid for servicemen on active duty and for their property not exceeding $1,000 in value. It must be made before two witnesses when testator is in fear of death or with death imminent from an injury suffered the same day. It must be written down within 30 days and proved not less than 14 days after death nor more than six months after testament.

Nebraska–   Valid for wages or personal property of soldiers or sailors, or for property exceeding $150 when acknowledged before three persons called by the testator as witnesses and made during his last illness at home or when sick elsewhere. Probate is not allowed for 14 days to permit process to be issued to the widow and others interested so they may contest. But probate must be completed within six months unless oral testament written down within six days.

Nevada–   Valid for property not exceeding $1,000 if made during the last illness and proved by two witnesses to the making within six months. Must be reduced to writing within 30 days after spoken.

New Hampshire–   Valid for property not exceeding $100 unless acknowledged by the testator before three persons called by him as witnesses, or made during his last illness at his dwelling place or when fatally ill away from home. It must be written down within six days and proved within six months of the testament.

New Jersey–   Invalid.

New Mexico–   Not recognized.

New York–   Valid for personal property for members of the armed forces on active duty in actual combat or mariners at sea when made before and proved by two witnesses. Invalid and unenforceable after one year following discharge if a soldier or sailor and if he has capacity to make a will at that time. See the discussion on holographic wills in New York State.

North Carolina–   Valid when proved by two witnesses to the making of the will in the last illness of the deceased where he lives. After six months it is invalid unless it is written down within ten days of being spoken. Cannot be proved until there has been publication for four weeks in newspapers to call the widow's and kin's attention to it so they may contest.

North Dakota–   Valid if the deceased was on active duty if a soldier, or at sea if a sailor, and feared death or was in imminent peril of death from injuries suffered the same day he made the will. For property not exceeding $1,000. Must be proved by two witnesses to the making of the will, one of whom was asked by the deceased to bear witness that such was his will. Testament must be reduced to writing within 30 days.

Ohio–   Valid when made in the final illness, and written and signed by two witnesses, not mentioned in the will, within ten days and proved within six months.

Oklahoma–   Valid for soldiers in the field or sailors at sea who have reason to fear imminent death, or expect it from injuries suffered that day. Valid for property not exceeding $1,000 in value, when proved by two witnesses present at the making of the will, one of whom was asked by the testator to bear witness that such was his will.

Oregon–   Valid for soldiers on active duty and sailors at sea when reduced to writing within 30 days and probated within six months. The widow and kin must be given notice to enable protests.

Pennsylvania–   Valid when made during the last illness or under peril of death. Two or more witnesses are required to prove it. The will has to be proved within three months after the death and written down within ten days of the making of the will. It is void if it attempts to dispose of more than $500 in personal property or any real estate.

Puerto Rico–   It must be shown it was impossible to write the will. Where the testator was in imminent danger of death, the will may be executed (without a notary) before five witnesses who were residents of the place where the will was executed. The testator must die within two months of making the will; it must be probated within three months of death. Also, it must have been reduced to a public instrument according to the law of civil procedure.

Rhode Island–   A soldier, sailor, or airman may dispose of his personal estate as he might have done at common law.

South Carolina–   Valid, except that if property exceeds $50 in value the will must be proved by three or more witnesses to the making who were requested by the maker to act as witnesses. The will must be made in the last illness in the house where the testator dies, and the will must be proved within six months. This period is extended to one year if the will is written down within six days of the making. The widow must be notified before probate.

South Dakota– Valid for property not exceeding $1,000 in value for soldiers in the field or sailors at sea, when in imminent peril of death or expecting it from injuries suffered that day. Two witnesses present at the making of the will are required to prove it, one of whom was requested by the testator to be witness, and the will must be written down within 30 days of the making. It must be filed for probate not less than 14 days after death and not more than six months.

Tennessee– Valid only for personal property when made in imminent peril of death from which death resulted. Must be made before two witnesses and reduced to writing by one of them within 30 days of the testament and proved within six months of death. Limited to $10,000 for military personnel in active service during war and $1,000 otherwise. There can be no probate for 14 days, and the will must have four weeks of publication in newspapers to alert widow and kin.

Texas– Valid when spoken during last illness at the home of testator, or elsewhere if his last illness occurred away from home, except that when personal property exceeds $30 in value the will must be proved by three witnesses within six months after it was made. This proviso is waived if the will is written down not more than six days after it was made. Probate must wait for 14 days, and heirs must be summoned to contest. Soldiers on active duty may dispose of chattels without regard to the rules on wills.

Utah– Valid for property not exceeding $1,000 in value when the words are written down within 30 days of the making of the will and it is probated not less than ten days after death nor more than six months after the making.

Vermont– Valid for personal property for a soldier and for a mariner at sea, but not exceeding $200 in value for anyone else and only when written down by a witness to the making of the will in the six days following the making and presented for probate within six months.

Virginia– Valid for the personal property of soldiers on active duty and sailors at sea.

Virgin Islands– May be made by a soldier or sailor in actual military or naval service. Must be made within the hearing of two persons and the execution and tenor thereof proved by at least two witnesses. Invalid after one year.

Washington– Valid only for personal property not exceeding $200, when made during the last illness and proved by two persons who witnessed it at the bidding

of the testator, provided the words have been written down and the will is proved within six months. Service personnel may dispose of wages and personal property in this manner. The widow must be given notice to enable her to contest.

West Virginia— Valid only for the personal property of servicemen on active duty and mariners at sea.

Wisconsin— Valid for servicemen in any amount. Otherwise valid if property does not exceed $150 in value, unless the will is proved by three persons who witnessed the making at the bidding of the deceased. Then it is valid up to $500. A bequest for more is only valid if to a spouse. The will must be made during the final illness, in the home of the deceased or where he lived for the ten days past or where the fatal illness occurred. The words must be written down within six days of the making and the will probated not less than 14 days nor more than six months after the death of the testator. The kin must be notified to contest.

Wyoming— Not recognized.

Taxes It is very important that you consider the tax implications of bequests that you make in your will. Even with small estates, tax savings can be made. Your attorney can best advise you. He may suggest that gifts be made during your lifetime rather than at death. In any event, do not overlook this aspect when you are ready to set down your wishes in your will. You want your beneficiaries to receive all that they are entitled to, and your care now will make all the difference then.

Death without a Will   If you make no will, or if it is found invalid, then the Probate Court, sometimes called the Surrogate's Court, will appoint an administrator to dispose of your estate in accordance with the laws of intestate succession, which means in accordance with the way the State Legislature has thought people would want their worldly goods distributed. The Administrator will undoubtedly be required to post a bond to insure the faithful performance of duties; the bond is an expense against the estate. See also Chapter 11.

There are ways of disposing of your assets during your lifetime to prevent their being included in your estate at death. Keep in mind that such legal disposition, while valid, may not avoid taxes unless careful consideration is also given to that aspect.

How to avoid probate   You can set up an *inter vivos* (during your lifetime) trust providing for the principal sum to be held by a trustee with the income to be paid to you during your lifetime, and then on your death paid over in full to someone else. A trust can be revocable or irrevocable. You can hold your real estate or stocks and bonds in joint names so that the whole will belong to the survivor. A bank account can be set up payable on death to a named party. Life insurance can be payable to named beneficiaries instead of to your estate. If you give away the ownership right in the policy when you take it out, not only can you avoid having the proceeds in your estate and avoid an estate tax, you may also be able to avoid a gift tax, because the policy has no cash value when you take it out.

Trusts   In addition to *inter vivos* trusts, there are also testamentary (covered by your will) trusts. These are helpful as a means of postponing the vesting of the principal sum in any beneficiary. The principal can be held intact, and the trustee pays over the income to the person or persons designated—or the income can be accumulated to build up the capital. A trust is especially helpful when there are minor children involved because they must have a guardian, and administering minors' assets can be difficult, expensive, and subject to Court supervision unless there is a trust fund. Of course, one must be sure to comply with the laws of one's state as to the length of the trust and any accumulation. The law has long been opposed to the "dead hand" controlling property for too many generations. Usually a trust must be measured (have the length) of no longer than the lives of people who are alive at the time the trust takes effect.

CHAPTER 11

Death Without A Will

Should you make a will? Don't state laws take care of designating who gets your property after you die? If you are not very rich, does it still pay to have a will? The answer to all three questions is, "Yes"; however, the reasons for the answer may not seem apparent at first.

If you could tell where and when you were going to die, it would not be very difficult to put your affairs in order and have your estate distributed as you wish. There are, however, many little things that do not seem important now but which may create problems when you are dead. Your joint bank account may expire (be spent) before you do; property you presently own may be sold; you may buy additional property before you die.

State laws, which are substantially the same, provide for the distribution of your property in the event you die without a valid will (intestate). However, what the law decides is the legal way to distribute your property may be a far cry from what you would want.

If you have a wife and minor children, the law generally requires that your children receive the lion's share of your property and that a guardian—generally your wife—be appointed by a court. Your wife (or other guardian) would be required to furnish a bond and comply with statutory guidelines for the use of your children's share of your estate. Your wife would be unable to use any portion of your children's share except for their welfare and would require permission from the court, from time to time, even to use the funds on behalf of your children. In addition, your wife would be required to file a statement of account for all of the funds that were set aside for your children.

There is nothing in the United States Constitution that forbids a state legislature to limit, condition, or even abolish a person's power to dispose of his property by will anywhere within the state's jurisdiction. The right to inherit the property of a dead person is created by statute.

If you leave no heirs whatever—recognizable under the law—then, by statute, your property reverts to the state.

A wife is never the heir of her husband, legally speaking. Only a blood relative is an heir in the traditional sense of the law. The wife's position, however, has been improved from what it was in earlier times by new legislation that has followed today's tendency to place husband and wife on an equal plane in every respect, including property rights.

The widow's rights   Formerly, when the ownership of real estate represented a greater portion of the husband's wealth, she had her dower right in an interest for life in a third of his land. Today such a provision is considered inadequate and unjust because a husband may be outstandingly wealthy in securities and cash, and own no real estate whatever. Under the old law, in such

a situation, a man could leave his wife destitute by the simple expedient of making a will in favor of other persons.

Nowadays, in New York, for example, a widow is entitled to a portion of her husband's estate that is fixed by statute. If he has made provision for her in his will, she has a right of election—a right to choose either the legacy under his will or the portion allowed her by the statute.

A surviving wife, when there are children and her husband dies leaving no will, receives in many states generally one-third or one-half of her husband's personal property, depending on the amount of the property, in addition to an interest in any real property he may have owned during their marriage or at his death. The other one-half or two-thirds of the personal property and the real property, not affected by the wife's interest, is divided in equal shares among the children.

How a man attempted to defraud his widow

The attitude of legislatures and courts, in thus giving material protection to a wife, is apparent in a court decision on a case involving a man who sought so to arrange his personal affairs so that there would be no estate in which his wife could claim a share. The man had four children by a former marriage. He transferred his property to them during his life, while at the same time retaining control of the property thus transferred.

The court, in its decision, struck directly at this evasion of the rights of the wife. It declared they may not be destroyed by transfers under which the grantor deprives the widow of these rights, and the attempt to elude them is a fraud. As a consequence, the husband, with respect to the widow, must be regarded at the time of his death as being the owner of the property in question. If the husband had given the property away without retaining control, the decision would have been different.

The rights of the surviving husband

The rights of a husband in the estate of his wife are, in general, comparable to those of the wife in the property of her husband when she is the survivor. The details of these rights are provided for in the statutes of the different states where the spouses have their residence.

A husband is no more the "heir" of his wife than she is of her husband except as either is made so by the statutes of the state where they reside. In general, throughout the states, if there is no will and there are no surviving children or parents, the husband receives the wife's entire estate. If there is a will, he has his choice of taking what is left him under the will or of taking the share the state law permits him to elect.

The husband's share when there are heirs

The law in some states is, if there are heirs, the husband has the use for his life of a third of the property his wife owns at the time of her death. When he dies, the property in which he has this interest passes to the heirs of the deceased wife according to the provisions of her will. If there is no will, it goes to the heirs who inherit her property under the statute. This right of the husband is much like the old "right of curtesy," where the husband had a life interest in the property that his wife owned at her death.

The children's share

When a parent dies without a will, one-half or two-thirds of his estate (the exact amount varies in the different states) is apportioned in equal shares among his children. The remaining part of the estate is divided among his spouse and parents, as we shall explain later.

Children born after the father's death

The law in relation to a child born after the death of his father is that for all beneficial purposes of his birth, he is legally the issue and heir of his father.

The right of an unborn child is shown in a case that took place in

Montana. When Charles Normandin died, he left behind him a wife and an unborn child. Immediately upon Charles' death, his brother, Peter, seized his property and kept it as his own. Eight months after Charles died, his daughter, Agnes, was born. Twenty years later, Peter died. Two months after Peter's death, Agnes presented her claim to the executrix of Peter's estate for the half of the estate of her father to which she was entitled and which Peter had appropriated.

"Agnes," said the court, "is deemed to have been living at the time of her father's death, although she was not born until eight months thereafter. She enjoyed all the rights of inheritance conferred upon living persons." Accordingly, she received the portion of her father's estate that was due her.

Can unborn children have heirs?

An unusual situation occurred in Alabama when, two months after the death of Frank Pinkston, his child was born, only to die within a few hours, the child's mother also dying soon afterward. Pinkston had a half-interest in a tract of land and at his death the property, under the law, went to his heirs. Claim to this interest was made by the heirs of Pinkston's wife on the ground that the mother had inherited this share of the property through the child, being the heir of the child unborn at the time of Pinkston's death.

Posthumous children (children born after their parent's death) have the same right of inheritance of property as the parents, and the same right of inheritance is vested in their heirs. This unborn child, the court ruled, was a living person "for most purposes of property."

The rights of adopted children

The law has had to provide for a peculiar circumstance in the case of adopted children. These children often have two sets of parents—the foster parents who adopted them legally, and the natural parents whose offspring they are. Adopted children are favored by the law. For the purposes of inheritance, they are, by and large, considered to be descendants of their adoptive parents but not "of the blood." It is a general rule, too, that they inherit from their natural parents as well. As to what their situation is with respect to inheriting from others, see Chapter 4 on Children.

How children share in their grandparents' estate

When children die before their parents, the law generally gives to their children or grandchildren the share in the parents' estate which the children would have received if they had survived their parents.

Iowa's statute in relation to the share of grandchildren in the estate of grandparents dying without a will is typical of state laws throughout the country. It says that when the parents of the grandchildren die before the grandparents, the grandchildren's portion of the estate is the share their parents would have received had they outlived the grandparents and died in possession of their share.

A further provision is that, if there are no children, the inheritance passes back to the parents or other ancestors of the deceased, and then on to their descendants.

Who inherits an illegitimate child's estate

What happens to the estate of a child of illegitimate birth who dies without a will? The following case provides a good illustration.

An illegitimate son died in Minnesota, leaving no wife, parents, brothers, or sisters. At his mother's death he had inherited all her property. He was survived by her brothers and sisters, and children of these brothers and sisters.

The Minnesota law is essentially the same as the law of most other states. It says that if any illegitimate child dies without a will (intestate) and without spouse or issue who inherit under the law, his estate shall descend to his mother, or, if she is dead, to her heirs.

The word "heirs," as used in a statute providing that the property of an illegitimate child shall pass to the heirs of the mother in case of her death, in general includes those persons to whom the law would give title to the mother's estate by way of descent if she should die without a will. By virtue of being the persons designated by the statute, the heirs of the mother inherited the property of the illegitimate child.

Under the old law an illegitimate son or daughter had no heirs except his or her children. To overcome this injustice statutes such as this have been enacted. It is still the law that an illegitimate child does not inherit from a father who does not leave a will. In many states if the father formally acknowledges the illegitimate child, it can inherit.

The line of inheritance

The order in which property is passed to the various blood relatives upon the death of its owner without a will demands the application of the rules of the statutes of each state in every instance. There is, however, a general scheme followed by all these statutes. Interestingly enough, it parallels pretty closely the ancient course of descent of the kingship to English sovereigns.

**When spouse
and parents survive**

A typical statute, in California, provides that if the deceased leaves a surviving spouse and no issue, one-half the estate goes to that spouse and one-half to the parents of the deceased in equal shares. If either parent is dead, his portion goes to the survivor, or if both are dead, to their issue. In case there are no children or spouse, the parents receive the whole estate. If they are dead, the brothers and sisters of the deceased get equal shares in the estate, and if these too are dead, their children inherit.

**Going back to
earlier generations**

We see, then, that although the course of the descent of property tends downward, through one's children, it may swing up and down again, among the several generations. When there are no children, grandchildren, or other descendants, the right of inheritance shifts to the parents, and if they are deceased, the inheritance goes down to brothers and sisters or to their descendants, and so on.

If there are no descendants of the grandparents who may be recognized as heirs, the right of inheritance swings upward to preceding generations and down to their descendants until it ultimately finds a resting place.

**Common ancestors
become heirs**

The rules of descent and distribution of the property of those dying without wills have the rigidity of mathematics, while on the other hand the conditions and circumstances to which these rules must be applied are of infinite variation. In some instances they are bewildering.

In Pennsylvania, a tract of land was owned by James Custer. Later, James died, leaving no wife, children, brothers or sisters. His father had survived him, but the property had been inherited by James from his mother, and, under the law in Pennsylvania, "No person who is not of the blood of the ancestors or other relations from whom any real estate descended, or by whom it was given or devised to the intestate, shall take any estate of inheritance therein."

Under that prohibition the father had no claim to the land. By ancient law, the court pointed out, property goes back under such conditions to a common ancestor of the man who has died. Then from that ancestor it passes down.

By this computation, James Davis, a great-grandfather of James Custer, was his next of kin and entitled to the estate, and from him it descended to his heirs.

This rule has since been abolished by statute in Pennsylvania.

Many of the old English rules such as this requirement that the one inheriting land be of the whole blood, or primogeniture—the rule that the eldest son inherits all the land—have been abolished in the United States.

When there are no heirs

Our law today retains an ancient provision that when there is no one to inherit the property left by a man or woman dying without a will, the property passes or "escheats" to the state. In England, long ago, property to which there were no heirs eventually reverted to the local lord or the Crown; in the United States, our states have assumed this position of a final heir.

If, then, you are without kin, the state will inherit your property should you die without a will. It is wise to act now if you have put off from year to year the making of your last testament, and you possess friends, or favor charities or organizations, whom you want to benefit at your death.

Only a will carefully drawn can give you any security as to a disposition of your estate in accordance with your desires. And while considering the means of disposition, thought can also be given to the very important aspect of the tax situation and how to provide for it and what will be left in the estate after payment of the estate taxes.

CHAPTER 12

Common Legal Problems of Death

When you die, it is hoped that your relatives will not immediately fight over your property. It is also hoped they will be more concerned about an appropriate funeral and burial in the fashion you would like. The law, however, is not very helpful in these areas.

The law must offer guidance amid the conflicting desires and claims of those who survive. The law is often compelled to determine precisely when a death occurred. In disasters or cases of continued absence, the layman is likely to presume death without proof of its actual occurrence, but the law must make the final decision. The law, too, is called upon to determine by whom the funeral and burial solemnization shall be arranged, and whether the body of the deceased may be transferred to another resting place. We have already discussed some of the problems that death may raise; here we shall examine other common after-death problems.

The body of a dead person belongs to no one under any property right. The great weight of authority in this country is that a person can dispose of his own body by will. Further, a wife or husband who survives or those who are the nearest relatives have the right to determine who shall have the custody of the body in preparation for burial.

Autopsy

When there is doubt as to the cause of death, the law requires an autopsy before a death certificate can be issued. In general, an autopsy must be made before burial, unless good and sufficient reason can be given to the court why a body should be disinterred. Serious suspicion of murder is such a good reason, but most other reasons will not be sustained.

The consent of surviving relatives is required for the performance of an autopsy by hospital authorities, as it is for all other autopsies, unless performed by a coroner. Generally, when an autopsy is performed, the results are not available to the public. They are available only to the authorities if there is reason to suspect a crime, and to the surviving relatives.

One interesting case showing how the law restricts disturbing a dead body involved a suicide. A guest at a fishing camp in Louisiana lingered at the boat dock, while others who had been out fishing with him went on ahead to the cottage. Shortly after they reached it, a pistol shot was heard. The body of the man who had stayed behind was found lying by a path, with a bullet hole in his head. Soon afterward, he was buried.

Four weeks later the insurance company that had issued this man a policy demanded an autopsy as a condition of paying benefits. If it could prove suicide, the widow was not entitled to collect. But she refused to give her permission. When she sued for the insurance, the company made her refusal its defense.

The company's request for an autopsy, held the court, should have been made immediately after death and it ruled that no authority should be given to disinter or disturb the body after burial, saying, ''A body when suitably buried ought to remain undisturbed, except for necessary or laudable reasons.'' Generally, now, by statute, it is a crime to interfere with a burial or to disinter without authority.

Who arranges for burial?

The place of burial and the arrangements for the services that accompany the ceremony are the privileges of the nearest relatives, in the absence of directions left by the deceased in his will.

A father died, leaving a daughter and son who made the funeral arrangements in the usual way. For some undisclosed reason the executor of the deceased's estate took to himself this right of the children and changed the arrangements. Later, suit was brought against the executor to recover the money he had expended from the estate for this purpose without authority. The court decided in favor of the children.

Removing a dead body

The problems involving a dead body do not stop with the funeral. In Georgia a few years ago, a husband purchased a cemetery lot he believed suitable for the burial of his wife; he himself wished to be interred in the adjoining lot. After his wife was buried, however, he learned that the second lot had already been purchased by another.

He asked for a permit to transfer his wife's body to another lot. The Supreme Court commented on his plea. ''To permit the husband to reinter the body is but to grant him the right to exercise his choice to a place of burial on the lot owned by him, which would permit his body, when his own death occurs, to be placed nearby. He seeks now no profanation nor any indignity to the dead, but merely the fulfillment of his original purpose.'' His request was granted.

How the courts decide on disinterment

The factors involved in the granting of permission by courts for the disinterment and removal of a body already buried are, first, the wishes of the dead person, second, those of the surviving spouse and, last, those of the next of kin.

For twenty years Major Koon of the United States Army made his home in Detroit, with his wife, Velma Doan Koon, and with her and her family at Richmond.

He died and was buried in the cemetery lot of the Doan family at Richmond. Then for the first time Velma and her family learned that Koon had been divorced long ago and there were children of that marriage.

None of these children had attended their father's funeral, but over a year later they asked to disinter the body, cremate it, and ship the ashes to California. On the ground that the major was properly buried where he would probably have chosen to be, and that the widow's wishes were paramount, the court refused to grant the children's request.

The courts, as we have noted, are loath to disturb the quiet of the grave unless there are good reasons to decide otherwise. The presumption is against a change.

Surviving relatives are prone to forget the wishes of the deceased, and to regard his body as their property. Not so the courts. In Virginia, a widow sought to shift the family burial plot to follow her changing religious beliefs. The courts did not favor her suit.

The controlling factors were different in the case of a woman who died and was buried in Kansas, after living most of her life there. Before her death she had expressed the wish to be buried in California. When one of her daughters applied for the right to remove her mother's body to Los Angeles, the court granted her permission. All the governing rules were satisfied: (1) It was the wish of the deceased; (2) the wish of the next of kin (no spouse survived); (3) the rules of the cemetery (which must be considered when made a part of the contract of purchase of the plot) did not forbid it; (4) the tenets and usages of the religious body conferring the right of burial likewise did not forbid it. It should be noted, however, that ecclesiastical rules and regulations are not controlling, at least where they come into conflict with principles of equity and other pertinent matters.

Death presumed from absence

When a person disappears, leaving no information of his whereabouts, a legal determination of his death or continued survival often becomes necessary. This occurs not only when the remaining spouse wants the marriage dissolved, but also in many business relationships where the fact of death is of outstanding importance.

A typical case

Arrested for a violation of the Virginia state liquor law, a man named Sherrill Goodwin was released on bail pending his trial. Several days before the date set for the trial, Goodwin packed his bag and disappeared, leaving a note telling his wife that he was going away, but that he would send her some money as soon as he secured work, and that he loved his family as he always had. At the trial he was found guilty and sentenced to sixty days of hard labor with the convict road force. Nine years later, Goodwin's wife sued for the insurance payable at his death on the policies he had carried.

In all states, the death of a person is presumed—unless the contrary can be shown—if he has disappeared and has not been heard from for a prolonged period. The statute in Virginia, which is the common law rule applicable in most states, says that any person residing in the state who goes away or disappears for seven successive years and is not heard from shall be presumed to be dead in any case where his death shall come in question unless it can be shown that he was alive during that period.

Whether Goodwin was alive or dead was for the jury to decide. Their verdict was that he was dead and his widow was entitled to the insurance.

**How
death is presumed
from imminent peril**

The problem of deciding whether a missing person may be presumed dead, and when he met his death, is relatively simple in cases involving "imminent peril." What this term means is clearly shown in the case that follows.

The *Sixeola,* with a Coast Guard crew aboard, was torpedoed in World War II. Two weeks after the catastrophe, the wife of one of the *Sixeola*'s crew members received a telegram from the commandant of the Coast Guard, saying that her husband was missing following action in the performance of his duty. The commandant promised to furnish her with further information as soon as possible.

This telegram was followed six months later by a letter saying that 28 members of the crew, including the woman's husband, were reported missing. "Due to the length of time and the circumstances of the attack these missing crew members are presumed lost."

In the suit brought to recover the insurance on the life of the missing man, these facts were held to be sufficient proof that he had died at that time.

Not in all cases is the law of imminent peril applied so readily as those affecting military personnel presumed killed in action. The following case is an illustration of a typical incident.

A forest fire was ravaging the country around Spokane, Washington. Many had lost their lives and volunteers were striving to check the flames. Thomas Fanning told a friend in Spokane that he was going to volunteer to fight the fire. The next day Fanning could not be found at his boarding house and he was never seen again.

Fanning's absence and the lack of any information of his whereabouts set the date of his death, by law, at the end of seven years. In this case the imminent peril of the forest fire showed the probability of his death, as the submarine attack on the vessel with the Coast Guard crew showed the probable death of those who did not survive, but the date of Fanning's death was determined by the legal presumption in the absence of supporting evidence.

Proximate peril The minister of a church in Idaho was happily married and had two children to whom he was devoted. He was a healthy optimist, 32 years old, of exemplary habits, and with a fondness for fishing.

One afternoon he rented a small rowboat, pushed off from the shore, and rowed out into a neighborhood lake. He was last seen late in the afternoon a quarter to a half mile out. The next morning he had not returned. The boat was found off shore, the minister's coat hanging over the side, one oar missing. A two-week search for his body was unsuccessful.

When his widow sued for the insurance on her husband's life, the court held she was entitled to collect. Summarizing the cases where death is presumed upon the occurrence of an approximate peril, it said: "Two settled principles applicable to a case of this nature are: That a person who was alive when last seen is presumed to continue living until the contrary is shown; and that one who disappears and remains unheard of for seven years and whose absence is unexplained, is presumed to be dead. Where the proof shows that the absentee encountered some specific peril to which it may reasonably be thought he had succumbed, death may be inferred short of the expiration of the seven-year period."

Circumstantial evidence of death

The perils from which the law infers death are not merely physical ones. Nowadays, situations of emotional or mental stress are widely recognized as a basis for presumption of death.

The disappearance of a resident of Bangor, Maine, was marked by no physical peril. The man's home life had been happy, but during the closing years of the Depression of the thirties he had become despondent. He was insolvent. His home was mortgaged. He had borrowed from friends, relatives, and banks.

"I realize if I live much longer I'll not have much of a good time. It wouldn't bother me if I were to die tomorrow," he remarked to a friend. He left Bangor for Boston, hoping to obtain financial help. Later his wife received a wire from him stating: "No luck. Leaving tonight. Boat. New York party. Home Friday. Love."

This man's personal luggage was found a few days afterward in his room on the boat but he was missing. These facts, in conjunction with his disappearance and his mental attitude at the time, established his death in the suit brought later by his widow to recover his life insurance.

According to the law, while the presumption of life continues, the fact of mere disappearance does not prove death. But disappearance where there is no information about the absentee, although search and inquiry are made, together with other circumstantial facts, such as the evidence of suicide in this case, may be sufficient to establish death.

The problem of relatives killed in a common disaster

The order in which the deaths of a husband and wife occur when they perish in a common disaster, such as the sinking of a ship, a fire, or an automobile accident, determines who inherits their property. But the answer to the question of who dies first is in most instances of this kind really a conjecture. The only adequate solution to the problem is a provision for such contingencies in the wills of both the husband and the wife.

If the husband dies first, the wife inherits the widow's share of his estate, however short the time may be by which she survives him. Then, at her death, whatever property she possesses, together with what part of her husband's estate she is entitled to, passes not to his heirs but to hers.

A father, mother, and two daughters were driving by automobile from Chicago to Bowling Green, Kentucky. The road was wet and slippery. The car skidded and turned over. There was a flaming explosion of gasoline and all four occupants of the car were burned to death with no witnesses of the tragedy.

All the victims were considered to have perished at the same time. No circumstances existed to contradict this presumption.

The claims were decided by the rule that is generally followed in such instances. In case of the death of two or more persons in a common disaster, according to this rule, there is no presumption either of survivorship or simultaneous death. In other words, representatives of the wife's estate, if they claimed the insurance, had to show that she survived her husband. If they could not, the property of the husband passed to his heirs, as it would if she had not survived.

Exceptions: Louisiana and California

Some of the legal principles of survivorship in the state of Louisiana are exceptions to the general rule of law in this country that all in a common disaster are supposed to perish at the same time unless the contrary can be shown. The laws of this state follow the legal codes of France. By these laws, the youngest is presumed to live the longest, and the oldest to die first. A man is presumed to survive a woman when both perish in a common disaster. California, following the laws of Spain, formerly had a rule similar to that of Louisiana.

A Louisiana case

On board the steamship *La Bourgogne* that sailed from New York for France in July, 1898, were a mother and daughter from New Orleans. Each had made a will giving all her property to the other, with an alternative disposition if neither survived the other.

In mid-ocean the *La Bourgogne* collided with another vessel and sank. No facts existed for determining whether mother or daughter survived the other. Both perished.

Under the law of Louisiana, which is an exception to the general rule in this country, it is provided that if several persons respectively entitled to inherit from one another happen to perish in the same event and it cannot be ascertained who died first, the circumstances of the fact determine the presumption of survivorship. If those who perish together are older than fifteen and younger than sixty, the male must be presumed to have survived where there is an equality of age or a difference of less than one year. Otherwise, the younger is presumed to survive the older.

In deciding the controversy that arose from the *La Bourgogne* tragedy, the Louisiana court said that it must be presumed that the daughter survived the mother since she was the younger, and they were older than fifteen and younger than sixty.

Transplants

Leading into the next chapter on Gifts is a problem usually associated with death, although it is a gift that might be made by a living person, and that is the problem of anatomical gifts, a form of transplantation.

Because of the world-wide interest stemming from the first human heart transplant performed by Dr. Christiaan Barnard in 1967 at Capetown, South Africa, studies were done on the legal aspects of the use of human organs, tissue, and blood for the purpose of implanting them in another human. The National Conference of Commissioners on Uniform State Laws approved a Model Uniform Anatomical Gifts Act on July 30, 1968. Prior to that time, although the majority of the states had passed laws permitting a living person to give a gift of his body or portions of it, the laws were so different in terms, that it was clear that some uniformity was needed. A copy of the Model Act is available from the National Transplant Information Center. Essentially, it provides that:

> (1) any person 18 or over may donate all or part of his or her body after death for research, transplantation, or placement in a tissue bank; (2) a donor's gift takes precedence over the rights of others, except where a state autopsy law may prevail; (3) if a donor does not make arrangements, his survivors, in a specified order of priority, may; (4) doctors who accept gifts of organs or tissues, relying in good faith on the documents, are protected from lawsuits; (5) the fact of death must be determined by a doctor who is not also involved in the transplant; (6) the donor may revoke a gift and the gift may also be rejected. An important clause permits the donation to be made by a will (without waiting for probate) or other written and witnessed document "which may be a card designed to be carried on the person." The document may, but need not, specify a recipient such as a hospital, medical school, or individual needing the gift. If no one is named, the attending doctor may accept it.

In 1970, New York State adopted as part of its Public Health Law, a section on Anatomical Gifts.

CHAPTER 13

Gifts

An English court, many years ago, attempted to formulate a legal doctrine in light of ordinary human reactions by stating that, "There cannot be a gift without a giving and taking."

This simplest concept of ownership is thus materialistic and identified with physical control. When young children trade things, the standard way to "transfer title" is to hand over the item. A child who no longer physically possessed the item would not derive comfort from the fact that he or she was still the lawful owner. Following this line of thinking the owner is the one with physical possession. To make someone else owner you physically transfer the property; and, if you lose possession you are no longer the owner. Very few people are interested in hearing about a legal distinction between "title" and "possession."

The modern notion of ownership shifts the emphasis to the functional criteria of what the law requires before putting one man in the shoes of another with reference to any particular property. Thousands of gifts are made daily in this country by people with only the simplest ideas of ownership, and generally without legal advice. Many people who would not think of considering a will without going to an attorney do not even realize that a legal problem exists in gifts of personal property. People have been making gifts all their lives without legal advice, and giving, to most of them, means delivering possession.

The necessity of delivery in gifts of personal property has always been adhered to in the United States. The typical law would therefore be as follows: to succeed in effectuating a gift, the claimant must show (1) the alleged donor's intent to give, and (2) delivery of either (a) the gift, e.g., cash, or (b) an instrument of gift, e.g., a stock certificate.

A gift or not a gift?

Remember, when you make a gift, it is not a gift if you reserve a right to take it back. The giving must be complete—there is no halfway ground. It is either a gift or it is not a gift.

Twelve hundred dollars and 40 shares of stock were transferred to Wilma MacPherson by her aunt one month before she died. Later, the executor of the aunt's estate claimed that both the cash and stock Wilma had received were not gifts.

The aunt was over 70 years old, with no children or relatives except some nieces and nephews. Of these, Wilma had been the only one to show any kindness to the old lady, and during every illness had cared for her. The assignment of the stock had been carefully prepared and executed, and the aunt herself had withdrawn the cash from the bank and deposited it to Wilma's credit.

The transfer of this money and stock was a valid gift, the court declared. Such a transfer must be intended as a gift—and as a gift in the present, not in the future. Further, it must give to the one who receives it full ownership and control. There is not a valid gift without a complete delivery, even though every other step essential to the validity of the gift has been taken. If the gift is not actually delivered, it is not a gift. "Intention cannot supply it; actions cannot supply it; it is an indispensable requisite without which a gift fails."

False "gifts"

By way of contrast, let us examine the facts of a case that came before the Federal court in Florida, where for 15 years a father had made so-called gifts of the stock of his business to his children. In every instance he had endorsed the stock certificates before witnesses, declaring them to be gifts to his children. Then he had taken the certificates and put them into his own safe-deposit box. He kept the dividends for himself, while he gave his children promissory notes for an equivalent amount, and deducted these dividends from his income tax returns because they were "gifts."

According to the law, the court said, these transfers were not gifts. One who makes a gift must do everything possible to give the ownership and control of the gift to the person receiving it. The father here had made no delivery of the stock to his children. He continued to deal with the securities and the income as his own; hence this income was taxable to him.

A vital element in many such attempts at making gifts is the trait deep-rooted in every possessor of property to hang on to the possession of it—the wish to be a giver and still keep the gift.

A gift with a condition

For many years Louise Johnson was a close friend of Augusta Scharf, an old lady in poor health. One day, when Louise Johnson called, Mrs. Scharf handed her the following note: "I give Mrs. Henry Johnson [Louise Johnson] the sole right to my bonds, all of them, for my expenses in case I pass away. Augusta L. Scharf."

Below this she had written, "If Mrs. Scharf should get well and strong again, I will return to her the four bonds as she requested. If she passes away, I am to give Anna Zalinski the $1,000 bond, a gift to her for her services during her poor health during the last three years. She was always willing and kind through very trying circumstances. Louise, the expenses I want you to pay are Anna [Anna Zalinski], and have my name put on my tombstone. My funeral expenses must come from the house as well as other bills when the house is sold."

With this memorandum Mrs. Scharf gave her friend the four bonds she had mentioned. Since Louise Johnson accepted them, her signature to the document was not necessary. Two weeks later Mrs. Scharf died.

Mrs. Scharf's attempt to make a gift failed. The cause was the all-too-human trait already mentioned, the desire to hold on to one's property even though one gives it away. It cannot be emphasized too strongly. For a gift between living persons to be valid there must be a giving up of possession, a relinquishment of all control both present and future. The gift must be placed beyond the power of the giver to recall it.

A gift must be accepted

The law requires in the making of a gift not only that the giver release all ownership and control but, more, that the one to whom the gift is made should accept it. Before the gift is accepted, if the giver changes his mind, or dies, the gift is revoked. It cannot be revoked once the gift has been accepted. Acceptance of a gift is as essential in the eyes of the law as is the offer by the giver. Not until there is an acceptance by the one who receives the gift does ownership pass.

When gifts are a burden

The courts will not infer, in the absence of proof, that a designated recipient has accepted a gift or legacy which is not only without any monetary value but which would be a millstone around his neck.

A resident of Pennsylvania died, willing his property to his wife. The estate was hopelessly insolvent. The holder of a mortgage on land that was part of the estate sued the widow for the past due taxes on this property. The property was already mortgaged far in excess of its value. According to the court that tried the case, the widow could not have accepted such property as a gift and so she bore no responsibility for it.

Showing acceptance

The receiver for a Michigan bank sued the widow and children of a stockholder for assessments made on the stock which they had received from him. They had received and spent the dividends two years before the assessments were levied. By accepting the dividends, they showed they had accepted the stock and were therefore liable for payment of the assessments.

The necessity for acceptance before a gift can be complete is similar to the acceptance of an offer before a contract becomes a binding obligation.

Gift of bank deposits

When you decide to make a gift or a gift is made to you, always keep in mind the rule that the object of the gift must pass completely from the control of the giver and be entirely within the control of the receiver of the gift. In the gift of bank deposits and the determination of whether such gifts are valid, the courts emphasize this transfer of ownership more than any other feature of the transaction.

Intention to make a gift

An old lady in California, realizing she had only a short time to live, decided to transfer her bank account into a joint bank account in the name of her sister, her nephew, and herself. She signed the necessary papers for this purpose and gave them to the teller of the bank on a Friday afternoon after banking hours. Before the bank opened the following Monday the old lady was dead.

Because she had delivered to the teller of the bank both her bankbook and the withdrawal order for the transfer of the account, the gift was complete. The required delivery, actual or symbolic, to one to whom the gift was made, or to someone for his benefit, with the intent to make the gift, had taken place. The deposit here had passed from the control of the old lady and was under the control of the three owners of the account. A gift may be made although the giver still retains some interest in it.

When a gift by check becomes complete

A gift by check is complete when the check is received and paid in the bank on which it is drawn. When this is done, the check is removed from circulation and canceled, and the transaction is closed.

The victim of a California automobile accident who was close to death gave to a friend a check payable to a third person, asking that it be deposited immediately to that person's account. At closing time of the bank that day the check was deposited. A few hours later the man who had signed the check was dead. Nevertheless the gift was complete. The check had been deposited and paid before the death of the giver.

Giving an engagement ring

The engagement ring has the character of a pledge—it binds the contract to marry. But with the dissolution of the bargain *by the woman*, her right to the ring disappears. By the law of some states she can be obliged to return it.

The other side of this problem is shown in a case that took place in Kentucky.

A couple there were engaged to be married. "Shortly thereafter," according to the county judge, "pursuant to a custom, to the origin of which the mind of man runneth not, the man presented a gift to the woman, the diamond ring here in question." Then later the man broke the engagement.

Later these two went squirrel hunting. Sitting under a tree, the woman had her engagement ring in her hand. The man took the ring and put it in his pocket, where it stayed until that judge decided the case and the woman received back her ring.

When a woman receives an engagement ring and then refuses to fulfill the conditions of the gift—to marry the giver—she must return the ring.

On the other hand, when the man refuses to carry out the marriage agreement, he forfeits the rights to the return of the engagement ring. However, in some states that have outlawed actions for breach of promise to marry, you may not be able to force return of the gift regardless of who is at fault. See further on this in Chapter 1 on The Law of Marriage.

Who owns the engagement ring of a dead woman?

In Illinois, on a Christmas eve, a man gave a dinner ring to the woman he had promised to marry, and later he gave her two other rings. Afterward she died, and he demanded that the rings be returned to him since the marriage had not taken place.

When the woman died she owned the jewelry, said the court. It was hers. She had broken no marriage contract nor had she refused to marry him. The man had no claim to the jewelry.

Other gifts during engagement

When gifts are made during an engagement—be they rings or any other objects—and they are gifts pure and simple and not part of the engagement pledge, or used to seal the promise to marry implicit in it, the general rule is that they remain the property of the recipient if the engagement should be broken off.

Making a gift of land

A gift of real estate, like any other gift, is not a gift until the transfer is complete. The land must be out of the giver's control and in the control of the one who receives the gift. This can best be done by the giving of the deed to the land, properly signed and authenticated.

Gift by word-of-mouth

A transfer of land cannot be made by word of mouth. There must be a delivery of possession or some act symbolizing that delivery. .Further, there must be an acceptance of the gift and acts of the receiver of the gift in reliance on the validity of the gift, such as the making of improvements to the extent that it would be a substantial injustice if the gift were revoked. This is because arrangements with respect to land are required by law to be in writing to be enforceable.

Improving a gift of land

In North Dakota, a mother gave her son and daughter-in-law some land, making the gift by word of mouth. The son and his wife made investments in building improvements. However, they paid the mother no rent for the land. When she ordered them to vacate, the son obeyed, but the daughter-in-law refused. Suit was brought to oust her, but these efforts proved to be in vain. There had been a reliance by the son and his wife on the gift of the land by word of mouth. They had taken possession and spent money on its improvement and development. To hold the gift void under such circumstances would have been a substantial injustice.

When a gift is irrevocable

A situation similar in many details occurred in Maryland, except that in this case the gift was conveyed by a written document. A father executed and delivered to his daughter deeds of two houses he owned in Baltimore. Later the father remarried and wanted his land back. The daughter, apparently not in sympathy with her father's new marriage venture, refused to reconvey the property. The father sued to recover it, but he did not succeed. The gift of land, being in writing, was complete and irrevocable.

If delivery is postponed

The circumstances are different when delivery or possession of a gift is postponed. An elderly woman had her attorney prepare a deed of her property to a close friend and instructed him, when she executed the deed, not to deliver it to her friend until she gave him further orders. Here there was no gift. The owner never delivered the deed, nor did her friend have the opportunity of accepting it.

Conditional gifts

A gift with conditions tagged to it, we have seen, may lose its character as a gift because of these conditions. However, if, by the transaction, the gift immediately becomes the property of the one to whom it is given, it is a legal gift.

Possession does not always make a gift

To the rule set forth in the preceding paragraph there are certain exceptions that must be explained. One of them is illustrated in the following case. A husband and wife in New York State signed the statement, "I give into the possession of my wife 90 shares of Bethlehem Steel common to hold in her possession until after my death. After my death, that 90 shares of Bethlehem Steel common are to become the personal property of my said wife, Jennie, but in case I should survive her, then, after her death these 90 shares of Bethlehem Steel common are to be returned to me and become part of my estate."

This was no gift. The wife was merely to act as custodian of the stock unless her husband died first. There was a delivery and an acceptance but there was no intent to make a gift except if the husband's death should occur before his wife's.

What power to revoke means

A very similar case concerned stock given with the understanding that the giver should receive all the dividends, and if he survived the person he gave the stock to, then the stock should be returned to him.

Such a plan, said the court, constituted no gift. The stock was merely held for the owner's lifetime with an agreement that the holder could transfer it to himself if the giver were the first to die. The giver could have revoked the transaction at any time during his life, for until he had been divested of all title, dominion, and control, the gift could be revoked. If a gift can be revoked or nullified, there is no gift.

Interest retained in a gift

The retention by the giver of a beneficial interest in property, or a right to share in the income or proceeds from it, is held by the courts not to be inconsistent with a valid gift.

Geraldyne Pratt was the daughter of a western railroad president. She lived with her parents and had only a small income of her own. Her mother wrote her the following letter:

Dear Geraldyne: I have transferred to you 200 shares of Texas Oil Company stock as a gift—with this reservation—that when you sell the stock you invest the proceeds in United States government securities to so remain during your life, with the further understanding that no part of the principal shall be disposed of either by sale or used for a loan. The income, use as your best judgment may dictate. Should death occur to you before either your father or myself, then the securities will revert to me, otherwise to him. If married and no issue, the preceding paragraph will prevail. If issue, the securities will be left in trust for the issue. Your mother, Mrs. J. A. Edson.

In a Federal court action concerning the income taxes on the securities involved in the transfer, the court said that here was an unmistakable gift. In regard to the provision for the return of the securities on the daughter's death, it was pointed out that all the factors that make a gift were present: (1) a giver competent to make a gift, (2) a clear and unmistakable intention on her part to make it, (3) a person capable of taking the gift, (4) a conveyance, assignment, or transfer to the receiver of the gift with no power of revocation by the giver, and (5) a relinquishment of the control of the gift.

Gifts in contemplation of death

Another and frequent type of conditional gift is one that becomes effective at the death of the giver—gifts *causa mortis*. Such a gift made in contemplation of death by the giver is valid although it is intended to be a revocable gift if the giver should not die.

The essential features of such gifts are as follows:

(1) The gift must be of personal property;

(2) possession of the property must be delivered at the time of the gift to the donee (recipient) or someone for him and the gift must be accepted by the donee;

(3) the title to the property must vest in the donee at the time of the gift. To constitute a gift *causa mortis* it must also be shown in addition to the above elements that the gift was made from a premonition of death from present sickness.

There is an essential distinction that should be stressed here between gifts of this character and gifts in general. Ordinarily, once a gift is made, the ownership of the gift is in the person receiving it. Here ownership is conditioned on the death of the giver. If the giver recovers from the illness that gives him the premonition of death under which the gift is made, the transaction is revoked and the giver becomes again the owner.

These rules were laid down in a case concerning the estate of a Mr. J. M. Thomas of Danville, Virginia. Mr. Thomas had put in his safe-deposit box an envelope containing securities, and on the envelope, with a list of the contents, was endorsed, "The personal property of my wife, Florence Thomas." He had been seriously ill and knew "he was down for good for some time."

He gave his wife a key to the safe-deposit box. Shortly before his death he asked, "Florence, where are your keys? Remember those keys are very precious for you to hold, for you might need them in order to get in the box in my safe to get possession of what I told you I have left you in the box." This statement was important evidence in the case.

In concluding its opinion on this case, the court said, "Looking at the evidence in connection with the surrounding circumstances, we think it shows that Mr. Thomas intended to make his wife a gift *causa mortis* of the stock and bonds in question and the same should be upheld."

A gift by a person not then expecting death, but which is to have effect on his death, is not valid. The reason is that such a disposition is testamentary, or similar to one made by will, and therefore requires all the legal formalities necessary to execute a will.

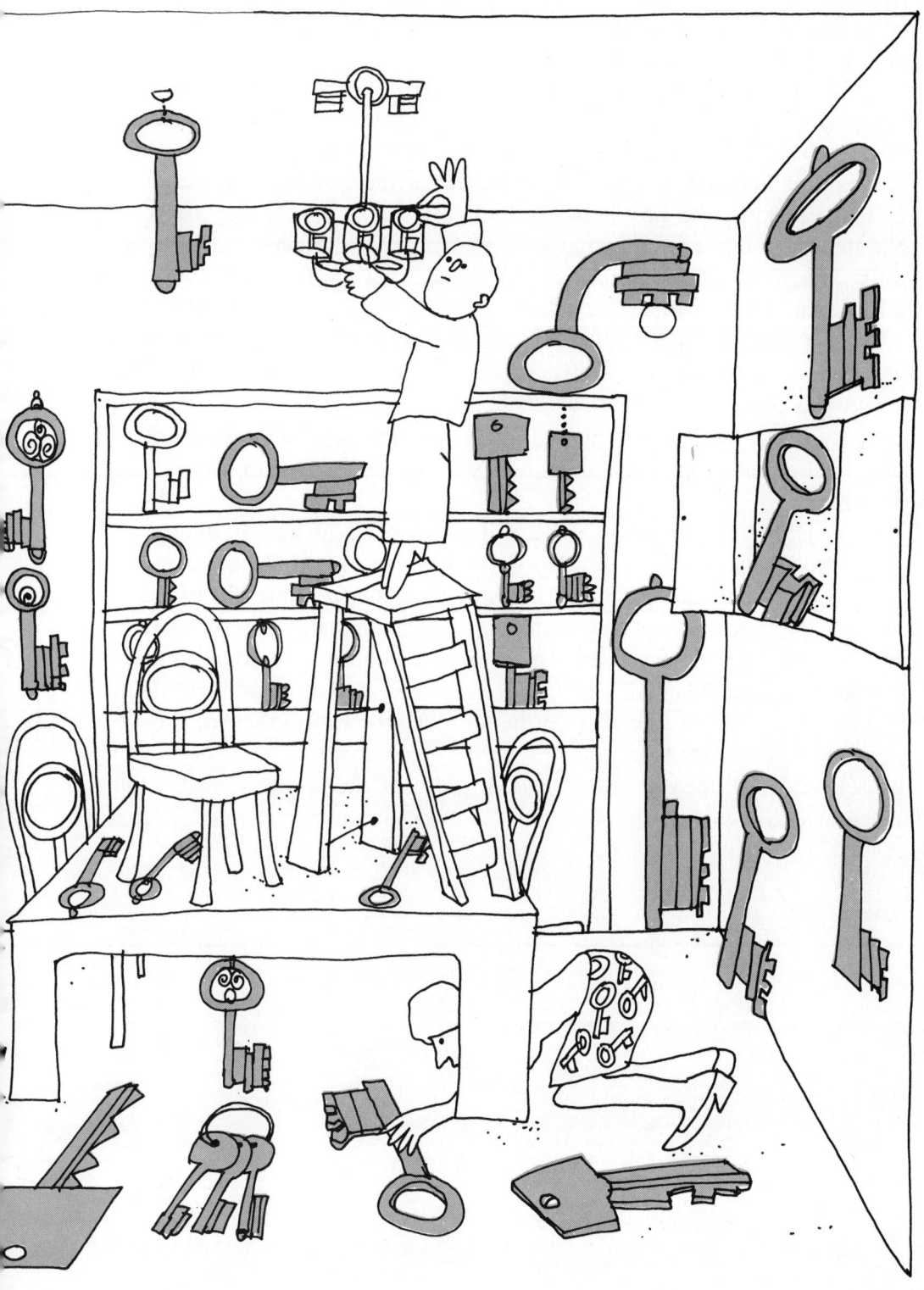

**An interest in
undivided property**

When a part of a property is given as a gift and the whole property remains undivided, a special problem is created for which the law provides. How this provision operates is shown in the following case, concerning an interest in bonds of great value.

A Mr. Collins of Chattanooga told his wife that he intended to give her half of the bonds he possessed. They went to the bank where he had the bonds and he turned half of them over to her. She clipped the coupons of her half. Some she deposited in the box and the rest she cashed, spending the proceeds. Collins gave her a key to the box, and her share was left with the other half, which Collins retained as his own. This disposition of the securities continued until Collins died two and a half years later.

At that time the state collected an inheritance tax on all the bonds, and the administrator of Collins' estate sued to recover as much of his tax as was represented by the bonds belonging to the widow.

This transfer by Collins to his wife of an undivided half of these securities was held a valid gift even though it was an undivided portion of the property.

Generally there can be no physical delivery of an interest in undivided property. If a half were separated by delivery, there would be a gift of half, not of an undivided interest in the whole. Further, the gift of many chattels (property, except real estate), such as an animal, is not susceptible of division. The physical delivery of a part interest in a living animal would be impossible. An undivided interest in a chattel or in a claim against some third person can be the subject of a valid gift and, though delivery is necessary to complete a gift, a "constructive" delivery, such as delivery of a deed or bill of sale in place of the property itself, will be sufficient.

The Mentally Ill
And The Law

The law gives to the word "incompetent" a special meaning that is different from our everyday usage of the term. Legally, an incompetent is a person incapable of managing his own affairs in his own interest. One person may be more keenly alive than another, more aware or more intelligent, yet both are unquestionably competent in the eyes of the law if they can conduct their own business in a relatively capable manner.

There is, so far as the law is concerned, no rule of mathematical precision that enables us to measure exactly how competent or incompetent an individual may be. The law's definition of "incompetent" is adequate for most practical purposes. A typical state statute declares this term to mean "any person who, though not insane, is by reason of old age, disease, weakness of mind or from any other cause incapable, unassisted, to properly manage and take care of himself and his property, and by reason thereof would be likely to be deceived or imposed upon by artful or designing persons." This definition is applicable in all states.

As might be expected, the question of whether or not a person is incompetent arises often in connection with the transfer of property.

Some years ago, in California, a mother of nine children deeded to one of her boys a parcel of land worth between $4,000 and $6,000 from the property she owned, which had a total value of ten times that amount. The other children made an effort to have their mother adjudged incompetent and the transfer of this land set aside.

While the mother was unable to state exactly the amount of her net income, she did remember clearly the various tracts of land she owned. As for her lack of business judgment in the management of her property, criticized by those of the family who sought to have the transfer to her son set aside, the court said that she was the owner of the property and had the right to manage it as she pleased. She could dispose of it, the court declared, as she thought fit, unless she was liable mentally to be deceived or imposed upon by "artful or designing persons."

A lower court had appointed a guardian for her. This appointment was canceled with the statement that, "Generally speaking an adult person has the right to control his own person and affairs and that right should not be taken from him except upon a showing that the statutory grounds warranting a restriction of his liberty of action was for his own protection."

Lack of judgment and incompetency

The courts, as you see, demand evidence of a very substantial nature before they will decide a person is incompetent. More must be shown than a demonstration that a person is eccentric or holds unusual beliefs. In one case, a physician testified about an elderly woman whose competency was in question. He said that she was "very credulous and had shown a lack of judgment, and that her marriage to a man of 45 (she was 76 at the time and it was her third marriage) was a subnormality and showed an intelligence defect."

Did the judge agree? "The fact that the woman may have been disappointed in her hope for happiness in her third marriage to a man much younger than herself could hardly be considered substantial evidence of incompetency," commented the judge. "The arrangement which she made with a man to manage and care for her ranch and act as her chauffeur for a half-interest in the ranch might indicate poor business judgment. There must be something more than poor business judgment to establish incompetency."

What the law presumes

Every man is supposed, legally, to be sane and mentally sound and to continue so until the contrary is shown. When the court decides he is insane or incompetent, then he is presumed legally to remain in that condition until the court determines that he has regained his sanity. No consistent pattern has developed regarding the acceptance by one state of the decision of another state that an individual is incompetent. Some states will accept the decision of another jurisdiction, while other states choose to make their own determination of the issue.

Can an incompetent change his will?

A resident of North Carolina made his will. More than 20 years later, he was legally declared an incompetent, unfit to manage his own affairs because of his age and infirm condition.

At the time this man was found to be incompetent, he asked his wife for his will. He wanted to destroy it and allow his estate to be distributed as if there were no will. This woman was his second wife, and he had children living born of a first marriage. The will he wished to destroy provided that his property should go at his death only to the wife and children of the second marriage. He had made no provision in his will for the children of the first marriage.

His wife refused to give up the will. The man died and the children of the first marriage sought to show he had revoked the will by seeking to destroy it. The court refused to set the will aside, however, following the legal rule that if a person is too feeble mentally to make a will, he is too feeble to revoke one already made. Further, the court pointed out that when a person has been found incompetent, this condition is supposed to continue until a court finds a different condition to exist.

Can an incompetent commit adultery?

If incompetency or insanity prevents a person from appreciating the nature and effects of his acts, it constitutes a strong defense against any accusation. Mentally incompetent persons are not convicted under any criminal law—they are placed under proper medical supervision and control. The law has come to look upon legally incompetent individuals as sick people. Persons considered legally insane are not held responsible for their actions. Therefore, such persons cannot be convicted of crimes.

A decision by a New York court some years ago involved the adultery of a woman who had been declared mentally ill. In a divorce action the infidelity was admitted but excused by the court on the ground that the woman was legally irresponsible.

This decision followed one handed down more than 100 years ago with a ruling that is still the law of this country. The old case concerned an Alabama wife who committed adulterous acts for several months. At that time, she was mentally ill, suffering from hallucinations, and for a long period of time had enjoyed no lucid intervals. Under such conditions there could be no more a forfeiture of her marital rights, said the court, than if advantage had been taken of her by drugs or force.

However, in many states, the showing of some mental illness is not automatically an adequate defense in a divorce action based on adultery, unless it is shown that the party who committed the adulterous act was not actually capable of understanding the nature and consequences of the act when it was committed. A number of courts have rejected the argument that a history of mental illness and disorder is sufficient evidence to excuse the adultery. These states require additional proof that demonstrates that the party was actually unaware of the consequences of the act.

Recovery from insanity

We have said that when a man is declared to be legally incompetent, the law presumes this condition to continue until it is shown to be otherwise. For a restoration of his rights, it must be proved to the satisfaction of the court that he has recovered his sanity.

The explanation of this rule is that incapacity is a fact likely to continue to exist. When the victim asks for a change of his status, he must prove that it is different from what it was. Otherwise he could impose upon those trying to protect him and put upon them the burden of proving his incapacity as often as he saw fit to file a petition for his release from these limitations.

A typical case that came under this rule concerned two brothers who had been found by a Massachusetts court to be incompetent. Later they made an effort to obtain their release. The court asserted that after they had been found to be insane it became their task to prove they were competent and sane—not the task of those opposing their release to prove in each instance that they were incompetent. Their suit was denied by the court because they could not prove sanity.

An appeal of the decision regarding the legal competency of an individual may be brought on behalf of the person involved by a friend or relative. Courts have discretionary power to grant to the person bringing the appeal the costs of the action. These funds can be taken from the property of the individual who had been declared incompetent.

How guardians of incompetents are chosen

The choice of the person to be appointed guardian of an incompetent, to care for his welfare and property, is generally left to the discretion of the court.

It is the court that decides whether the management of the incompetent's property shall be entrusted to the guardian appointed for his personal custody or by still another person. Most frequently, the person who takes care of an incompetent is a close relative or friend, while the custodian of his property must have a special qualification—he should be possessed of the judgment and experience necessary to administer properly the incompetent's funds. The welfare of incompetent persons and the matter of their property are objects of particular care and attention on the part of the courts.

Objectionable guardians

A close relative is not always the most desirable guardian for an incompetent, as the facts in the following case show. In a case in the state of Washington, a son sought to be appointed his mother's guardian. Evidence was presented that proved the relationship between the mother and son was not particularly close. The father had objections too. Consequently, the son was not appointed. The court, as the law provides, used its own discretion in its selection of a guardian.

Ordinarily, a person indebted to an incompetent is not selected to be his guardian, but such a choice is not impossible, being subject to the general rule that appointments be made in the sound discretion of the court and with the incompetent's happiness and material welfare as the paramount consideration.

Why appointments are revoked

The court's interest in an incompetent does not end with the appointment of a guardian. If a guardian becomes guilty of fraud or misconduct, is found unqualified for his position, or applies for relief from the trust, the court will appoint a new guardian.

The manner in which a Kentucky court exercised its discretion in one case was clearly open to criticism. It appointed an 86-year-old man, confined to his bed with a fractured leg, as the guardian of an incompetent sister 83 years old. Such a man was obviously incapable of fulfilling a guardian's duties, and when persons interested in the situation brought it to the attention of the higher court, this appointment was set aside.

In another case, where a wife and children, acting with an attorney, arranged for the appointment of the attorney as the guardian of the aged husband and father, they did this in an effort to secure a division of his property among themselves, rather than with a view to the mental and economic welfare of the incompetent. This appointment, conflicting with the aim of the law, was also set aside.

When the incompetent is not notified

When a guardian dies, resigns, or becomes unable any longer to fulfill his role, a successor may be named without notice to the incompetent. Since the incompetent is incapable of caring for himself or his property, or representing himself, such notice would be useless. So the court decided, when an attempt was made to set aside the appointment of a guardian chosen by the court without notifying the incompetent. The court stressed the governing factor in these cases: "The matter of who is to act as guardian lies very largely in the sound discretion of the court making the appointment."

Who owns an incompetent's property?

The problem frequently arises of who has title to the property of an incompetent. Ordinarily, when someone dies, title to his personal property belongs to the executor. His real property belongs to the heirs, subject to sale for the debts of the deceased. Does the ownership of an incompetent's property pass to his guardian, the way a dead man's personal property passes to his executor? The answer is often of vital importance, not only in the management of the incompetent's property, but in the enforcement of his rights.

The law says that a guardian is merely the custodian of the real and personal property of his ward. The incompetent still owns his property. He is merely deprived during his incompetency of its management and control.

When the property needs immediate attention during a proceeding to determine competency, courts often appoint a temporary receiver to care for it.

A guardian, or "committee," as he is sometimes known, was appointed for a man committed to a hospital for the insane in Virginia. Two years later the court decided this man had regained his sanity. The guardian, however, refused to return his property. Here the situation was governed by the rule that the incompetent still owned his property and had been merely deprived of its control during his illness. When he was declared sane, he automatically regained his rights to its control, and the duties and authority of the guardian were dissolved.

How an incompetent is committed

The liberty of all is protected by Constitutional and legislative guarantees. This protection is supposed to be extended to the victim of a mental malady to the same extent as it is to a person endowed with physical and mental health. A person whose competency is being considered in a legal procedure is therefore entitled to the same protection as one who is charged with a criminal offense. The laws of the various states prescribe the different ways a mentally ill person may be committed to a mental hospital. Sometimes these laws have been found to operate in situations in a manner that effectively denies the full protection of the law to possible incompetents.

Recently, a Federal court in Pennsylvania found that thousands of mental patients had been placed in that state's mental institutions under procedure that violated due process of law. All these patients were committed by their families, with the concurrence of two doctors, but without a court order and against their will. Due process of law was violated because the persons involved had no chance to present evidence of their competency.

Each state now has its own method of committing incompetents. A trial may be required, or an examination before a committing magistrate,

or some other procedure involving a legal hearing. Evidence is presented that is made part of the record. The evidence consists of the testimony of physicians and psychiatrists, as well as of ordinary witnesses. The statutes governing the procedure must be obeyed down to the last detail.

A woman inmate of a state hospital was brought before a court for a determination of the legality of her confinement. The person seeking to obtain her release was her 18-year-old son, her sole support. It was revealed that the woman had not even been present at the hearing when she was determined insane and ordered confined in an asylum. The commitment had been made on the mere conclusion of a social worker that the woman was in need of treatment in a mental hospital. This was a violation of the law, and the woman was released.

One alleged to be an incompetent has a right to a lawyer. The court must appoint one for him, unless the court feels that he has made an intelligent judgment not to have one, which is difficult for an alleged incompetent. If a person is improperly committed, he is generally entitled to sue the state for damages.

When a hearing is not given

However loosely the statutes in this area may be interpreted, then, they do not permit a person to be deprived of liberty without legal due process. If a court permits a person to be confined in a mental hospital without strictly following the required procedure, there is always recourse to a higher court. Some form of trial or hearing is always required before a person can be declared an incompetent.

Are contracts of incompetents valid?

There is no hard-and-fast rule covering this question. The decision will rest largely on whether the party who dealt with the incompetent acted in good faith. If that party did not realize that he was dealing with an incompetent, the contract is more likely to be upheld.

A man who was to be confined to a mental institution was negotiating for the purchase of a hotel in Atlantic City, New Jersey. His wife and son, under advice from their attorney, wrote to the real estate broker for the hotel, notifying him of the mental condition of the man with whom he was dealing. Nevertheless, the hotel owner closed the deal. The New Jersey Supreme Court, in an action to set aside the purchase, ruled that, even if the sale were fair, it was invalid. The judge said that the wording of the letter sent by the buyer's family, which the hotel owner had seen, "was plainly such as would lead a prudent person to the belief of (the man's) insanity."

A person furnishing the means of livelihood to an incompetent is entitled to recompense, as if he were furnishing it under an agreement. Board and care were given for 11 years by a son to his father, a speechless paralytic. The older man was not confined to his bed, but was mentally infirm.

Another son had been appointed custodian of the father's property. When the father died, this son was asked by the first for payment, out of the father's estate, of the expenses he had incurred over the 11 years he had cared for his father. The custodian refused to give him such sum, but the courts awarded it to him.

The principle that a mentally ill person is not responsible for his contracts is a shield for that person only so long as he actually is mentally ill. The occurrence of the illness may have been long before a formal court ruling of incompetency, and the court decision can be applied retroactively to nullify contracts made between the inception of the incompetency and the date of the court's decision. The shield dissolves as soon as the person recovers sanity. This may also occur long before a court ruling.

In Minnesota, a woman borrowed some money. When effort was made by the lender to recover this money, the woman pleaded incompetency. She had long before been restored to full mental health, but she pointed out that the guardianship she was under—her husband's, in this case—had not officially been terminated. The court refused to release the borrower from her obligation to pay.

When an incompetent commits a crime

We have seen that a mentally ill person is incapable of committing a crime in the eyes of the law since he lacks the necessary intent. However, merely showing that the person involved was not in control of all his faculties at the time the crime was committed will not protect him. He must meet the standard of being "legally insane" at the time the crime was committed, to avoid punishment. The elements of this standard vary from state to state. The rule of "not knowing right from wrong" is still prevalent in most jurisdictions, although it has come under much criticism lately.

The protection afforded by the law extends beyond the rule that the defendant had to have had the necessary intent at the time he committed the crime. If he is mentally ill at the time of his trial, he cannot be tried even if he was sane when the crime was committed. The case is postponed until he recovers from his disability. The law says that an incompetent can neither plead to an arraignment, be subject to trial, receive judgment after trial, nor undergo punishment as a criminal.

Until the prisoner does recover, he is kept in a mental hospital or other prescribed place of detention.

Further, as we have noted, when a person has once been legally adjudged an incompetent or insane, the presumption of sanity enjoyed by every normal individual is gone. In its place is a presumption of insanity, and the recovery of sanity must be proved before the incompetent can again be held responsible for his acts or permitted to defend himself in a criminal trial.

The rule governing the recovery of damages for injuries inflicted by a person mentally ill represents a clear appraisal of both sides of the situation. There is a seeming hardship in compelling one who is unaware of his irrational acts to pay for their consequences. Yet it would be more unjust to deny redress to the one who has suffered the damage and is in no way responsible for it. Hence, the rule is that an insane person is liable in damages for wrongs he commits to the same extent as any normal person.

Does an incompetent pay punitive damages?

A barn on a Wisconsin farm was set on fire by a man subsequently committed to a state hospital for the criminally insane. In an action by the owner against this incompetent's guardian, the court followed the rule of the lunatic's liability for damages for his wrongdoing. The cost of the barn had to be paid out of his estate.

It should be pointed out, however, that in a case brought against an incompetent the courts will not award punitive damages—that is, damages a wrongdoer is obliged to pay as punishment, rather than as compensation. No suit will be sustained where a malicious intent on the part of the defendant is a necessary element to recovery of damages, since this cannot be shown to be present in a person mentally ill.

An incompetent's liability for murder

When a mentally ill person kills someone, the liability that is owed the next of kin of the victim is governed by the general rule on wrongdoing. In an Illinois tragedy, a lunatic killed another man, then shot himself. The victim's next of kin were awarded damages for the loss they suffered by the death of their relative.

An insane person—to cite the court's opinion—has no will; for that reason, he cannot commit a crime. Nevertheless, his estate is liable for the damages he inflicts.

Slander by a deranged person

A false accusation of stealing was made in Tennessee by a deranged man. The victim of this slander brought suit against his accuser. In deciding the case, the court stressed the fact that intention is an element of slander. The defendant, it decided, could not be liable in damages because "the insanity of the incompetent at the time of speaking the words complained of is a complete excuse when the speaker is entirely insane and, when partially insane, that fact is considered in mitigation of the damages awarded."

Is an incompetent responsible for any damage he causes?

A man in West Virginia, who had gone insane, shot his friend. The injured man was taken to a hospital where, after a month, he died. No criminal prosecution for murder could be initiated, since the man responsible for the killing was insane. However, a civil action was brought for the suffering caused to the deceased man and for the potential income he could have earned had he remained alive.

The court, in upholding a verdict of $20,000 against the insane man, ruled that although no punitive damages could be charged against the defendant, an award for damages actually suffered by the dead man and his family could be made. The reason for allowing such recovery of damages against the incompetent was that while both the killer and the deceased were legally innocent, the responsibility for the loss was placed on the one who caused the action involved.

Is the marriage of an incompetent valid?

A California man took part in a wedding ceremony that was held in an old garage. He had to be prompted continually during the ceremony for his responses. In an action to have the marriage declared invalid, the judge noted that the evidence presented indicated that the man "was unaware of the fact that he was being married and he interjected remarks concerning matters foreign to such a solemn occasion." Evidence was also presented that revealed that the man's new wife began stealing his property immediately after the ceremony. The court annulled the marriage, declaring that such evidence was ample to show that the man was not of sufficiently sound mind to engage in a legal marriage ceremony.

The rule employed in most states is that the validity of the marriage depends upon whether the parties understand the nature of the marriage contract when they enter into it. This includes an understanding of the duties and responsibilities it creates. If a person deemed incompetent may be said to have understood these matters at the time of the ceremony, then the marriage is legal.

In some jurisdictions, "marriages" of persons ruled unable, legally, to engage in a valid wedding ceremony may become legal if the incompetent cohabits with his spouse after he regains his competency or during his sane periods.

How dependents of incompetents are supported

Many states have rules providing that people must support certain close relatives if they are able to, even though those relatives are adults.

Applying these rules to the care of the family of the incompetent, the law holds that the family is entitled to maintenance from the income of his property. Beyond that, the court has power to make provision out of the surplus of such an estate for those whom it supposes the incompetent would have provided for had he been sane.

A famous case of the right of a guardian, with the approval of the court, to contribute from an incompetent's estate to the support of the relatives was that involving Ida A. Flagler. Seventy-eight years old and incurably insane, this woman possessed an estate of more than $11,000,000 with an annual income of approximately $500,000.

A second cousin of the incompetent was a woman of middle age with an unemployed husband and an adopted daughter. The only income of this family was $15 a week, earned by the wife. Coal bills, doctors' bills, and house repair charges had piled high.

"If Mrs. Flagler today could decide upon the disposition of her great estate, moral or charitable considerations would dictate her decision only to the extent that she felt their force," was the comment of the court on the application of this family for an allowance from the estate of Mrs. Flagler.

"Her great affluence might impel her to relieve the distress of her cousin; the law would not compel her to do so if she decided otherwise. The court may not be moved by its own generous impulses in the disposal of the income of the incompetent. In reaching a decision the court may give to moral or charitable considerations only such weight as it finds that the incompetent herself would have given them. Allowances for the support of collateral relatives of the incompetent have been made upon the theory that the lunatic would in all probability have made such payments if he had been of sound mind."

On this opinion, provision was made for relieving the destitution of this family.

If allowances are made to adult children

An adult daughter sought an allowance from the estate of her incompetent father. The court granted her the allowance, but with the provision that any sums of money paid by the guardian should constitute an advance against any inheritance she might receive upon the death of her father. This is the general rule in this country when allowances are made to adult children capable of supporting themselves.

CHAPTER 15

The Law
of Libel and Slander

"Sticks and stones may break my bones, but names will never harm me," runs an old saying. It is far from true. Name calling, under certain conditions, can damage one's reputation seriously. Then it becomes slander or libel, and the ground for a legal action to collect damages. Any retraction of the statement must clearly indicate that the statement was incorrect. However, the damage may be done.

Libel and slander are two different offenses. Libel is restricted basically to written statements, but it can be committed by means of signs, pictures, or other representations of a person or his acts. Slander is limited to statements made by word of mouth. In their basic conditions they sometimes overlap.

Because it is in more permanent form and so presumably more harmful, written defamation is actionable without proof of special damage. All that must be shown is that the words were written and that they were defamatory to the person to whom they referred. As to spoken defamation, unless the slander is of a certain class, it is not actionable without proof of damages. Those falling within the special class of slander are known as "per se," meaning harmful "by itself."

The courts have been considering whether a spoken television broadcast is libel or slander. While not permanent as in writing, broadcasting reaches many more persons and can be more harmful than a mere spoken statement. If it is not libel, then it must fall within the specified class to be actionable without proof of damages.

A New York court has given a definition of libel that expresses, in general, the law of this country. It says: "Any written or printed article is libelous or actionable if it tends to expose the subject to public contempt, ridicule, aversion, or disgrace, or induce an evil opinion of him in the minds of right-thinking persons and to deprive him of their friendly intercourse in society." It must also be shown that the words were understandable to the general public and were meant to be understood in a derogatory sense. The party who was the subject of the statement does not have to show that people actually took the words to be true.

To any charge of defamation there is an important defense: It is the truth. A case of defamation, generally, does not exist when the statement on which it is based is true from start to finish. The burden of proving the truth of a defamatory statement rests on the defendant in a suit. To mitigate the damages that may be allowed, the defendant is permitted to show that the plaintiff has a bad character and reputation.

Where the defamer is shown to have been motivated by ill will or malice, courts and juries may award punitive damages—damages as a punishment—in addition to those actually incurred.

Truth and libel

A resident of Louisiana complained to the court that "his good name, fame, credit, and reputation" had been injured in the sum of $25,000 by a letter sent not only to him but to his sisters and brothers also. This letter, which referred to one written by the plaintiff, declared:

"One can expect such a letter as you have written, in view of the fact that you failed in the filial devotion that you owed your late mother by refusing to pay your 1/5th percentage of her funeral bill. Your excuse for not paying this bill was the ridiculous statement that you had not been consulted in making the funeral arrangements."

The plaintiff asserted that although he had on several occasions refused to pay the bill, he had ultimately done so, and therefore the letter was libelous.

In dismissing this action, the court declared that the truth was a complete defense. This so-called libelous letter did not deny he had ultimately contributed his share of the funeral expenses, but stated simply that he had once refused to. Since he admitted this, there was no libel.

The consequences of a libel suit

"In this man quackery reaches its apotheosis. He continues to demonstrate his astuteness in shaking shillings from the pockets of credulous Americans notwithstanding the efforts of various governmental departments and agencies." So ran the leading paragraph of an article in a prominent monthly magazine, which went on to describe at length its further objections to this individual.

In the libel suit the man brought against the publication, the testimony amounted to more than 1,000 printed pages. It revealed the background of this "charlatan" much more fully than the magazine article had done. Not only had he received his medical degree from a "diploma mill"—for 16 years he had performed sexual rejuvenation operations on from 5,000 to 6,000 persons, charging them from nothing to $750 apiece.

He had enjoyed a monthly gross income of approximately $100,000, and had stimulated this medical practice by pamphlets, newspapers, and radio broadcasts. Then both his medical license and his license for an independently operated radio broadcast station had been revoked.

It was further shown in court that he had been indicted in California for the illegal practice of medicine. At the time of the publication of the article for which this libel suit was brought, the evidence pointed out, he was advertising by Mexican radio broadcasts that he would treat prostatic troubles by letter at two dollars a case.

Said the court: "We think the facts are sufficient to support a reasonable and honest opinion that he should be considered a charlatan and quack in the ordinary and well-understood meaning of the words.''

This case, like many other libel suits, illustrates the folly of seeking to repair damage to one's reputation by taking court action. Even if one wins a libel suit—which this man did not—the airing of the testimony often does further damage to the character of those concerned, whether that testimony is true or false.

Libel in a few words

A daily newspaper published a paragraph declaring that a well-known actress, married for six years to a man of good reputation, was the "latest lady love" of another. The publication of this statement, said the court, was a libel. It was established that the lady concerned was of good reputation, and the newspaper report, the court ruled, had unnecessarily brought to its victim humiliation and mental suffering.

No ground for libel

In another instance, a large, metropolitan daily newspaper printed the story of Catherine, who ran a boarding house. It reported that Catherine had been courted by a man who, although she did not know it at the time, was wanted by the police in Chicago for the murder of his wife five days before. This man was later apprehended, tried, and hanged for his crime.

Catherine sued the paper, claiming she was libeled by the article—held up to scorn and ridicule. But the court pointed out that all the paper said was that Catherine had been courted by a murderer five days after he had committed the crime. Although the man was described as a murderer and an archfiend, there was in the entire article not one word of discrediting comments on Catherine's own character or conduct. She did not have a valid case at law.

Insinuation as libel

A New England newspaper published an article about a candidate for public office. It said that a neighbor of this candidate had built his house with two driveways on one side and none on the other, and had planted trees in the space between the two driveways as a screen against the candidate's prying eyes, to protect the housemaid from annoyance.

This insinuation, that the candidate spent his time as a "Peeping Tom," was held to be a libel by the court, reflecting as it did on his reputability as a member of the community. He was resting his claim for public office on the respect and confidence of his fellow-citizens, which the newspaper article tended to take away from him.

The court must make the decision as to whether the words were used in such a manner as to be defamatory. The person who claims to be defamed cannot lift words out of context. The entire setting in which the words were used must be considered in the decision.

False and malicious publication

An Alabama paper provided the ground for a libel suit when it published an article declaring that ''An Arabian sheik asked a friend here to buy him an American girl for his harem,'' and named the friend. It went on to say that while this American friend ''will not take the responsibility of selecting Sheik Iman's chief wife, he will be glad to make contact with the Arabian for those interested,'' and it included the friend's telephone number and post office address.

''The very idea of a harem,'' said the court, ''is as repulsive as is the purchase of a girl to be carried from America to some distant country to complete a harem of four wives.'' A false and malicious publication that anyone stood ready and willing to abet such a program was held an actionable libel.

Incomplete insinuation is not libel

A practicing physician in Chicago who was a former citizen of Warsaw incurred the ill-will of a Polish-American publication by accepting a cross as a decoration from the Polish government. Referring to him, it wrote in its columns that "For some years former 'honor vivas' [complimentary decorations] of this kind have emitted a specific stench. Characteristic of them is an epigram of Pushkin, one of the greatest of Russian poets, written on the occasion of giving a high decoration to one of the Russian dignitaries serving the government well.

> *"Oh Lord God Jesus Christ*
> *You have used a thief on the cross*
> *And now you have new trouble*
> *To save a cross on a thief."*

The word "thief" in this poem did not charge the recipient of the medal with that crime. His act was not larceny. Unless the word was used to convey the idea that the doctor was a thief and guilty of a crime, said the court, there was no libel.

What is slander per se?

Slander, we have said, relates solely to spoken words. An assertion, to be slanderous per se, that is, to be ruled slanderous without the showing of any evidence besides the fact that a third party heard the statement, must come within one or more of these four classes: (1) words imputing the commission of a crime; (2) words imputing infection by a loathsome or contagious disease that excludes the person from society; (3) words proclaiming unfitness for office or employment or words derogatory of a person's fitness for a trade or profession; (4) words imputing unchastity (spoken of a woman).

As with libel, a statement cannot be slanderous if it is true. However, certain states will not admit the truth as a defense if malice is an element in the statement on which the accusation of defamation is based.

When the defamatory words are not slander per se, then proof of special damage is necessary in order to have a case. The special damage must involve monetary loss. If the defamed person can demonstrate that his business fell off because of the slander, or that it resulted in the loss of some particular contract, then he can recover for the damage. But the fact that the defamed person was humiliated by the statement, or that his friends avoided him, is not sufficient evidence.

A statement might appear on its face not to be defamatory, but may be ruled slanderous per se when additional facts are shown. This could be the case, for example, if a person spreads a false story that a certain woman gave birth to a son. If it is proven that the woman was unmarried and those who heard the story were aware of this fact, then the statement becomes slanderous per se. This seemingly nondefamatory report actually imputed unchastity to the woman. A few states, however, always require the showing of special damages in any defamation case in which apparently innocent words are shown to be defamatory.

False accusation of a crime

A rancher published a report in which he falsely accused one of his neighbors of poisoning cattle and added that "if he thereafter is known to be guilty of any more villainous conduct or any more stock poisoning, he will be dealt with as justice may demand." The court found the statement to be defamatory, and would not allow the introduction of evidence of other crimes as an indication that the neighbor was a criminal. The judge in the case stated that "I am aware of no rule of law which would allow proof to be made of specific offenses and particular acts of dishonesty, not connected with the transactions under investigation."

An essential condition of slander

Words, to be either slander or libel, must be made public—they must be communicated to, and understood by, at least one person other than the one of whom they are spoken or written. Condemning another to himself alone may breed trouble, but it is neither slander nor libel.

An employee of an oil company, during World War II, made remarks on the conduct of the war that were offensive to his associates. "He wished Hitler would take the European countries and come on over here and take the United States," was a typical comment. The superintendent of the company told the man he was being discharged for these un-American speeches. Whatever the superintendent said was heard by no one except the employee. The suit brought by this employee for slander by the superintendent was unsuccessful. There had been no publication of these statements, no third person had heard them—hence, no slander.

No witness, no slander

The manager of an Ohio hotel discharged an employee. "You stole the butter and that is not the only thing you ever stole around here." This statement, like that of the oil company superintendent, was heard by no one but the discharged waiter; hence there was no injury other than the discomfort and hurt feelings of the man who had lost his job.

**Slander
with others present**

In North Carolina, the manager of a grocery company called an employee into his office. "Last week two boxes of bananas went out of the warehouse. They went out on trucks. It shows you are letting the drivers take them out and sell them—then split with you. The drivers you have over there are crooks."

The manager was sitting with his back to the doorway of his office and, in the doorway, unseen by the manager, was another employee. Here was a publication of words imputing a crime that sustained the employee's suit for damages.

**Repetition of a
defamatory statement**

A newspaper that subscribed to a press service printed an article, which it attributed to the press service, stating that a respected resident of the area had just defaulted on thousands of dollars worth of loans. The story was untrue, but the person described was hurt in his business. The court found that the newspaper was guilty of libel, even though it attributed the article to another party. The fact that the newspaper printed the article was sufficient grounds for a finding of defamation. (However, newspapers sometimes have a defense of "fair comment," which is discussed later in this chapter.)

Every repetition of a defamatory statement is also a further defamation.

**Defamation
of deceased**

It is the general rule that a libel or slander upon the memory of a deceased person, which makes no direct reflection upon his living relatives, gives them no cause of action for defamation either on their own behalf or on behalf of the deceased. However, if the words, by implication, defame a living person, they may be actionable. For example, the statement that a deceased person was never married may be grounds for a claim by his daughter that she was defamed.

**Words that
are slanderous**

An installment furniture merchant, repossessing his merchandise on a default of the buyer in payment, said in the presence of another man and two small children, "You damned old bitch, you—I'm going to take my stuff and I'll beat you with my cane before I get out of here."

This statement in the presence of others, and the fact that the legal definition of "bitch," when used in this manner, is a lewd woman or common prostitute, constituted a slander for which the woman so addressed was allowed to recover damages.

The term "rat" was once applied to an opposing attorney. Though ill-chosen and harsh, said the court, this invective did not constitute slander. The word "rat," in itself, did not impute a crime, unchastity, a loathsome disease, or dishonesty.

The general standard used for words that are slanderous is that the person spoken about must be defamed in the eyes of an important and respectable group in the community in which he lives. Each state has its own standard of what constitutes "an important and respectable group."

Imputing a disease to someone

The element of libel and slander in the imputation of disease does not arise when there are merely general reports of pestilence or disease and of public-spirited efforts to rid the community of such scourges, as in a newspaper. It is only where the words represent an effort to destroy the happiness and community standing of the person concerned that valid grounds are supplied for a lawsuit.

In general, slander or libel, to be such, must not refer to a minor disease, but to a serious contagious infection, like leprosy or syphilis.

Libel of a class of people

A prominent sportswriter made the following statement in an article about boxing that appeared in a national magazine: "I must be truthful. Boxing is the garbage pile of sports. The few who transcend it have my respect. Still it damages more young men than it helps. It is the sanctuary of the scoundrel and it always has been a toy of the rogue."

A professional boxer sued the writer for defamation. The court ruled that "the article contains matter highly defamatory of various unnamed characters in the professional boxing sport. That is no basis for libel because an impersonal reproach of an indeterminate class is not actionable."

To obtain a judgment for a defamation that refers to a group or class of people, a person must show that he was in the class that was defamed and that he can be specifically identified as one to whom the statement has particular application. The writer here referred to the sport of boxing in general. This one boxer could not prove that he was one of the people to whom the derogatory remarks of the writer referred.

Venereal disease and slander

An insurance investigator, calling on a woman in relation to the payment of the insurance on her husband's life, said, in the presence of a third party, "Our association is absolutely not going to pay your husband's claim because the company has proof that you and your husband have syphilis." This untruthful statement charged these people with a loathsome disease and was actionable slander.

A more virulent assault was made by an Iowa woman on her son's wife. Among other remarks, she said of the younger woman, "She's nothing but a whore. She runs around with other men, has a bad disease, and is nothing but dirty trash."

The daughter-in-law answered with an action for slander in which the jury awarded her $3,000. The mother-in-law appealed. The higher court refused to change or modify the verdict, and added that the jury under such circumstances might well have added "exemplary" damages—a punishment for the wanton attempt to injure the character of the daughter-in-law.

When a man's business is injured by defamation

A charge that a person is unfit in his trade or profession can do more than injure his reputation. It can also be expected to interfere with his earnings and to alienate persons who would otherwise patronize or employ him. Therefore, this is perhaps the most serious category of libel or slander from the viewpoint of actual damages.

A business may be defamed by words that cast aspersions on the character of the firm, or upon the character of its employees, if the words refer to its method of doing business. But businesses cannot be defamed by words that would affect the purely personal reputation of an individual.

Libel by a business service

Dun & Bradstreet, the financial reporting service, erroneously reported that an electrical supply company in Kansas had filed for bankruptcy. The company sued for libel and received a substantial damage award from a jury, and the Federal Court of Appeals for the Tenth Circuit affirmed the judgment. The United States Supreme Court refused to consider the matter, which means, in effect, that the freedom of the press privilege heretofore discussed does not extend to financial reporting services.

Fair criticism, not slander

A magazine article criticized the publications of a psychiatrist about soap opera broadcasts of various networks. These programs the psychiatrist had analyzed in psychiatric terms that were long and unflattering. The title of the offending magazine article was "Dusting off Dr. B."

"If Dr. B. can find nothing wrong in publicizing the miseries of the doomed, the drugged and the damned through the medium of books and motion pictures," the magazine observed, "why don't he let radio have a frustration or two? There ain't nobody here but us chickens, boys. If we may break a metaphor over the reader's head, it seems much as if radio and Dr. B. were in the same bed except that Dr. B. is working the other side of the street."

Then, in reference to his psychiatric studies, the article said, "In any case, it seems quite possible that Dr. B. will contrive to turn the entire trilogy into a trauma of obfustication [*sic*], full of big words that us poor folks in radio don't hardly know the meaning of—just another teleological concatenation of sesquipedalian lucubrating—all whizz and canal water."

Offended at this ridicule, the doctor sued the magazine, but his action was unsuccessful. The article was held not libelous because it did not exceed the bounds of fair criticism to which any other person of public prominence may be subjected with impunity, nor did it shame or disgrace the author, in the court's opinion.

There is a famous legal maxim that says that an individual has a right to swing his arms—but that right ends where the next man's nose begins.

Fair and unbiased criticism is healthful. But when the criticism goes beyond the bounds of truth and fairness, it goes beyond the point "where the next man's nose begins."

How Congressmen are protected

Congressmen have certain immunity under the Constitution of the United States. Remarks that they make as part of official meetings of the Senate or the House of Representatives, or the committees of either, may not be made the basis of a slander or a libel suit, even though they may seem scurrilous. On the other hand, defamatory remarks made by the same persons in other places may be grounds for a suit.

Major officials in the executive branches of state and local governments and all Federal employees have recently also been granted immunity from suits for defamation. However, this immunity only extends to statements that are fair comment made in the legitimate course of their jobs.

The right of fair comment

The New York Times carried a full-page advertisement charging that the Commissioner of Public Affairs of a Southern city was responsible for illegal actions by the police force of that city. Some of the statements made in the advertisement were untrue. The Commissioner sued the newspaper and those who paid for the ad for defamation. The Supreme Court, in an effort to promote what it called "uninhibited, robust and wide-open" debate on public issues, ruled that the Commissioner could not recover for defamation, since the free speech guarantees of the Constitution "prohibit a public official from recovering damages for a defamatory falsehood relating to his official conduct unless he proves that the statement was made with 'actual malice'—that is, with knowledge that it was false or with reckless disregard of whether it was false or not." If the person accused of defamation felt that the statement was true when he made it, he is thereby protected from a charge of defamation.

The rule was recently put very succinctly by Justice White of the United States Supreme Court as follows:

> For public officers and public figures to recover for damage to their reputations for libelous falsehoods, they must prove either knowing or reckless disregard of the truth. All other plaintiffs must prove at least negligent falsehood, but if the publication about them was in an area of legitimate public interest, then they too must prove deliberate or reckless error. In all actions

Privilege and malice

for libel or slander, actual damages must be proved, and awards of punitive damages will be strictly limited.

A well-established principle of law is that a person may publish defamatory statements in the performance of a legal or moral duty when he believes such statements true—if the publication is made without malice.

Such privileged communications include those of an attorney to his client, a doctor to his patient, a priest to his communicant, public officials to their superiors, or witnesses in a trial to a judge and jury. They also include the communications of a husband to his wife on matters involving their household or marital relationship, or of parents to their children. A businessman enjoys the same privilege in communicating with his partner.

Fact versus opinion

Shortly before the entry of this country into World War II, a book, *The Trojan Horse of America*, was published. In the book occurred the following, "We have examined some of the criteria by which the Communist Trojan Horse may be identified. Let us now consider the marks of the Nazi Trojan Horse. Does the organization through its letters and literature laud the achievements of Adolf Hitler? Take for example an illustration from the magazine which bears the name of *Southern Progress*. 'Adolf Hitler is the George Washington of Germany and maybe of all Europe,' declared this obscure paper."

Promptly the owner of this magazine sued the author for libel. Then came the difficulties in the prosecution of the action. Whether the *Southern Progress* publication was an advocate of the Nazi party of Germany or whether it was not, was a matter of opinion, not one of fact, according to the evidence in the case. That a book is worthless, is harmful to a good cause, or helpful to a bad one, is an opinion. This libel action, being based not on a misrepresentation of fact, but on opinion, failed.

Calling someone a Communist

Changed public opinion can make statements slanderous or libelous that, at a former time, would not have exposed the person so charged to public contempt or ridicule. The law of libel and slander develops with the trend of public thinking.

With the close of World War II began a new phase in the law of libel, that no man should call another a Communist, unless he was such in truth, without being prepared to pay damages.

Before the war, the law saw this matter in a different light. In 1939 a libel action in New York was based on the published statement that a man was affiliated with the Communist Party. The court said of this statement, at the time, ''The Communist Party under existing law may function as a political party. . . . It may like any other established political party proclaim its principles and invite public approval of them. At least while it possesses that status and those rights it cannot be held that it is defamatory *per se* to say of one that he is affiliated with or a member of the Communist Party any more than it would be to say that he is a member of any other legally recognized political party.''

In 1945, after World War II had ended, the United States Circuit Court of Appeals was asked to decide whether an article in a widely circulated magazine contained a libel of a Massachusetts lawyer because it said that ''The Political Action Committee has hired as its legislative agent one S. G., who but recently was a legislative representative for the Massachusetts Communist Party.''

Much water had gone over the dam of public opinion since the 1939 decision. Here the Federal court held this statement to be libel, ''unless there is a difference between saying that a man is a Communist and saying that he is an agent for the party or sympathizes with its objectives and methods.'' It added that ''any difference is one of degree only.''

This Federal decision was later followed by a determination by the courts that laid down this rule: ''Having regard for current public attitude—transitory as it may be—the courts have held that a false charge that one is a Communist is basis for a libel action. And it is of little moment whether the statement describes plaintiff as a Communist or as one having communistic sympathies and affiliations.'' Either statement is a valid ground for court action.

The courts still must look at the impact of the statement upon the community to determine whether it is libelous. A false statement that a person is disloyal, or that he favors Communism above the existing American government, will clearly be defamatory. However, the decision as to whether a false statement that someone is disloyal is defamatory will rest upon the interpretation that the public will place on that statement. Recently, a newspaper printed an article that stated that former Soviet Premier Khrushchev was a ''friend in the Kremlin'' of a noted American scientist. A Federal court ruled that this statement, alone, could not be considered libelous.

Defamatory statements made in political broadcasts

A candidate for the U.S. Senate in North Dakota, who was granted equal time on television, accused his opponents of disloyalty. The station let him make the statement because the law requires that all candidates be given equal time to speak on radio and television. One of the other candidates sued the station for defamation.

The Supreme Court stated that "while denying all candidates use of stations would protect broadcasters from liability, it would also withdraw political discussion from the air. If a station owner could protect himself from liability in no other way but by refusing to broadcast candidates' speeches, the necessary effect would be to hamper the congressional plan to develop broadcasting as a political outlet, rather than to foster it." The Court therefore ruled that no claim can result from any statement that is made by a candidate during a political broadcast.

CHAPTER 16

Real Estate

Buying and selling real estate involves many legal considerations in which almost everyone, at some point in his life, is involved. The technical aspects of a real estate transaction are complicated; however, a general understanding of the nature of such a transaction can help avoid many financial and emotional mistakes.

There are numerous terms associated with buying and selling real estate that a prospective purchaser should know, such as deed, binder, tenancy by the entirety, covenant, title, easement, mortgage, eminent domain, and condemnation, to name a few.

The purchase and sale of real estate usually begins with a contract of sale.

The binder

The purchase of a house frequently begins with the prospective purchaser signing a written memorandum of the transaction, called a ''binder,'' at the time he pays the deposit. The contents of the binder can be very important and may be used against the purchaser in connection with the preparation of the formal contract of sale.

Binders are generally not enforceable unless they contain the minimum terms of the transaction, namely (1) the parties involved, (2) a description of the property, (3) the purchase price, and (4) the method of payment. Even if a binder refers to a contract, it can, in itself, be a contract and a very unsatisfactory one at that. If a deposit is necessary, let your check serve as the receipt and sign no papers without the services of an attorney.

Formal contract of sale

Once the parties have agreed to consummate a real estate transaction, they should sign a contract of sale providing for the delivery of the property or ''closing of title'' at some specified time. The purpose of the contract of sale is to embody all of the aspects of the transaction in a written document and to enable the buyer to arrange for financing and to insure that the seller has proper title to the property before title actually passes from the seller to the buyer. Whatever is left out of the written contract of sale, be it oral assurances or ''understandings,'' is unenforceable and has no effect after the contract is signed.

Tenancy by the entirety

It is common practice for a husband and wife to purchase or take title to a house in their joint names. A deed that lists the buyers as ''Robert Jones and Jane Jones, his wife'' creates such a tenancy by the entirety whereby each possesses the entire property and after the death of one the survivor takes the whole property. There are estate tax considerations in taking property in the form of a tenancy by the entirety, and a husband and wife should contact their attorney before signing a real estate contract in this form.

Description of the property

Before you buy property you should be fully aware of what you are buying. If the description of the property being purchased is inaccurate or incomplete, you may be buying less than what you think, or may end up using someone else's property, or your neighbor may be using property that, in fact, belongs to you. It is always advisable to obtain a survey so that the buyer knows the real estate building that he is buying. In many cases, the seller has a survey and will deliver it to the buyer.

What is the actual purchase price?

The contract of sale should clearly state the amount of money to be paid and the method of payment. If the purchase price is listed at $40,000 and a separate clause refers to a mortgage of $20,000, it is unclear whether the buyer will have to pay $40,000 or $60,000. Great care should be taken to avoid any such ambiguity in connection with an existing mortgage and to make it clear that the purchaser is to be credited with any existing mortgage or purchase-money mortgage (a mortgage given by the seller to the buyer to secure the unpaid balance of the purchase price).

The purchaser should be careful when purchasing property with a preexisting mortgage to have competent assistance to review all of the terms of the mortgage and to receive satisfactory proof from the seller showing the reduced amount of principal, the interest rate, and maturity date, so that the purchaser knows how much he actually has to pay on the existing mortgage.

Closing title

The time and place for paying the purchase price and delivering the deed (a document signed by the seller transferring title to the property to the buyer) are also set forth in the contract of sale. At the closing of title, adjustments should be made in any fees, taxes on property, principal, costs, interest, or other expenses.

The deed

There are a number of essential facts you should always bear in mind when you take part in a transfer of land. First of all, you should make or receive a deed to establish the transfer—or conveyance, as it is often called at law. The deed represents or symbolizes the land itself. When a deed is delivered, it is, effectively, the delivery of the land.

It is indispensable that this deed be in writing. It must be properly signed and should be witnessed. Make certain, also, that it is acknowledged before a notary public and entered in the official records of your locality. Copying of the deed into the public records gives legal notice of ownership to all who may be concerned with the land in the present or the future.

Land deeds fall, roughly speaking, into three classes: (1) warranty deeds, (2) bargain and sale deeds, and (3) quitclaim deeds. Each of these is different from the others. Each has a different purpose and each has different requirements.

A warranty deed not only conveys the property, but contains a covenant by the seller that he owns the property and that his title is free of any liens or encumbrances other than those specifically set out in the deed. Should the buyer find, after he makes the purchase, that there are encumbrances or liens other than those specified in the deed, he is entitled to recover from the seller whatever he is compelled to spend in satisfying these claims, which the grantor or seller represented to him as not existing.

Bargain and sale deeds are simple conveyances of title to land by the owner, but contain no representations or warranties such as those set out in warranty deeds, except possibly a warranty that the seller himself has done nothing to encumber or create a lien against the property. With this form, the purchaser gets, in addition to the rights of the seller, the benefit of any rights an innocent third party purchaser may have against creditors of the seller who didn't record their mortgages, etc.

A quitclaim deed is generally used where there may be some claim against a parcel of land, resulting from the complexities of descent or similar conditions. It conveys simply whatever ownership, however qualified, the seller may possess in the property.

Form of warranty deed

A covenant of warranty and of "quiet enjoyment" runs with the land —it is a warranty of title and quiet enjoyment not just to the immediate purchaser but to all subsequent owners of the property.

In states where the wife still has her dower right in her husband's property she must join him in signing it and be a party to the deed.

The form of these deeds may be modified to some extent by the requirements of statutes in the different states, but the following form of a warranty deed is substantially the same in all the states:

This indenture made in the *City* and *State of New York* this *2nd* day of *September, 1971,* between *John Jones*, residing at

801 West 10th Street, Borough of Manhattan, City of New York, the "Buyer," and *Edward Levey,* residing at *783 York Avenue, Borough of Manhattan, City of New York,* the "Seller."

Witnesseth, that the Seller, in consideration of *Five Thousand ($5,000) Dollars* lawful money of the United States, paid by the Buyer, the receipt of which is hereby acknowledged, does hereby grant and release unto the Buyer, his heirs and assigns forever, all that certain lot, piece or parcel of land, with the buildings thereon erected, situate, lying and being in the *Borough of Manhattan, City and State of New York,* and bounded and described as follows:

Beginning *at a point fifty feet from the intersection of . . . (insert description of land conveyed).*

Together with the appurtenances and all the estate and rights of the Seller in and to said premises.

To have and to hold the premises herein granted unto the Buyer, his heirs and assigns, forever.

And the Seller covenants as follows:

First, that the Seller is seized of said premises in fee simple* and has good right to convey the same.

Second, that the Buyer shall quietly enjoy the said premises.

Third, that the said premises are free from encumbrances.

Fourth, that the Seller will forever warrant the title to said premises.

In witness whereof the Seller has hereunto set his hand the day and year first above written.

John Jones (L. S.)

(In the presence of:)
Lester Smith
David Chase

State of *New York*   ⎫
                       ⎬ ss:
County of *New York* ⎭

On this *2nd* day of *September, 1971,* before me personally appeared *John Jones,* to me known and known to me to be the individual who executed the foregoing instrument, and duly

---

*This means "absolutely." See Dictionary of Common Legal Terms at the end of this book for the meaning of other legal words used.

acknowledged to me that he executed the same for the purposes therein named.

Regina Ilan
Notary Public

The protection a warranty affords A deed of Alabama property contained provisions warranting title and quiet enjoyment, and that the property was free from encumbrances—all the standard guarantees. Later the purchaser died and the property passed

to his heirs. They in turn conveyed the property to a man named Poyner. At that time, six years after the original conveyance, it was discovered that when the first deed was made, the city had a lien on the property for street paving expenses.

Poyner, the owner of the property, sued and recovered an amount sufficient to satisfy the lien. The court pointed out that such a warranty covenant runs with the land into the hands of the heirs and any assignees and may be the grounds for suit when the breach of such a covenant occurs.

Form of bargain and sale deed

The following form of a bargain and sale deed is substantially that used in the various states, subject to statutory modification:

This indenture made in the *City* and *State of New York* on the *10th* day of *October, 1971,* between *Kenneth Kraus,* residing at *400 Riverside Drive, Borough of Manhattan, City of New York,* the "Seller," and *Donna Kirk,* residing at *211 Central Park West, Borough of Manhattan, City of New York,* the "Buyer."

Witnesseth, that the Seller, in consideration of *Forty Thousand ($40,000) Dollars*, lawful money of the United States, the receipt of which is hereby acknowledged, does hereby grant and release unto the Buyer, her heirs and assigns forever, all that certain lot, piece or parcel of land with the buildings thereon erected, situate, lying and being in the *Borough of Manhattan, City of New York,* and bounded and described as follows:

Beginning . . . (*insert description of land conveyed*).

Together with the appurtenances and all the estate and rights of the Seller in and to said premises, to have and to hold the premises herein granted unto the Buyer, her heirs and assigns forever.

In witness whereof the Seller has hereunto set his hand the day and year first above written.

Kenneth Kraus (L. S.)

(In the presence of:)
Thomas Esmond
Henry Andrews

State of *New York* } ss:
County of *New York* }

On this *10th* day of *October, 1971,* before me personally appeared *Kenneth Kraus,* to me known and known to me to be the person who executed the foregoing instrument, and duly acknowledged to me that he executed the same for the purposes therein set forth.

Edward Smith
Notary Public

As in the execution of the warranty deed, in states where the wife still retains her dower right in her husband's property, she must join in, and be a party to, the conveyance.

What is a quitclaim deed?

A quitclaim deed does not necessarily convey the land, but simply the right, title, and interest of the seller or grantor, if any, in the land. As in the other types of conveyance of land, the wife should join in the deed and be a party to the conveyance where she still retains her dower right in her husband's property.

Form of quitclaim deed

The following is substantially the form of the quitclaim deed employed throughout the country:

This indenture made in the *City of New York* on the *14th* day of *May, 1971,* between *Lewis Goldsmith,* residing at *809 Springfield Street, Borough of Manhattan, City of New York,* the "Seller" and *Robert Price,* residing at *7572 Merrick Street, Borough of Manhattan, City of New York,* the "Buyer."

Witnesseth, that the Seller in consideration of the sum of *Ten Thousand ($10,000) Dollars,* lawful money of the United States, paid by the Buyer, the receipt whereof is hereby acknowledged, does hereby remise, release and quitclaim unto the Buyer, his heirs and assigns forever, all that certain lot, piece or parcel of land with the buildings thereon erected, situate, lying and being in the *Borough of Manhattan, City of New York,* and bounded and described as follows:

Beginning . . . (*insert description of property conveyed*).

Together with the appurtenances and all the estate and rights of the Seller in and to said premises.

To have and to hold the premises herein granted unto the Buyer, his heirs and assigns forever.

In witness whereof the Seller has hereunto set his hand and seal the day and year above written.

Lewis Goldsmith (L. S.)

(In the presence of:)
Edith Gordon
John Thompson

State of *New York*
County of *New York* } ss:

On this *14th* day of *May, 1971,* before me personally appeared *Lewis Goldsmith*, to me known and known to me to be the individual who executed the foregoing instrument, and duly acknowledged to me that he executed the same for the purposes therein set forth.

Harvey Greenfield
Notary Public

Are oral deeds legal?

Do not accept an oral transfer of ownership of land. The law does not recognize such a conveyance as a deed. A typical state statute in relation to the execution of deeds says: "An estate in real property other than an estate at will or for a term not exceeding one year, can be transferred only by operation of law or by an instrument in writing subscribed by the party disposing of the same . . ." All states have similar "statutes of fraud" requiring that conveyances of real estate be in writing. They are intended to prevent "fraud" in testimony about oral transactions.

How a deed should be executed

In Indiana, the boundaries of a tract of land were not clear. The owners involved settled upon their titles by an oral agreement, but no deeds were exchanged.

Here the court laid down the rule that is accepted as the law of the country in relation to the execution of deeds: that an instrument to transfer the title to land must not only have a grantor, a grantee, and a "thing granted"—it must also be signed by the grantor or someone he directs to sign for him. Further, it should be witnessed and acknowledged before a notary or other public officer as required by the statute and delivered to the grantee. Some courts, following their statutes, will not insist upon the witnessing or acknowledgment, but for your own protection you should always have these.

Signing with an X

An aged owner, nearly deaf and blind, wished to deed property in Oklahoma to his son. Unable to sign the deed himself, he used an X for his signature before witnesses and acknowledged the document to be his deed before a notary public. Later the validity of this deed was questioned because it had been executed by a cross rather than the signature of the owner of the land.

This objection did not prevail. Where there has been an acknowledgment and the grantor is able to make a deed, the conveyance is secure against any defects in its execution, said the court. Further, when a document in the form of a deed is attested and delivered, the courts consider it a deed if the control of the property passes from the original owner on the delivery of this deed.

An X signature by one unable to write his name is always valid in law.

Acknowledging a deed

The acknowledgment of a deed—the statement made by the grantor of land before a notary public or other officer authorized to certify to such statements that the execution of the deed is the free act of the grantor—is not generally necessary insofar as the actual transfer of the property is concerned.

A rule laid down in one case where no acknowledgment was made in the conveyance of real estate says that a deed to real property that has been executed and delivered is valid between the parties to the transaction although neither acknowledged nor witnessed.

In another case the court held that a deed signed and delivered, although not acknowledged before a notary, was adequate to transfer title to the property.

When acknowledgment is necessary

A similar decision was made in a case where a deed was neither acknowledged nor witnessed. Here, however, the court indicated that an acknowledgment is necessary for the recording of a conveyance for notice of the conveyance to later purchasers. This is a point you cannot afford to overlook. Suppose a deed is made and delivered by a grantor, and later this same grantor makes a second deed of the same land and delivers this second deed to another grantee. The grantor is committing a fraud, but if the first deed has not been recorded and the second grantee is innocent of the fraud and has no knowledge of the previous deed, when he records his deed he acquires legal title to the land. The first grantee has no such title.

An acknowledgment of a deed by a grantor, the court explained, is not essential to pass legal title between the parties to the instrument. Attestation and acknowledgment are formalities required by the statute to entitle the deed to be recorded so as to operate as notice to subsequent purchasers, but are not essential to transfer the title between the parties.

A deed must be delivered

The delivery of a deed is necessary for the transfer of the ownership of real property. While the delivery to the grantee personally is not necessary, there must be some act of the one conveying the land that signifies a surrender of his ownership and control of the property. Such an act is known as a "constructive delivery." The word "constructive" is applied at law to a condition or act the court assumes on the basis of other conditions or acts that have actually taken place.

If you take part in a transaction involving a deed, make certain that it is delivered. That is the safest course. However, the courts have declared that a valid transfer of real property can be made even without the knowledge of the grantee. The case that follows provides an illustration of this rule.

An example of constructive delivery

A woman owning land in California made a deed of land to her brother and herself as joint owners. She left this deed with the notary before whom she had acknowledged it, and asked him to have it returned to her.

The brother to whom the joint interest in this property was thus conveyed had no knowledge of the transfer until three years later, when his sister died. There was no necessity to show acceptance. "There may be a constructive delivery as well as an actual delivery so long as acts are shown to indicate the intention of the grantor to vest title by the instrument."

Delivery by an agent

The owner of some real estate in Georgia wrote the following letter: "Dear Brother: Am not feeling so well. Asthma is bothering me. Am in town having a paper fixed up. If anything happens to me you have this paper recorded at once and turn over to Stella (his wife) if she is living. Mark the envelope so you will know what it is and take care of it. Am mailing it to you. Your loving brother, J. W. C."

A properly executed deed was enclosed in the letter. Less than a year later, C. died. Two days after his death his brother had the deed recorded and left instructions that it be returned, after recording, to Stella, the wife. This was done.

The brothers and sisters of the man who had died sued to set aside the deed on the ground that it had never been delivered by the grantor. Deciding in their favor, that there had been no delivery of the deed and that title and ownership of this land had not passed to the wife, the court explained that when the deed was sent by C. to his brother, he made his brother an agent to have the deed recorded and delivered to his wife. When C. died, his death revoked that agency and the authority of his brother to act for him ended. Hence, there was no delivery of the deed, either physically or constructively, and the effort of C. to convey the land to his wife failed. The letter could not, of course, operate as a valid will, either.

There is a significant lesson here. A deed is an important document. Any matters pertaining to it should be taken care of directly, without relying on a person who is not an attorney.

Recording of deeds

The deed you receive when you buy real estate should be recorded immediately—that is, delivered to the proper officer of the county where the land is located, with instructions to put the deed on record. This officer is sometimes known as the County Register or Registrar and sometimes as the County Clerk.

There is an old adage that a man may be honest but he should be kept honest. We have referred to the fact that when the owner of land has given deeds of the same land to two different grantees, the second deed is obviously fraud—because by it the grantor is selling something he no longer owns, and if the second grantee has his deed recorded before the first grantee records his, the land belongs to the second grantee unless he is in some way a party to this fraud or had knowledge of the earlier conveyance.

"The basic purpose which led to the enactment of the recording acts was to prevent persons owning lands from selling them more than once," is the laconic observation of a New York court.

Before a purchaser can assert a claim on such a second grant, it must be clear that he is innocent of any knowledge or of any wrongdoing. This statement was first made over 100 years ago. It concerned a person who purchased some land at a sheriff's sale and then sought to put off that land a grantee under a previously executed but still unrecorded deed of the land. Here the purchaser from the sheriff knew in advance the deed was not recorded. He was a party to the fraud and thus acquired nothing by his purchase.

What is a covenant?

A covenant is an agreement to do or not to do a particular act, according to the courts. Covenants may stipulate the character of the buildings or improvements that may be made on the land, as well as those that may not be made. They may state who may live in the buildings on the land, or what use may be made of the land. They may contain a wide range of restrictions and yet be a basic condition of the conveyance.

If you, as a grantee of land, fail to do as agreed under the covenants in the deed of your land, you may be penalized by the loss of the property, by damages for your violation of the covenant, or by a prohibition by the court—an injunction—against the continuance of the violation. What the penalty will be depends on the nature of the covenant and the judgment of the court.

A typical covenant

Typical of covenants of this sort was one in a deed of Connecticut property that said: "For a period of twenty years from and after the date hereof the grantee will not erect or maintain or permit to be erected or maintained any building except a one-family dwelling."

First the grantee of this deed received into his house three "paying guests." Next he rearranged the interior and inaugurated what was a boarding house in the full meaning of the expression. This use of the house violated the covenant in his deed restricting the use of the building to one family, and an injunction was issued against a continuance of this use.

Injunction granted

The covenant in a deed of land in Oklahoma restricted the use of the property to residential purposes. "No building shall ever be used or occupied for any purpose except for that of private residence exclusively, nor shall any part or portion thereof be used for business or trade of any kind whatsoever."

The residents on this tract objected to the construction there of a gasoline filling station by an oil company, and sought an injunction. They declared such a use of the property was contrary to the covenant into which all the adjacent landowners had entered, and it was on this ground that the injunction was granted.

Covenants binding in the future

An agreement was made by the owner of property on the bay at Mobile, Alabama, not to use his property for any public or commercial purpose except for the reasonable and proper use for bathing by his family. Two years later the owner adopted a plan of renting the beach for public picnics and bathing parties.

Such an agreement restricting the use of land "runs with the land," said the court and is binding on all who have notice or knowledge of the restriction. Further, by the execution of such an agreement the owners of the property bind not only themselves but succeeding owners of the property. By recording deeds containing restricting covenants, you give legal notice of them to all subsequent purchasers or grantees when purchasing property intended for a particular use. It is important, therefore, that the land records be searched for the existence of any such restrictions when you purchase property.

Forfeiture of title

A deed of property at Beverly Hills, California, provided: "All buildings to be erected on Doheny Drive shall be exclusively for private residence." It contained the further provision that a breach of this condition after 30 days' notice and a failure to remedy the breach would forfeit title to the property—it would then revert to the original grantor.

This covenant was later challenged, but to no avail. Restrictions governing the character, location, and cost of buildings to be constructed in accordance with the general plan for a specific neighborhood in cities have been universally held to be valid and binding. Also, provisions for forfeiture of title by the owner for failure to comply with such restrictions may cost him his property.

How covenants are abandoned

After covenants of this character are made, conditions often arise that justify the courts in holding the restrictions abandoned because of changes in the character of the neighborhood. A typical case concerning such a condition is the one that follows.

In Pasadena, California, various real estate owners made a contract or covenant by which they bound themselves to restrict to "persons of the Caucasian race" the use of a neighborhood owned by them. Later there was an influx of people of other races into this neighborhood. When some of the owners protested against these violations of the covenants in the deeds, the court refused to interfere.

Such interference, the court declared, would serve only to harass and injure those living in the vicinity. The enforcement of this covenant was not justified when the character of the neighborhood had changed by virtue of altered conditions in no way connected with these covenants. Today, of course, such a limitation is unenforceable. See Chapter 9 on Your Civil Rights.

When restrictions are unenforceable

In 1855, a deed made for the conveyance of property in Baltimore, Maryland, contained a covenant restricting it for small private residences. The houses in this vicinity were at the time occupied by single families, and the yards were filled with flowers, shrubbery, and trees. Thirty years later these families were gone. In the place of the onetime homes were rooming and tenement houses, a gasoline filling station, and a used car lot.

The courts, when requested to, refused to enforce the restrictions. It was held that they had been inserted into deeds to maintain the locality as a residential district. The vicinity no longer had that character—the restrictions were no longer reasonable or enforceable, now that the reason for their imposition was gone.

In general, restrictions of this type can exist for no longer a time than the nature of the circumstances and the purpose of their imposition indicates them to be reasonable. Unreasonable restrictions, in the light of changed economic or other conditions, will not be enforced by courts through issuance of an injunction.

The meaning of easements

An easement is an acquired right or a privilege to enjoy or use land belonging to another. A path across the land of another used so long by the public that there is a right to its uninterrupted use, a roadway through another's lot, the protection afforded by the eaves of a house overhanging the land of another—all these are easements. That is why an easement has been called "a privilege without a profit."

For 30 years, near Bear Creek, in California, a Mr. Peck had used a lane over another owner's land, adjacent to his own. One day he found the road barred. Across the land was a locked gate.

The court maintained Peck had a right to the use of this path. That right had been acquired by him and others by an "open, visible, continuous, and uninterrupted" use for 30 years.

What makes an easement?

The use of another's property by one who claims an easement must be "adverse" to the owner of that property. Passing across a field on the express invitation or consent of the owner creates no easement. Doing

so for 20 years (the period of time usually prescribed in which an easement will acrue), will create such a right, provided the exercise of that right has been "open, adverse, and continuous," for all that time. An easement is said to arise thus by "prescription"—that is, continued use against the legal rights of the landowner to prevent it if he chooses.

Easement in the use of a building

An easement also arises from the use of common stairs and hallways by those passing through a building. In Lowell, Massachusetts, John and Thomas Nesmith built adjoining buildings and provided for a common entrance, landings, and stairways. Half of the space so used was allotted to the property of one and half to that of the other.

All went well until a successor to one of these owners wished to tear down the building. The other owner refused to permit him. The court was called upon to decide who had the law on his side.

"If the structure ceases to exist," reads the decision in this case, "the right ends as there is nothing upon which it can be exercised. This is because the owner of the building is not obliged to replace it when it ceases to exist by reason of decay, earthquake, tornado, fire, or its destruction otherwise caused without fault or act of the owner."

This is the general viewpoint of the law on this matter. However, the question of whether the owner of the property subject to an easement of this character is free voluntarily to destroy the building and not restore the easement is not uniformly decided. The court here held that the owner of the land was free to demolish the building without obligation for the restoration of the hall and stairways for the use of the adjoining owner. In some states a contrary rule has been established.

The best solution to this problem is to follow the method usually adopted by owners who want to prevent easements—closing the passageway for an appreciable length of time at not too infrequent intervals. By so doing you break the continuity that is an essential feature in the establishment of a right of way or easement of this character.

Easement by implication

Easements are in some instances recognized by the courts as arising by implication. The following is a good example of such an easement. When part of a tract of land is sold to another, and there is no other reasonable way of access available to the purchaser, the seller by implication gives to the grantee a right of way across his own land to the plot sold.

How a mortgage operates

A mortgage of real estate is simply equivalent to the deposit of land by its owner (or mortgagor) as collateral for the payment of a loan. A mortgage is merely security for a debt. You buy land and pay, let us say, half the purchase price in cash. The payment of the remaining half of the price that you still owe, you secure to the person who puts up the money (the mortgagee) by giving a mortgage on the property for that amount. This loan or mortgage you pay off as stipulated in an agreement, which may or may not be a part of the mortgage. When it has been paid off, the lender's interest in the property ends.

It is of fundamental importance, when payments are completed under a mortgage, that the mortgagor obtain and file a "satisfaction piece" from the mortgagee. Otherwise he may have no clear proof that his title to the property is free of encumbrances. A "satisfaction piece" is merely legal terminology for a formal document that the mortgage has been paid and the lien released.

Kinds of mortgages

Mortgages on land, and on the buildings situated on the land that at law are considered a part of the realty, may be as many as there are lenders to the owner of the money thus secured. These mortgages, however, are entitled to priority in payment in the order in which they are given. They are generally designated as a first mortgage, a second mortgage, and sometimes a third.

A mortgage given in part payment of the purchase price of property is a "purchase money mortgage" and has priority in payment over any subsequent mortgage other than those already on the land when it was purchased.

Improving property already mortgaged

Should improvements be made to the property, buildings erected, or similar additions made that enhance the value, the mortgage covers these as well, and the security of the mortgagee is correspondingly greater, unless such improvements are expressly excepted from the lien of the mortgage by agreement between the mortgagor and the mortgagee.

Who inherits a mortgage?

A real estate mortgage is personal property, as is any other form of security, such as a bond, or a stock, or bank deposits. Upon the death of the owner of the mortgage, it passes to the beneficiaries under the will of the mortgagee as would any other debt owed to the estate.

Foreclosure of real property mortgage

The foreclosure of a mortgage is made to collect money that has been lent the owner of the property, when he fails to repay the holder of the mortgage as stipulated. In such an action the property is taken from the owner and sold at auction. From the proceeds of the sale, after payment of the court and sale expenses, the debt for which the mortgage was given as security is paid.

In some instances, where property is rented to tenants and is producing a current income for the owner, a receiver is appointed by the court to collect these rents and hold them until the final disposition of the proceeds of the sale. However, when the value of the land is sufficient for the payment of the mortgage debt, this remedy is seldom granted by the court, nor is it granted when it is apparent that the income from the property is already being paid on the taxes and interest, and in reduction of the mortgage.

The foreclosure decree, made by the court, determines the amount of the debt, makes provision for the payment of attorney fees and costs, and orders the sale of the property with directions as to the notice of sale, the place where the notice must be given, and the time allowed between the giving of the notice and the date of the sale. This decree will also specify the time and place for the sale, or leave these details to the decision of the master or referee—the officer appointed by the court for the conduct of subsequent proceedings until the making of the final foreclosure decree, after the sale.

The foreclosure sale

A public notice of the place and time of the mortgage foreclosure sale must be given in accordance with the decree or, in some states, with the provisions of the statute. This notice is often given by publication in a newspaper "printed in the county" or "of general circulation," or by posting the notice in a specific and prominent place.

The foreclosure sale is made by public auction. If no bidder appears, the auctioneer adjourns the sale to another date.

If the proceeds do not cover the mortgage

In some, but not all, states, if the mortgage contains an agreement by the mortgagor to pay the debt—or if the debt is represented by a separate written obligation, called a bond—there is a personal liability on the mortgagor that goes beyond the proceeds of the foreclosure sale. It requires payment by him personally of any deficiency that may occur. In other states the right of the mortgagee to this deficiency judgment is not recognized. If the foreclosure sale yields proceeds in excess of the mortage and fees, this money belongs to the mortgagor.

The mortgagor's right to redeem the mortgage is ordinarily closed and ended with the sale on foreclosure. It is sometimes held by the courts that the mortgagor may be permitted to redeem after the sale but before the final foreclosure decree is made by the court.

When a deed is given as a mortgage

A mortgage of land is, in practical effect, a conveyance of the land to whoever lends the money, while the person making the mortgage continues in possession of the land, with an agreement that if and when the money is repaid to the lender, as agreed, the conveyance is void and of no effect.

Often an absolute deed is given as security for the repayment of a loan on real property, by agreement or understanding between the owner of the property and the lender of the money that the deed will be returned or canceled when the money is repaid. When such an arrangement is made, the legal problem of what the instrument is—deed or mortgage—may arise, particularly at the time the borrower attempts to exercise ownership or the lender attempts to foreclose.

The purchaser of a piece of real estate in Florida erected on his land a two-story brick building. Shortly before the building was completed, he mortgaged it and the lot for a loan. Sometime later, when he was unable to reduce the mortgage, he gave the lender a deed of the property with the agreement that the lender manage the property, collect the rents, and apply them to this unpaid loan.

Six years later the borrower asked for an account of the money that had been collected and the balance that he owed on the loan. This the creditor refused, saying that he had taken the deed in payment of the loan.

Here the court asserted that "an instrument given for the purpose or with the intention of securing the payment of money is a mortgage."

If the mortgagee buys the property

The mortgage does not pay the debt; it is simply security for its payment. As we have already indicated, if the proceeds from the sale of the security are not enough for the payment of the balance, the deficiency remains as the borrower's obligation, which he must pay, just as he must pay any other debt he owes.

An owner of property in Philadelphia borrowed $4,500 and gave as security a mortgage on her property. When she failed to pay, the property was sold at foreclosure and bought by the lender of the money. Later, after the borrower had died, the administrator paid the deficiency and demanded the return of the property. This the court refused to order.

A mortgage not fully paid on a foreclosure sale of the property can be a personal claim against the mortgagor for the deficiency, even if the mortgagee himself buys the property at the sale.

How a mortgagee's claims are limited

State statutes, however, in many instances impose limitations on the amount of the judgment or claim that may be granted the mortgagee after the foreclosure and sale of the property and the credit of the proceeds on the mortgage, for which he looks for payment to the mortgagor.

Real property taxes The power to levy a tax on real property is generally delegated by the state legislature to local authorities—city, county, or town—subject to whatever limitations or restrictions the legislature may see fit to impose. The levy is made for the calendar or fiscal year.

Notice of the assessment against each taxpayer is posted or advertised. This is frequently done by making the tax rolls or books in which the assessments are listed available to inspection by the public—and to the taxpayers particularly—at some public office during business hours on certain days.

Should any taxpayer feel himself aggrieved by the assessment against his property, he has the opportunity, within a stated time, to file his objections with the tax authorities and be heard on his complaint. After this hearing, the tax may be reduced or left undisturbed, although it is still subject to review by the courts at the instance of the aggrieved taxpayer.

The usual grounds upon which complaints are made by taxpayers is that the property has been overvalued and the amount of the assessment is unjust.

How real estate value is assessed The highest price the property would bring free of encumbrances at a fair and voluntary private sale for cash, or its fair cash market value, is ordinarily the criterion of its value. In estimating the value of land, the assessors take into consideration the location, quality, conditions, improvements, and use—all the factors that affect the market value or that would influence the minds of purchasers.

Unless the land has been recently purchased, the original price paid by the purchaser is not conclusive of the value at the time the assessment is made. However, the purchase price may be considered in fixing the value.

Foreclosure sale for taxes On and after a named date in the statute, unpaid taxes on a real estate become a lien on the land. Substantially, these taxes are a first mortgage. If the tax is not paid within the time set by the law, the land may be sold for the nonpayment of the taxes.

The statutory requirement is that the tax collector shall make a list of the lands on which taxes remain unpaid, with a description, in each instance, of the property and the name of the owner. After the list has been advertised, either by posting in some prominent place or by publication in a newspaper, or both, the land is sold at public auction and the unpaid taxes deducted from the proceeds.

It is generally provided by law that after the sale the former owner has a period of time within which he may pay the taxes and the expenses of the sale, interest, advertising, and other charges, and secure the return of his property. Except under special circumstances, the owner must exercise this privilege within a specified time, limited by the law, or else lose his property. This period of time varies according to the statutes of the different states.

Buyer beware

The classic contract rule is that the buyer takes the property as is and any defect that exists will not affect the validity of the contract of sale, as long as the seller has not misrepresented that no such defect existed. Recent decisions, however, have begun to modify this rule of caveat emptor and to protect the buyers of new houses to imply a warranty of quality or fitness. This will depend on the law of your state.

Condemnation and eminent domain

An owner of real property may have proper title, pay all necessary taxes, mortgage payments, or whatever and still lose his property. The right of the Federal or local governments to take property for the public interest upon payment of just compensation is inherent in government. Under the Fifth Amendment to the United States Constitution, the government may exercise its power of eminent domain as long as it pays the owner just compensation.

The laws governing eminent domain generally derive from the late 19th century when open lands were plentiful and were being claimed for canals, roads, and railroads. Now, with a highly urbanized society and many more agencies with the power of eminent domain, vast amounts of private property have been claimed for interstate highways, urban renewal projects, schools, parks, and many other public-interest uses. The value of the property being condemned has led to numerous lawsuits and hardships to private property owners. The owner of real property must realize that his rights of ownership are subject to a higher state authority that may, on occasion, require the owner of property to give his specific property for the interest of the public at large, but with just compensation.

What is "just compensation" becomes a question of expert opinion as to values and comparison with other property in the vicinity.

In one case, the owner of property had protested a high valuation or assessment of his property for tax pruposes and had succeeded in having the value reduced. Thereafter, the government had taken his property in eminent domain proceedings for a public purpose of slum clearance. The owner now wanted a much higher valuation for his compensation.

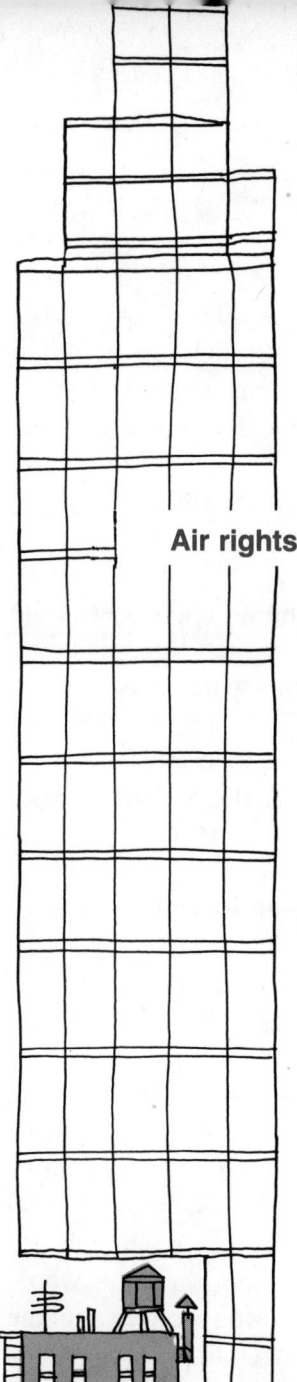

The court determined that the value for tax purposes and the value for condemnation purposes were not necessarily the same, because different factors were involved. It is common knowledge, for example, that in many areas of the country, for tax purposes, property is underassessed.

Air rights

Urbanization has also led to many modifications of classic real estate concepts, one of the latest being the development of air rights. The first air rights law was adopted by Illinois in 1927, allowing railroads owning real estate to sell, convey, and lease estates above and below the surface. Increasing pressure for usable building space in urban areas led to the enactment by Congress, in 1958, of a law granting to the Interstate Highway System the right to establish parking facilities for motor vehicles above and below the highways of the System. Both Federal and local governments expanded the use of air rights and established a trend toward treating air rights as real property subject to the same treatment as other real property.

Air rights are described as air space or development rights to above a specified horizontal place and such surface rights and land needed for support and access for the street and to ensure compatibility with subsurface use.

In 1970, New York City amended its zoning law to allow the transfer of unused and/or development rights from a site that could not use such rights to one that could, thus creating a greater economic use of limited space.

Examples of air rights projects are: the Pan American Building over Grand Central Station, and Madison Square Garden and Pennsylvania Plaza over Pennsylvania Station, both in New York City; the Prudential Center in Boston; the Chicago Merchandise Mart of the Marshall Field Company over the Chicago and North Western Railway tracks; and the Chicago Daily News Building over the Chicago Union Station.

Condominiums and cooperatives

Another form of development is the condominium concept of owning real property. This ancient concept, known since the Roman Empire, has taken on new life since World War II. A condominium is a form of real estate ownership whereby an individual acquires title in fee to an apartment in a multiple dwelling with a right to participate in the use of common facilities. It is an attempt to make apartment ownership similar to private home ownership. Owners buy and sell freely, subject only to contract arrangement with other owners of condominium apartments. Each owner arranges for his own financing and mortgage with the previous owner. Owners of condominium apartments are subject to real estate taxes and other real property expenses, in addition to fees to maintain common aspects of the building, such as heating, and maintenance of hallways, lobbies, and the exterior of the building. Before entering into a contract to buy a condominium apartment, it is wise to have your attorney review all of your obligations and responsibilities, both legal and financial.

Cooperative apartments

A variation of the condominium approach to owning an apartment is the cooperative apartment building. In a cooperative, a group of people come together to purchase a whole building and allocate the apartments or areas of the building to the respective purchasers in accordance with the financial responsibility of each owner. The usual form of a cooperative involves separate shares or interests in the common facilities and leases of specific apartments. The two types, that is, shares and leases, usually must be transferred together. The owners of the shares then elect a governing board to set policy and rules for the running of the building, and it generally functions as a private, closely held corporation.

The owner of a cooperative apartment, however, does not "own" it in the usual ownership sense. It is more like being a stockholder in a corporation with a right to possession of an apartment as long as you remain such a stockholder. You can sell your interest, the purchaser being subject to approval of the board of directors (pursuant to the corporate charter and by-laws), and with it goes the right to possession of the apartment allocated to those shares. There are tax advantages to this, because local real estate taxes and interest on a building mortgage are deductible, to the extent applicable, from income tax. Any mortgage is on the whole building and not on the individual apartment in a cooperative, so the corporation and not an individual owner-tenant, makes the arrangements for the mortgage. If you borrow money to buy your cooperative, it is a personal loan and not a real estate loan. However, some states, like New York, where cooperatives are in vogue, have recent statutes allowing loans tied into a specific cooperative apartment.

Can I get my down payment back?

In an ordinary real estate transaction, the down payment on a purchase that is not completed, is not refundable to the purchaser unless the contract specifically provides for a refund. This is so even if the seller sustains no damage. For example, when the purchaser does not go through with the deal, the seller may possibly sell to someone else at a higher price, but he can still keep the down payment even though there was no loss to him.

The rule in personal property matters is the opposite. The down payment must be refunded (unless the contract provides otherwise), but the seller can show the damages sustained by virtue of the failure of the purchaser to go through with the deal, which damages may be covered by the down payment.

How do you treat the purchase of shares of stock and a proprietary lease in a cooperative apartment?

In a recent New York case, the purchaser defaulted because of a downturn in business conditions and wanted the deposit back, subject to any actual damage. The seller claimed it was like an interest in real property. The court held that the stock certificate and lease were more like personal property, partly on the basis that, without proof of actual damage, forfeiture of a deposit is like a penalty and a penalty is unfair unless clearly required by law.

This leads to chapter 17 on Personal Property.

Your Personal Property Rights

As a general rule, the term "real property" includes land and buildings. All other forms of property or assets are "personal property." If property is movable, it is likely to be considered as personal property. This class includes animals, ships, furniture, merchandise, and the like, as well as such things as stocks, bonds, patents, copyrights, claims for damages, etc. It even includes debts.

This distinction between personal and real property becomes vital in the settlement of estates and the payment of debts, as it is the personal property of a deceased person that is used first in the satisfaction of claims and the payment of funeral and administration expenses.

The same distinction is also important in determining what is included by deeds of real estate and the traditional phrase used in them: "Together with the appurtenances and all the estates and rights of the party of the first part in and to said premises."

The definition of personal property by a typical state statute is: "The words 'personal property' include money, goods, chattels, things in action, and evidences of debt." ("Things in action" means claims or rights with a money value—we shall discuss these further along in this chapter.)

This definition determined the meaning of a clause in an agreement between a father and his son that, in return for the support and care of the father for the remaining years of his life, the son should have all the personal property of the father at his death.

The contract was made shortly before the entrance of this country into World War I, and the father died a few months after that war ended. One of the things the father owned was a farm. During the period between the execution of the agreement and the death of the father, receipts from farm products reached an unprecedented amount, due to the high food prices of that time. This definition that personal property included money compelled the court to determine adversely the claims of other members of the family that the accumulation of money, since it was derived from the farm, was not personal property and not included in this agreement.

Is timber personal property?

A landowner in Arkansas contended that a lien on his land for unpaid taxes did not apply to standing timber but solely to the soil—that standing timber was personal property.

The term "land," the court declared, meant not just the land itself but everything that was attached to it "by the process of nature or art." The standing timber was attached to the land and was as much a part of the land as was the soil itself. This is also the case with growing crops, as we shall see later.

On the other hand, a purchaser of land in Georgia claimed ownership of pulp wood cut from his tract months before he took title to the property. But the law holds that timber, when cut down, is personal property and does not pass under a deed of the property. "Anything detached from the realty," said the court, "becomes personal immediately upon being detached therefrom."

**Property in its
full meaning**

The boundary line that courts and legislatures have drawn for the man in the street as a clear distinction between what he can own to the exclusion of all others, and what belongs to everyone to the exclusion of none, often disappears in a fog of uncertainty. In general, we may say that property includes practically all valuable rights—the term relates to every possible interest a person may have, tangible or intangible. For example, a Georgia state court recently held that the right to practice law is a property right.

**Is a professional
name property?**

A name, too, can be property. Two men, whose names had acquired a notable advertising value in radio, assigned to a broadcasting company the exclusive management of their services, their trade names, and their productions, and agreed they would make no contracts with other broadcasting companies.

They then proceeded to make another contract for the publication of their broadcast material under their own names. The court forbade the use by them of either their names or the script, as these rights had been assigned to the broadcasting company, and were property rights belonging to the company and entitled to protection by the court.

In this same category of property rights may be placed the trademarks and trade names of the business world in general.

**Patents, trademarks,
and copyrights**

This area is a specialty in the law, so much so that lawyers are permitted to state that they specialize in this field.

The Constitution of the United States provides in Article I, Section 8, Clause 8 that Congress shall have Power

> To promote the Progress of Science and useful Arts, by securing
> for Limited Times to Authors and Inventors the exclusive Right
> to their respective Writings and Discoveries;

This covers patents for inventors and copyright for authors. It does not cover trademarks, the authority for which comes from the power of Congress "to regulate Commerce."

Trademarks and how to register them

A trademark is a name, symbol, sign, or device attached or applied to goods for sale in the market. It serves to distinguish these goods from similar ones made by others, and is a means by which they may be identified with their particular manufacturer or producer.

The courts have based their prohibition of the infringement of trademarks on the ground that the trademark owner has an exclusive property right in the mark. They have also based it on the ground that the public is entitled to protection against fraud by the false representations of unscrupulous merchants or manufacturers seeking to "palm off" on the public their own products as those of another.

Generally any phrase, mark, word, or device that will serve to identify the origin or ownership of the goods to which it is applied may be adopted as a trademark. On the other hand, it can be used only if it will not prejudice the rights of others who may already have established the same or a similar symbol as a trademark. Further it must not be a word in common or general use which is descriptive of the product.

The Federal Trademark Act, also known as the Lanham Act, provides for the registration of trademarks by owners who have acquired their title by virtue of actual use in interstate commerce. The application for trademark registration must be made to the Commissioner of Patents, be signed by the applicant, and specify the name, domicile, location, and citizenship of the applicant or, in the case of a firm or corporation, the place of business. Further, this application must state the class of merchandise and provide a particular description of the goods comprised in the class for which the trademark is appropriated, and the length of time the mark has been used, as well as a description of the mark itself. The application must be accompanied by a drawing of the trademark, signed by the applicant, and five additional specimens of the mark as actually used and as are required by the Patent Commissioner, together with a fee of $35.

Such a Federal trademark when issued has a term of 20 years, provided that during the sixth year an affidavit is filed to the effect that the trademark is in use or explaining its non-use. It may be renewed for additional 20-year terms within the six months prior to expiration by showing of continued use. The renewal fee is $25.

In addition to Federal registration, there are state trademark acts and rights at common law for trademarks.

What happens when trademarks conflict?

If it appears that the trademark owner is entitled to registration, the mark is published in the official Patent Office publication. When, however, an application is made for the registration of a trademark that is substantially

identical with a trademark already registered for other goods, or has such close similarity to a mark already in use as to be likely to be mistaken for it, it is termed an interference. For the purpose of determining priority rights under such circumstances, any person believing his rights damaged may oppose the registration of the mark by filing a statement of the grounds on which he bases his objections.

If the trademark will not result in confusion, the Commissioner has the duty to grant registration. But where the prior user shows that his interests would be injured by the registration of the mark, then the opposition will be sustained and registration refused.

In court actions for infringement of a trademark, as the United States Circuit Court of Appeals for the Second Circuit, which covers New York, Connecticut, and Vermont, recently stated, many factors are taken into consideration:

"The prior owner's chance of success is a function of many variables: the strength of his mark, the degree of similarity between the two marks, the proximity of the products, the likelihood that the prior owner will bridge the gap, actual confusion, and the reciprocal of defendant's good faith in adopting its own mark, the quality of defendant's product, and the sophistication of the buyers. Even this extensive catalogue does not exhaust the possibilities—the court may have to take still other variables into account."

Patents   An inventor has a right, separate and distinct from any rights under the Patent Law, not only to use and sell his invention but to deprive the public of its use by keeping his invention a secret. He will be protected by the courts in this right, which we shall discuss further along in this chapter.

Aside from his right in a secret process or invention, any exclusive right to the production and sale of an invention can be secured by an inventor only from the government through letters patent.

The law states that (a) "any new and useful process, machine, manufacture, or composition of matter, or any new and useful improvement thereof," (b) any asexually reproduced "distinct and new variety of plant other than a tuberpropagated plant" and (c) "any new, original or ornamental design for an article of manufacture" can be patented.

No patent can be obtained for any method or device that lacks the essential feature of innovation or discovery. The mere alteration of shape or form is not sufficient.

In an interesting situation reported in the press, an application for a patent to raise sunken ships by pumping polystyrene foam pellets into compartments of the ship's hull in order to displace water until the buoyancy was sufficient to raise the hull, was thwarted by Donald Duck. It seems that a while before in a Donald Duck comic strip a similar method was used but instead of polystyrene it was ping pong balls. Accordingly, there was nothing novel or original to the basis of a patent.

In relation to designs, the thing to be patented must have the essential feature of novelty. The term for a design patent is at most 14 years, while for a regular patent it is 17 years.

The right to a patent is granted by Congress only to the inventor, and letters patent issued to one who is not the inventor are void. In order for anyone to be the original inventor, he must have conceived it. However, a mere conception of the mind is not an invention, and it does not become an invention or a patentable object until it is represented by some physical implement demonstrating its practical efficiency and utility. The idea must be reduced to a thing. Mere suggestions are not inventions.

The obtaining of a patent is by an application for letters patent to the Commissioner of Patents in Washington. The application must be in writing, signed by the inventor or by his representative, and must consist of a petition, specifications, oath, and drawings, together with a fee of $65.

Patent applications and claims for patents are complex and written in a manner which requires special knowledge. A patent attorney should be consulted in this connection.

The petition must be addressed to the Commissioner of Patents, must be written in English, and must state the name, residence, and post office address of the petitioner. It must designate by title the invention sought to be patented, contain a reference to the specifications for a full disclosure of the invention, and be signed by the applicant or his representative.

The specifications must be a written description of the invention and point out the part or combination which is claimed the discovery. The patent may be assigned by its owner to another person, but a record of the transfer should be promptly filed with the Patent Office. If not filed within three months, the assignment is void against a later innocent assignee who paid something of value.

Literary property and copyright

The exclusive right of printing or otherwise multiplying copies of an intellectual production and publishing and selling them is defined as copyright. This right is available, however, only by virtue of the provisions of the Copyright Act. Under the law this exclusive right is granted to the author—not only to make copies and sell them, but to translate, dramatize, perform, represent, or deliver dramatizations in public, or to make records or means for their mechanical reproduction.

Further, under the common law, which is now reinforced by the Copyright Act, an author has a property right in his work before it is published. He will be granted relief by the courts against anyone who either deprives him of that right or, by fraudulently obtaining possession of the results of his work, attempts to use or publish it without his consent.

The first Federal Copyright Act was enacted by Congress in 1790 and the last comprehensive revision in 1909; this law, with its amendments and modifications, still continues in force. Copyright protection has been continually extended. Besides both the published and unpublished works of an author, it now includes books, maps, charts, dramatic and musical compositions, engravings, cuts, prints, photographs and their negatives, paintings, drawings, chromos, statuary, and medals or designs.

Until recently there was no copyright in a recording because the recording was not considered a work in itself, but only a means of reproduction. As McLuhan has said, ''the Medium becomes the Message,'' and so ''sound recordings'' published after February 15, 1972 are protected.

While musical compositions, in order to be copyrighted, must be original, copyright is not confined to productions that are essentially new, but may be extended to any arrangement or adaptation of older compositions. The arrangement for a pianoforte of an orchestral score of an opera is an original composition within the purview of this law.

The size of a painting is not material, nor whether any pictorial production is a work of art. Nor will the fact that a work of art is also utilitarian prevent it from being copyrightable.

There is no power under the Constitution by which Congress may grant a perpetual copyright. The term for which this right has been granted has always in the United States been divided into an original and a renewal period. The statute provides for a 28-year term with a renewal for a further period of the same length obtained by filing for it in the twenty-eighth year of the first term.

The Congress of the United States has been considering legislation to revamp completely the Copyright Act of 1909, to, among other things, change the term of copyright for new works to the life of the author plus 50 years in order to accord with the European practice, and to extend the copyright term in subsisting works to 75 years. For this reason, there have been extensions of the renewal term for works still protected by statutory copyright so that they would not go into the public domain in the meantime. This extension has run from September 19, 1962 to December 31, 1972 thus far. The extension applies only to works already in the renewal term. This means that if you are interested in copying without permission a work in the public domain in the United States, you must look to see when it was first copyrighted. As a rule of thumb, if it was in 1905 or before, you are safe to use it. Adding 56 years (28-year first term and 28-year possible renewal term) to 1905 gives us 1961, and the extension did not start until September 19, 1962.

Copyright forms and instructions are available from the Register of Copyrights, Library of Congress, Washington, D.C. For registering a work published in the United States, the form must be filled out and sent with two copies of the work and six dollars.

Copyright is actually obtained for a published work by the fact of making the work available to the general public and by providing therein a proper copyright notice, which for a book consists of the word "Copyright" or letter "c" in a circle, thus, ©, plus the year of publication and the name of the copyright owner. This notice must be in the appropriate place, which for a book is the title page or page thereafter. For a sound recording you use the letter "p" in a circle, thus, ℗.

An improper copyright notice invalidates the copyright. Copyright registration in Washington, D.C., is a mere formality coming after copyright has been obtained as described.

The letter "c" in a circle, ©, gives protection under the Universal Copyright Convention (U.C.C.) which came into force September 16, 1955, to which the United States and now some 60 other countries are parties. The so-called Communist bloc countries are not members except for Hungary. A work first published in countries which are not members of the U.C.C. and with which the United States has no treaty, is not protected in the United States.

An interesting example of this involved Shostakovich, the famous Russian composer. Because we have no treaty with Russia, his music had no copyright protection in the United States. Twentieth Century-Fox used his music as background in the movie "Iron Curtain" about Soviet espionage in Canada. He could not stop its use by means of copyright law so he tried to claim that his reputation was being injured, because he, a Soviet citizen, had his music used in an anti-Soviet film. However, his action was unsuccessful.

The right of ownership

The ownership of property, whether the property be real or personal, carries with it the right to exclude others from its possession, use, or enjoyment. The right of ownership is a right guaranteed by the Fifth and Fourteenth Amendments of the United States Constitution. The Fifth Amendment protects against the United States and the Fourteenth Amendment protects against the individual states.

Stolen property cannot be transferred

Certificates of railroad stock standing in the name of two children were pledged by their guardian with a bank at Pittsfield for a loan on behalf of the children. Three days after the loan was made, the cashier of this bank stole the certificates and pledged them elsewhere as security for a loan to himself.

Five months later the guardian paid her loan and left, as she supposed, the stock certificates in the custody of the bank. A year later the persons holding these certificates as collateral for the cashier's loan sought to transfer them to their own names. This was refused because of the lack of a court order permitting such a disposition of the stock by the guardian who had endorsed them. They then asked the cashier to obtain the necessary probate decree authorizing the sale of the stock. This he did by forging the petition, and by this fraud the stock was transferred.

Two years later the cashier committed suicide and his theft of the stock certificates was disclosed. The children owned the stock. They had never parted with its ownership. Those who had made the loan to the cashier pleaded their right, but they could not secure ownership from a thief who held no title. "A bona fide purchaser for value from one who has taken property in such a way acquires no title to it," said the court, decreeing in the children's favor.

Title to stolen money

The rule in most jurisdictions, that the owner of personal property cannot lose title without his consent, has been the law for more than 500 years. There is, however, an exception to this rule for currency and negotiable instruments. One who has given value to acquire stolen money or negotiable instruments and who took the stolen property honestly, without knowledge that it was stolen, normally acquires the right to that property.

Stolen bankbook

In a recent case that went to the highest court in the state of New York, a marine engineering officer, returning from a voyage, stayed at a hotel in New York City, and on awakening discovered that his personal effects had been tampered with and that, among other things, his bankbook for an account with a New York City bank had been stolen. First thing the next morning he appeared at the bank to inform them and discovered that $12,000 had been withdrawn from his account. He sued the bank for the money, and the defense was that the signature had been carefully compared and found virtually identical with the one on file before the payment was made.

Unlike the situation with a negotiable instrument, where those who honor such a signature do so at their own peril and are accountable to the person whose name is forged, in the absence of legislation, the rule for a bankbook is whether the bank was negligent. The jury decided in favor of the depositor, and the bank appealed. The highest court in the state of New York stated that evidence merely of comparison of signatures was not sufficient, and that under the circumstances the withdrawal of $12,000 out of a balance of $12,700 required that the bank establish that they followed prudent banking practices, which would involve additional inquiries, comparison of personal data in its records, etc.

When personal property becomes real property

Property often lies astride the boundary line set by law between real and personal property. A dwelling built on a permanent foundation is unquestionably real property. The material of which the building is constructed was personal property before it was assembled into a building. The point when it ceases to be in one class and becomes property in the other is carefully indicated by the law, but so many special cases arise that special interpretations are often required.

The general rule   The general rule used to determine whether fixtures are a part of the real estate or are chattels is demonstrated in the following case.

The owner of a house bought a heating furnace under an installment contract providing that the seller owned the heater until the price was fully paid. This contract also stated that the heater remained personal property and did not become a part of the house in which it was installed until payment was completed. The owner of the house failed to make the payments not only on this contract but on the mortgage on the house which he owned.

The seller's efforts to recover this heating plant met with the opposition of the owner of the mortgage, who claimed the furnace was a part of the house by which his mortgage was secured. In its decision that the furnace was a part of the real estate and beyond the power of the conditional seller to recover, the court gave three tests by which it could be determined when property thus attached to land or a building becomes real estate and loses its character as personal property.

First, the property must be annexed to the land.

Second, it must have "an appropriate application to the use of purpose of the realty to which it is attached."

Third, the owner must have an actual or apparent intention to make it a permanent part of the realty.

Is it detachable?   A gasoline tank and pump used by a garage were not the property of a purchaser of the land on which they were situated. The removal of the tank, said the court, could be effected by digging, and of the pump by unscrewing a few bolts. The equipment was neither essential nor a permanent part of the garage of which it was an adjunct, as was the heating plant in the previous case.

In general, the rule in the majority of states is that if the attached property (such as heating plant, refrigerator, stove, air condiooner, lighting fixtures, etc.) can be detached from the building without damage to the land or building, then it keeps its character as personal property and does not become real estate by reason of its original installation.

A rather interesting question regarding this issue was recently decided by a New York court. That court ruled that the rights in a cooperative apartment were personal property, not real property, since they were to terminate after a certain number of years. See the chapter on real property.

Ideas as personal property

Under some circumstances ideas are property, and the owner of an idea is entitled to protection against its exploitation by others. A leading case which established this principle declared that "when an idea, which may be neither patentable nor subject to copyright is more than a mere abstraction, and is reduced to detailed form, and is novel, the law gives effect to a property right in it." Here there is a striking analogy between the ownership of ideas and the ownership of wild animals. Capture an animal in the woods and keep it in a cage—then it is your property and no one but yourself has a right to its possession. But let the animal escape to the woods whence it came, and it again becomes the property of whoever takes it for his own.

Secret ideas or processes which are undisclosed to the public and "know-how" withheld in confidence by its possessors are similar in the application of the law. The employees of an organization engaged in chemical research had the exclusive possession and knowledge of secret formulas for production. Some of the employees engaged in the use of these formulas left the company and organized a competing business. Commenting on their use of these secrets, a New York court pointed out the well-established law that property rights exist in secret formulas and former employes who learned them in confidence would be enjoined from their use in competition with the owner. In the absence of a prior agreement to the contrary, an owner of a shop or factory generally owns the right to the use of any discoveries made by his employees while they are working for him. To preserve these property rights, however, the processes and formulas must be kept secret. When a knowledge of them comes into the possession of the general public, the property right evaporates. The right of a person to his ideas as property so long as they are secret or fended from public exploitation by agreements to that end is illustrated by a decision of the highest court of New York State some years ago in an action brought against the Equitable Life Assurance Society for their use of an advertising idea where ownership of the idea was claimed by another. The suit was unsuccessful, for the plaintiff had revealed his idea before making any agreement with the Society.

In this case, the essentials that must exist for an exclusive property right in ideas were outlined as follows: "Without denying that there may be property in an idea or trade system or secret, it is obvious that its originator or proprietor must himself protect it from escape or discovery.

If it cannot be sold or negotiated or used without discovery, it would seem proper that some contract should guard or regulate the disclosure. Otherwise it must follow the law of ideas and become the acquisition of whoever receives it.''

Courts have ruled that by revealing an idea on a confidential basis the originator does not lose his rights in it.

If you wish to protect a valuable idea, therefore, be sure that it is not disclosed to the prospective user until you have entered into a contract providing for your compensation on its use. An attorney should be consulted immediately, if you have a valuable idea or secret, which another person is using without your permission.

Discoveries and inventions

This same rule of law governs the ownership of discoveries and inventions. A suit was brought to prevent the use of certain inventions in petroleum production by competitors. While the process may not be one entitled to protection as a patent, suggested the court, it may still be entitled to protection as a trade secret.

Facts of great value, like a lost purse on the highway, declared the court, may lie long unnoticed upon the public commons. Hundreds pass them by until one more observant than the rest makes a discovery. The inventor and the discoverer are both entitled to protection, one by the patent law, the other by injunction against the violation of this secrecy by which the owner holds his discovery in captivity. However, protection is given only against those who have learned the secret because of a confidential relationship with its owner. There is no protection against a person who honestly and through independent investigation acquires the same secret.

One of the early decisions in this country was that a "secret art" is property and that a contract can be made that the receiver of any knowledge of this "secret art" will not divulge his information.

Registered mail

One of the problems is proving that you created your idea at the date you claim and also in showing what was in the idea. One way to do this and keep a record of it, is to enclose a copy of your expressed idea in an envelope and send it to yourself by registered mail. When received, the registered letter is put away in a safe place without breaking the Post Office seals on the envelope. The date on the envelope will show that the content was conceived and at least expressed by that date and the seals will demonstrate that the content was then as you now claim and not a later substitution.

Are crops personal property?

While crops are growing, they are land. When they are harvested, they are personal property.

Growing crops ordinarily pass with a conveyance of the land. They may, however, be sold separately from the land as may standing timber. A lawsuit was brought in Arkansas against the Western Union Telegraph Company for damages to crops. A levee had been weakened because a hole was dug in it for a pole to hold the wires of the company. As a consequence the riverbank gave way and the overflowing river destroyed the crops in the adjacent fields.

The company's defense was that the destroyed crops were real property and for that reason the lawsuit must be in the county where the land was located. This contention was sustained by the court in holding that the unmatured crops were part of the land.

If a non-owner raises crops

The law relating to the status of crops raised by one who is not an owner of the land featured in a suit in the state of Washington. Stanfield and Dodge, in possession of land in Chelan County, had raised and harvested a fruit crop which they sold to the Fruit Production Company. In May of that year Harrison had bought this land. While he had never been in actual possession or occupation of the land, he nevertheless gave the Pacific Fruit and Produce Company a chattel mortgage on this growing fruit crop.

In determining the ownership of this crop the court asserted that the owner of the land, when he is not in possession of it and it is cultivated by a stranger, has no right or title to crops harvested before he takes possession; that it makes no difference whether the one growing and harvesting the crops is in possession or is a trespasser.

Can a trespasser own crops?

In Missouri, Claude McCullock raised a seven-acre crop of corn on the land of others. He had been a tenant of a former owner, and continued in possession of the land after its sale in February of the year he raised and harvested this crop.

When the owner of the land sued him for the value of the corn, the court held that McCullock was the owner of the crop. "Where one in possession of land, even as a mere trespasser, cultivates and brings to maturity a crop and severs it from the soil, he thereby becomes the owner of the crop. But if he abandons the possession of the land before the crop is matured and severed from the soil, it then becomes the property of the owner."

Other states, however, have not been as lenient toward such trespassers. In California, for example, all rights which a tenant has to crops he is raising normally end at the time of the termination of his leasehold. In New York, a trespasser does not have a right to possession of the crops he has raised against any party who was an owner of the property while the crops were being grown. He does have title superior to anyone who acquires the property after the crops have been harvested.

Claims and rights of action

The law, we have seen, classifies property as real and personal—land and the improvements that are a part of the land are real property—all other property is personal. Personal property includes not only things themselves—as money, household goods, wearing apparel—but it also includes the right to the possession of these things. Your wages or salary are personal property. The right you have to wages or salaries that are earned but not paid to you is also personal property. Claims for damages or for anything with a money equivalent are also your property. Claims and demands are known in the law as "choses in action," or "things in action."

Certificates of deposit –personal property

The will of an Alabama resident contained the following: "I also will to my said wife all other personal property of which I may die seized or possessed except any notes or mortgages that may be payable to me." Part of the property of this man was certificates of deposit of a local bank, amounting to $6,000. (Certificates of deposit are a bank's written statements or acknowledgments of the deposit of specific sums of money.)

His relative claimed these certificates were notes and mortgages which he had excluded in his will from the property he had bequeathed his wife. The court, however, held them to be personal property represented by a right to the collection of the money at their maturity.

Conditional and installment sales

Goods bought and sold in the usual way belong to the buyer when they are delivered to him. The difference between an ordinary sale and a conditional sale is that by a conditional sale the goods do not belong to the buyer until he has paid for them, and the contract for the sale states this. The buyer has possession of the article but the seller owns it. It is his security for the price the buyer has agreed to pay.

If you do not keep up installments

The remedies of the seller when the buyer's payments are not made as agreed are: (1) the seller may retake the property and end the contract; (2) he may retake the property, sell it, apply the proceeds of the sale to the amount remaining unpaid and sue for the balance, if any; or (3) he may bring a lawsuit for the unpaid balance.

What is a chattel mortgage?

A chattel mortgage is a mortgage on personal property. Like the conditional sales agreement, it is often used by a seller to obtain the payment of the purchase price by the buyer.

The following provision or its equivalent will usually be found in chattel mortgages: "For the purpose of securing payment of the amount set forth herein, the mortgagor does hereby grant, bargain, sell and mortgage unto the said mortgagee the above described property, provided that if said mortgagor shall well and truly pay the said sum, then this instrument shall be void, otherwise to remain in full force and effect."

Some states also require that certain specific information be included in all chattel mortgages. Before any such document is prepared, care should be taken to see that it is not unenforcable because of failure to comply with the technical requirements of the jurisdiction in which it is drawn.

Why recording is necessary

A chattel mortgage leaves legal title with the mortgagor. It gives the mortgagee only a security title.

Under a conditional sales agreement, the seller may retake the goods. But under a chattel mortgage, if he retakes the property, he normally sells it and applies the proceeds of the sale to the unpaid balance and then brings suit for whatever remains unpaid. This unpaid balance may include the costs of reclaiming, storing, and reselling the property.

Care should be taken, when the document creating the chattel mortgage is drawn, to make it clear that it is indeed a chattel mortgage and not a conditional sales contract.

In 1952, a Uniform Commercial Code was approved by the National

Conference of Commissioners on Uniform State Laws, who work to improve and to simplify the state statutes in various fields. The purpose of this Code was to simplify, clarify, and modernize the laws governing commercial transactions. Over the years, it has been adopted in every state of the Union, and in the Virgin Islands. In New York State, its effective date was September 27, 1964, which made it applicable to all business transactions entered into or occurring after that date. Instruments or agreements, such as chattel mortgages and conditional sales contracts, are now "security agreements."

The statutes in most of the states require that, when security agreements, conditional sales or chattel mortgages are made, that the contract or a copy be filed on the public record as directed by the statutes. Unless it is recorded in this way, the seller loses any rights he has to retake possession of his property if it is seized or levied on by others for the buyer's debts.

The place of record is generally the office of the village, town, or county clerk, or the office where deeds and mortgages of real estate are recorded.

What happens when a conditional sales agreement is not recorded is illustrated by a case that occurred in Colorado.

A bond and mortgage company bought $1,000 worth of office furniture under a conditional sales contract, paying $300 down and agreeing to pay the balance in monthly installments of $56.

The landlord of the building the company occupied had inserted a clause in his lease that he had a lien for any unpaid rent on all the tenant's property. The company neglected to pay the furniture merchant and overlooked paying the landlord. The landlord changed the lock on the office door and took the furniture. Thereupon the furniture merchant sued the landlord for his furniture.

The merchant had failed, however, to put his conditional sales agreement on record. For that reason, as far as the landlord was concerned, the agreement whereby the merchant reserved the right of retaking his goods was void. For his remissness, the merchant, and not the landlord, suffered the loss.

Because of many consumer complaints of advantage being taken by sellers, the law in a number of states is now in a state of flux on the right of sellers to enforce the sales contract. See further on this subject in Chapter 19 on Loans, Lenders, and Credit.

One of the problems has been that of the "holder in due course" or the "bona fide purchaser." Suppose you are sold shoddy merchandise under a chattel mortgage periodic payment plan with notes that you signed for payment. When the time comes for you to make a payment, you refuse and stand ready to defend on the ground that the merchandise is almost worthless. However, you find that you are sued on your notes by a bank that acquired the notes by paying your seller for them. You cannot raise the defense against this bona fide purchaser, and so you have the burden of starting a suit against the original sellers if you can find them. Some states like New Jersey are changing this rule and making the bona fide purchaser in this kind of a situation subject to the defenses you would have had against the original sellers.

Another problem is the door-to-door salesman who catches you off-guard and makes a quick sale. You now in some states, like New York, have a period of time to cancel the agreement on more mature and reflective thought.

Cognovit note

The United States Supreme Court recently declared that a "cognovit note" did not violate the provision of the Fourteenth Amendment to the U.S. Constitution which prevents deprivation of property without due process of law.

The cognovit is an ancient legal device by which a debtor consents in advance to the holder's obtaining a judgment without notice of hearing and possibly even with the appearance on the debtor's behalf of an attorney designated by the holder. The idea of it is to permit the holder of a note to obtain a judgment without trial on possible defenses which the signer of the note might assert. It is somewhat similar to a "confession of judgment." The cognovit note goes back to the time of Blackstone and was even mentioned by Charles Dickens in his "Pickwick Papers." There has been a great deal of critical comment with respect to it because it means that the debtor is waiving the opportunity to raise proper legal questions and defenses against the collection of the note. Some states specifically authorize the cognovit, such as Ohio from which the challenge arose to its constitutionality on which the U.S. Supreme Court ruled. Other states disallow it and some make it a crime to have it signed, for example, Indiana, New Mexico, and Rhode Island. The majority of states, for example, Connecticut, Michigan, and Minnesota, however, regulate its use, and many prohibit the device in small loans and consumer sales, because that is where it has its most objectionable use. The U. S. Supreme Court stated that the use of such a note was not per se unconstitutional, where the facts of the commercial transaction showed that there was a proper use of it. However, the Court indicated that the debtor should still have an opportunity, even if in a separate action, to raise his claims against the creditor. Also, it stated that if there were defenses such as prior payment or mistaken identity, those could be asserted in any event.

Abandonment of property

Personal property is considered to be abandoned when two conditions are satisfied: (1) the owner intends to abandon the property, and (2) he actually leaves or throws it away. Under such circumstances the property belongs to whoever finds it.

When crops are abandoned

A tenant of land in Texas abandoned the land he had been farming together with a crop of unpacked cotton. Another man picked and marketed this crop and was held by the court rightfully entitled to the proceeds. The abandonment of the crop had divested the owner of his title, and the finder could hold it as his own.

Who owns a derelict vessel?

The sinking of the schooner *Willis* on Lake Erie long ago is a famous example of the application of the law of abandonment. A November storm sweeping over the lake wrecked the schooner six miles from the shore in 60 feet of water. The owners gave up all hope of saving either the boat or its cargo. Nine months later, others located and raised the ship, finding on board $865. The ship, said the court, was a derelict, and belonged to the first finder who took possession of her.

Found property

Another famous illustration of the law of the right of finders to claim lost property as their own occurred in Alabama before the Civil War. The law announced at that time is still the law of this country. A slave boy found a package of the banknotes of the bank at Huntsville, Alabama, and promptly delivered them to an official of the bank. Later the bank refused to surrender this money to the slave's owner, but in the subsequent suit it was adjudged the owner's property.

Loser and finder

In another famous case, a chimney sweep found a diamond and took it to a goldsmith. The stone was "a jewel of the finest water." The goldsmith offered the boy three cents for the ten-carat gem. This the boy refused and asked the return of his diamond. The goldsmith refused to give it up and the boy sued. The decision, which has been adopted as authority since that time, laid down the law "that the finder of the jewel, though he does not by such finding acquire an absolute property or ownership, yet he has such property as will enable him to keep it against all but the rightful owner." This subject of lost property is discussed at length in another chapter.

The care you owe another's proprety

The kind of care required of someone in the possession of another's personal property has been defined as follows: (1) extreme care, when the use of the property is solely for the benefit of the one to whom it is loaned; (2) ordinary care, when it is for the benefit of both owner and user; and (3) nominal care, with a liability only for gross negligence, when the property is put into the custody of one not the owner solely for the benefit of the owner.

Your responsibility for rented property

Road contractors in Massachusetts rented construction machinery. While this property was in use, they claimed it continually "broke down." On return of the equipment to the owners, parts were found broken, others missing, and the entire machinery was in serious disrepair.

The owner of the machinery, asserted the court, was entitled to the return of his machinery in as good condition as it was when leased to the contractor except for "ordinary wear and tear." When the contractor failed to return it in that condition he became liable for the repairs necessitated by his improper use of the property.

The hirer is not an insurer

On the other hand, when you rent personal property from another, you are not an insurer of that property against loss of any character, except that which occurs through your own neglect. You are obliged, however, to use the ordinary diligence of a prudent man in the care of the property.

If property in your care is stolen

An old legal adage says that one who has in his custody the property of another is not liable for "thefts, acts of God or the public enemy, or where goods are taken by violence." This old rule has been somewhat modified, but it is still the law—the user of another's personal property is not an insurer against loss by theft or fire.

The owner of an automobile left his car in a garage on a Saturday.

Monday morning the car was found overturned in a ditch in a neighboring town.

The garage proprietor, the preceding week, had hired a 16-year-old boy. He had inquired of the boy's former employer and had been told that the boy was "Absolutely O.K. as far as he was concerned. Good worker. No trouble as to dishonesty and would rehire him if he needed help."

This boy and two others had broken into the garage, found the ignition key to the car, and driven it to a nearby town, where they turned it over in a ditch and left it. The next morning they were arrested by the state police.

The garage owner was exonerated of any liability to the car owner for the theft and damage. Saturday he had closed and locked his garage. No one was in the building when he left. The boys had entered by the commission of an act of burglary in forcing open the window. The garage owner was not an insurer of the car, but liable only for the exercise of reasonable and prudent care, which he had used.

Damage to another's property by fire

The owner of a nightclub at Evansville, Wyoming, rented a roulette table, checks, chairs, dice table, "21" table, and other furnishings for the club. Later the building was destroyed by fire and the rented gambling paraphernalia badly damaged. The court absolved the nightclub owner of any liablilty, basing its decision on the universally accepted rule that "A hirer is bound only to ordinary or reasonable care."

Goods placed in the care of a person other than their owner require the same care the custodian would exercise over his own property. If he fails to return them, or returns them in a damaged condition, it is his duty to furnish an explanation of what has happened. But if the loss or damage does not arise as a consequence of his negligence, the owner himself must bear the loss.

Power of attorney

To handle your property, or to act for you in other ways, you may appoint an agent orally or in writing. It is preferable to have a power of attorney, which may be executed in substantially the form given below, as an official authorization of your agent.

Any person who is legally capable to act for himself may act as an attorney. Of course this excludes an incompetent or mentally ill person. Children may act as agents, too, provided they have reached the age of discretion.

The person given the power of attorney acts in your place. He has your authority. It is, legally, as though he were you. His powers are limited, however, by the actual authorization, which may restrict them to the performance of one or two acts in your behalf, or many, depending on how you word the power of attorney. Within these limits, you are liable for the acts performed by the person who holds the document.

Your power of attorney should be signed and witnessed. It should state precisely what powers you are transferring to your attorney or agent. It is advisable that the document be notarized. The laws of certain states require this for transactions in real estate.

An attorney's power to act for his principal may be revoked by giving notice to him. Persons who are dealing with the attorney should also be notified of the revocation, if the acts defined by the document have not yet been concluded. If you do not notify all concerned in a revocation, you may be responsible for any acts your attorney performs honestly under the power conveyed to him.

A power of attorney is revoked automatically by the death of his principal, by conclusion of the acts described in the document, or by the expiration of any limit of time set forth in the document. If the principal is declared incompetent, revocation is likewise automatic.

Form of power of attorney

KNOW ALL MEN BY THESE PRESENTS, that I, *Charles E. Brown, of the Borough of Manhattan, City and State of New York,* have made, constituted, and appointed and by these presents do make, constitute, and appoint *Henry DeWitt,* of *the said place* my true and lawful attorney for me and in my name, place and stead, to do *(state here matters in which authority is granted)*, giving and granting unto my said attorney full power and authority to do and perform all and every act and thing whatsoever requisite and necessary to be done in and about the premises as fully to all intents and purposes as I the said *Charles E. Brown*, might or could do if personally present, hereby ratifying and confirming all that my said attorney shall lawfully do or cause to be done by virtue hereof.

IN WITNESS WHEREOF I have hereunto set my hand and seal the *6th day of June, 1972*.

Charles E. Brown (Seal)

Sealed and delivered in the presence of:
George Murphy
State of New York
County of New York

On this *6th day of June, 1972*, before me *Stephanie E. Kupferman*, a Notary Public in and for the State of New York, duly commissioned and sworn, personally came and appeared *Charles E. Brown*, to me personally known and known to me to be the same person described in and who executed the foregoing power of attorney and he acknowledged the within Power of Attorney to be his free act and deed.

In testimony whereof, I have hereunto subscribed my name and affixed my seal of office the day and year last above written.

Stephanie E. Kupferman

Notarial Seal
Notary Public

How to use a proxy In the conduct of stockholders' meetings in a corporation, every holder of stock has a vote for each of his shares. Often it is difficult for the individual stockholder to attend the meetings personally. In order that his vote can be taken in the election of directors and in other matters requiring the consent of the stockholders, he is permitted to execute a proxy in the following form, allowing another to represent him and his interests. In other words, a proxy is a power of attorney for the purpose of voting. It may be restricted to one meeting or more by inserting the necessary words in the following form. It should be witnessed and, if required, notarized.

Form of proxy Know all men by these presents, that I, *Charles E. Brown,* do hereby constitute and appoint *Henry DeWitt* attorney and agent for me and in my name, place, and stead to vote as my proxy at *any election of Directors of the Transatlantic Corporation,* according to the number of votes I should be entitled to cast if then personally present.

In witness whereof I have hereunto set my hand and seal this *6th day of June, 1958.*

Charles E. Brown (Seal)

Signed and delivered in the presence of:
George Murphy

Income taxes Incomes are taxed by the Federal government and, in many localities, by state governments as well. As a rule all income is taxed, subject, however, to such exemptions and deductions as the statutes permit. The deductions and exemptions should be checked each year before filing a return, since some changes in the statute since the last tax return was filed may have been made by Congress or the state legislature.

The gross income subject to these taxes is defined by the Federal statute as "all income from whatever source derived (including but not limited to the following items):" (1) Compensation for services, including fees, commissions, and similar items; (2) Gross income derived from business; (3) Gains derived from dealings in property; (4) Interest; (5) Rents; (6) Royalties; (7) Dividends; (8) Alimony and separate maintenance payments; (9) Annuities; (10) Income from life insurance and endowment contracts; (11) Pensions; (12) Income from discharge of indebtedness; (13) Distributive share of partnership gross income; (14) Income in respect of a decedent; and (15) Income from an interest in an estate or trust.

Deductions and exemptions must be carefully itemized in your tax returns. Records and receipts should be kept as part of your permanent files, since they may be required by the authorities to confirm your statements.

The following checklist includes the deductions from taxable income that are subject to such legislative changes as may from time to time be made.

Interest–
Interest paid or accrued within the taxable year by the taxpayer is deductible from income, except as otherwise provided.

Alimony–
It is generally held to be deductible from a spouse's income when paid by a court decree or as an incident to court proceedings. When paid by private agreement, it is only deductible for agreements made after August 16, 1954, when the law was changed to allow it.

Business Expenses–
A wage-earner's expenses, if necessary in his employment, may be deducted. For example, the cost of business cards that his employer does not compensate him for, may be deducted. Expenses paid or incurred in the conduct of a business are generally deductible provided they relate to the business and are directly connected with its conduct. Money paid during the tax year for the production and collection of income or in the management and maintaining of property is generally deductible. For example, the charge for a safe-deposit box, if it is used to store income-producing securities, may be deducted.

Attorney Fees–
When fees paid to lawyers are an ordinary and necessary business expense, or are for the conduct and management of a business, such payments are generally deductible.

Wages— Compensation paid to employees for services as an ordinary business expense are deductible. In some instances, where such payments are bonuses or pensions, these, too, are deductible. Mere gratuities, however, or payments of this character made for purposes other than the conduct of a business, are generally not permitted as deductions. The right to deductions of this kind extends to extra and additional compensation, provided always that it is incurred as a usual and necessary expense of the business.

Contributions— Contributions made by the taxpayer to bona fide charitable, educational, or scientific institutions are deductible within certain limits. They must be carefully itemized in your returns, which should state the name and address of the organization, and how much was contributed. Keep receipts or canceled checks so that you can later prove your contributions.

Entertainment— In the same manner as other expenses, travel and entertainment costs are generally deductible when they are necessary business expenses and made in good faith.

Rents— Payments made as rent for property used in the carrying on of a business are deductible expenses provided the taxpayer lacks title to, or any equity in, the property.

Losses— Deductible losses, which include various types of business and noncommercial losses, must be losses incurred during the taxable year and be actually realized during that year. The mere possibility of loss is insufficient. The actual loss must be determined. Losses incurred in a given year may be "carried back" or "carried over" for a certain number of years. A qualified attorney or accountant should be consulted to determine the most advantageous method of applying losses against the income of prior or future years.

Loss to Property— Loss from the destruction of nonbusiness property or damage to its value—except where the loss is what may be classified as a steady deterioration—is generally deductible from income. Deductions over depreciation are allowable for property used for business or other income-producing purposes. Losses incurred through theft or embezzlement are deductible if the loss was incurred directly by the taxpayer. Losses from theft are considered to have occurred in the year that the loss was discovered. Losses incurred through illegal loans and similar instances of this character are not items that may be deducted from income. Wagering losses are allowed, but only to the extent of the income that which a taxpayer gains from wagering during the year that the losses were incurred.

Taxes–

Debts or parts of debts owed to the taxpayer which become worthless during the taxable year are deductible, but the taxpayer must strictly comply with the statute in the ascertainment of the character of those debts as well as the year in which the deduction may be taken.

Certain taxes are allowable deductions to be applied to the year in which they are paid or accrued. The taxpayer should secure definite information on which taxes are deductible, and which are not, under the applicable statute.

Social Security

Almost every kind of employment, including self-employment, is covered by social security. Some occupations, however, are covered only if certain conditions are met. Earnings for domestic workers, for example, are covered to the extent that they exceed $50 for any employer during a calendar quarter. Farm employees are covered if, during a year, they work at least 20 days and their employer pays them $150 or more. Your local Social Security Office will answer any questions regarding eligibility.

What Social Security benefits are paid?

Monthly Retirement Benefits–

These are payable in full at age 65, and reduced benefits are available at age 62, to persons whose income does not exceed the maximum limit established by the government. You do not have to stop working to become eligible. The maximum limit is subject to change and your Social Security Office should also be consulted on this matter.

Monthly Survivor Benefits–

These are payable to the following relatives of a deceased person who had been paying his social security premiums:
(1) the widow when she reaches 62 (or as early as 60 in a reduced amount);
(2) the unmarried children who are under 18 (under 22, if they are full-time students);
(3) the children 18 or over if they become disabled before age 18 and continue to be disabled;
(4) the widow at any age if she is caring for a child under 18 (or a child 18 or over who became disabled before he reached 18);
(5) the widow as early as age 50 if she has a severe disability;
(6) the dependent parents who are 62 or over;

(7) the dependent widower at 62 or over, or as early as age 50 if he is disabled.

Monthly Disability Benefits— These are payable, before age 65, to a person with a severe disability that has lasted or is expected to last at least 12 months. The spouse and children of the disabled person may also be eligible for benefits.

What is Medicare?

Medicare is a two-part health insurance program for older persons. Everyone age 65 or older who gets monthly social security or railroad retirement benefits automatically has the hospital insurance portion of Medicare. This portion helps pay for hospital care and certain follow-up services. Those people who reach age 65 after 1967 who are not eligible for the monthly benefits of social security may still qualify for this portion of Medicare if they were covered by social security for a certain number of months. Again, your Social Security Office should be consulted for current specific regulations.

The second part of Medicare helps pay bills for services of doctors and for a number of other medical items and services. No prior coverage is necessary for these benefits.

Is there a right to one's privacy?

Many states have adopted laws which grant certain protections to individuals to enable them to maintain control over knowledge about them. A magazine once published an unauthorized, somewhat embarrassing, photograph of a female movie personality in connection with a false story regarding a crime which was unrelated to the picture. The photograph was authentic but it was not one which the magazine would have been able to take if it had not used devious means. In a suit for damages by the movie

star, the court ruled that the actress' right of privacy had been invaded, since the picture was unauthorized and could not have been taken in public. If it were merely an unauthorized photograph of her taken on the street, her right of privacy would not have been invaded.

Several jurisdictions now also have laws which prohibit the unauthorized use of a person's name to promote the trade or business of another. A famous football player, for example, would have a claim in these jurisdictions that his privacy was invaded, if a company claimed that the player used its product although he never gave his permission to make that claim.

The privacy right has also been extended to protect people from unauthorized tapping of their phones or eavesdropping and from having others peering into their homes.

Limitations on the privacy right

In a much publicized case, Notre Dame University tried to prevent the release of a book and a movie which portrayed the students and administration of the University in a farcical manner. The Notre Dame president was given passing mention twice in the book and the students were consistently portrayed as fools. The court said that in this case there was no privacy right invaded. The mere use of the name of a person is not protected, unless it is employed in a manner which indicates something bad about the person; therefore, the Notre Dame president had no privacy right violated. The Court there felt that "viewers know they are not seeing the real Notre Dame, (and) there is nothing in the film from which they could infer anything about the institution." It was ruled that the privacy right of Notre Dame, as an institution, was not violated merely by the use of its name. The privacy right of the University could only have been violated if its name were used publicly in a manner which would have been offensive or objectionable.

What special rights do veterans have?

The Federal government has devised a system which grants special privileges to those who have served in the armed forces. These include educational assistance to veterans, or to the spouse and children of diseased or completely disabled veterans, special loan guarantees for purchases of homes, and disability benefits. There are also insurance payments for the families of deceased veterans. The particular rules covering all these areas change periodically. All inquiries regarding these benefits should be made to the local Veterans Administration Office.

CHAPTER 18

Lost Property

Lost property, according to the law of many states, is entirely different from property that is mislaid or left behind unintentionally. In general, the courts hold that property is lost when the owner has deprived himself of its possession by accident, neglect, forgetfulness, or by any other means, without any intention to put it down or abandon it. Property is not "lost," however, when its owner voluntarily puts it down somewhere with the intention of picking it up, and afterwards does not remember where he left it. Such property is mislaid or "left."

As you can readily see, to determine where the dividing line lies between "lost" and "mislaid" property is at times difficult. Basic definitions vary in the laws and decisions of the different states. New York State found the distinction too vague and now treats both lost and mislaid property as "lost" property. Other states still retain the distinction.

A pocketbook was thoughtlessly left by a customer in a barber shop at Lebanon, Tennessee. The barber picked up the pocketbook, spent the money in it, and was arrested and convicted of larceny. Here the pocketbook was not lost, nor was the barber a finder within the meaning of the law. The pocketbook was "left," not "lost," said the court that tried the case. "To lose is not to place or put anything carefully and voluntarily in the place you intended and then forget it—it is casually and involuntarily to part from the possession."

Who owns lost property? A different situation involving lost property occurred some years ago in Missouri. A wrecking company in Kansas City purchased an old residence and proceeded to demolish it. The demolition work disclosed a metal box that had been concealed in one of the walls. The box held money, gold certificates, and other valuables, with a total value of $12,700. No one knew when or by whom the box had been placed in the wall. In this instance, the box and its contents were unquestionably "lost property." The wrecking company was the finder and entitled to possession.

An old decision sums up the conditions under which lost personal property belongs to the finder. It says that a stray animal or other thing found, to come under the law providing for the disposal of such things, must appear to be without an owner, like the wild animals that range in the forests or fields. Where the owner is known, the strayed animal or other lost thing cannot properly fall within the legal meaning of the term "lost goods."

The general rule is that the finder has a sufficient right of possession to enable him to retain the property against all but the rightful owner. If there are two or more finders, and the original owner is unknown, those who found the property have equal rights in it.

Anyone to whom the finder sells the lost property acquires the same rights in it that the finder had; that is, he has a superior title to it against all but the original owner.

Finding money in the street

On a February afternoon, some years ago, H. L. McDonald, walking along Figueroa Street in Los Angeles, found seven $1,000 bills lying on the sidewalk. He proceeded to the Turf Club, changed one of the bills, made a new acquaintance with whom he was soon fast friends, and told him of his find. Leaving this "friend," he returned to the hotel where he lived, shortly after midnight.

A few minutes later there was a knock at the door. A man named Paul Beach entered, showed a detective's badge, and demanded the money McDonald had found. McDonald surrendered four of the $1,000 bills and told Beach there were no more. The next morning Beach called again with a woman companion whom he introduced as the daughter of the man who had lost the $7,000. McDonald gave up the other $3,000. A few days later Beach was arrested for grand larceny and was convicted and sentenced to prison. The money was the legal property of McDonald since the owner was unknown. He had a right to its possession against all except the true owner.

The finder's duty

While the finder of lost property owns what he has found against all but the true owner, the law places on him the duty of making an effort to discover the true owner. The phrase commonly found in the statutes of the different states is that the finder must make a "reasonable effort" to ascertain who the true owner is. What specific efforts the finder shall make, the statutes either leave to his own judgment and determination of what is a reasonable effort, or they specify the procedure that should be followed in attempting to find the original owner. In any case, the person who finds the property must always take reasonable care to see that the property is maintained in adequate condition.

There is sometimes a penalty attached to failure to comply in those states which require some search for the rightful owner. A typical provision of the law concerning the finder says: "A person who finds lost property under circumstances which give him knowledge or means of inquiring as to the true owner, and who appropriates such property to his own use or to the use of another person who is not entitled thereto without having made every reasonable effort to find the owner and restore the property to him, is guilty of larceny."

A man who was mentally unbalanced, laboring under the delusion that people were trying to take his money from him, drew $600 from a Wisconsin bank, then boarded a train. At a station stop he jumped through the car window, fled along the tracks, and hid the roll of bills under one of the rails. One of those who helped to apprehend the incompetent found this money and retained part of it. He was convicted of larceny.

Who takes charge of mislaid property?

On a public desk in the National Exchange Bank at Albany, New York, a careless depositor left $50 in bills. A man named Loucks picked up the money and gave it to the cashier for safekeeping until it was claimed by the owner. Two years later the money had not been claimed and Loucks demanded its return to him. The bank refused.

Deciding Loucks was not entitled to the money, the court called attention to the distinction made by the law where lost articles have been dropped on a shop floor, left in a public hotel room, or on a railway train. When articles are left in such places under circumstances that suggest that the true owner will later return to claim them, they are not "lost," and the proprietor of the shop or other person in charge is the proper custodian. If the property remains unclaimed, it goes to this custodian.

This right of the person in charge of a place to take custody of, and eventually title to, lost objects found on the premises under his care has its limits. A plain, unmarked, white envelope in which was enclosed $500 in currency was found by the employee of a bank in Toledo, Ohio, on the floor of a lobby near the bank's safe-deposit vaults. She turned the money over to a bank official. Years later she sued the bank for this money.

The money, asserted the court, was found on the floor of an entryway through which passed not only customers of the bank and of the safe-deposit company but those who were customers of neither organization. If a lost object is found in a public or semi-public place, the proprietor, or neighboring proprietor, does not automatically become its custodian on behalf of the true owner. The right of possession and custody of the finder was superior to that of the bank or shopkeeper. This was held to be the law even when the finder is an employee of the owner or proprietor of the premises.

Finders are not always keepers
When lost property is found, it must be taken into custody of the finder. Otherwise the property remains in the public domain, available to the ownership of whoever else claims it.

The steamship *America*, with a cargo of lead, sank in the Mississippi. Between 25 and 30 years later, a wrecker named Brazelton located the wreck. To establish his company's claim, he fastened a buoy to the ship by a weight resting on the submerged hull, postponing the work of raising the vessel until a later period. Before he had taken possession of the property, others took over the wreck and claimed the right to both cargo and ship.

These last claimants were awarded possession of the property under the rule that "To be able to acquire possession of property, two distinct things are required: the intention of possessing it as owner and the corporeal possession of the thing."

Establishing proof of ownership

It is a rule of law that no one can be deprived, without his consent, of lost property he has found in a place common to all—except by the true owner. However, suppose the true owner turns up. He has a claim to his property, but first he must establish his right of ownership. When property in the possession of someone who is not its real owner cannot be readily identified, as, say, an automobile can by its serial number, it is not always easy for the real owner to establish his right. Often, the property in question is money, and there is no proof of ownership except the circumstances under which it has been lost and found.

A World War I veteran, Christopher Williams, was discharged from the Army and confined to a hospital as a tuberculosis patient for eight years, until his death. He lived frugally and saved much of the government compensation he received during these years. Two months before he died he withdrew from the bank $2,112.71 in gold certificates. At his death the hospital authorities took charge of his personal effects, which included an old traveling bag. This bag, with other personal items, was forwarded to his home in Kentucky. Four years later his brother sold the bag to Virgil Baugh.

After Baugh had used the bag for five years, his wife one day appeared at the bank with $1,040 in gold certificates and asked for their exchange into silver certificates. She explained that she had been cleaning an old traveling bag her husband owned. Feeling something bulky in the bottom, she investigated it and found inside the lining a hole covered with adhesive tape and in it $2,140 in $20 and $50 gold certificates. She related the circumstances under which her husband had acquired the bag from Christopher Williams' brother.

The news of the find spread through the town. Then the administrator of the veteran's estate sued to recover the money. The defense was interposed that the money had not actually been identified as Williams' property. However, the evidence of its original ownership was considered by the court as amply establishing the right of the administrator to recover the money.

This incident is typical of many. Lacking positive identification, the owner's proof of possession must rest on circumstantial evidence—the story of the road the property traveled from its disappearance until it was found.

Rewards and expenses of finder

If a reward is offered for the recovery of lost property, the finder who returns the property may sue to collect the reward money. The law considers that a contract exists between the original owner and the finder when the lost item is produced in response to an offer of a reward. Most states, however, do not give the finder a lien on the lost property. He must return the item and then sue if the reward is not paid.

When recompense is made

In the early days, in Oregon, two horses were lost while their owner was crossing the plains. A man named Watts found the horses, but the court refused him any allowance for his expenses or labor in their care. The court declared that no principle of law was better settled than that the finder of lost property could claim no recompense for either his services or his expenses except when this had been promised.

This rule sometimes makes the restoration of lost property to the rightful owner a serious burden. Nor does it become less by a principle announced by another judge: "Where one person gratuitously performs an act of kindness for another, the law, as a general rule, does not recognize the right to compensation for such an act."

In some states, however, statutes have been enacted providing for recompense to finders of lost property for expenses they have incurred in its care and return. In Iowa, for example, originally the laws expressly provided that a finder of lost property was entitled to no reward unless the reward was voluntarily given. A later statute is that the finder is entitled to "ten percent upon the value thereof," and may demand that amount as a condition for the return by him of the property to the owner.

Who owns "treasure trove"?

Treasure trove is money or coin, gold, silver, plate, or bullion found hidden in the earth or in a house or other private place. It may also be concealed in other articles, such as bureaus or safes. Its original owner must be unknown, and it must have been hidden or concealed long enough to indicate that the owner is probably dead or impossible to locate. Treasure trove is not lost property in the sense we have been discussing. Under ancient law, when found, it belonged to the king, but if he who had hidden the treasure was afterwards discovered, the original owner and not the king was entitled to it. In the United States, the right of the state or Federal government to property of this character has seldom or never been claimed. The finder is entitled to such treasure against anyone but the true owner, in the absence of a statute to the contrary. However, much depends on where the treasure is found, and whether it is actually treasure trove or simply lost property. The distinction between these two categories has been maintained in several states, while others now group all lost property under one set of laws.

When buried treasure is found

A celebrated case concerned two boys, Hugh Gray and Darwin Yoran, who found under a plank in a barn two tin cans, each containing $1,000 in currency. They took these cans to the father of one of the boys, who deposited the money with the county treasurer and advertised its finding in the state journal. This advertisement did not turn up the original owner. However, the owner of the barn in which the money had been found sued to obtain it under the lost-property law, claiming it should be his since it was discovered on his property.

The court in this state decided to maintain the separate treasure-trove category and declared that the statutes pertaining to lost property did not apply in this case. The money was treasure trove, the court said, since its original owner was unknown and it had been hidden for a long time. It belonged to the boys who had found it.

But a person who merely finds articles of value embedded in the soil, which are not considered treasure trove, acquires no superior title to the property. There is an assumption made by the law that the owner of the property on which the item is found is the rightful owner of the article.

If you lose property in a restaurant

In 1958, New York State enacted the Lost and Found Property Act. The Act abolished the old common-law distinctions between "lost property," "mislaid property," "abandoned property" and "treasure trove." It also eliminated distinctions between "public" and "private" premises and set up a procedure for the return of found property to the true owner. It also gave authority to the Police Department to take custody of found property and after a reasonable period of time to distribute it where there was no contest as to who should receive it. The general intent was to give the finder a right superior to everyone but the true owner, regardless of where the property was found. There were certain exceptions. If the finder's presence on the property where something was found by him was a crime (e.g., a thief), the finder's rights, if any, would belong to the person properly in possession of the premises. If a public employee or official found property during the course of his duties, the group or entity for whom he worked was considered the finder, and the same could be the case for an employee who should have delivered the lost property to his employer.

In 1969, an interesting case reached the Court of Appeals, the highest court in the State of New York. A contractor had been employed to remodel the basement of a private home. He found almost $5,000 in small bills concealed under an old wash basin, which had been there for some time. The owners of the house did not know of the money, although they had been in the house for some ten years.

In considering the question of whether the contractor or the house owner should receive the money, the Court reviewed the early common-law rule to the effect that if property was found in a private place, the owner or occupant of the premises where the property was discovered had the right to it, except as against the true owner. But the Court held that the new rule applied, and that it was the finder who now had the right superior to all except the true owner, rather than the owner of the premises.

New York lost and found

The proprietor of a restaurant is not liable for the loss of the coat and hat of a customer unless it is checked with a restaurant employee or the employee acknowledges that he will take care of it in some other manner. The proprietor may also be liable if his employees are negligent in their general care of the property of patrons that is temporarily laid aside.

A customer failed to give his overcoat to the waiter or check it at the coat and hat stand, but hung it on a hook near his table. At the end of his meal, he found his coat gone. The restaurant owner was not liable for this loss. He would have been, however, if the overcoat had been given into the custody of a restaurant employee.

Another case involved a restaurant where there was no checking place for patrons; however, along the walls and around four columns in the center of the room were rows of hooks for hanging coats and hats. On the walls were placards saying, "Not Responsible for Hats and Coats." These were not noticed by a customer who hung his overcoat on one of the hooks about two feet from his table. After finishing his meal, he noticed that his coat had disappeared. He sued the restaurant.

If the customer had wished to retain control over his overcoat, said the court in deciding the action, the hooks were there for his convenience. Or on the other hand, if he had wished to give it into the exclusive possession of the proprietor and so place on him any liability for its loss, he could have done so. But he could not keep control of his coat and hold the proprietor of the restaurant liable for its safety. Under the circumstances, the restaurant was not liable.

Situations such as these are commonplace. Proprietors of restaurants, by the very nature of their duties, cannot stand guard over coats and hats hanging unchecked about the room. In most restaurants of any size, checking stands are provided, thus relieving guests of the burden and worry of coats, hats, umbrellas, wraps, and other apparel. By using these facilities, the customer makes the proprietor liable for any loss that occurs through neglect or failure to return the apparel to its owner.

When baggage gets lost

When you are traveling by air, train, bus, or boat and give your luggage to the agent or check it for delivery at your destination, the carrier to whom you have entrusted it is responsible for its delivery. He is liable to you for its value in almost all cases in which it is lost, provided that you do not contribute to its loss. The exceptions to this rule are for losses which result from such extraordinary incidents as acts of God or from special actions taken by a governmental authority. Even in these exceptional cases, if negligence on the part of the carrier placed the baggage in the position where the loss occurred, the passenger may still be able to recover.

A woman checked her bag and its contents with a bus agent. When she reached the end of her journey, the bag was missing. If the passenger has control of baggage to the exclusion of the carrier, said the court that heard her case, then the railway or bus company is not liable for the loss. But when a passenger delivers a bag or suitcase to a bus agent, as in this instance, the bus company and not the passenger must bear the loss.

Custody of baggage determines liability

The baggage delivered before a passenger has bought his ticket comes under the same rule of law with the same liability of the carrier, unless the carrier lets the passenger know of special liability limitations, such as the fact that it will not become responsible for the baggage until the passenger pays his fare. A passenger normally has the right to deliver his baggage to a bus or railroad in order that he may have a reasonable time before the departure of the train or plane, or before the sailing of a boat, for obtaining a ticket. From the time the luggage is delivered to the carrier, the responsibility for its safety no longer belongs to the passenger.

The owner of a trunk reserved space on a train from Detroit to Cleveland and left it with the railway baggage agent about six hours before the time of departure. An hour after he left this luggage with the railroad, it disappeared. For the loss of the trunk and its content, the railroad was held liable in the suit brought by the traveler for its value.

On the other hand, if the owner of baggage does not deliver it to the carrier but retains it in his custody, he cannot hold the bus or railroad liable for his loss. A woman boarded a bus at Pulaski, Tennessee, for Birmingham, Alabama. She had with her a bag which she left hanging from an arm of the seat. Later she discovered it was missing. The court held she was not entitled to recover for this loss from the bus company.

In another lost-baggage incident, the bus driver requested the passengers to leave the bus, saying he would hand them their luggage and asking that each passenger identify his bag as it was handed out. When almost all the passengers had received their baggage, one woman was offered a bag not her own—her bag had disappeared.

The court, deciding in her favor, pointed out that, if the driver asked the passengers to leave the bus and to let him distribute their luggage, he assumed control of it and the company became responsible for any loss.

Traveling on different trains

When baggage is checked for a trip through and over connecting railroad or bus lines and is lost, it is impossible for the owner to know by which bus or railway company the baggage was lost. Under these circumstances, the owner of the baggage can always seek recovery from his loss from the first carrier. Under the law, the initial carrier, the first bus or railway line on which the owner travels—the one to which the baggage is delivered at the beginning of the journey—is liable for any loss of baggage that may occur on the trip, regardless of any different or connecting railway or bus lines over which the traveler may proceed. The first carrier sells the passenger a through ticket and checks the passenger's luggage to his destination and, irrespective of where the loss occurs, it is liable for the passenger's loss.

How liability for loss of baggage may be limited

It is a general rule that a railroad, airline, or bus company may limit its liability for a failure to perform its contract for the safe transportation of a passenger's luggage. This limitation of liability for the loss of luggage is stated on the baggage receipt. An extra charge is made when baggage is valued at an unusual amount or at a greater value than a specified sum. If it is not paid, the carrier's liability for loss is limited to the stated maximum.

This limitation for liability, however, cannot be made by the bus or railroad except with the consent of the passenger. While the courts have in some instances held that the liability for loss may be limited by a general notice—on the baggage receipt, for example—that notice nevertheless must be brought to the attention of the passenger.

Are hotels liable for lost or stolen property?

Many jurisdictions hold a hotel proprietor responsible for the safekeeping of the goods of his guests. They make him almost the insurer of the baggage of those who stay at his hotel, unless the property is lost by an extraordinary incident, such as an act of God, or by the negligence of the guest himself.

The liability is based on the right of the hotel proprietor to charge for the accommodations of the guest. It is one aspect of those accommodations. Jurisdictions which apply this liability feel that whoever stays at a hotel and pays for a room is entitled to this protection of his property.

This rule had its origin in the early days when the roads and country were infested by thieves and highwaymen. In those times, the innkeepers, frequently in collusion with the thieves, would set traps for unsuspecting wayfarers. By establishing this liability, the courts gave protection to travelers, who, being unfamiliar with the neighborhood, were not in a position to judge the character of the innkeeper from whom they sought lodging.

In other jurisdictions, a hotel owner is only liable for losses if he failed to exercise "adequate" care of the property of his guests. While these jurisdictions demand that less precaution be taken by the proprietor, they will still require that he be extremely careful with the property of his guests before absolving him of liability for any loss.

A sign, displayed either in the room of the guest or in public places about the hotel and which states that the establishment will only be responsible for valuables that are checked with it, may be adequate notice in all jurisdictions to relieve the proprietor of liability for the loss of all valuables that are not checked.

Regulations regarding the depositing of valuables with the proprietor for safekeeping do not apply to the clothing and articles which guests normally use daily, nor do they apply to money in reasonable amounts needed for ordinary expenses. These would normally not be checked and the proprietor may, therefore, still be responsible for them.

Regardless of whether the hotel owner is held to be responsible for a high standard of care or just adequate care, there may be statutory limits of liability.

Who is liable for parking-lot losses?

An automobile owner, when he leaves his car in a parking lot, should always read the stub he receives for the return of his car. Frequently these stubs carry printed notice of limitations to the liability the proprietor assumes in the care of the car left in his custody.

On one such stub was printed, "Parking Contract. Read it. We are not responsible for the car, its accessories, or contents while parked in our lot. No employee has any authority to vary or increase our liability. Additional parking charge begins at 7 A.M. No attendant on duty after 6 P.M."

The car owner who had received this stub in the morning returned

for his car after six o'clock that evening. He could find no one on duty at the parking lot, and his car was gone. He had paid the charges in advance, and at the request of the parking-lot attendant had left the keys of the automobile in the ignition switch so that the car might be moved for the convenience of the attendant.

The court held, in the suit brought by the car owner to recover his loss, that when the owner left the ignition key with the attendant, at the latter's request, the proprietor of the lot assumed the responsibility of taking the same care of this car that a reasonably careful man would take in the care of his own automobile. Since he had failed to do so, he had to make good the loss of the car.

The keys decide the responsibility

The law is different, however, when the owner of a car pays the parking fee and leaves his car in whatever place is designated, taking his keys away with him. In such a case the parking-lot proprietor is not liable for the loss of the car by theft. The reason for this is that the owner of the car has the custody of his car when he enters the parking lot, and by retaining the keys he never surrenders possession of the car to the lot proprietor.

There are exceptions to this rule, as the following case shows. A car owner left his car in a parking lot. This lot was about 200 feet square, enclosed by an eight-foot wooden fence that had but one exit. There was an attendant on duty 24 hours a day. The car was gone when its owner called for it. The car owner, the court held, was entitled to recover the value of the car irrespective of whether or not he had left his keys. He had a right to expect, from the equipment of the lot, that his car would receive the care and watchfulness he was led to believe he was paying for. There is, the court declared, an implied obligation on the part of a parking-lot proprietor to keep safely and return the property which he has taken into his custody, except when the property is lost or damaged without negligence on his part, as from a disastrous fire.

As you see, much depends upon the facts of a case. Nor will all courts view them the same way. A simple statement of the rule of law governing the responsibility for the safekeeping of an automobile in a parking lot is that the liability follows the keys—give the keys to the parking-lot employee and the parking-lot proprietor is liable; keep them yourself, and you assume the risk, unless negligence of the lot owner or his employee can be shown.

CHAPTER 19

Loans, Lenders, and Credit

When you borrow money, you should, first of all, consider the amount of interest you will have to pay. But sometimes, the way interest is computed is so complicated the layman is at the mercy of the lender. Also, different laws apply to different lending agencies.

Usury is the charging of a rate of interest higher than the law allows. The usual rate of interest charged on an ordinary loan for every $100 borrowed varies from state to state. The maximum rate is fixed by law, generally at between 6 and 9 percent for regular bank loans. A lower rate may be agreed upon between the borrower and the lender. In the case of pawnbrokers and money-lenders, however, a part of the transaction is the pledge of jewelry, household goods, and personal property, and it is in transactions of this character that a greater rate of interest is permitted by law.

Banks

In the case of banks or savings and loan associations, loans may be made on salaries or wages for any amount that the earning ability of the borrower justifies. In many jurisdictions, it is illegal to assign, as security for a loan, any wages that are to be earned in the future.

The interest rate varies depending upon the credit rating of the borrower. That amount is often deducted at the time the loan is made. For example, on a loan of $100 for a year with interest at the rate of 6 percent per year, the borrower receives $94 and at the end of the year pays the bank back $100. Thus the actual rate is greater than the stated annual rate of 6 percent since the interest is actually being paid on a loan of only $94.

Loan companies

The interest rates charged by loan companies and pawnbrokers vary in the different states and with the size of the loans, but are generally from 2 to 2½ percent a month or 24 to 30 percent a year. In Alaska the rate charged for small loans is 4 percent a month or 48 percent a year. In Arizona the annual interest permitted by law is 36 percent for small loan companies and 12 percent for credit unions.

One has to be very careful when entering into a loan agreement with any lender, even one well established in the community. In 1969, when money was tight, interest rates soared. Homeowners who had signed mortgage contracts thinking their interest rates were fixed learned otherwise, to their dismay. Many savings and loan associations had inserted in their mortgage contracts a clause variously known as an "escalator rate clause," a "variable rate clause," or an "adjustable rate clause." What this meant to the homeowner was that the holder of the mortgage was legally free to raise the interest rate on mortgages.

You should read your mortgage contract very carefully and seek legal advice before entering into any loan agreement which could affect your home ownership for years to come.

Government agency contracts   Veterans Administration and Federal Housing Administration insured mortgages do not contain escalator clauses.

Small loans   These are loans for under a specified amount, usually less than 1,000 dollars, which are strictly controlled by statute. They carry a fixed rate of interest, and some states provide that the interest need not be payable in advance. The statutes are aimed at protecting borrowers of small sums who may not fully appreciate all of the intricacies in the world of finance.

The lender must be licensed and must deliver to the borrower at the time of the loan a statement showing in clear terms the amount and date of the loan and the time of maturity, the nature of the security, if any, the name and address of the borrower and the lender, and the rate of interest charged. The borrower must receive receipts for all payments which must indicate the amount applied to interest and any of the money that is being applied to reduce the principal. The receipt must also show how much of the loan remains unpaid. Some small-loan statutes will not allow a lender to have more than one contract of indebtedness with the same person or with a husband and wife together.

Fees in addition   Some statutes allow the lender to charge fees over and above the loan, such as notary fees and recording fees of the security for the loan. But these additions are very few in order not to overburden the debtor.

What about insurance?   Sometimes a lender will require that a borrower, before getting the loan, purchase insurance as security for the loan. However, if it is not reasonably necessary, then the loan can be considered usurious, since adding the insurance premium on to the payments causes the interest rate to be higher than allowed by law. What makes the insurance unnecessary is that the borrower already has assets exceeding the amount of the loan.

Some lenders say they will procure insurance for the borrower, charge the borrower for it, but then fail to buy the insurance. These loans are also usurious.

Attorney's fees

Attorney's fees incurred by a lender through a delay by the borrower in making his payments are often made an additional charge. This method is seized upon by some money-lenders as a ready means for securing a greater return on loans than the interest which the law allows. There may actually be no attorney involved, or a greater charge made than the attorney's fee requires. Statutes have been enacted to control dishonesty in fixing this charge on loans.

A small-loan note given in New Jersey contained a clause that on the entry of judgment there should be included reasonable costs including attorney fees of $15 plus 15 percent of the amount of the judgment. The borrower challenged these fees.

The statute in New Jersey, which is typical of laws of this kind, says: "In addition to the interest herein provided for, no further or other charge or amount for any examination, service, brokerage, commission, expense, fee, or bonus . . . shall be directly or indirectly charged . . . except on actual sale of the security in foreclosure proceedings or upon the entry of judgment." The right of the money-lender in this state to additional charges was confirmed by the court with these words: "The statute itself puts no limit to either the amount or character of the charges upon the entry of judgment."

The lenders here had scrupulously followed the provisions of the statute for no charge in addition to the note and interest until the entry of judgment. In other instances in this state, these additional charges were made on the default of the debtor irrespective of suit or the entry of judgment. The penalty for this violation of the statute was the loss by the money-lender of the money he had loaned.

Collection charges

Another incident that is fairly common in connection with this type of transaction occurred in Louisiana. The Unity Plan Finance Company, a small-loan organization in Louisiana, had inserted a special clause in the notes they issued. It said that, should the borrower fail in making his payments promptly as agreed, he must pay the company, as liquidated damages, five cents for each dollar in arrears. This was "to cover the cost of collection without employment of attorney."

The Louisiana courts held that if this additional amount, together with the interest payable by the borrower, exceeded the 3½ percent allowed by the statute, the money-lender could not recover his loan. However, when such additional charges represent attorney's fees paid for the bringing of suit and the entry of judgment arising from the borrower's default in payment, the rule is that such a stipulation is valid and enforceable. But when these charges are made before suit is brought, they are a violation of the statute if the additional charges and interest exceed the interest rate allowed by law.

However, the courts in Pennsylvania, Connecticut, and Massachusetts, among others, have determined that their Small Loan Acts prohibit the charging of attorney's fees as well as other charges or fees.

Other loans
Many people borrow money on personal property, by means of chattel mortgages, as well as on real estate. Insurance policies are often made the basis of a loan. These subjects are discussed elsewhere in the book, and you should consult the table of contents under the appropriate topic, such as Your Personal Property Rights or What You Should Know About Insurance.

Truth in lending

These days most stores sell their wares on credit or through charge accounts. In fact, money paid over the counter is almost going out of style. This is another area where the buyer must beware. Most states have established ceilings on the maximum rate of interest merchants can charge for merchandise sold on credit. Some states have no ceilings on any type of credit purchase.

In May, 1968, President Johnson signed into law the Consumer Credit Protection Act, also known as the "Truth in Lending Act." This Act will be of substantial benefit in eliminating the confusion that has existed in consumer loans. The Act is divided into four basic areas. The first area requires the disclosure of credit terms in almost every type of consumer credit transaction, including the disclosure of credit terms in advertisements. The second area deals with extortion-type credit transactions, providing criminal penalties for violators. The third area limits the garnishment of an individual's wages (garnishment, discussed later, is usually the withholding of a portion of an individual's salary to pay a debt). The fourth section creates a commission to study consumer credit.

Various other legislative attempts on a state level have been made in order to protect the unwary borrower. In 1968 the National Conference of Commissioners on Uniform State Laws, and the American Bar Association approved the Consumer Credit Code as a uniform law. The code covers credit sales and loans made to individuals for consumer purposes. It requires disclosure of finance and other charges, limits finance rates, controls credit insurance, advances remedies for consumers, and curtails creditors' remedies. The comprehensive nature of this code will probably lead many states to adopt it.

Credit contracts sold

Many times a retailer will extend credit to a purchaser and then sell that credit contract to a finance company, thereby absolving himself from any further responsibility to the customer. The customer then must pay the finance company, and will be forced to continue paying even if the product or services is defective or inadequate. Of course the finance company does not service the item, and the customer may be left holding the bag. Before you buy any item on credit, especially one that will need to be repaired from time to time, you should ascertain what provision the retailer makes for repairs. It may be better to do without the item than to be taken in by an easy credit seller. (See further on this in Chapter 17 on Your Personal Property Rights.)

Holder in due course

A legal doctrine known as the ''holder in due course doctrine'' allows a finance company to take over your installment sales contract without taking over the responsibility of correcting any defect on your purchase. For example, if you buy a used car from a dealer on the installment plan, he can immediately turn your note over to a finance company. If your car is defective and you have the dealer's guarantee, you are still required to pay the finance company.

In light of these abuses, many states, including New Jersey, Connecticut, Massachusetts, Utah, and Vermont, have eliminated the holder in due course for the home improvement industry, if not for all goods. The Consumer Credit Code, described above, prohibits the use of negotiable promissory notes.

Credit cards

Recently the credit card was characterized as the cream of the crop for thieves. Stolen credit cards can eventuate in enormous bills before the card is voided or the thief is caught. Because of the ease of use, the wide acceptability of credit cards, and the rate of thefts, various states have enacted legislation making it a felony to steal, receive, or unlawfully possess a credit card owned by another person. There are also penalties for forging, altering, or counterfeiting credit cards.

Read your contract when applying for a credit card. There is usually a clause stipulating that, if the card is lost or stolen, you are liable for all purchases charged either until the card is found or until the organization issuing it has received notice in writing of the loss or theft. Recent Federal legislation has placed a limit on this responsibility, and the credit card organizations must notify you about the limitation.

Debt consolidation agencies

What happens when you get over your head in charges, credits, loans? Agencies have advertised themselves as the solution to debtor's problems. They are also called debt consolidators, managers, liquidators, poolers, pro-rators.

They claim that they will pool all your debts and, with a small regular payment made in your behalf to your creditors, pay off your obligations over a stated period of time.

At present, 21 states outlaw these agencies, and many cities do also. These states are: Arkansas, Delaware, Florida, Georgia, Kansas, Maine, Massachusetts, Missouri, New Jersey, New Mexico, New York, North Carolina, Ohio, Oklahoma, Pennsylvania, Rhode Island, South Carolina, Texas, Virginia, West Virginia, and Wyoming. A number of states regulate their business dealings, and many state legislatures are considering their prohibition.

Before you sign any agreement with a debt consolidation agency, you should be fully apprised of all their charges, how much they will be taking as a fee and how much of your payments will go to your creditors, and how able they are to deal with your creditors and the long-term progress of your debt reduction. You should also check with your local Better Business Bureau for any information they may have on the company. They may be able to tell you whether the people you owe will deal with such a company.

Repossession

Most states allow a seller to sue for a deficiency judgment even though the deficiency may be small, with the result that after all expenses are included the costs may be substantially greater than the original purchase price and, in addition, the property is taken away from you. An example of this is where a finance company repossesses a car after the buyer had paid almost the total purchase price, say, $2,000 on a $2,500 car. The finance company then resells the car to the original dealer for $400, and the buyer still must pay the unpaid balance even though an open negotiated sale of the car may have netted close to $1,000.

If ever you suffer a repossession, send the finance company a certified or registered letter requesting them to use their best efforts to get a fair price. If possible, attend the sale, with a friend, or a lawyer for support.

Garnishment

This is a means used by creditors to obtain repayment of debts. A creditor will make a claim on the debtor's property that may be in the hands of a third party, or on monies owed by a third party to the debtor. Usually it is used to reach unpaid wages of an employee who is in debt.

A creditor garnishees, or causes a summons to be issued to, an employer ordering him to pay to the creditor some of the wages owed the debtor. Needless to say, this creates ill feeling on the job, since it is a nuisance for an employer to make out two paychecks. Also, it lets the employer know how much in debt his employee is, and this can lead to the employee being fired.

The states have laws that regulate the amount of money that can be garnisheed. They differ. In Arizona, the law permits the garnishment of 100 percent of both a husband's and a wife's wages. But since this means that there is then no income left for normal living expenses, the debtor can petition the court and have 50 percent of his salary paid to him. Pennsylvania and Texas exempt all wages from garnishment; Florida exempts the wages of the head of the family; Illinois exempts 85 percent of wages; New York exempts 90 percent of wages; Wisconsin exempts 60 percent or a maximum of $100. If there are dependents, the exemption cannot exceed 75 percent of all family income; Kentucky exempts a maximum of $67.50 a month; New Hampshire exempts $20 a week; Iowa exempts $35 a week plus $3 for each dependent.

Being in debt is a hard enough row to hoe. But having your salary garnisheed does indeed make life difficult. Sometimes it is possible to work out a satisfactory repayment plan with your creditors. However, be very careful of the agreement that you sign to be sure you will not be paying back more than you owe. Also, on occasion, creditors will print up their own summonses and not file them with the court; the court therefore does not exercise its protective control of the garnishment process. If your wages are being garnisheed, it will pay you to see someone at your local Legal Aid Society to be sure that everything is in order.

Can a wife garnishee her husband's pension?

Some states, for example, Pennsylvania, have declared that pension funds are free and exempt from claims of creditors. But is a wife who has a valid support agreement a creditor? Some states will not allow a wife to attach her husband's pension, but others say that a wife must not become a public charge and that if the husband has pension rights, he can be made to exercise them and obtain the cash surrender value of the plan in order to meet the wife's support needs.

What is a co-maker? Sometimes a lending organization requires an endorsement of a borrower's note by a person who knows the borrower. Before you become an endorser or co-maker of such a note, consider your responsibility. Borrower and co-maker are identical in the liability they assume for the payment of the loan. The co-maker signs the note and the borrower signs the note. The lender may demand and collect from either or both.

Time limitations on recovery In every instance where there is the right to bring a suit for the enforcement of a remedy, the collection of money, the recovery of damages, or where there is any other claim or cause of action, the law prescribes a period of time within which such a suit must be brought. This is called a statute of limitation. The object of these laws is to prevent an unscrupulous person, long after the records and recollection of the transaction are lost and forgotten, from bringing a lawsuit that either would be impossible to defend adequately or would not be susceptible of a fair decision. These laws do not extinguish the claim. After the collection of a loan of money is barred by the statute of limitations, you may still owe the money, but the law prevents the lender from collecting by bringing a suit.

The periods of time allowed for bringing suits differ, both in different states and in different transactions. Actions for money loaned or other simple contract debts are ordinarily barred after the expiration of six years from the time the action could be instituted.

However, the promise by the borrower to pay the loan, or a partial payment, in many instances removes any limitation of this character that may then exist, and the period in which the action may be brought is renewed after such an acknowledgment of the debt for another corresponding period.

Loopholes in the law of usury The laws in the various states impose upon pawnbrokers or makers of small loans penalties for an overcharge of interest. However, borrowers do not always manage to obtain the redress the laws afford.

A man and his wife in Washington, D.C., borrowed $300 from a money-lender. By devious negotiations the lender charged them a rate that amounted to 67 percent, or the equivalent of $200 a year as interest on a $300 loan.

After the note had been made, the money-lender sold it, before it was due, to a third person, who paid value for it and knew nothing of the usurious interest charge.

The negotiable instrument law is substantially the same in every state, and the buyer of a note before it becomes due, if he pays value and has no notice of any defenses of the maker, such as usury, holds it free of such a defense.

This was the position of the buyer of this note. The court, deciding the borrowers must pay, and pay in full, said that however unfortunate it might be, they were helpless to defend themselves against this outrageous transaction, since there was no law that afforded them relief. The liability for payment of the entire amount was theirs to meet.

In Nebraska, the usury statutes were amended to read that the debt involved would not be canceled if usurious interest was charged. The principal would be due but not the interest, and if it has already been paid the borrower is entitled to a return of the usurious interest or charges after paying the loan. In a case that came up under the statute, the borrower wanted the court to void his contract to buy a mobile home and award him title to it since there was usurious interest involved. On an installment contract the payments made usually go first to pay off the interest and then the principal. The court said in this case that the money would be applied wholly to principal because of the usury.

When you pawn a valuable

A pawnbroker is not liable to the owner of a pawned object for its loss by fire, robbery, or any other cause unless this loss is a result of negligence on his part. A money-lender is not an insurer—he is merely a custodian.

Over 75 years ago, a man named George Frederick had a pawnshop on Bleecker Street in New York City. Susan Abbett borrowed money from him and gave as security a gold brooch, two silver watches, a pair of earrings, and a pair of silver cuff links. Three weeks later the pawnshop was robbed and this jewelry, with other pledges, was stolen. Susan Abbett sued the pawnbroker.

Said the court: All that has ever been required by the law on the part of a pawnbroker has been that which is required of warehousemen, the exercise of ordinary diligence and care. Since the pawnbroker in this case had taken reasonable care of the pledged property, he bore no responsibility for its loss.

Pawned objects destroyed by fire

In New Orleans, Frank Monrose summed up a transaction with Elisha Crocker in this receipt: "Received of Elisha Crocker $312 to be repaid in 60 days from this date, and as collateral security for the repayment I do hereby place into his hands the following articles, viz., one pair diamond earrings, two diamond rings, one diamond breast pin, two pair gold buckles, one pair gold earrings with breast pin. Signed, F. Monrose."

Before the 60 days had expired, Crocker's house and its contents were wholly destroyed by fire. The statutes of Louisiana, conforming substantially to those of the rest of the country, say that the lender with whom the property is pledged is only responsible "for loss or decay of the pledge which may happen through his fault." The money-lender here was not liable for this loss since in no way could it be blamed on his lack of care of the pledge.

**Can a pledged
article be withheld?**

Does the pawnbroker have a right to withhold a pledged article upon payment of the loan with interest and surrender of the receipt or pawn ticket?

Martha Buchanan pledged jewelry with the Provident Loan Society in New York as security for a loan of $2,000. Later she offered the Society her receipt or pawn ticket and the amount due on the loan with interest. The pawnbroker refused to deliver the jewelry, claiming others had an interest in it. Under such circumstances, declared the court, the Society was liable for the value of the goods.

**When a pledged
article is sold**

Any agreement you make with a pawnbroker about the disposition of the article pledged by you as security for the loan you make should be clearly understood and in writing. If the pawnbroker is unwilling to put this agreement into writing, then confirm it yourself by letter to him.

**Is notice
of sale necessary?**

A ring was pawned at New Haven, Connecticut, for a loan payable in six months, and the borrower received a pawn ticket endorsed: "Goods pawned will not be kept longer than six months from the date of the ticket, but will be sold at private sale, and no further notice will be given."

The pawnbroker held the ring for eight months. When it had not been redeemed in that time, he put the ring on sale and disposed of it in the usual course of business. Three months later, 11 months after the ring had been pawned, the borrower sought to redeem his ring but found it had been sold.

The pawnbroker contended the loan had been made on the terms endorsed on the pawn ticket. The borrower insisted there was an agreement that the ring would be sold only at public auction after notice to the borrower and that the endorsement of the pawn ticket did not apply and had been waived.

The court held that a contract with a pawnbroker gives him the right to sell the property pawned if the loan is not paid within the time agreed. In the absence of any agreement to the contrary, the property pledged must be sold at public sale after notice has been given to the borrower not only of the intention to sell the pledge, but of the time and place when the sale will occur.

Observe your redemption date

Observe closely the time within which a loan must be repaid as well as any provisions for "days of grace" given the borrower by statute, which extend the time for payment beyond the period agreed upon. Under some statutes, 60 days beyond the due date is allowed as "days of grace" before the pledge can be sold. However, the number of days varies with the state.

On September 1, a man named McPike, for a loan of $100, pawned a diamond ring worth $350. The pawn ticket provided for payment of the loan 30 days after date and stated that it was subject to forfeiture if interest was not paid within 90 days. (This included 30 statutory days of grace.)

McPike died four days before the expiraton of the 90 days. Ten days after the expiration, his wife called at the pawnshop and was told she was too late—the ring had been sold. Neither the borrower's death nor the efforts of the widow could stay the time when the pawnbroker could sell the ring.

If you borrow money and promise to repay it, your obligation is not less if the agreement is written down informally in the form of an IOU. It is valid evidence of a contract of a loan and a promise to repay.

Gambling debts

An IOU for a gambling debt incurred illegally cannot be used to enforce payment. However, many gambling debts, although not enforceable legally, are enforced by physical abuse or threats. Be wary of entering into any such agreement.

CHAPTER 20

Animals

In the eyes of the law, animals are personal property. However, the law makes a distinction between wild animals and tame ones. The bear cub or the rabbit in the forest—animals in their wild state—belong to nobody. For them to become your property, you must catch them and keep them. If they escape and become wild again, your right of ownership comes to an end. The next person to capture them has a right of ownership superior to yours.

However, if you capture a wild animal that escapes from a zoo or a circus, or one that has been tamed, it is a well-established principle of law that you do not become its owner. By this principle, if you keep rabbits in your backyard and they escape into the street or a neighbor's yard, they do not become the property of the person who catches them.

No one has a right to enter your land to hunt wild animals. Such entering, without permission, is trespassing.

Bees are property, too, if you have caught them or have them in your possession. If they leave your land, they are yours as long as you know where they are. Still, you have no right to trespass on someone else's land to recover bees that have escaped.

Tame animals—chickens, ducks, and other barnyard fowl, as well as sheep, cattle, horses, goats, and other animals used for food or labor—rank unquestionably as personal property, and, in general, they enjoy all the protection of the law afforded such property. The case is different with dogs, however.

Dogs Dogs are generally considered domestic animals, or personal property, but they are not in exactly the same class as horses, sheep, and cows. They are, rather, classed with monkeys, parrots, singing birds, and "similar animals kept for pleasure, curiosity, and caprice," to quote the words of the Supreme Court. Cats belong in the same class.

Of dogs, Justice Brown of that court wrote: "They differ among themselves more widely than any other class of animals and can hardly be said to have any characteristics that are common to the entire breed. While the highest breeds rank among the noblest representatives of the animal kingdom and are justly estimated for their intelligence, sagacity, fidelity, watchfulness, affection and, above all, for their natural companionship with man, others are afflicted with such infirmities of temper as to be little better than a public nuisance."

For these reasons, special rules of law have been developed concerning dogs.

Why your dog should be licensed

Cities and states generally provide, either by ordinances or statutes, that the owner of a dog must file with the town or city clerk, or a similar officer, a statement of his ownership and a description of the dog. The owner must also pay a license fee for the privilege of keeping the dog for a stipulated period, usually a year, and for this a tag is issued that is attached to the collar of the dog. Failure to register a dog and pay a license fee is penalized by fine or by withholding legal protection of the dog. Or the municipal authorities may have the right to impound or kill the dog.

Damages for an unlicensed dog

A Newfoundland dog renowned for pedigree and pups and named in the *American Kennel Blue Book*, Countess Lona lived with her master in New Orleans. Following him along the street one day, she stopped on a railroad track and, failing to notice an oncoming train, was hit and instantly killed.

At that time, in New Orleans, a city ordinance provided that no dog should be at large unless provided with a tag furnished annually by the city treasurer for $2. The Countess had no tag. By this ordinance of the city, she was an outlaw.

Her owner, a man named Sentall, sued the railroad for his damages for the loss of the dog and recovered. That judgment was reversed by the Louisiana appellate court and ultimately came before the Supreme Court of the United States. The Supreme Court affirmed the decision of the Louisiana appellate court that Countess Lona without her tag was outside the protection of the law and that her owner could not recover damages for her death.

In brief, the fate of a dog and the protection of the law will be determined by the specific provisions of the law of the locality.

If a dog is killed negligently

A pole on which was strung a lead cable was maintained by a telephone company in a yard used as a run for two hunting dogs, Nancy and Pooch. The telephone company made some repairs on this cable. Four weeks after the repair work was done, Nancy died from lead poisoning. During that time Pooch, too, became sick, and the week after Nancy's death he died. A search of the yard where the telephone company had done its repair work disclosed quantities of lead parings and bits of solder. The owner of the dogs brought suit against the company.

A statute saying that no action could be maintained for the loss of a dog not equipped with a tax tag was invoked by the telephone company in its defense. That statute, the court held in this case, cannot be intended to exonerate persons who kill or injure dogs through negligence. The telephone company was liable for the value of the dogs.

Dogs have not been given the overall protection of such domestic animals as horses and cattle, but they nevertheless are property and, when equipped with tax and license tags, have their own right to legal protection.

Dog enticement

Two valuable hunting dogs died after eating poisoned bait which had been placed on a ranch in Montana. The owner had requested the Department of the Interior to place the bait to kill coyotes. A hunter who had no permission to be in the area with his dogs claimed that nevertheless he should be paid damages for the loss of the dogs since the bait odor was detectable for 200 to 300 yards and his dogs had been enticed by it. The court said that the bait was attractive to the dogs, but that there had been care to post the area, warning of the poison, and that if the hunter had obtained permission to hunt on the ranch, he would have been further aware of the danger. The moral is that some things do entice animals just as there are attractions for small and unwary children, but you, as the owner, may not be able to collect damages for your loss if there has been no negligent conduct or if you have been at fault.

Some courts have allowed recovery on any injury caused by a wild animal. Others have required a showing that the owner of the animal was negligent or that the injured party did not incite the animal.

If an owner knows his animal is dangerous, although the type of animal is not normally considered vicious, he is obligated to exercise due care to control it. If, however, the animal is normally peaceable and attacks under provocation, the owner is not responsible. "Dangerous" in this case may even refer to the playfulness of the animal. A Pennsylvania man owned an "overfriendly" Great Dane which weighed more than 105 pounds. He let the dog into his house, and it jumped on the owner's 74-year-old housekeeper. The housekeeper fell, breaking her arm and leg. The court allowed the housekeeper to recover damages, noting that the owner was aware of the characteristics of the dog and that he was negligent in not controlling it.

Cows on the highway

In some of the southwestern and western states, where cattle-raising is a major industry, cows are permitted to run at large, and the owner of land cannot recover for the damages they may cause to his property unless he had it fenced. In other words, the duty in these states is to fence the cattle out, not to fence them in. This, however, is not the rule in the industrial states of the East, and those states with large manufacturing centers. The old bucolic rule is illustrated by the following case:

An automobile driver on an Alabama highway collided with a cow, then sued the animal's owner for the damage his car had suffered from the impact.

"The common-law rule that animals must be on the owner's premises is not the law in this state. The rule is rather reversed," said the Alabama court. "Animals are permitted to run at large unless prohibited by statute."

The court held the cow owner not responsible for the damage. The cow had a right, as did the automobile owner, to be on the highway, and her owner was not negligent because she was there unless he knew she had propensities that would result in damage.

This is no longer the rule in Alabama, which now provides for impounding animals running at large on state and Federal highways.

In many states which have open-range policies, when a motorist injures a cow, he not only cannot collect for his damages but he must also pay for the cow at the going beef rate.

When a hired animal causes injury

The owner of an animal, when he hires it out to you for use, is responsible for the damages caused by the animal's viciousness if he knows or should have known that the animal was vicious. In general, he is under an obligation to find out whether an animal is inclined to be dangerous, and to give you such information about the animal. He is also under an obligation to furnish you a reasonably safe animal. If the owner informs you that the animal has vicious tendencies and you use it anyhow, you assume the risk of the consequences.

Horseback riding at one's risk

At a riding school, a woman who had lived on a farm and had been familiar with horses all her life was offered a mount she had difficulty in controlling. Another mount was offered her, but she refused it. Finally, when she was riding the first horse, he reared and wheeled; the woman, unable to keep her seat, was thrown to the ground.

This woman was not a novice, said the court when she brought suit against the owner. In order for her to recover damages for her injuries, it had to be shown that the owner of the horse had a knowledge of his vicious propensities, which knowledge the rider did not possess. Since

before her accident, the plaintiff had a clear idea of how the horse would behave, she had no claim against the owner.

In another case, a young, inexperienced rider was given a horse at a riding stable. It was regularly used by youngsters frequenting the stable. The horse reared soon after the youngster mounted him, and the boy was thrown to the ground, breaking his arm. His parents sued. They might have been able to recover, since the boy was a novice and the court conceivably would have said the stable was under a duty to give him a calm horse. However, it was determined that the horse reared because the boy kicked it. Since the boy incited the horse, no recovery was allowed.

The normal hazards of sports

A 13-year-old girl receiving instruction at a riding academy brushed against a tree while riding a horse and was hurt. The horse was calm, well-behaved, and had no vicious habits.

The court held that there was no fault on the part of the owner and that the girl could not recover damages for these injuries. The owner did not agree to become an insurer against every accident that might occur, the court pointed out, and there is always some hazard in horseback riding, as in most sports. One who participates in any activity voluntarily must be charged with assuming all normal risks of that activity. The animal was reasonably safe, so no charge could be leveled against the owner on this score.

Animals that may be destroyed

A mad dog or any other vicious or dangerous animal that is running at large and menacing the lives of others is a public menace and may lawfully be killed.

Statutes, local laws, and ordinances have recently been adopted throughout the country for the destruction of cattle affected by tuberculosis. The United States Supreme Court has already asserted that the police powers of the states justify the destruction or abatement of whatever may be regarded as a public nuisance. Within this power lies the right to condemn infected cattle, on which the welfare and health of the people depend.

A California act, for example, provides that cattle infected by tuberculosis should immediately be segregated and each animal appraised and slaughtered within 30 days. The owner is then reimbursed by the state for one-third of the difference between the proceeds of the sale of the salvage and the appraised value, but not more than $75.

Cruelty to animals is punishable

The old English law from which our own has grown held little or no concern for the sufferings of animals and the prevention of the cruelties inflicted upon them. A few centuries ago, men could torture animals with impunity. The situation is far different today, and our states have laws that protect animals and provide for the punishment of those who treat them cruelly.

In addition to the damages for which one is liable when the animal is another's property, the punishment under the criminal laws for cruelty of this character extends from offenses for which a fine is imposed to imprisonment at hard labor. Under a statute in California relating to these offenses, a man who had maliciously placed poison in a water trough for use by horses received a prison term. Recovery has also been allowed against persons who negligently leave poisonous substances on streets or highways, or who spray or dust plants, if injury to animals results.

What "cruelty" means

But what constitutes cruelty to animals? A famous court decision sets out a definition that has long served as a guidepost. "The torture must consist in some violent, wanton, and cruel act necessarily producing pain and suffering to the animal." Cruelty may refer to a wide range of acts. It may be beating an animal, or it may be failing to take care, in a civilized way, of an animal in your charge. If you do not provide your dog with proper food, drink, or shelter, for example, this is generally considered cruelty, depending on the circumstances, and particularly the suffering inflicted on the dog.

A typical case of cruelty was based on a complaint lodged against a man in Indiana charging that he had imprisoned dogs in a wagon. There was not enough space for them in it, and he failed to supply them with sufficient food and water. They became sick, and some of them died. Found guilty, the owner had to pay a fine.

Unusual treatment is not always cruel

Complaints of cruelty are often made without any basis in fact. Animals may be treated in an unusual way, but if it does not involve "wanton and unnecessary torture," it may not be cruelty under the law.

A store temporarily lodged a two-week-old chick in a glass container as an advertising feature. This container was 19 inches high. Inside was food, water, and a wire netting on which the chicken could stand. There was also three-way ventilation.

A society for the prevention of cruelty to animals complained to the courts of the cruelty this treatment inflicted on the chicken. The manager of the store was arrested and tried as the responsible party. It was shown that the chicken weighed twice the standard weight of its contemporaries, and a university expert testified that it was in good health. The case resulted in no conviction, since cruelty normally involves the wanton and unnecessary torture of an animal.

Many humane groups have sought to enjoin rodeo performances because they allege that the animals are cruelly treated. Bullfighting has also been banned in the United States because of the alleged cruel and inhumane treatment accorded the participating animals.

Trespassing domestic animals

Two families lived on adjoining lots in North Carolina. Each had a flock of chickens. After the garden peas and other vegetables had been planted, the chickens of each family became increasingly irksome to the other. In one of the families was a small boy who displayed sadistic tendencies in ridding his father's garden of the neighboring chickens. One of the chickens he chased into a brush pile, where he grabbed it by its legs and crushed its head with his heel. He pulled off the head of the next. Another he impaled on a sharp stick.

"This boy had no more right to destroy the trespassing chickens," said the court, "than he had to destroy his neighbor's cattle. The remedy is by impounding them till the damage is paid or by action for damages." This, in general, is the law regarding animals that trespass. Ordinarily, one cannot freely kill or injure trespassing animals. However, many jurisdictions have held that, unlike in this North Carolina case, a person has a right to kill a trespassing animal if in defense of the person, his family, or his property.

Killing an animal nuisance

A dog racing through a sheep pasture was shot and killed by a boy who believed that the dog was after the sheep, since, in the past, the dog had made periodic raids on them. The owner maintained that this time the dog had actually been innocent, engaged solely in a hunt for rabbits.

The killing, however, was held justified by the court, irrespective of whether at the moment the dog was after sheep or otherwise employed.

"When a dog acquires the egg-sucking or sheep-killing habit," the court declared, "he becomes a nuisance and may be destroyed as such."

There is, however, no rule against trespassing by a dog, provided he does no harm. The point in this specific case, on the other hand, is that there was good reason for regarding the dog as a menace.

When wild animals cause injury

Earlier in this chapter we said that animals are assigned by law to two classes, tame and wild. If you have the custody of wild animals, you are required to exercise extreme care—much more than you have to with tame animals, unless these are known to have a vicious disposition.

At a Virginia resort, two bears, both wild and vicious, were kept on the premises, and the guests were encouraged to feed them sweets and soft drinks. The proprietors gave no warning of the vicious dispositions of the bears. They were kept in a pen of two layers of poultry wire reinforced by hog wire.

A guest was standing with his back to the pen. One of the bears sprang to the fence, forced his paw through the wire, and severely scratched and tore the face and clothing of the guest.

The court held that, while there may have been some contributory negligence on the part of this guest, "the keeper should have exercised a very high degree of care in the manner and place of keeping such animals." Damages were awarded the injured guest.

Wild animals in the national parks

The United States has been sued for injuries sustained as a result of encounters with bears in some of the national parks. In one case a man was bitten on his arm while he was dozing in his car. He and his family had gone to Wyoming on a cattle-buying trip and were returning to Nebraska by way of a sightseeing trip through Yellowstone National Park. The wife was driving, the children were in the back seat, and the car was in a line of traffic which was stopped to watch some frolicking bear cubs. The family did not see the adult bear approach the car and bite the father. The man sued for his injuries, claiming that he should have been warned not to have his window rolled down, and that the park rangers should have taken measures to see that the bear was taken to a remote part of the park. The court did not feel there was any negligence. The government was not in the same position as a private person who has a choice whether to harbor a wild animal. Keeping the park in its natural state is in the public interest, and therefore having the park bears roam at will is not negligence. The rangers had no notice that this bear was dangerous, and there were many warnings posted to the effect that bears are wild animals and that tourists were not to feed or encourage them. Here, because of the overriding public benefit, there was only a duty of ordinary and reasonable care.

In another case, a small child was visiting the National Zoo in Washington, D.C. She was with her grandfather, from whom she became separated momentarily. They were in the lion house. The child slipped past a guard rail and got too near one of the cages. In roughing playfully with her, the lion injured her fatally. At that time there were no wires to prevent the lion from reaching outside the cage, although there were warning signs in the area. The case was settled out of court, but it did result in added precautions being taken to prevent another such tragedy.

An accident despite reasonable care

A carload of cattle was being shipped from Houston, Texas, to Tennessee and was unloaded overnight into a cattle pen at Vicksburg, Mississippi. The next morning, while they were being reloaded, a steer escaped and, running at large in a suburb, attacked and gored a small child.

This steer, contended those acting on behalf of the child, was a wild animal, savage and vicious. "Cattle," answered the court, "emerged from the classification of wild animals into that of domestic animals centuries ago. Whether such a domestic animal may return to the classification of wild animals is not before the court."

Since reasonable care had been taken and the misfortune did not arise from the negligence of the employees of the railroad or the stockyard, the case did not provide grounds for the recovery of damages for the child's injuries.

Handlers must be skilled

Some animals were on exhibition at the Cleveland Brookside Park. Among them was Osa, a onetime wild elephant who, with a veneer of civilization, still retained the habits of the jungle. A boy bought a ticket for a ride in the howdah on her back, but, when he was seated there, Osa reared on her hind legs and, trumpeting loudly, she bolted for the gateway to the elephant house. The howdah was torn from her back and her passenger was hurled to the ground. The elephant attendant, who lacked training, had been unable to control her.

The rule emphasized by the court in this case—the rule that governs in all such instances involving damages from the behavior of wild animals—is that a superior skill and knowledge is demanded of a keeper of wild animals. Since Osa's attendant was untrained, the proprietors of the exhibition were liable for damages.

Photographs of an animal

A dog owner arranged for photographs of her dog and paid for them. The photographer made copies of these pictures available to an advertising agency for a fee, which agency used the pictures in advertisements for its clients. The court held that the dog had no right of privacy, but that the right in the specific pictures by contract belonged to the dog owner, who had paid for them, and she could prevent use of the pictures against her wishes by innocent parties such as the advertising agency and client and, in addition, collect damages from the photographer.

Care by a veterinarian

Your vet must use such reasonable skill, diligence, and attention in his care of your pet as may ordinarily be expected of careful, skillful, and trustworthy persons in their professions. If he does not, then he is answerable for the consequences of his want of skill or care. Even if he is not a graduate of a school of veterinary medicine, if he is a practicing vet he will be expected to conform to the proper level of treatment. He can also be liable for an improper diagnosis.

Nuisances

Dogs, regardless of their number and whether they are kept for pleasure, profit, or as a public service, may become a private nuisance, and the court will issue an injunction against the nuisance. "Nuisance" means the use of property by someone so as to interfere unduly with the property or enjoyment of someone else. Anyone keeping noisy, odorous, mischievous, or annoying dogs may be subjecting his neighbors to a private nuisance if the comfortable enjoyment of their homes is lessened, or if the value of their property is substantially diminished as a result. You must be a person of normal sensibilities, however, to claim you have been offended. If you ask for an injunction, the court's decision will not depend on whether you complained about the nuisance earlier, or whether other neighbors agree with you that there is a nuisance. What is important is that you can identify the offending dog or dogs and can show that you are a normal person.

A family in Louisiana was awakened every morning between 4 and 6:30 A.M. by the barking of a neighbor's German shepherd, who was kept in a fenced backyard. Other neighbors testified that they had a feeling of security with a watchdog in the area, but nevertheless the court found that the dog was a nuisance, and the owner was enjoined from allowing his dog to bark early in the morning. The court suggested that he keep him in the house.

In another case, a pharmaceutical company kept laboratory dogs in order to test drugs used in treatment of animal diseases. There were odors and noises from the kennels and runs, and some summer-home owners sought to have an injunction issued against the company. In this case the court found that the business had a right superior to the homeowners, since the company had tried to keep the dogs quiet and since they were involved in scientific development.

In each such case, the court will weigh the considerations on both sides to determine whether to order a removal of the animals.

What about pets in an apartment?

If you have a lease which forbids animals, then you had better adhere to it; the courts hold that provisions like this are not unreasonable. If you breach the provision, the landlord may be able to repossess the premises.

Sometimes the landlord will consent to the breach. Where the lease requires written permission, the landlord can give oral permission for you to keep a pet. Also, if he has knowingly allowed your pet in the apartment for a long period of time, the court may consider that he has waived the requirement that you obtain permission. If he has asked you to move because you have a pet and then accepts rent for a time past your notice to vacate, he will be considered to have waived the provision, and you will not have to move.

Read your lease and be sure of provisions concerning pets, be they dogs, birds, or even snakes. Permission once given may be revoked if your dog and your landlord do not get along.

Charitable trusts for pets

The courts have held that a charitable trust or bequest established by a competent person for the care and protection of pets is valid and will be enforced.

CHAPTER 21

Names

The purpose of a name is to designate a person. You may be known by a variety of names, none of which appears on your birth certificate. Yet, under the law, any of these names generally will be valid. You may collect money due you, sue, or be sued under these names, so long as they are names by which you are known.

A policy was issued in Alabama by the National Life and Accident Insurance Company on the life of Mary Sloan. Her husband was the son of a man named Hartley and also the stepson of a man named Sloan. He was known to his acquaintances by either surname, and his wife's name naturally followed the same changes as her husband's among their friends.

When she died, the insurance company objected to paying the policy on the ground that she was really named Mary Hartley, while the name of the woman it had insured was Mary Sloan.

The court held the company liable for the payment of the insurance since the name in the policy was one by which the woman was known. The general rule is that insurance companies may only be absolved of their obligation to pay in such cases if the use of an incorrect name led them to believe that they were insuring a person other than the deceased. Otherwise, the use of an incorrect name is considered inconsequential. The same rule applies to disputes over grants of property and to contracts. There again, if the designated party is clearly identified by the name used, a minor error will be inconsequential.

Using the wrong name in a lawsuit

A Mrs. Fern Kirk rented property at DeWitt, Arkansas, to W. H. Bonner. When her tenant was in arrears for his rent for over a year, she brought suit. The woman had used interchangeably the names Kirk and Kirkpatrick. She had signed the lease of the property with the name Fern Kirk, but she brought suit for the recovery of the rent in the name of Kirkpatrick. On this discrepancy of names the tenant sought to avoid his liability in the defense of the suit.

The purpose of an individual's name, the court pointed out, is to designate the individual, and whatever name the woman used was immaterial, so long as it served that purpose.

Once it is realized that a minor mistake in the name was made, it is a mere formality to have it changed on the record.

Names and voting

This judicial tolerance toward the use of names stops short of the names to be used by voters at the polls. Courts cannot lend their aid to voters concealing their identity under the cloak of an assumed name.

A few years ago a woman in New Jersey asked the court for an order that her vote be accepted under the name of Love Faith. This was a new name she had adopted, and she had refused to disclose to election officials her real or previous name.

Denying her this right, the court ruled, "There is no more reason why the individual who now chooses to be known among her associates by the name of 'Love Faith' should fail to disclose her past identity by registering under her previous, ordinary name than should the members of the Roman Catholic sisterhoods, all of whom carry out their civil voting privileges under their ordinary civil names."

Many people these days take different names for religious or other reasons—witness Muhammed Ali, originally known as Cassius Clay. Names may be changed by legal procedure or simply by use. When the latter, whether the change will be recognized depends on the law of the jurisdiction involved and on whether the change has a fraudulent purpose.

How the law views middle names

In general, middle names have no special importance to the law. The courts find one Christian name sufficient. If a middle name or initial is inserted, omitted, or even used incorrectly, whether in a criminal or a civil proceeding, the courts pay no attention to the matter, as a rule.

A confession of burglary made to a district attorney in Texas was signed "T. L. Gallagher" and submitted as the confession of Tommie Gallagher. An effort was later made to set aside the conviction on this discrepancy of names.

The court held that the middle initial was of no consequence, according to the well-established rule that the law recognizes only one Christian name.

Incorrect middle initial

Frank E. Coxe was named in a suit over the collection of taxes assessed against property owned by Frank Coxe. This discrepancy in the presence or absence of the middle initial was disregarded by the court with the comment, "Middle name and middle initials are immaterial."

Omitting a middle initial on a check

Lewis L. Wagner, losing some money in a dice game at Miami, Florida, paid his obligations with a check signed "Lewis Wagner." He omitted his middle initial deliberately, anticipating that the bank would refuse to pay the check since his usual signature included the initial. The bank paid the check. He sued the bank to recover the sum involved, but lost the suit. The law, the court indicated, regarding the insertion or omission of *L* in his signature as, in this instance, of no moment.

Error in a title or degree

Names are often accompanied by titles like "Doctor," "Professor," "M.D.," "Reverend," and so on. They are no more a part of a name than "Colonel," "Governor," or "Honorable." While they are descriptive of the man, his name is the name he receives at birth. The law holds that any variation in name, with or without title, is not material unless, as may happen in some court cases, it can mislead a jury to do some substantial injury to the accused.

Is "Mrs." part of a name?

The name of a married woman is her given or Christian name, her family name before marriage, and the family name of her husband, which she acquires upon marriage. Thus, if her maiden name is Isabelle Smith and she marries a man named Brown, her full legal name is Isabel Smith Brown. For convenience and the information of others, she may precede her name with "Mrs." but this prefix is no part of her name.

Courts have held, in a few cases, however, that a married woman could legally use her maiden name while still married if her husband had abandoned her. It is normally preferable for a woman to use her married name, even if she is separated from her husband, at least until she is legally divorced.

On the other hand, a woman can normally choose to use "Mrs." even after she is divorced. But some courts have prohibited women from using their married name, although not from using the prefix "Mrs.," if they were divorced as a result of their adultery.

One court has made the typical observation that "Mrs." is not a name but a mere title and, not being used exclusively by married women, raises no presumption that the person using this title is married at the time. "It includes widows and divorcees as well as married women. It indicates that the party using it is a woman who has been married, but leaves it doubtful whether she is married at the time or not." Of course, the new form "Ms." deliberately leaves the identification of marital status as vague as "Mr." does for the male.

"Junior" and "Senior"–parts of a name?

The suffixes "Junior" and "Senior" are also merely descriptive and no part of the user's name. To omit or add such a suffix is normally a harmless error in civil and criminal proceedings. The use of these suffixes may

be necessary if there would otherwise be confusion regarding whether the father or the son is being designated.

Abbreviations   Under most circumstances, abbreviations are recognized by the courts as synonymous with the names from which they are derived. For example, in one case, when "Ed" was used for the Christian name of Edwin P. Gaston, and this use was challenged, the court held that the "ordinary and commonly used abbreviations of Christian names" are permissible.

This, however, does not apply in all instances to the use of the mere initial. A letter of the alphabet, one court observed, does not make a name. However, the use of the initial letter to represent a name is so common that it can generally be regarded as the abbreviation of the Christian name.

A check was written by Mary A. Wall, signed "The Mining Securities Company, by M. A. Wall," payable to Mary A. Wall, and cashed at the bank on which it was drawn. The woman was not entitled to the money, and the company sued for its recovery. The defense asserted that nothing before the court showed that the M. A. Wall who had signed the check and the Mary A. Wall who received the money were the same person.

"It is sufficient to describe a person by any known or acceptable abbreviation of his Christian name," declared the court, holding that in the Wall case the name and the initials represented identical names.

Compare this situation with that in the Clifford Irving case, where McGraw-Hill, a publishing firm, in payment for rights to an alleged autobiography of Howard Hughes, made out a check in a very substantial amount to H. Hughes, which check was endorsed "Helga" Hughes, who turned out in reality to be Clifford Irving's wife Edith.

Exceptions to this rule have been made. In these exceptional cases, evidence, in addition to the mere similarity of names must be presented to indicate who was the person that was actually designated.

The rule consistently held by all the states under all circumstances involving names is, as we have observed earlier, that the name is the correct Christian and family name with either the correct initials or full middle name.

Is a misspelled name valid at law?

The correct name of a man involved in a summons and a suit for the partition of land in Minnesota was Albert B. Geilfuss, while the name that had been used was Albert B. Guilfuss. The question which ultimately came before the Supreme Court for determination was whether or not this irregularity was vital. The Supreme Court held that the mistake in the name did not affect the validity of the Minnesota court's decision. The due process clause of the Constitution that requires notice to be given to a party to a suit, the Supreme Court said, "does not impose an unattainable standard of accuracy. If a person is served personally with process in which his name is misspelled he cannot safely ignore it."

This is the general rule. Court rules of procedure permit corrections in misspelled names of plaintiffs or defendants so long as the proper person has been served with the process or writ.

Nicknames

A nickname obviously derived from a Christian name may be used as the correct and legal designation of an individual. However, as mentioned earlier, it is better to use the actual Christian name and avoid possible misunderstanding.

A woman named Mary Elizabeth Hedges was known to her business associates as Elizabeth Hedges and also as Bess Hedges. She had dropped her first name, Mary, and had retained her middle name, Elizabeth.

A creditor secured a judgment against Bess Hedges. Elizabeth Hedges owned real estate in the county in which the judgment was recovered. If it could be assumed that the person against whom this judgment had been recovered and the owner of the land were identical, the judgment was a lien on the property.

The New York court was called upon to determine whether or not this judgment against Bess Hedges was a lien on land owned by Elizabeth Hedges. Some names, the court said, have nicknames that are synonymous with the names themselves; others, such as Cliff for Radcliffe, Ganz for Gansevoort, Will for Wilbur or Wilfred, are not. On the other hand, Bess and Elizabeth have been equivalents for centuries, and a judgment against Bess Hedges is a lien on property owned by Elizabeth Hedges.

The deciding factor in each case will be the extent to which the use of the name clearly identifies a particular person. If there is still some question, extrinsic evidence will have to be presented to indicate who is the actual party involved.

The rule laid down on the use and misuse of names and nicknames, to quote the words of one authority, is, "If two names are in original derivation the same, and are taken promiscuously to be the same in common use, though they differ in sound, yet there is no variance." This is the rule generally applied by the courts.

Other names held to be similar equivalents are Willie and William, Bill and William, Charlie and Charles, Dan and Daniel, Frank and Francis, Jack and John, Ed and Edward and Bob and Robert.

Fraud and change of name

The law is well settled in this country that a person's name is his to change or continue as he may see fit, except where there may be statutory restrictions on such action or where a name is changed for the perpetration of a fraud.

The substitution of a name that serves to implement a fraud comes under the same condemnation of the law as does the fraud itself. Dewey Librizzi, having been convicted of crime in New Jersey, later changed his name and became to his acquaintances and business associates Dewey La Rose. Under this name he operated a garage, made agreements with supply firms, leased property, and carried his bank account. With his original name already on the state list of drivers whose licenses had been revoked, he made a new application under the name of Dewey La Rose. In support of his application he asserted that he had never had his license revoked or suspended.

Faced with the charge of having made a false motor vehicle license application, he contended he had a right to change his name under the law. The law is clear, answered the court, that in the absence of a statute or judicial determination to the contrary, there is nothing in the common law which prohibits a person from taking or assuming another name. But if this is done for the purpose of committing a fraud, it is illegal, the court pointed out, rejecting La Rose's plea.

Changing your name by court process

In a majority of the states, statutes have been enacted prescribing the method by which you may change your name other than by simply adopting and being known by a new name. You accomplish a statutory change generally by filing an application with the court named in the law, which thereupon makes an order changing your name as you request.

Your request, however, is not granted by the courts as a matter of right, but rests in the discretion of the court to which you apply. In one instance, a man named Taminosian made an application asking that his name be changed to Mohammed Nadir. His application was rejected when this change was opposed bitterly by the wife and children, who, said the court, were entitled to consideration, especially when no sufficient cause for the change had been shown.

A court order changing your name has the advantage of furnishing an official record of the change which will establish beyond question your identity under either the old or the new name, should this be necessary.

In a few instances it has been held that once the change is effected by court procedure under a statute, the person must be known by his new name and by no other. Under such circumstances, any further change must be made by application to the courts, and the right to a voluntary change without this procedure is lost.

The New York law outlines the usual form for an application to change one's name. The applicant must state his name, age, and residence, the name he wishes to assume, whether or not he is a citizen of the United States, whether married or single, whether any judgments have been recorded against him under the name he is seeking to change, whether he is a party to any pending legal action, and whether he has any monetary obligations under the name he is seeking to abandon.

Some other states also require that the reason for the change be given and that the petitioner state whether he has been convicted of a crime under his present name. Most courts will allow the name change unless there is a substantial reason to deny it.

When the application for a change of name is made by an infant, the child must be represented by one or both parents, depending on the state, or by a guardian. When the parents disagree on the change, the welfare of the child is considered by the court.

A father generally has a superior interest in maintaining the parental surname in the child, even if the mother has custody. However, courts will allow a change in the last name of the child against the wishes of the father in cases where the use of the father's last name may be embarrassing or harmful to the child, as, for example, when the father is an infamous criminal.

CHAPTER 22

Your Rights
and Remedies
Under Your Lease

A person seeking to rent an apartment or a house is often confronted with a situation where he is without counsel, has very little to negotiate, and finds that the landlord adamantly refuses to alter the landlord's "standard form" lease. In this take-it-or-leave-it situation, the tenant often justifies his entering into an onerous lease by saying that it is only for a short period of time. The ability to insert a few clauses beneficial to the tenant at the beginning of the term of the lease may, however, avoid a good deal of exasperation.

A few of the basic considerations of the tenant are that he obtain (1) possession of the premises at the agreed time (2) in the condition specified, and, if possible, (3) a right to sublet or assign all or a part of his interest in the lease.

The lease of an apartment or house is simply a contract between two parties, the owner of a building, generally called the "landlord," and a tenant. The tenant agrees to pay a specific sum, called "rent," generally in equal monthly installments, and the landlord agrees that the tenant may have the use and possession of the apartment or house for the time stated in the lease. The landlord is known as the lessor, and the tenant as the lessee.

A mass of law has grown up governing the mutual obligations and duties of both parties to a contract of this type. A breach of this contract, however, does not in every instance create a forfeiture of the contract. When a tenant agrees to pay his rent in advance on the first day of each month, his failure to pay until some later date does not permit the landlord to take possession immediately and leave the tenant homeless. The only punishment the tenant may suffer is dispossess proceedings, or a legal action by the landlord which requires the tenant to pay his rent, with the only penalty some few additional dollars for the legal expenses the landlord has incurred on his account.

The landlord on his part may fail to furnish the heat, the water, or the service that the tenant has anticipated or that are stipulated in the lease. For many of the minor inconveniences of this character, the tenant's only remedy is to select another dwelling when his lease expires.

Statutes, however, generally provide that the landlord is criminally liable for a failure to furnish adequate heat, water, or sanitary conditions, besides various services the legislatures of the different states have imposed upon apartment-house or multiple-dwelling owners. For failure to comply with these requirements, various penalties are prescribed.

Although the ordinary lease of a dwelling contains conditions and obligations to which both tenant and landlord agree, when you sign your lease and pay your rent you have virtually complete control of the premises for the period of occupancy set out in your lease. No one can interfere with your enjoyment or possession of the premises or your access to them, any more than anyone can interfere with your occupancy of a dwelling for which you had paid in full.

How to protect your security

A prospective tenant is often asked to give a landlord a deposit of, usually, one or two months' rent as security for the fulfillment of the tenant's obligations under a lease. Such an agreement for security is legal and enforceable. The tenant should, however, always arrange the terms of his lease so that he will receive value for the money he advances or deposits. The money should be on account of an obligation that is discharged by the payment of deposit—for example, it might serve as the payment of the last few months' rent—and the lease should say this. Such an arrangement keeps the tenant from losing his money or being obliged to go to law to recover it if there is a change of landlords.

As of September 1, 1970, New York State required that a landlord deposit all security for rental payments on residential real estate in interest-bearing accounts in the name of the tenant.

Where governmental rent controls are in effect, there is usually a provision, as part of the control on rents, limiting the deposit to one or two months' rent.

Must the landlord oust trespassers?

A tenant signing a lease of an apartment or house naturally assumes, when he pays the first month's rent, that the landlord is obliged to give him possession. This assumption is correct, but only within certain limits. The landlord is not obliged to evict a former tenant or a trespassing third party who has no right to possession of the premises.

At Hempstead, New York, Abe and Dorothy Fergang had leased a store; the lease expired on June 30. A man named Teitelbaum had leased this store for a term to begin the following day. The Fergangs refused to vacate. Teitelbaum brought eviction proceedings, was unsuccessful in the lower court, appealed, was granted a new trial, and finally, when the Fergangs did not appear for the new trial, he secured a warrant of eviction for them. The premises were vacated the following January, six months after his tenancy had begun.

Teitelbaum then sued his landlord for the damages he had suffered because of the landlord's failure to give him possession. The court held that since there was no implied obligation on the part of the landlord to oust a trespasser, his failure to do so did not make him liable in damages to the tenant.

The tenant, by virtue of his lease, has title to the property leased, and it is his duty to make full use of the remedies the law affords for gaining the possession he is entitled to under the law.

A number of states have modified this general rule to provide for certain rights of the tenant against the landlord who has failed to give possession, such as the right to cancel the lease. In reality, the tenant has bargained for possession and not the right to sue someone.

Should rent be paid in advance?

The payment of rent by a tenant is a discharge of his obligation under the lease for the possession of the property. Rent is not an obligation or a debt until it becomes due and payable by the terms of the lease.

The attempt of a landlord to collect rent that would accrue in the future under a lease, but had not yet become due, was denied by the court. The rent was no debt, the court declared, until the future time when it became payable, and even that event was not a certainty.

For this reason, any incident that deprives the tenant of possession will end his obligation to make rental payments unless there is some provision to the contrary in the lease.

This principle makes an advance payment of rent to a landlord a hazardous concession. After such a payment has been made, but before it becomes due, the landlord may sell the property or he may lose possession and ownership through foreclosure of a mortgage; there may be a fire or some other unforeseen contingency. Then the tenant has to sue the landlord to recover his money.

In the case of a mortgage foreclosure or the sale of the property, the tenant may readily become liable to the new landlord for the payment of rent as it becomes due, despite advance payments.

When rent is due

A written lease generally provides that the rent shall be paid in advance, usually on the first day of the month. It is an almost universal rule of law, however, that unless a lease expressly provides for payment of rent in advance, the rent will be payable at the end of the period for which it is reserved, whether it be a week, a month, a quarter, a year, or longer. If, as is usual, the rent is due monthly and the lease does not call for payment in advance, it will be due at the end of the month. The actual use of the premises is what the tenant agrees to pay rent for. Consequently, until this period of use is complete, no rent is payable unless it is otherwise agreed.

If no date is set   A lease of property for a term of years provided for a total rent of $20,000. Stipulated payment dates for $19,000 of this sum were set out in the lease, but no time for the payment of the remaining $1,000 was set under the lease. The payment of this $1,000, the court held, was for this reason not payable until the tenant's term of occupancy expired.

Refund in eviction cases   When rent is paid in advance, and a tenant is evicted, he is entitled to a partial refund. This refund should be equal to the rent-paid period of residence he is deprived of by his eviction. For example, if a tenant pays rent on the first of the month and is evicted on the fifteenth, he is entitled to a refund of the rental for the rest of the month after the fifteenth. Of course, this assumes the tenant has no further liability under a lease.

Accidental destruction of premises   The accidental destruction of the premises does not release a tenant from his liability for rent unless the lease provides for this. However, in the absence of a clause providing for no further payment of rent, if the premises are destroyed, an obvious injustice is inflicted on the tenant. For this reason, in many of the states, statutes have been enacted relieving him of the need to continue paying rent in such a situation.

Your duty to pay promptly   In most instances, rent is made payable on the first day of each month. Failure to pay on this date is a breach of contract, and the landlord is entitled to evict. However, if payment is made later in the month and the landlord accepts it without protest, this is a waiver that deprives him of the right to base eviction proceedings on nonpayment on the first. However, he can reinstate this provision for payment on the first by a demand to that effect in advance of a subsequent payment date.

Who must make repairs?   Under the common law—our traditional law, derived from England—a tenant takes the apartment or house he has leased as is. The common law still prevails in a majority of the states, and landlords are not obliged to make any repairs on the property. However, in some states the common law has been modified by statute, and landlords must make repairs. Also, in the absence of provision for repairs, the tenant covenants to make repairs in the tenant area and the landlord's duty to make repairs extends only to portions of the premises over which he retains control, e.g., common hallways, lobbies, elevators.

If a building becomes uninhabitable due to lack of repair, the tenant, at common law, could vacate the premises and in an action for nonpayment of rent assert the defense that the landlord caused the premises to become unfit for occupancy. This is referred to as a "constructive eviction." In 1971, a New York City tenant challenged this doctrine when, without moving from the premises, he alleged that the landlord breached the covenant of habitability and fitness for use by his failure to repair and maintain the building. The court ruled in favor of the tenant, citing the contemporary housing conditions in New York City and the chronic housing shortage. Under these conditions, the remedy of "constructive eviction," under which the tenant can claim that the premises have become uninhabitable and that therefore he has the right to move and to refuse to pay future rent, is an illusory remedy. As long as the tenant is required to move out to have this defense, he is in an unfortunate position, because there is no place to which to move. In these situations, the tenant seeks only habitable housing and not a defense against a lawsuit for rent.

In a recent case, the United States Supreme Court denied the right of tenants to withhold rent from a landlord who fails to make repairs. In a case involving the Oregon law, two tenants in Portland sued in the Federal court to have a state law held unconstitutional which allowed the eviction of tenants who failed to pay rent. They had stopped paying their $100 per month rent because the landlord had failed to make the repairs after city officials had declared the premises unfit for habitation.

In a 5-2 decision (Justices Lewis F. Powell, Jr., and William H. Rehnquist, recently appointed to the Supreme Court, did not take part in the decision), the Court made it clear that it was not prepared to assist the legal reformers who had helped to liberalize landlord-tenant laws. Justice Byron R. White, writing for the majority, stated: "The Constitution does not provide judicial remedies for every social and economic ill. We are unable to perceive in that document any constitutional guarantees of access to dwellings of a particular quality or any recognition of the right of a tenant to occupy the real property of his landlord beyond the term of his lease without the payment of rent."

The Court made it clear that "The assurance of adequate housing and the definition of landlord-tenant relationships is a legislative, not a judicial, function."

Some jurisdictions allow a tenant to make repairs and offset them against

the rent due the landlord. In New York, where a landlord had refused to repair a toilet in a residential apartment, the tenant was forced to hire a repairman at her own expense. The tenant was held entitled to offset the cost of the repairs against the rent due. The Court stressed that the traditional doctrine that distinguishes a landlord's right to receive rent from his duty to repair and maintain a building in accordance with local housing codes had received increased criticism, and it rejected the common-law idea of the landlord/tenant relationship for a more modern doctrine based upon mutual rights and obligations.

TV antennas and air conditioners

When you rent an apartment it does not include rights outside the premises unless specified. So, unless your lease so provides or unless rent control rules apply, you do not have the right to install a television antenna on the roof or an air conditioner which extends much beyond the window frame.

Control of rented premises

The control of the premises is the tenant's, and the responsibility for the welfare and safety of passers-by that might be imperiled by the improper use of the premises can be placed on the tenant and, in some cases, on the owner also.

Is a landlord liable for injuries?

In one of our southern states, a store building was leased. This building had a parapet wall of 8 to 14 feet. An adjoining building, which was 10 or 12 feet higher than the leased building, was destroyed by a fire which weakened the parapet wall. The tenants complained to the landlord of the danger from a collapse of this wall, but he made no repairs. In a severe wind storm, a month after the fire, the wall collapsed, crashing through the roof and the two upper floors of the rented store building, and killing one of the occupants on the first floor.

In the suit that followed, the court pointed out that under the common law, where there is no statute to the contrary, the landlord is not under any obligation to make repairs. In the absence of such a statute, a landlord is not liable to his tenant for personal injuries sustained because of the defective condition of the leased premises. However, if there is an agreement to make repairs which the landlord undertakes to fulfill and he does his work negligently, to the injury of the tenant, he bears the responsibility. This is the law, and it is enforced even if the landlord makes the repairs voluntarily, at the tenant's request. If the landlord, after agreeing to make repairs, fails to do so, and the tenant is injured, the landlord is liable.

In a case decided under a statute which required a landlord to keep the building and every part thereof in good repair, a landlord was held liable for $10,000 damages for the rape of a girl by an intruder who was presumed to have gained access to her apartment through a broken window. The landlord had been notified numerous times of the defective window and, since the window was part of the building and the landlord had sufficient time to make repairs, he was held liable. The judge said that failure to repair the broken window was a cause of the admission of the rapist.

A landlord's agreement to make limited repairs

Sometimes a landlord agrees to make certain repairs of a limited nature. This agreement does not bind him to make any other repairs. The extent of these repairs determines also his liability for negligence or personal injury.

For example, a landlord in Massachusetts agreed to make some repairs to a house, but did not agree to repair a piazza railing. Later the tenant was severely injured by a fall when this railing collapsed.

The landlord was not liable for the injury. He had not agreed to do this particular repair work, and could not be called negligent because he failed to make repairs that he had never agreed to make. The mere fact that he had made some repairs was no evidence that he would make more.

May you withhold rent?

A tenant agrees to make periodic payments of rent under his lease, and the landlord, on the other hand, agrees that he will furnish the tenant with various services, including adequate heat. Suppose the landlord fails to do his job—what recourse do you have? The laws in the various states are not uniform on whether rent may be withheld when the landlord fails to furnish some of the services he has promised. In some cases the tenant is required to pay the rent either to a court or to an escrow agent who will hold the money, pending court determination. Recently, tenants in many states have been withholding their rents in what have been called "rent strikes." When, as a consequence, the landlord brings action for eviction for nonpayment of rent, the tenants will assert the landlord's defect of service either as a defense to the suit or as a counterclaim. If your landlord disregards your complaint about lack of services, such as heat, ask the local health authorities or your lawyer for advice.

How to end a lease early

If your landlord is willing, you can end your lease before the stated date by an oral agreement with him. No formal writing is needed. You merely leave the premises and return the keys to the landlord, who accepts possession. However, it is safer to have a statement in writing from the landlord that you are released in order to avoid later claims. Most leases provide for rent to continue, even if you move out before their expiration.

When rent ends

During the last years of World War II, Barbara King occupied a one-family house. Her landlord sold the property, and the next August the new owner told her he wanted it for his own use and asked her to vacate. At the time, she was unable to do so, and she remained in the house, paying her rent regularly. On the following December 8, she sent the owner a check for eight days' rent, moved out, and gave him the keys. On her check for the rent she had endorsed, "Final payment in full for rent." The landlord, still holding her check, sued for $110, the full December rent.

The rent had been paid in full to the termination of tenancy, said the court. The landlord was not entitled to rent for the portion of the month that remained after the tenant had surrendered—and the landlord accepted—possession of the premises.

How the landlord's acceptance is proved

In general, the best possible token of a landlord's acceptance of surrender of premises is shown by his taking possession of the property and again assuming all the authority of an owner in possession.

In one case, a tenant told his landlord that he had an opportunity to buy a house and asked if a surrender of the rented premises would be acceptable for the unexpired term of his lease. The landlord apparently consented to the suggestion. The tenant moved out in November, gave the keys to the landlord, and paid the rent until the end of the month. Later the landlord sued him for the balance of the rent under the lease.

The court held that the landlord, in taking possession of the property and seeking a new tenant, "without any agreement express or implied that the tenant's rent was to continue, released the tenant from further liability."

Oral agreement to end lease

A plumbing store in Franklin, Kentucky, was rented for five years at $35 a month during World War II. After some months the tenant told his landlord that, with plumbing and heating fixtures "frozen" by the government, he could not continue the lease of the store unless the rent was reduced to $15 a month. The landlord replied, "If you can't pay the $35 a month, you can move out and I'll go into business myself."

The tenant replied, "I'll move out." To this the landlord answered, "All right."

In the suit the landlord brought later for the rent that accrued after the tenant vacated the premises, the court held the offer of the tenant and the consent of the landlord represented a surrender and acceptance of the lease, and that the landlord's action for the subsequent rent could not be maintained.

What holdover tenancy means

When you have to make arrangements with your landlord for the continuation of your tenancy because your lease is going to expire, be sure to make them a reasonable time before the date of expiration. Do not leave such arrangements to chance and the last minute. The courts of the various states have laid down different rules of law to govern the liability of a tenant under such circumstances, and not all are what you might desire.

Most states have a rule that when a tenant voluntarily continues in possession of property after a lease for one year or more has expired, and does so with the consent of the landlord, a tenancy for an additional year is created. This is known as a "holdover tenancy." Such a tenancy may be ended on notice of either landlord or tenant prior to the end of the year. The length of time between the giving of notice and the termination of the tenancy is governed in some cases by statute. The tenancy is also ended if the tenant moves out at the end of any holdover year, according to the rule in the majority of states. In some states the rule is that when a tenant continues to occupy premises with the landlord's consent after the lease has terminated, the tenant becomes automatically a tenant from year to year, and his tenancy can be terminated only on notice.

In a few states the rule is that when a tenant holds over after his lease expires, a tenancy at will or sufferance is created which can be ended with a notice by either the landlord or tenant to the other.

In most instances, the termination of these holdover tenancies is governed by statutes that prescribe when and how notice must be given. It is important to follow these rules to the letter.

When notice is not adequate

For six and one-half years a tenant had occupied premises. On October 1, he gave notice to his landlord that he was vacating the premises on the following January 1. The law of the state required a six-month notice rather than the notice of three months which the tenant gave. As a consequence, the notice was ineffectual, and the tenant was liable for the rent for another year. This emphasizes the care a tenant must take under such circumstances to follow the statutes of the state in which the property is located.

Restriction on landlord

The holdover rule works both ways. The landlord is bound to another one-year term if he accepts rent after the expiration of the original lease term. He cannot then evict the tenant during the additional term created by the holdover.

The rule about holdover for one year also applies to leases for a term of months or weeks or any period less than a year. In such cases the holdover and the payment and acceptance of rent after the end of the original lease creates a new term for one month or one week, as the case may be.

Rent control and holdovers

This doctrine of holdover tenancy has no application if, when the original lease term expires, the tenant is authorized to continue in possession by any Federal, state, or local rent control laws. In these cases he becomes what is known as a "statutory tenant," and the tenancy can be terminated at any time without further liability by his removal from the premises. The reason for this exception is that the rent control laws prevent the landlord from dispossessing the tenant at the end of the lease term, and hence he is not held to have given his implied consent to the holdover by the acceptance of rent.

Subletting and assignment

If your lease prohibits subletting or assigning of premises, you must obey this provision. If it contains no such provision, you are free to sublet all or part of the premises. A sublease is a transfer of only a part of the lessee's estate or interest in the premises, with a right to take it back at some time before the term of the lease expires, while an assignment is a transfer by the lessee of his entire interest remaining in the lease. When a tenant sublets or assigns his interest in the lease, generally he is still primarily liable for all of the covenants and terms of the lease, and only upon specific agreement with the landlord can the tenant be relieved of this liability.

The only restriction imposed by law on a tenant who sublets is that the use of the property by a subtenant or assignee of the lease shall not be of a different character than that provided by the lease. In other words, the subtenant must observe all the terms and restrictions of the lease as the original tenant would.

Subletting against landlord's wishes

Generally, if you assign or sublet when the lease prohibits you to, this act does not of itself terminate the lease. It merely gives the landlord a right to terminate. He must do this in the manner prescribed in the lease. On the other hand, the violation of a provision against subletting will not permit the landlord to declare the assignment or sublease void and at the same time allow him to continue the exercise of his rights under the original lease.

In other words, the landlord may terminate the lease and thereby release the tenant of any further obligation for the payment of this rent, but the landlord cannot collect rent from the tenant and at the same time deny the tenant the benefits of the lease under which he is collecting that rent.

How a landlord waives the subletting restriction

A landlord may waive his right to withhold his consent to an assignment or sublease. He may even give his consent after a specifically prohibited assignment or sublease has been made. The landlord's waiver may be made either by words or acts that clearly evidence his consent. The law finds a waiver when the landlord, having knowledge of the subletting in violation of the lease terms, accepts rent from the tenant.

Taking in roomers

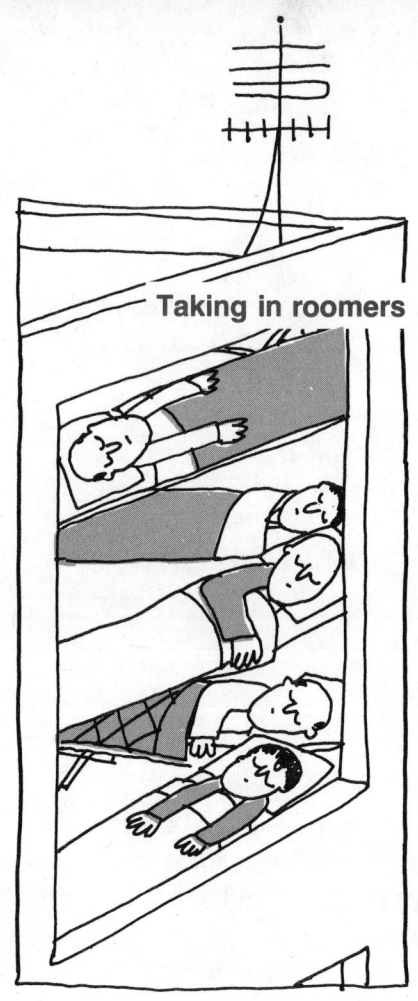

Some of the rooms in an apartment in the District of Columbia were rented by the tenant to roomers or lodgers. The landlord demanded the eviction of the tenant, claiming this use of the apartment for roomers was a violation of such a clause against subletting contained in the lease.

A roomer or lodger, asserted the court, is not a tenant. The letting of a room to a lodger is not a subletting that entitles the owner to posession as a breach of the covenant against subletting. The tenant here had the exclusive possession of the apartment in which she rented rooms to lodgers. The lodger had only a right to use or occupy the room—a mere license to use it which gave him no control of the premises, such as would be enjoyed by a tenant under a sublease.

License or lease?

A case involving two businessmen illustrates further the difference between a lease and a license. A wholesale shoe manufacturer consigned to a retailer a stock of shoes under an agreement that the shoe manufacturer should "lease a sufficient amount of space in the store and the store windows for the sale and fitting" of his shoes.

The retailer failed to pay the rent of the store. The landlord seized the stock of shoes for the unpaid balance, claiming that the manufacturer was a subtenant and his goods subject to the landlord's lien for rent.

Calling this arrangement between the shoe manufacturer and the storekeeper a lease did not make it so, asserted the court. When the use and occupation of premises is given for a special purpose in which the owner is concerned, and the owner retains control and legal possession, no tenancy is created. This rule applies equally to the relation of lodgers and proprietors of rooming houses.

The tenant's obligations after eviction

A lease provided that should the tenant be dispossessed or evicted, he should pay a sum equivalent to the rent still due—which should be applied to the expense of obtaining possession, then to the payment of the rent—and he should be liable for any deficiency.

The tenant who received this lease deposited $800 in security. Eventually, he was evicted. In this situation, not only was he deprived of possession of the property, but the security he had deposited was applied to rent that accrued after he had been dispossessed.

When this tenant sued to recover his money, the court pointed out that the obligation of the tenant to pay rent for the full-lease term may be made to survive a notice of termination or eviction, while the landlord retains the security to cover this obligation.

The tenant, we have said, is entitled to a credit for any rent received from another person to whom the landlord lets the premises. It is not the landlord's obligation, however, to find another tenant.

Rent control and statutory tenancy

It is important to bear in mind that the rules of law set forth in this chapter are the general rules concerning the landlord and tenant.

These rules have been temporarily modified by rent control statutes, primarily for the benefit of tenants, which usually deprive landlords of the right to dispossess tenants except for nonpayment of rent and in certain other specified circumstances, such as use of the premises for himself or his immediate family, demolition of the building, etc. Landlords also are deprived of the right, where the premises are subject to rent control, to set the terms of the tenancy.

There is no standard national rule in matters of this kind, and your local rent office, or your attorney, should be consulted.

CHAPTER 23

What You should Know About Insurance

There are various types of insurance which you come in contact with in your day-to-day activity. Life insurance, accident insurance, health insurance, and unemployment insurance are probably the best known and most widely used. If you own a house, you probably have liability, property, and fire insurance. Most car owners carry personal liability, fire and theft, and collision insurance, even if these are not required by state law. This chapter will outline basic information to help you understand the purpose and coverage of insurance.

An insurance policy is a contract and, like any other contract, may be void if it is made with fraudulent misrepresentations by either of the parties. The insurance company cannot be held to indemnify you against a loss when the risk it agrees to indemnify under its policy is not the actual risk as it was represented by you in your application.

Not all misrepresentations will deprive a person of his right to benefits. Many people misunderstand the questions in the applications and thus supply faulty answers, or they forget to include details that may later turn out to be significant. Omissions and other misrepresentations may be minor or major, and their effect on the right to collect depends on the circumstances, as the cases that follow will show.

A life insurance policy was issued on the life of a man who, less than six months afterward, died of cancer. In his application for this insurance, he had represented to the company that for 12 years previous he had consulted no physicians except in one instance—when he was ill with influenza. The court, in holding the company not liable for the face amount of the policy, pointed out that his failure to mention this cancerous condition in his application was a concealment of a material fact that might well have been a contributory cause to his death, and increased the risk assumed by the company.

"Whether the misrepresentation relates to health or to some other fact or condition, the final test is *whether there was an increase in risk*," the court declared.

When there is a minor misrepresentation

An application for an accident and health policy failed to state that, a year before the application, the applicant had suffered an injury to his foot. Two days after the policy was issued, the insured, while working for an engineering organization, fell and was seriously injured. The insurance company maintained he was guilty of a misrepresentation in the application because he had omitted any mention of the foot injury.

It could not be proved that the foot injury was responsible for the man's fall. The omission was therefore held by the court not to be a material misrepresentation that would justify the company refusing to pay benefits.

Each decision, when there is a charge of misrepresentation, depends, as we have said, upon the facts of the particular case.

An innocent misrepresentation may be damaging

A warranty in your policy is a material statement and is vital to the contract. Breach a warranty, and the insurance company can void your policy. If your policy says that any declaration you make concerning your health is a warranty, and you give inaccurate information about your health, you are endangering your right to collect, even if the misrepresentation is unwitting. Here is an unfortunate example of how a person may be penalized even though he is innocent:

Many years before Ettman applied for a disability insurance policy, he was unable to read the writing on the blackboard at school. His mother took him to an eminent eye specialist. This doctor found that the boy was suffering from a disease that would eventually cause him to lose his sight. But at the request of the boy's mother, the doctor withheld this information from him.

During World War I, Ettman's eye condition prevented him from serving in the armed forces. His statement at the time he applied for his disability insurance policy was that he was nearsighted. Asked why the Army had rejected him, he said, "I knew I was nearsighted, and I didn't think they would use anybody in the Army that had glasses."

Later, when his sight failed him, he sought to collect benefits. The company contested his right, alleging misrepresentation when he originally applied.

The court held that this man could not recover under his policy. His statements about his health in the application for insurance were warranties, or material statements. Though the insured might have had no knowledge of their falsity or of his condition, his statements were a breach of warranty.

Reinstating a policy

A year before his death, a man who held a life insurance policy was afflicted with Hodgkin's disease, which is incurable and inevitably fatal. Six months later, his policy lapsed because of nonpayment of premiums. In his application for its reinstatement, the following question appeared: "Within the past two years have you had any illness or have you consulted or been treated by any physician or physicians?" He answered it with a "no."

When the insurance company refused to pay benefits and a suit was brought against it, the court declared this man's answer in the application "was patently untrue and for more than two months prior thereto the insured was a 'sick man.' The misrepresentation of the insured that he had not consulted a physician had the effect of increasing the risk." For this reason, the decision favored the company.

An important exception

There is an important exception to this right of an insurance company to refuse to pay benefits under a policy when it has been secured through misrepresentations by the insured. This right may be automatically waived if the company continues to accept premiums paid after it has notice or knowledge of such misrepresentation.

A man suffering with ulcers applied for and was granted a policy of life insurance. Five months later he developed severe symptoms. He was taken to a hospital, where he died in a few months.

The insurance company contended his death was caused by a condition that had existed for over ten years. However, while the insured was confined to the hospital, his wife, who had been paying the premiums on his policy, told a representative of the company about her husband's condition. She also told this agent that her husband had made misrepresentations when he applied to have his policy reinstated after it had lapsed because of nonpayment of premiums a few months before. She asked the agent if his company would continue the policy and accept her future payments. After this conversation, three premiums were paid by her and accepted by the company before her husband's death.

Legally, when the company received, in the person of its agent, notice of the misrepresentations of the insured, it possessed grounds for the forfeiture of the policy. Whether or not the agent conveyed this information to the office of the company was immaterial. Before the law, a company and its agent are the same thing. When the company continued to accept the premiums and allowed the matter to rest without doing anything further, its right to forfeit the policy was lost.

The difference between brokers and agents

The average person often assumes, to his grief, that the insurance broker is the agent of the insurance company by which he is insured and that the transactions he has with the broker are transactions with the company. While it is true that under some circumstances the broker is the agent of the insurance company, yet in others he is solely the agent of the insured. Do not take anything for granted. Get from the company written assurance that your broker is their authorized representative. If he is not, the safe and proper method in the conduct of insurance transactions is to carry them on directly with the company itself. Pay your premiums to the company directly. Send proofs of loss to the company yourself and make your requests for changes or modifications of your policy to the company. In this way you will eliminate the question that often vexes even the courts—whether the broker is the agent of the insurance company or of the person who is insured.

Whose agent is he?

The proprietor of a lunchroom asked a friend who was an insurance broker to secure for his automobile a policy of fire and theft insurance and also a policy of property damage. The broker applied for both policies, but the property damage policy could not be issued until after an investigation. The broker, however, did not tell the insured of the delay in the issuance of the property damage policy. Two days later a property damage loss occurred.

The lunchroom proprietor, suing for the damages he had suffered, contended that the risk had been accepted by the company through the broker as its agent. He was acting on the erroneous assumption of most laymen that such a relationship exists between the broker and the company.

The court held the lunchroom proprietor had no claim against the insurance company since the broker was the agent not for the insurance company but for the lunchroom proprietor. Here a distinction was made by the court that is of vital importance in transactions like this:

"Ordinarily the relation between the insured and the broker is that between principal and agent. An insurance broker is ordinarily employed by a person seeking insurance, and one so employed is to be distinguished from the ordinary insurance agent who is employed by insurance companies to solicit and write insurance by and in the company."

When the broker is the company's agent

It is a general law, as the courts have pointed out, that a broker is the agent of the policy holder and not of the insurer. Generally, he acts for you. However, when he receives the executed policy for delivery to you, he becomes for that purpose the agent of the company.

Another general rule of law about insurance brokers is that, when a company gives a policy of insurance to a broker for delivery to the insured, the broker is authorized to collect the premium on the policy at the time he delivers the policy. To that extent a broker may be the agent of the company.

Who can be the beneficiary

If you take out an insurance policy, to collect benefits you must have an insurable interest in the person or property it covers.

This means simply an interest in any person whose death or injury, or any property whose loss or destruction would cause you serious disadvantage or direct financial loss.

This basic rule of law has eliminated to a large degree speculation in the buying and selling of insurance policies. Also, before this rule was established, it was objected that policies were often nothing more than wagering or gambling policies, by which any disinterested insurer stood to profit if the event he insured against, and in the hope of which he paid premiums, happened to take place. Moreover, it used to be alleged that if a person named as a beneficiary in a life insurance policy had no serious interest in the continued welfare of the one insured, there was created a serious temptation to take human life in order to receive the benefits of the policy.

What is an insurable interest in life insurance?

In line with this rule, two safeguards are imposed on the issuance of life insurance policies. The person taking out insurance naming himself as beneficiary must stand in a close family or financial relationship to the person whose life is the subject of the policy. The beneficiary must also acquire the insurance with the consent of the person insured. Everyone may rightfully and legally provide in his insurance policy for those who are related by ties of blood or affection, not excluding illegitimate children.

As a general rule a person may lawfully take out a life insurance policy on his own life and make it payable to whomsoever he wishes even though the beneficiary has no insurable interest, provided the insured party acts in good faith without intent to defraud the insurance company. When the insurance is taken out on the life of another, an insurable interest must exist.

The purpose of requiring an insurable interest is to prevent insurance being a lottery in which a person may bet on the probability that a certain event will occur. The idea of insurance is to protect people against substantial loss, not to give them a chance on a windfall.

In a recent case in New York, a man took insurance on an automobile; when the automobile was stolen, the insurance company refused to pay on the ground that the man had no insurable interest in the automobile, because, when he bought it, it was a stolen car. Now if he knew it was stolen when he bought it, he obviously would not be entitled to collect insurance when it was stolen from him. If, however, he was an innocent purchaser without knowledge that the car was "hot" property, was this possession sufficient to give him an insurable interest? The court stated that he had a substantial economic interest in the vehicle and that he had the right of ownership as against everyone but the true owner, and that this gave him a sufficient interest to make it insurable.

Insurance may be taken out on the life of a debtor, but it must be reasonably proportioned to the amount of his obligation to his creditor.

In one case, a brother attempted to collect the proceeds of an insurance policy that he had taken out on the life of his sister.

"A brother has no insurable interest in the life of his sister merely because of the relationship," was the ruling of the court that rejected his claim. "In order for a brother to have such an insurable interest, it must appear that he is her heir at law or dependent on her in some way, or that the relation of debtor and creditor exists between them."

Can business associates insure each other?

An agreement between C. G. Cooper and Clarence Lebus provided that Lebus was to construct a restaurant building and a filling station, and Cooper was to conduct the business. The profits were to be divided equally between the two men. Also, an insurance policy was issued on Cooper's life for the benefit of Lebus.

At Cooper's death, the proceeds of the policy were paid to the administrators of the estate of Lebus, who had also died. The administrators of Cooper's estate sought to recover the money on the claim of no insurable interest on the part of Lebus.

Holding that the administrators of Cooper's estate were not entitled to this money and that Lebus had an insurable interest in Cooper's life, the court asserted that any person had such an interest in the life of another when he was a creditor and had a financial interest in the preservation of the life of the insured.

It is common, therefore, in accordance with this law, for business partners to insure their lives, each for the benefit of the other. This has importance where the success of a business is dependent on both or all partners. Such policies are also used in order to permit the heirs of the deceased partner to be paid the value of his share in the enterprise so that the surviving partner can continue the business without division of its assets.

Study your policy

Before you accept a life insurance policy, read it through carefully. Pay particular attention to the exceptions, the causes from which death may result that are not covered by the insurance. If there is any doubt or uncertainty, insist that the company write its policy in clear and unequivocal terms in every respect, specifying precisely under what circumstances they will pay the death benefit, and under what circumstances they will not.

Such a clear and well-defined statement of the circumstances under which your beneficiaries will receive the money you wish to provide, may spare them considerable difficulty later on. Your insurance company agent will usually help you with the policy, but you should be certain that you have taken all the necessary steps yourself.

Double indemnity

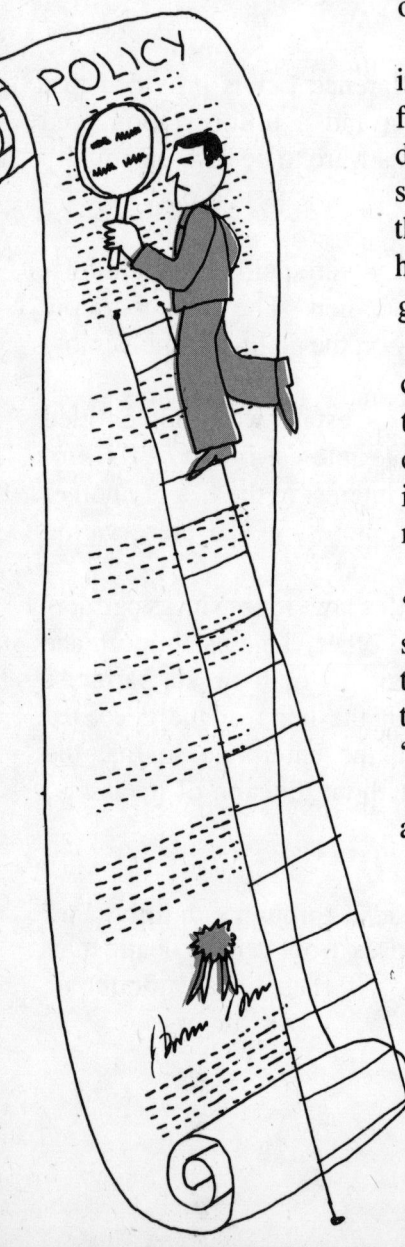

Many life insurance policies provide for double indemnity—payment of double the face value of the policy—when the death of the policy holder occurs through an accident.

Across the cover page of one policy was stamped in purple ink "Double indemnity for fatal accident." In the body of the policy this provision for double indemnity was limited to occasions when the death "has resulted directly and independently of all other causes, from bodily injury effected solely through external, violent, and accidental means, provided, however, that such double indemnity shall not be payable if the insured's death has resulted directly or indirectly from the taking of poison or inhaling gas, whether voluntarily or otherwise."

The insured was killed by the inhalation of carbon monoxide gas. The court criticized the glaring ambiguity and the contradiction in the representation stamped in purple ink on the cover of the policy and the terms of coverage set forth in the body of the instrument. It pointed out that the insurer could easily have avoided ambiguity by adding to the stamped matter some brief expression calling attention to the limitations.

"Even a careful reading of the whole instrument," the court declared, "would probably leave in the uninitiated mind the belief that the especially stamped phraseology was intended to afford a measure of protection broader than that indicated in the printed matter of the policy." The insured was therefore held entitled to the double indemnity provided by the policy. "The stamped matter must be taken as part of the policy."

The usual rule when there is ambiguity is to construe the document against those who prepared it.

**What accidental
death means**

The child of a policy holder was a patient in a hospital. She urgently needed a blood transfusion for her recovery. His blood being found suitable, the policy holder offered it for the transfusion. A preliminary examination showed his heart to be normal.

While the insured was on the operating table, and before a teaspoonful of blood had been withdrawn, he died. The court held that the beneficiary under the life insurance policy of this man was entitled to the double indemnity that was provided when death was caused by "external, violent, and accidental means."

"The interpretation," said the court, "must be that of the average man who would say that a death has been caused by accidental means when the deceased died in such a way that his death is spoken of as accidental."

Suicide

As a matter of general law, on an ordinary life insurance policy, the burden of proof to sustain any exception is on the insurance company. There is also a presumption against death by suicide, so that if the insurance company contends that the accidental death was due to suicide, they have the burden of proving that the insured took his or her own life. However, where double indemnity is involved, the beneficiary has the burden of proof to show that the provision applies.

**If you pay your
premium late**

The details in the carrying out of insurance contracts are governed very largely by the provisions of the policy itself. In the payment of premiums, the time and method is usually specified in the policy. Whether or not you are late in paying your premium, and therefore whether or not your policy has lapsed, will depend on the postmark of the envelope in which the premium was sent, the receipt, or on any other stipulation that has been made a provision of the policy.

**How soon the company
is liable**

How soon the company becomes liable under a new policy is also governed by its provisions. The liability may exist when the first premium is paid or it may exist independent of the payment of this premium; the policy may be delivered and the company become liable for the risk with a time provision for the payment.

In the absence of a statute or provision in the policy or application to the contrary, payment of the first premium is not generally necessary to make the contract of insurance valid or effective.

When a lapsed policy still has value

Many life policies contain provisions against forfeiture. That is, in the event you should fail to pay the premium, the insurance contract is not canceled but you are given a lesser amount of insurance, that is, paid in full. The value of the policy is figured by the amounts previously received by the company in premiums—although this value may be only a fraction of the face of the policy when it was originally issued to you.

By contract or statute a grace period may be provided covering the time between the date the premium is due and cancellation of the policy.

Can creditors claim your insurance?

A policy of life insurance naming someone other than the insured as beneficiary is ordinarily considered the property of the beneficiary. For example, when the amount of the policy is for the benefit of the wife, the husband is considered to have made the payments as the agent of the wife. In many instances, however, the amount that may thus be allocated for the benefit of the wife, in the event of interference by creditors of the husband, is limited by statute.

When the policy is payable to the estate of the insured it is his property. It is subject to the claims of his creditors, and to his own disposition as security for any loans or similar business uses which he may undertake.

Ordinary or whole life insurance

This type of insurance allows the insured to accumulate a portion of the premium and give the policy some intrinsic or surrender value, which increases over time, in addition to the amount of insurance which is payable on death and which is reflected in the face value of the policy. Ordinary life insurance costs about three times as much as term insurance in the same face amount, which has no value unless you die.

There are beneficial aspects in an ordinary life insurance policy in addition to surrender value. The interest component of ordinary life insurance is neither taxed to the insured or the beneficiary. Once an ordinary life insurance policy has been issued, the insured need never take another physical examination, and as long as the conditions of the policy are met, the insurance company cannot cancel your policy.

Term insurance

This is a form of life insurance, effective only for the term or period for which the premium is paid, with, possibly, the option of continuing the insurance from term to term. But at the end of the term the liability of the company ceases.

Under these policies, the company retains the right to decline a renewal.

Since term insurance is for a stated period—a number of months or whatever time is presented by the premium which is paid—the premiums are lower in amount than for a regular life insurance policy and the coverage of the policy is limited. Term insurance is pure death insurance with no intrinsic value.

Endowment insurance

The contract for this type of insurance is that the insurance company will pay a specific sum to the insured when and if he attains the age stated in the policy, or, if he dies before that time, the company agrees to pay the sum to the beneficiary named in the policy. Actually, it is insurance for the continuance of life rather than its ending, and it is an investment and a form of saving as well as life insurance.

There is no "best" type of insurance. Everyone differs in his needs and requires different protection. It is always best to discuss your insurance needs with a reputable broker or agent, or your lawyer, who can help you evaluate the various aspects of different types of life insurance.

Property damage–automobiles

A fundamental rule about policies indemnifying damages to property is that, when their clauses are doubtful in meaning, they are interpreted in favor of the insured. Such policy clauses, however, must be interpreted in such a way that each clause is given effect, as far as possible.

The difficulties and misunderstandings that can arise out of ambiguous clauses are many, and often cannot be foreseen. The wisest course in selecting a policy is to look for a broad and general coverage restricted by as few exceptions as possible.

This is as true of policies covering automobiles as it is of policies covering other kinds of property.

Car damaged by unknown cause

A parked automobile insured under a casualty insurance policy was damaged by an unknown cause while the owner was absent. The policy contained a provision making the insuring company liable "for any loss of or damage to the automobile and the equipment usually attached thereto . . . except that this company shall not be liable for loss by collision."

The insured sought to establish that the damage was not from collision.

This the court refused to concede. "A collision," it was pointed out, "implies an impact. Both bodies may be in motion or one in motion and the other stationary. Clearly it matters not whether the car or the other object is in motion. The damage to the insured car was caused by collision with another object."

Property damage claims arise from such infinite varieties of circumstances that each incident must stand by itself.

Only broad general rules of law can be laid down applicable to all instances.

When a car is used as a public conveyance

Frequently, policies covering liability for property damage to automobiles contain a clause saying that no liability is incurred by the insuring company if the automobile is "used as a public or livery conveyance for carrying passengers for compensation," or they have other clauses with similar limitations.

The courts have been careful to construe this to mean that a vehicle is held out to the public as a mode of transportation available for use by a wide class of people. Use of a vehicle for a limited class of people

selected by a predetermined standard does not make the vehicle a public conveyance. In Missouri, a driver who used a vehicle to commute with a group of friends who contributed toward driving expenses was not held to be driving a public vehicle. In New York, a personal car operated by a woman to transfer her children with other children to and from a day camp was held not a public conveyance.

Despite the fact that the use of a vehicle was restricted to the members of a country club, a California court found that any member of the public could patronize the club, thus eliminating the selectivity of the group and placing the vehicle in the class of a public conveyance.

In determining whether a conveyance is public or private, the importance of charging a fare varies from state to state. In Louisiana, the charging of a fare is essential in determining a conveyance to be a public conveyance; in California, the charging of a fare is not an essential element.

Automobile collision and casualty insurance

A company insured an automobile owner against damages from collision. However, the policy stated the company would not pay if the collision occurred when the automobile was driven by a person violating the provisions of the law relating to age or occupation.

In this case, the policy holder's car was involved in a collision when it was being driven by his daughter. Since she was only 15 years old and had not received a driver's license, he could not recover his damages.

Another policy insured against loss or damage to an automobile from collision or upset or from the "stranding, sinking, or burning or derailment of any conveyance in or upon which the automobile was being transported."

The owner of the policy, driving his truck and trailer onto a ferry-boat, was directed by a ferry employee to stop. He did so. In some way the stopping of his large vehicle loosened the stakes to which the ferry-boat was tied. The boat drifted into midstream, and the truck and trailer, left thus half on and half off the boat, dropped into the river.

The insurance company contended that the accident was not one covered by the policy. The court, however, held that it was, since the damage was ultimately caused by the ferry and its employee, and the driver was entitled to recover from the company the amount of his damage.

One automobile insurance policy provided for indemnity "for any loss or damage to the automobile except by collision, breakage of glass, loss caused by missiles, falling objects, theft, explosion, earthquake, wind storm, hail, water, flood, vandalism, riot, or civil commotion."

The policy holder's car was parked on a steep grade facing downhill, the front wheel turned against the curb, the hand brake set, and the gears engaged. A three-and-one-half-year-old child crawled into the car and managed to release the brake. The car rolled down the hill, collided with a parked car, and stopped. The damages resulting from the acts of this child, the court held here, were covered by the insurance policy and the accident was not within the exceptions made to its coverage.

No-fault insurance

After many years of discussion a number of states have adopted "no-fault" automobile insurance. States' plans vary, but basically they provide that an insured victim can collect out-of-pocket losses from his own insurance company, whether or not he was negligent, quickly and with little additional expense. Traditionally, drivers carry liability insurance protecting them in case they negligently injure someone. Victims recover damages only when they can prove that an accident was not their fault—often a costly and time-consuming task.

When you carry liability insurance—and in many states it is compulsory—you are protecting yourself against your own fault. In any suit brought for injuries or property damage suffered because of another person's fault, the victim, in order to recover damages, must show, first, that the other person was negligent, and, second, that he (the victim) did not contribute to the accident by his own negligence. If the victim establishes his case, the compensation he receives is paid by the other person's insurance company.

The theory behind no-fault insurance is that, in view of the great number of automobile accidents and in view of the difficulty of apportioning responsibility, payment of damages should be dealt with in the manner of workmen's compensation cases. Under no-fault plans, the victim is compensated regardless of whose fault the accident was. The amount, however, is generally limited to loss of income and out-of-pocket medical and hospital expenses. (In traditional automobile negligence suits, there are, apart from these basic costs, often additional grounds for recovery of damages, such as those caused by pain and suffering. The determination of monetary compensation for such nebulous damages may be relatively difficult, but the resulting awards may be substantial.)

One exception to the rule requiring freedom from negligence is where the victim has died, because it is too difficult in this situation to prove freedom from negligence. Another exception is where the victim has lost his memory. In a recent case in New York, a trailer truck negligently blocked a thruway. An automobile collided with the trailer truck, and as a result, the driver of the automobile suffered loss of memory, among other injuries. He was in no position to testify as to his freedom from negligence, and under the circumstances the court treaded lightly on the obligation to show such due care on the victim's part.

Accident insurance

As we indicated earlier in this chapter, the words "accident" and "accidental" have no technical legal meaning but are used by the courts in the ordinary sense in which they are understood by the average man.

Justice Blatchford of the Supreme Court once defined an accident in the following way: "If a result is such as follows from ordinary means voluntarily employed in a not unusual or accepted way, it cannot be a result effected by accidental means; but if, in the act which precedes the injury, something unforeseen, unexpected, and unusual occurs which produces the injury, then the injury has resulted through accidental means."

It is against injuries arising from these "unforeseen, unexpected, and unusual" occurrences that accident insurance indemnifies the policy holder.

What is total disability?

A common provision in accident insurance policies is that benefits are payable only when the injuries "wholly and continuously disable the insured from performing any and every duty pertaining to his occupation."

A meat cleaver slipped and cut off the right-hand thumb of a butcher insured by such a policy. With this injury, he was unable to carry on his work as usual. He could do only such minor jobs as grinding sausage and cutting coarse meats.

The insurance company refused to pay under their policy, claiming he was not prevented from "performing any and every duty pertaining to his work," as provided in the policy.

The rule prevailing in most of the states in such a case is that the total disability contemplated by an accident policy is not to be interpreted according to the strict meaning of the phrase. The courts generally do not require the insured to be in a state of absolute helplessness for benefits to be payable. Rather, the phrase means "an inability to do all the substantial and material acts necessary to the prosecution of the insured's business in a customary and usual manner," say the courts.

In the butcher's case, the court held that the injury entitled him to the benefits payable under the total disability clause in his policy, for there was a substantial interference in the pursuit of his trade.

Benefits while under a physician's care

Another phrase in ordinary use in accident policies restricts the payment of benefits to the period in which the insured "shall be under the regular care of a legally qualified physician or surgeon."

An injured man was told by a surgeon to massage his injured hand and soak it in hot water, and with this advice the doctor discontinued his treatment. The man insisted that by following these instructions he was "under the regular care of a physician." But the court ruled this self-treatment was not the equivalent of being under the regular care of a physician, and denied the man a recovery of benefits.

"Continuously confined within the house"

Some accident policies provide for the payment of benefits only during the period in which the insured is "continuously confined within the house." An oil contractor was disabled by acute inflammatory arthritis. He had, however, taken automobile trips for his health and in a few instances had transacted some business on these trips. Defending his right to benefits under this clause in his accident insurance policy, he said, "All I did on those trips was just to ride in the car; somebody else always did the driving."

"Continuous confinement," as used in such clauses of accident insurance policies, does not mean actual confinement within a house. "The mere fact that he went out occasionally for the purpose of taking exercise and fresh air under the advice of his physician," said the court, deciding in his favor, "would not be sufficient to prevent recovery of benefits."

Fire insurance

A fire insurance policy is a contract by which an insurance company agrees to indemnify the owner of property, or anyone who has an insurable interest in property, against damage to it by fire. It is a contract with the policy holder alone and does not run with the property. However, when the property is sold, the policy may ordinarily be assigned to the purchaser, provided the consent of the insurance company is obtained. If this assignment is not ratified by the company, the purchaser has no rights under the policy.

As with other types of insurance, the person for whose benefit fire insurance is written must have what we have called an insurable interest in the property insured. You have an insurable interest in property when you will be benefited by its continued existence and will suffer a financial loss if it is destroyed. An executor, a receiver, a person owning merely an interest in a building, or any person in rightful possession has such an interest. But a mere trespasser has no interest that would sustain his recovery for any loss.

It is to your advantage to have the policy describe the property in comprehensive or in general terms. However, the description will not be extended to cover property outside what you and the insurance company had in mind when the policy was drawn up.

Payment of the premium to an authorized agent of the insurance company is adequate. The fact that a broker has the right to solicit insurance does not authorize him to collect premiums. The recommended practice is payment by a check to the order of the insurance company.

Any misstatement of fact by the insured that might induce the company more readily to write the policy and accept the risk will void the policy.

When a fire loss occurs, the usual requirement of the fire insurance company is that notice of the loss be given it immediately. No particular form of proof of loss is required, unless provided by the policy, but the proofs furnished should contain all the information available to the insured. Under such circumstances, you should bear in mind that the statements you include in any proofs of loss are binding. If you make them carelessly or inaccurately, this may prejudice your right to recover the insurance to which you are otherwise entitled.

Two kinds of fires

Surprising as it may seem, the courts distinguish between "hostile" and "friendly" fires. A fire insurance policy always insures against damages from a hostile fire, as distinguished from a friendly fire. In the words of one court:

"If a fire is a friendly fire, that is, one in a furnace or stove which is subject to control in such furnace or stove and one not escaping therefrom, it is not covered by these policies."

When a "friendly fire" causes damage

A store building was heated by a furnace that became overheated one night. Smoke and soot poured from the furnace room, and the showrooms of the store were covered with ashes and dust. In the lawsuit against the insurance company for the damages from this fire, the court held this a friendly fire. It did not come under the fire coverage of insurance policies on the store and its contents. "The basic point here, moreover, is that nothing burned," said the court.

If you drop an object into a fire

A package of antique jewelry accidentally left on the floor of a jewelry store was swept up by employees and thrown with the day's accumulation of trash and rubbish into an incinerator. The fire policy insured against "all direct loss or damage by fire." Under this clause, an attempt was made to collect damages.

In deciding the case, the court referred to the principle of nonrecovery for damages due to a friendly fire. The policy did not insure against a loss of this kind.

If a fire is for the ordinary purpose of heating, lighting, manufacturing, or incinerating, it is not a fire within the meaning of a fire policy. Had fire escaped from the stove and burned the jewelry, damages could have been collected.

Fire as a proximate cause of damage

The Ohio River had overflowed its banks at Cincinnati. A gasoline tank was torn from its moorings by the flood and exploded in flames 500 yards from the building of the insured. The fire spread rapidly in the direction of the building, and employees of the insured who were working in his store were ordered by the police and fire departments to vacate it. The inundating water reached a depth of five feet in the store, damaging the merchandise. However, none of the property was damaged directly by the fire or by the use of water in checking the fire. Still, it was because of the fire that the employees had not been permitted to remain and save the merchandise.

The court held that the fire was the "proximate" cause of the loss. "The phrase 'all direct loss or damage by fire,' or 'loss or damage by fire caused by order of civil authority,' is not restricted to a fire on the premises, and a loss will be held to be within such policies where a fire was the means or agency in causing the loss."

Thus damage to premises caused in combating a fire in adjoining or nearby premises can be within the coverage of the policy.

Extended coverage with a fire insurance policy

A fire insurance policy excepted from its coverage "loss by explosion or lightning unless fire ensue and in that event for loss or damage by fire only. If a building or a material part thereof fall except as a result of fire, all insurance by this policy on such building or its contents shall immediately cease." Most fire insurance policies today do not exclude lightning.

An explosion occurred, followed by a fire in which some additions to the building collapsed. The defense of the insurance company was that the collapse of these additions released the company from liability.

The court said that the doubts and ambiguities in an insurance policy must be interpreted in favor of the policy holder and that the company was liable here for whatever damages occurred to the building as a consequence of the fire.

Coverage for such accidents not involving fire is known as "extended coverage." It is obtainable by a rider to the fire insurance policy upon payment of an additional premium which is much less than the premium for fire coverage alone.

Theft

The phrases used in some theft insurance policies are not always as clear as they could be. Lack of uniformity in the decisions of the courts makes it hard to predict how they will decide in certain cases. As with other policies, follow this rule: Beware of words in your theft policy that are "weasel words"—terms that can take on unforeseen shades of meaning under the stresses and strains of a court suit.

Robbery is not "trickery"

What is or is not a robbery generally depends upon the meaning given the word by the insurance policy. It is important to study policy definitions carefully, as the following case shows.

The theft policy of a pawnbroker had a provision that "robbery as used in this policy shall mean a felonious and forcible taking of property: (a) by violence inflicted on a custodian; (b) by putting him in fear of violence; (c) by an overt felonious act committed in the presence of a custodian and of which he was actually cognizant."

One day, shortly before noon, a well-dressed man came into the policy holder's pawnshop and asked to see an unset diamond—he had heard about it through an acquaintance of the pawnbroker. In a small room of the shop the diamond was laid on a flat-top desk for exhibition. After some conversation the stranger picked up the diamond and, while inspecting it, attempted to light a cigarette. As he did so, there dropped from his hands to the desk an object resembling the diamond, but which later proved to be a mere bit of glass. The stranger left without making a purchase and, shortly afterwards, the pawnbroker discovered the real gem was gone. He tried unsuccessfully to overtake the thief with the aid of the police, but no trace of the man was ever found.

When the pawnbroker sued to recover the value of the stolen diamond, the insurance company claimed he had no right to collect since his suit was based on the clause in the policy insuring against loss through "an overt felonious act committed in the presence of the custodian." According to the company, the crime was one of trickery, and not robbery.

If the company had not defined robbery the way it did in phrase (c) of the policy, observed the court, its argument about trickery would have made more sense. But "no amount of argument, no matter how well presented, can alter the plain reading of the company's undertaking." The taking of the diamond was held to be an overt and felonious act against which the company had insured the pawnbroker.

Other courts might have decided this case differently, giving more weight to the part of phrase (c) which limits the felonious act to one of which the custodian is "actually cognizant." The lesson is clear—make certain what the actual meaning of the words in your policy are.

Theft and the unlawful use of an automobile

A boy was employed by the owner of an automobile to clean the car and entrusted with the keys of the car for that purpose. With some other boys he drove the car into the country and left it wrecked in a ditch.

The insurance company contended that it was not liable for damages. It said the boy's possession was lawful, and consequently his taking the car was not a theft. The court answered this defense with a quotation from the Supreme Court: "The phraseology of contracts of insurance is that chosen by the insurer, and the contract in fixed form is tendered to the prospective policy holder, who is often without technical training and who rarely accepts it with a lawyer at his elbow." The company was held liable under its policy for the theft of the automobile.

In another instance with almost the same circumstances, a boy employed to clean and polish a car took it for a joy ride and wrecked it. In this case a different court held the result of the boy's acts was not a loss for which the insurance company was liable under its policy of theft insurance.

Contradictory decisions such as these emphasize again the vital need of an automobile owner to have the coverage so clearly expressed in his policy that a layman as well as an insurance expert may be certain of its meaning and of the extent of its coverage.

Burglary insurance

An insurance policy against loss by burglary is interpreted by the definition of "burglary" under the statutes of the state in which the insured premises are located. Burglary, in general, is said to occur when a house is broken into by force at night for the purpose of stealing. In some of the states, burglary may be committed by day as well, and in buildings other than dwellings. Whether or not you can collect under your policy depends on the precise definition your state has made, and on other details of the statute.

For payment of benefits, burglary insurance policies sometimes require visible marks on the premises as proof of actual force made in entering the building. These requirements are not a limitation of liability, but are used only for the purpose of preventing fraudulent claims by policy holders. Sometimes there are losses with no evidence of burglary—probably the result of pilfering by clerks or the like. These cannot be considered losses by burglary, which requires entry by the use of force or fraud.

It is the rule that, where the policy may be interpreted in more than one way, the interpretation most favorable to the insured will be adopted by the courts, but a court will not make a new contract by a forced construction of the terms of the contract. For this reason a person taking out a policy should read its terms carefully and critically before accepting it and paying the premium.

In one instance of this sort, a court said, "The insured was not obliged to accept the contract of insurance; she might have secured more liberal terms elsewhere, but the courts are not at liberty to extend by construction the plain and well-understood meaning of the language."

One policy provided that there should be no claim for loss when the theft was the deed of members of the insured's household. A loss caused by theft when others were introduced into the premise by a member of the household was not to be recoverable under the policy by reason of this exception.

In many burglary policies the insurance company reserves the right to replace the stolen property. Furthermore, where the loss has been adjusted and paid by the insurance company, the insured cannot recover for additional items later found missing which he failed to include in his claim.

Credit insurance

Under a credit insurance policy, for a stipulated sum the insurance company guarantees a creditor up to a specific amount against losses from the insolvency of his customers.

Credit insurance policies generally classify losses into two groups. The first is the initial loss up to a certain amount, which the insured agrees to bear. The second is the loss in excess of this amount, but up to a certain limit, and it is against this loss that the insurer agrees to indemnify the policy holder. In other words, the insuring company indemnifies the insured for an amount above a named minimum and below a stipulated maximum sum.

The usual form of credit insurance limits the losses against which the insured is indemnified to those from customers who have received a certain rating by credit mercantile companies. Also, by some policies the losses against which the insured is indemnified are confined to those on sales to customers with whom the merchant has previously had business transactions.

For a clearer picture of what such a policy is, let us look at the terms of a typical one that came into court. It contained, in part, provisions that if the insured, by reason of the insolvency of those to whom he had sold merchandise on credit, suffered losses in excess of 1¾ percent of his total sales, but not more than $5,000, the insuring company would pay these losses. This agreement also provided that the credit extended by the insured should not exceed 30 percent of the capital rating of the customer, and that this rating should be above a specified amount.

A contract such as this is essentially the same as any other insurance contract insuring against a risk. It is a policy of indemnity against the loss of property. The peril of loss through insolvency is as definite and real to the merchant as the peril of fire, accident, or theft, except that he faces it much more frequently.

Under most of these policies, provision is made that the insured give notice to the insuring company within a certain period of time after learning of the insolvency of the customer. The purpose of this preliminary notice is to afford the insurer information that will enable it to investigate and take whatever precautionary measures may be possible to limit its loss.

Fidelity insurance or indemnity bond

A fidelity insurance contract is an agreement by an insurance company to indemnify the policy holder against losses he may suffer through lack of honesty, integrity, or fidelity on the part of his employees or officers of his organization.

The usual fidelity insurance policy provides that the company will pay to the employer or the person insured the amount of any loss of funds or damage to property he shall incur through the dishonesty of the employees insured against. This coverage includes loss through any act performed in bad faith by an employee, or—also in bad faith—any failure to perform a necessary act. It does not include losses through mere negligence, incompetency, or error of judgment on the employee's part. It is immaterial whether or not the loss occurs in the performance of any duty or trust especially assigned to the employee. The loss may involve the insured's own property, or property in his custody.

Frequently this type of insurance is in the form of an indemnity bond. But whatever the form—insurance policy or indemnity bond—the insurer guarantees the fidelity of the employees.

Where the policy covers losses from fraud or dishonesty, or from larceny or embezzlement, the liability of the company will not extend beyond losses from such causes. The frequently used terms of "fraud" and "dishonesty," however, extend beyond criminal acts, and the general rule is that when an agent collects money belonging to his employer and either uses it for his own purpose or refuses to turn it in, the insurance company is liable. On the other hand, when there are mutual demands of employer and employee against each other, and the employee's refusal to turn in money is made with the honest belief that his employer owes him an equal amount, the employee cannot be considered to be acting either fraudulently or dishonestly.

The policy or indemnity bond requires, as a general rule, that, in case of loss, notice shall be given to the insuring company in writing within a reasonable amount of time. The employer is not required to report mere suspicions unless they are strong enough in his opinion to justify the discharge of the employee.

In the application for insurance of this kind, statements are asked for about the character, past habits, and conduct of the person or persons insured against. If these representations are false, and known to be false by the insured, they may serve to release the insuring company from liability in the event of loss.

State unemployment insurance

The unemployment insurance laws, which have been enacted generally throughout the states, provide for a payroll tax by the state. The money acquired through this tax is devoted to the aid of those who are unemployed and who meet the qualifications set up by statute for receiving benefits.

Any worker, except those specifically excepted from the operation of these statutes, should immediately upon the loss of employment apply to the unemployment bureau of his state for information and forms necessary to file his claim for a share of these benefits.

The applicant, however, must be wholly unemployed—that is, he must be free to accept any employment that may be offered him through state agencies. Further, he is obliged to report regularly for assignment to any work in his field for which the bureau of the state has been requested to supply workers. If he obtains a job on his own initiative, he must bring this fact to the attention of the bureau at once. It is illegal to continue to collect unemployment checks while working, and a penalty will be imposed.

A worker becomes disqualified for unemployment benefits if he refuses, without good cause, any offer of employment for which he is reasonably fitted by his training and experience. With variations depending upon your state law, the grounds on which he may refuse work in his field offered by the unemployment bureau and still retain unemployment benefits usually are: (1) if the employment suggested to him has, as a condition, membership in a company labor union that would interfere with membership he may have in another union; (2) when there is a strike or similar industrial disturbance in the organization in which this employment is offered him; (3) when the place of employment is an unreasonable distance from his residence; or (4) when the wages offered are substantially less than those prevailing in the locality for that or similar work.

The tax for unemployment insurance is not levied against government payrolls and payrolls of nonprofit organizations operated exclusively for religious, charitable, scientific, literary, and educational purposes. Consequently, unemployed workers from these organizations are not usually entitled to benefits.

Benefits are continued for a stipulated period, except when the recipient is successful in securing employment. The amount of benefits is based on the wages or salary he enjoyed during the time of his employment.

The unemployment insurance system is now an established part of our social and economic structure. Yet when it was first introduced, there were some objections raised to it. In justification of the New York Unemployment Insurance statute, which is typical of those throughout the country, the highest court in New York pointed out that in 1936 (the year in which many of these statutes were enacted) unemployment had increased enormously in every part of the country. When such a condition becomes general and affects the whole country, said the court, the situation demands the exercise of the power of the state. During the Depression years, tremendous sums of both state and Federal money were expended in keeping housed and alive the families of the unemployed.

"Such help was absolutely necessary and it would be a strange kind of government, in fact no government at all, which would not give help in such trouble," said the court.

Liability insurance

This type of insurance is an indemnity against liability for bodily injuries or for damages inflicted upon the property of others. It has a wide application both in industry and in private activities.

The hazards of modern industry have created such risks for employers that a tremendous demand has arisen for liability insurance that will protect them against losses from causes beyond their control.

In this class of insurance are included the so-called public liability policies, which provide insurance against loss from the bodily injury or death of persons not employed by the insured, but involved in an accident through the negligence of his employees or others engaged in his business.

Liability insurance compensates an employer for damages he must pay to people injured due to the negligent acts of his employees. (Employees themselves are covered by Workmen's Compensation, discussed later in this chapter.) The premiums for injuries to employees are ordinarily a percentage of the compensation paid to them, and are computed on the payroll of the insured at specific rates proportional to the risk assumed by the employees, such as office workers, drivers, machine operators and so on.

The various functions of liability insurance extend to the liability of contractors, elevator liability, risks borne by landlords, losses from strikes, as well as from many of the infinite activities of everyday life. Liability policies are also issued to physicians, dentists, and lawyers, and cover losses arising from error or mistake. These are known as "malpractice" policies.

An automobile liability policy provides indemnity against loss, through injuries to others arising from the operation of the insured's vehicle by himself, by members of his family, or by others with his consent. Such a policy, however, does not indemnify the owner against damage to his own car by others.

Casualty insurance

Insurance of this kind ordinarily provides for payment of loss for damage arising from accident or some other unanticipated event.

Usually it provides benefits to compensate for damages to property from cyclones, hail, hurricanes, or lightning; the loss of domestic animals; breaking of plate glass; boiler explosions, and the like.

Essential facts about Social Security

The Federal Social Security Act provides that after December 31, 1939, every individual who is "fully insured," has attained the age of 65 and filed an application for the benefits provided by that law, is entitled to monthly payments from the time he becomes eligible for them until he dies.

The collection of the fund for the payment of these benefits is by a tax levied on the wages of employees as well as by a tax of an equal amount levied upon the employer.

This law was amended in 1956 to include practically all self-employed people (except doctors) who earn from self-employment four hundred dollars or more a year. (Special rules apply to farm-owner income.) In 1965, self-employed physicians were covered. Beginning in 1968, ministers were covered unless they request to be excluded for reasons of conscience.

Members of the armed forces are now included in the category of employees with the United States Government in the role of employer. Most other Federal government employees are covered not by this system but by a Federal retirement system.

Disability provisions

It is now possible to receive disability benefits as part of Social Security. Any worker who becomes severely disabled is eligible for monthly benefits under Social Security if he has worked long enough and recently enough, regardless of age. While a worker is disabled, payments can also be made to certain members of his family. A person disabled before the age of 18 does not have to qualify for disability benefits if his parents have worked.

A 1967 change in the Social Security law allows a disabled widow, dependent widow, or (under certain circumstances) the surviving wife of a worker who has worked long enough under Social Security to be eligible to get monthly benefits as soon as she reaches 50.

It is always best to contact your local Social Security office for additional information on disability benefits.

Relatives who can collect benefits

In addition to the Social Security benefits to which an "insured" is entitled, the wife or widow of the employee, when she becomes 65 years of age, is also entitled to payments—or, if she elects, payments in a lesser amount can start at age 62 for a wife or at 60 for a widow, or even to a surviving divorced wife under certain circumstances, if she was married for 20 years. The act also provides for the payment of benefits to every dependent child of the individual covered by the law.

The widow's benefit continues until her remarriage or death.

When the widow is entitled to any Social Security benefits in her own right—as when she has been employed, and by virtue of that employment and her age is entitled to benefits independently of her right as a widow—the payments she would otherwise be eligible to receive as the widow will be reduced by as much as is paid to her in her own right as an employee.

When the wage-earner entitled to Social Security benefits dies and leaves neither widow nor child, but does leave a parent or parents 62 or older, "chiefly" dependent on the deceased for support, the parents are each eligible for insurance benefits.

Friend's compensation for burial expenses

The Social Security Act further provides that if a person entitled to benefits dies and leaves no widow, child, or parent, then any person who may have paid the burial expenses will be reimbursed to three times the monthly benefit paid or which would have been paid to the deceased under this statute during his life, or two hundred fifty-five dollars, whichever is less.

Time limit on benefits of deceased

Claims to collect benefits due to the relatives or the friends of a person who has died should be made immediately after his death. If a claim is not filed within two years, it may not be recognized. In certain instances only, an additional two years to file will be permitted for good cause shown.

If you work after sixty-five

When the recipient of benefits accepts employment or is self-employed, he may earn up to $1,680 a year and still receive his full benefits. Beyond that, benefits are reduced, and if you earn more than $2,880 a year, no benefits are payable, except that in any month when you earn less than $140, no benefit check will be withheld.

There is continuing pressure on the Congress of the United States to remove these restrictions or else to increase the permissible amount of additional income, so you should check with your lawyer or the local Social Security office in order to keep abreast of changing regulations.

Outside sources of income—such as pensions, disability compensations, rents received by landlords who are not in the real estate business—are not considered wages or earnings and do not affect the monthly payments.

If the recipient of Social Security benefits is more than 72 years old, no restriction is placed on the amount of wages he may earn and still receive his monthly benefits.

Income tax There is no Federal income tax levied on the proceeds from Social Security.

Check up on your account Under the Social Security regulations, "Any individual or after his death, any widow, child or parent, upon making a written request, may obtain from the Social Security Administration a statement of the amount of wages paid such individual, and the periods of payment as shown by the records of the Administration at the time the request for information is received."

It is highly advisable that every employee write to the Social Security Administration for such a statement every two years or so. Errors have been known to occur in the Administration's records, or the employer may not regularly be sending in the tax. If rectification is not made within a few years of the date of the error, it cannot be made at all, and the loss is the employee's. The field offices of the Social Security Administration have a special form available for requesting a statement of your account. Only this form can be used.

No one entitled to benefits under this statute can transfer or assign any of the monies that may become due or payable under it, nor are any of these benefits subject to claims or attachments by creditors, or to the operation of any bankruptcy or insolvency statutes.

Health insurance Nearly all people 65 and over are eligible for health insurance under Medicare. Nearly everyone who reached 65 before 1968 is eligible for hospital insurance, including people not eligible for cash Social Security benefits. If you reached 65 after 1968 and are not eligible for cash benefits you will have to obtain what are known as "work credits" similar to those required before you receive cash Social Security benefits. Hospital insurance covers home health visits as well as the cost of services, as stated in the policy, rendered while the insured is in the hospital.

Medical insurance This is voluntary insurance, and no one is covered automatically. Anyone 65 or over is eligible. You pay a monthly premium, and the government matches your premium dollar for dollar. Once you enroll your insurance stays in force. This insurance is more extensive than hospital insurance.

When and how to apply for benefits The application for benefits under the Social Security law may be made by anyone anticipating retirement at a definite future date, but no application for this purpose will be accepted "prior to three months before the first month for which the applicant becomes entitled to receive such benefits."

Application for the benefits under the Social Security Act must be made on the forms prescribed by the commissioner and may be obtained from any office of the bureau. The amount of wages and the dates of payments may be established by any applicant by the records of the Administration or by any other acceptable evidence.

Evidence of the applicant's date of birth is required. Acceptable evidence includes (1) public records, (2) church records, (3) Census Bureau notification of registration of birth, (4) hospital records, (5) records of physicians or midwives, (6) family Bible, (7) naturalization records, (8) immigration papers, (9) military records, (10) passports, (11) school records, (12) vaccination records, (13) insurance policies, (14) labor union records, (15) and marriage records.

After your application has been filed, it is considered by the Bureau of Old Age and Survivors Insurance, and you are notified of its decision. This decision is final unless you ask for a review. In that event, you may ask either for a reconsideration or a hearing before a referee under the rules established for that purpose by the bureau. Further review is available beyond that in the courts.

Workmen's compensation acts

These state statutes have been generally enacted for the payment to an injured employee or his family of a specific amount for injuries he has suffered during his work, if the injuries incapacitate him from continued work and deprive him of further earnings, either permanently or temporarily. Workmen's compensation is a substitute for any other remedy the worker might otherwise have against his employer, such as a damage suit.

The underlying principle of these laws is that of insurance. The claim of the worker arises from his employment, and the compensation paid him is because of his loss or impairment of earning power. It is proportioned to the amount of his previous earnings and the gravity of the injuries.

The application for these benefits should be made by the workman, or someone acting on his behalf, to the labor bureau or whatever corresponds to such a state bureau or department, in the state in which the applicant resides or where he has been employed. There he will receive instructions for the preparation of his claim and for the filing of the claim with the proper state authorities.

By receiving workmen's compensation, you do not waive any claim you may have against a third party not your employer for negligence leading to your injury. You can still sue such third party, although your employer may have some interest in what you collect because of the compensation payments received by you. Consult your attorney on this.

CHAPTER 24

Motor Vehicles, Drivers, and Related Matters

Before you sign a contract to buy a car, be sure to read it carefully. Check for fringe charges, a dollar-a-day late charge on your payments, etc. Also, you will be wise to get all guarantees specifically set down by the seller in writing. Such guarantees are known as "express warranties," and the seller must back them up. If he fails to do so, you may bring an action to recover damages or, if you have not yet paid the purchase price, you may return the car and cancel the agreement.

Do not rely on the mere word of a salesman that a car is in good condition. The court may consider that what he said was just his personal opinion and not a commitment on the part of the company he represents. You need an official statement from the company or the individual seller if your complaint is to stand up in court.

In a recent case in a French court, a car buyer sued because his car got only 16 miles to a gallon of gasoline, whereas the car salesman had assured him he would get 24 miles to a gallon. The Paris judge ruled that gas consumption is one of the most important qualities of an automobile and is one of the most convincing sales arguments. The excessive consumption of gas made the car defective. The owner obtained a $1,000 judgment from the car dealer. Such substantial misrepresentations may be grounds for a successful suit by the buyer.

A manufacturer of automobiles or a dealer who handles cars as a business sells the product with certain implied guarantees, as well as the ones which are stated in the sales contract. Failure of any of these guarantees will be grounds for a suit. Among these implied warranties is the promise that the product is in acceptable condition for use, unless the manufacturer or dealer indicates any particular dangers or defects which he knows or should know about and which are not obvious to the buyer. This particular implied guarantee will not apply, however, if the buyer had an opportunity to inspect the product before the sale and could have found the defect upon inspection.

Perhaps the most important implied guarantee is for the general operating fitness of the car. This will apply, unless the seller specifically disclaims it.

All potential buyers should understand that if the car is bought from someone other than a dealer, such as the original owner of a used car, these implied guarantees are much less strict and particular caution should be used. You should always road-test a used car before considering buying it. In all cases, be sure to read the contract carefully before you sign.

These rules for the purchase of automobiles apply to almost all other new and used products as well. While the movement for consumer protection is gaining strength, there are many areas in which the buyer is still unprotected.

An interesting extension of the doctrine of implied warranty with respect to a new product involved a man who was working in a sewer and using an oxygen-producing mask made by the defendant. He died of asphyxiation because the mask did not work properly. The plaintiffs in the case were members of his repair crew, and they were injured while rushing into the sewer to save him. They sued the defendant manufacturer on the "danger invites rescue" theory based on the original wrong of breach of implied warranty that the mask would be acceptable for use. The court stated that whether they were suing on breach of implied warranty or on negligence in manufacture was not significant, because both were wrongful acts. The manufacture and sale of the defective mask placed the man in peril and invited his rescue by those who worked with him, and the defendant was held liable for damages sustained by the rescuers in their attempt to aid the victim.

If the product proves unsatisfactory

A buyer can bring action against the seller for failure of the product to meet either the stated contract guarantees or the implied guarantees, if he has notified the seller of the failure within a reasonable time after he discovers, or should have discovered, the defect. What a "reasonable" time is will depend on the nature of the defect. The first step that should be taken, if the defect has been discovered soon after purchase and the payment was by check, is to stop the check. If the buyer cannot get satisfaction from the seller, he may take any of the three following possible actions:

1. resell the product, if possible (noting the defects to the new buyer, of course), and obtain the difference from the original seller, between the price he would have received on resale if the product had been satisfactory, and what he actually did receive, or
2. sue for the difference between the actual value of the product with the defect and the original purchase price, or
3. if he cannot resell the product and does not want to keep the defective one, he can try to force the original seller to furnish a product which is in proper condition.

False advertising

Describing an automobile or any other product in glowing terms, particularly in a context in which it should be obvious to the prospective buyer and seller that an effort is being made primarily to glorify the product, is usually acceptable. Untrue or fraudulent statements, however,

may be grounds for an action in fraud and deceit by the buyer. The decision in each case will depend upon how the court feels the remark should have been interpreted by the buyer.

A bicycle manufacturer described his product as "having been subjected to the most severe practical tests." He added that "we guarantee them to be all that is claimed—perfect of their kind, unsurpassed and unsurpassable." A buyer of one of these bikes brought an action when the product did not prove to be of excellent quality. The decision in the case was in favor of the manufacturer. The court stated that merely to advertise an article as "perfect of its kind" or "unsurpassed and unsurpassable" is not such a representation as to be classified a guarantee of performance. The judge in this case added that these statements are "nothing more than the extravagant phrases with which dealers are prone to recommend their wares." He felt the buyer should have understood them in this context.

In an Indiana case, a court did find a farm product manufacturer guilty of deceit in advertising for claiming that his product would effectively treat a certain disease in hogs. The court here found that such a statement was more than a mere expression of opinion by the seller; it was meant as a representation of fact to be relied upon by buyers, and, therefore, amounted to fraudulent advertising.

How to transfer title to a car

When you purchase a car, used or new, apply at the most convenient motor vehicle license bureau for the transfer of its registration to you.

The name under which the car is registered is the name of the legal owner of record. In the event of loss or mishap, your ability to prove your ownership and your right to possession of the car becomes of paramount importance. A correct entry in the official records is the best way of proving your title. Almost every state now requires that, before any car can be sold, the potential buyer must obtain the formal certificate of ownership (which motor vehicle authorities maintain). This protects the new buyer. If it turns out that the car was sold by someone who stole it, the new buyer would not have priority of ownership over the rightful owner. He would also not have priority over a party who has a lien against the car, and any existing secured interest in the automobile would be indicated on the certificate of ownership.

Financing the purchase of your car

The purchase of an automobile made other than for cash may be financed with the assistance of an automobile-financing company, a loan company, a bank, or a credit union.

Under all circumstances, if the money needed for the purchase of a car can be obtained from a reputable bank or credit union, by all means borrow money from one of them. The bank lends a portion of the money needed for the purchase, and the borrower supplies the balance. The bank secures its loan by a chattel mortgage on the car. If you cannot meet the payments, the bank may start proceedings to repossess it. But aside from the interest that will be deducted from the face of the loan when it is made there is no other charge, or only a small one.

In financing the purchase through the aid of a finance company, be careful to check the amount you are asked to pay for interest. Examine with special care the "charges" over and above the interest. Carrying charges are today regulated in most of the states by statute. Federal law now requires that the actual interest you agree to pay be made clear to you. Do not accept a chart indicating repayments as a substitute for a simple statement of the interest rates.

Can you sell a mortgaged car?

Remember, too, that with the consent of the mortgagee or lender of the money, in the event the loan is secured by a chattel mortgage, you are free to sell your car before the payments are fully made, under any arrangement that meets with the expressed approval of the lender of the money. On the other hand, it is a penal offense to attempt to sell an automobile or any other property that is mortgaged unless you first obtain the consent of the person who holds the mortgage. Such a consent must always be set out in writing, signed by the lender, and made a part, preferably, of the bill of sale to your buyer.

What to do in an accident

If you are involved in an accident, do not make the mistake of failing to obtain the names and addresses of all or as many as possible of the witnesses. If you are insured against the casualty, immediately notify your insurance company. Further, be careful, when arranging for the repair of the damages done to your car, to have no work done other than the repairs made necessary by the accident. In this way you obtain a clear statement of your damages that will require no explanation in court of other charges, and will open no door for a cross-examination belittling the expense you have incurred. The opposing attorney will also be unable to create for the jury the implication that your claim included additional and outside items.

Damages

A suit to collect damages resulting from an automobile accident must be brought within a reasonable time of the date of the accident. Generally the time limit is three years. The laws of your state will mandate the exact statute of limitation.

Not all discomfort, nor every bruise that may occur, is a ground for the collection of damages. The operation of a bus or of a private car may be the cause of slight injuries to passengers by a too abrupt stop, but the way the driver handled the vehicle may have provided escape from greater injuries. If a too abrupt stop causes the passengers to be bruised or injured, and it is due to the operator's careless driving, then there is unquestionable ground for claims for injuries. If, however, the operator was not negligent—if the sudden stop and the injuries occurred in the proper and honest exercise of skill demanded to avoid an accident—there is certainly no liability on the driver or the owner of the automobile.

A driver is not an insurer of the safety of others, nor can any operator guarantee to his passengers an absolute freedom from injury or discomfort that may be the consequence not of his own negligence but that of others.

What "negligence" means

Negligence, a factor commonly encountered in suits arising from automobile collisions, has been defined as "the omission to do something which a reasonable person guided by those considerations which ordinarily regulate the conduct of human affairs would do, or to do something which a prudent and reasonable man would not do. Negligence is the absence of care.''

What is contributory negligence?

Contributory negligence is the act or omission amounting to a want of ordinary care on the part of the injured or complaining party which, concurring with the defendant's negligence, caused the injury. Without such cooperating negligence, the injury would not have occurred.

When an accident is unavoidable

When a person has taken every precaution and yet is involved in an accident, he cannot in general be held responsible for damages.

The car of a woman driving along a highway was suddenly struck by another automobile. The collision threw her car out of control so that for an instant it was diagonally across the highway and in the path of a third car, which hit it. The court ruled there was no liability on her part for the damages suffered by the driver of the third car, since the accident was not her fault. Said the court: ''Where is the absence of care or what did she do which a prudent and reasonable person would not have done? There is not the slightest evidence tending to show any negligence on her part.''

If violations are mutual

Where the parties to an accident are both guilty of a violation of the rules of the road, and both violations contribute to the injury, neither can recover damages even if one party's negligence was greater than the other's. There is a rule for apportionment of damages based on the degree of negligence, but it applies only in admiralty or maritime accidents.

The driver of a heavy truck traveling on a road 16 feet wide turned sharply across the road at an intersection without signaling the turn. Then, seeing a car to the rear, he swerved back into the road. The driver of the passenger car at the rear of the truck, traveling at about 30 miles an hour, was attempting to pass when the truck turned. To avoid being hit, he had to swerve sharply to the left, and he hit a telegraph pole.

Both drivers were held guilty of negligence in their disregard of the rules of the road: the truck driver because he failed to signal his intended turn to the left, and the driver of the passenger car because he passed at the intersection of a highway. For this reason, the passenger-car driver was not entitled to recover.

A passenger's rights and responsibilities

The injuries or damages that may be inflicted on others by someone operating a borrowed car are, in most states, the responsibility of the owner who loaned it. Where this is not the law, in order to prove that the owner is liable, it must be shown that the lending was in itself negligent—for example, the car was loaned to a child or an incompetent driver.

A driver normally must be reasonably careful of his passengers, and he is liable for injuries suffered by them as a result of his failure to observe such reasonable care.

However, the majority of states have passed "guest statutes," which permit a passenger to recover for only those injuries resulting from reckless or willful conduct or gross negligence on the part of the driver of the car in which he is a passenger. A demonstration that the driver failed to exercise reasonable care will not be sufficient in these "guest statute" states to allow injured passengers to sue the driver successfully. The idea behind the guest statutes is that, since the passenger is not paying for the ride, the host should not be held to a high standard of care.

In none of the states does the law permit a passenger to recover for his injuries if he failed to point out imminent dangers which he should have realized the driver would not notice. Legally, a passenger in this situation is said to have contributed to the accident and cannot recover for damages which resulted.

Joint adventure

An adventure in law is not the same as one you dream about in the company of Rock Hudson or Sophia Loren. It can also be called a joint venture or a joint enterprise. It is a joint undertaking by two or more people, and a determination of who controls the undertaking is of the utmost importance in defining it as a joint adventure. If both parties in

a vehicle have a common destination, are making a trip for a common purpose, share expenses, and can equally direct which route will be taken, then a court may very well decide the trip was a joint adventure, and the driver's negligence will be imputed to the passenger just as though he were driving. It does not matter, in such a case, that the passenger does not know how to drive if he can exercise control over the driver and the operation of the car.

Some courts have applied the term "joint adventure" only to situations where there is a business or financial interest in the trip or the use of the car. But most courts still say the use can be for pleasure as well.

Many courts do not like to use the term where married people are concerned, since the marital relationship is something special and has about it a general commonness of purpose. However, you should be aware that many courts will find a joint adventure even if the parties are married.

Members of a joint enterprise or adventure can sue one another and recover damages based only on allegations of simple negligence. This is an exception to the requirements of the states' guest statutes previously discussed.

Car pools Share-the-ride arrangements abound, and there is no general rule governing them. In some cases you will be considered a guest, and in others you will be considered an invitee, to whom is owed the duty of ordinary care. One thing that the courts consider in assigning responsibility is whether the purpose of the arrangement is social or whether the driver is simply being accommodating. In the latter situation, the passenger will probably be held to be a guest.

Another important factor is whether the passenger pays for the ride. Suppose you drive your car some days and ride with others the rest of the time. Payment can be money, services, or other benefits. The point is that you have an obligation either to pay for your rides or to reciprocate in kind. It is also important that you have a definite rather than a casual arrangement, and also that you pay regularly and in some fixed amount. Another aspect that the courts will look to in deciding whether the passenger is a guest is the relationship between the driver and the passenger. If there is a family relationship, the courts tend to find that the passenger was a guest.

Plaintiff was injured while riding in an automobile under an arrangement among six fellow employees. Five had cars and alternated driving, while the sixth, who had no car, paid 75 cents a week to be transported. When plaintiff, a regular driver, sued his driver, the court held plaintiff was a guest since the arrangement was "simply the exchange of amenities between fellow employees." Plaintiff lost his case because he could not prove his driver was grossly negligent.

In another case, a woman was injured while riding to work with her son-in-law. She rode with him regularly and from time to time gave him $1 for gasoline. She was held to be a guest.

In each case, the court will view the particular arrangement involved to determine whether a guest relationship existed.

What about taking the kids?

In a typical arrangement, neighboring parents agreed to take turns driving each other's children to school. There was an accident and a lawsuit. The court found that there was "a definite business relationship whereby each party was saved time and expense in the task of transporting her child to and from school." So the driver was held to the duty of ordinary care.

What about pleasure or vacation trips?

Sharing the expense of gas and oil consumed on a trip when that trip is taken for joint pleasure or social purposes is nothing more than an exchange of social amenities, and a passenger is still considered a guest. It might be different if payment constituted an important element for the giving of the transportation.

Two friends went to a bowling tournament out of state. They had made similar trips in the past and had alternated using cars and sharing travel expenses. In the suit that followed an accident, the court held that the plaintiff, who was injured while in his friend's car, was his guest. "Balancing of expenditures for mutual auto trips does not constitute payment for transportation."

The rules of the road

These days it is imperative that a driver drive defensively and that he obey the "rules of the road," not only for his own safety but to avoid penalties. The law of the road has been defined as "the custom or practice which has become crystallized into an accepted system of rules regulating travel on the highways." Legislative enactments have established these rules of the road officially in an effort to reduce accidents resulting in death, injury, and the destruction of property. However, not all drivers know these rules, nor do they know how the law views them under varying circumstances. Here we shall consider some of the common problems you may face, and what your rights and responsibilities may be when you are involved in different kinds of accidents.

The right of way when entering a highway

Under the statutes governing the right of way, the driver of a vehicle about to enter a highway from a private drive must yield the right of way to all vehicles on the highway.

At the intersection of a private road and a common highway, a truck and and a bicycle collided. The boy on the bicycle had come from the private driveway. Before leaving it, he had seen the truck approaching, but, believing he would have time to travel a hundred feet on the road and turn to the left into another street before he would be overtaken by the truck, he had shot ahead. He was hit by the truck, knocked from his bicycle, and injured.

When this boy sought to collect damages, they were denied him. The traveler on the highway has the right to assume—although not absolutely—that the other traveler, about to enter his path of travel from a private driveway, will yield to him.

Right of way and how it is limited

Right of way, when its abuse can lead to an accident, is a relative thing. The duty to avoid accidents or collisions at street intersections rests on all travelers who find themselves there at the same time.

When two automobiles collided at a street intersection, one of the drivers protested that the other had been negligent in not reducing his speed, irrespective of his right of way.

In its comment on this criticism, the court observed that not only is there no universal rule requiring a motorist who has the right of way to reduce the speed of his car under all circumstances at a street intersection, but that also, there is nothing in the law that entitles a motorist to proceed across a street intersection regardless of other circumstances. "The right of way possessed by a motorist is, like a 'green light,' not a command to proceed but a qualified permission to do so."

Another court has stated this rule to be that every traveler must take heed at a street intersection and that, even though he is first at the intersection or has the technical right of way, such facts are not of controlling importance.

Right of way and negligence

Late on a winter night a car was traveling an icy road between Battle Creek and Lansing in Michigan, where "slow" signals warned of danger. At a street intersection the driver stopped, glanced along an intersecting street and, since no other vehicle was in sight, he started his car. However, trees had obstructed his view. A cab was approaching. He noticed it when it was 150 feet away, and the ice of the pavement made it impossible either to stop or to speed ahead. The cars collided.

An effort was made by the cab driver to reverse the judgment awarded against him. He contended that the passenger-car driver had been guilty of contributory negligence in not exercising greater care at the street intersection.

Refusing to disturb the verdict of the court below, the appellate court said that no hard and fast rule exists that speed or statutory right of way determines negligence. Each driver must use such care as obvious conditions require.

Pedestrian right of way

Late on a misty afternoon a brickyard employee was returning home from work. The yard was on the north side of a highway, and the workman, starting to cross along a path used by his fellow workers for many years, glanced to the east and west for approaching automobiles. About one-eighth of a mile to the east was an approaching car—another was coming from the west about twenty feet away. Confident he could reach the center of the street before the arrival of the nearer car, he started across and had reached the center line safely when this oncoming car swerved to the left, hitting the man and knocking him to the ground unconscious.

The automobile driver's defense was contributory negligence on the part of the injured man—since he had glanced only once at the oncoming car. The defendant also declared that "pedestrians are obligated to yield the right of way to all vehicles on the roadway." However, the court held the rule of the road to be that the right of way is relative and not absolute and that it does not absolve anyone from the duty of exercising due care to avoid accidents.

In some places the right of way always belongs to the pedestrian, except where signals control traffic.

Signals and warnings

The rule of the road is, in general, that anyone traveling on a street or highway must cooperate with others. Those on the road possess mutual rights. A driver of an automobile has no rights on a highway superior to the rights of others engaged in the lawful use of the road. When a driver engages in an act that involves the safety of others on the road, he must give them a timely warning by a proper sign or signal, mechanically or by hand, as the situation requires.

Sounding the horn by a highway

An automobile driver approaching a highway from a private roadway or drive must sound his horn and give a signal that he intends to enter the highway.

A motorcycle, with its exhaust explosions audible at 400 feet, was traveling a highway at 35 miles an hour. An automobile entered the highway from a service station and gave no signal. It collided with the motorcycle. The motorcycle operator, said the court, had the right to assume that the driver of the automobile would not take the right of way without first giving warning of an intention to do so. It was the motorcycle operator's duty to sound a warning "only in the event it appeared necessary to give a warning."

Failing to sound a horn for pedestrian

One winter morning an elderly farmer started on foot to a nearby town leading a gentle seven-year-old cow by a four-foot lead rope. Another farmer was driving his car at 20 miles an hour. Looking ahead, the driver saw the man and the cow on the right side of the road. When he overtook them he slowed down to about five miles an hour and passed about 11 feet on their left, not sounding his horn, as this seemed unnecessary to him. Suddenly, when the automobile was abreast of the man and the cow, the cow gave a lunge, knocking her owner to the ground. His fall resulted in a fractured hip.

The trial court held there was no negligence, and that the automobile driver was under no obligation to give any warning of his approach. The cow owner appealed, and the appellate court declared this omission might or might not have been negligence—it was a question of fact for a jury to determine.

"A timely warning would not have been a vain thing," said the appellate court. "It would have given notice of a close approach of danger which the owner of the cow had no special reason to apprehend."

Another pedestrian

In a fairly similar incident, a pedestrian was walking on the right side of a highway. The driver of an automobile proceeding in the same direction attempted to pass on the left side about eight feet from the pedestrian without sounding his horn. Startled by the sound of the car, he jumped in front of it and was injured. Under the law of that jurisdiction, a pedestrian on a highway was required to travel on the left side of a highway. However, although he was walking where he should not have been, the court held that this violation did not mean that he could be run down at will. The law is that a motorist has a duty to exercise the care and precaution that circumstances require, and by all means to sound a warning on approaching a pedestrian.

When a horn is not sounded properly

An 11-year-old boy, riding a bicycle along a highway, was overtaken by an automobile which collided with him. He was thrown to the ground and killed. At the time of the accident, a strong wind was blowing in a direction away from the boy on the bicycle. The driver of the car had sounded his horn when he was 175 feet in the rear of the bicycle, but the wind apparently had prevented the signal from reaching the boy's ears.

The court held the driver of the car liable in damages for the death of the boy. "He was negligent in failing to give an audible warning as he approached and undertook to pass the bicycle."

Rear red lights and stopping

The driver of a truck stopped without giving any signal that he intended to do so. His negligence was responsible for an accident. Sued for damages, he based his defense on the fact that the red signal lights displayed when he applied the brakes were adequate notice to the car following in the rear.

The court held the truck driver guilty of negligence. A signal made by holding out a hand, said the court, "is not subject to speculation, but definitely advises the following driver of the intention to stop. Causing the red stoplight to go on is not the equivalent of the stop signal, and failure to give it is negligence."

Today, however, directional signals and flashing red lights are generally accepted as proper notification of a driver's intentions.

Lack of signals on turning

A truck driver, without checking his mirror to see if any car was behind him, made a left turn without signaling. At that moment, the driver of an automobile going in the same direction was attempting, after sounding his horn, to pass the truck. They collided. In deciding the automobile driver's suit, the court pointed out that a driver, before starting, stopping, backing, or turning from a direct line, must assure himself that he can act with safety and, when another vehicle is affected, he must give a signal of his intention.

Although the judgment of the trial court favored the driver of the passenger car, this decision was reversed on appeal and remanded to the trial court. The automobile driver's attempt to pass had been made at a street intersection. If the jury should determine this to be contributory negligence on his part, the appellate court declared, he could not recover damages.

Failing to signal at an intersection

A heavy truck was traveling on the right side of a highway at 15 miles an hour. At a crossroad, without giving any signal, the driver swung his truck sharply to the left. He had not seen a passenger car less than 75 feet behind him, going 30 miles an hour.

The driver of the passenger car sounded his horn and undertook to pass on the left at the intersection of the roads—it was too late for him to stop when he saw the truck driver make his turn to the left. The passenger-car driver swerved farther to the left, skidded from the pavement to the shoulder of the road, and hit a telephone pole.

In the suit by the owner of the passenger car, the court pointed out that the driver of any vehicle on a highway must signal his intention to turn from a direct line, or to start, stop, or back, by extending his hand and arm horizontally beyond the vehicle's left side.

Here, however, the driver of the passenger car failed to recover damages. He had been guilty of contributory negligence when he attempted to pass the leading truck at a street intersection.

Signaling to cars in the rear

When two or more cars are one behind the other on the road, the leading vehicle has no better legal position than the cars that follow it. The driver of each must take care not to stop, slow up, or swerve from his course without giving notice of his intention to those behind.

A bus followed by a truck at a distance of 100 feet was traveling about 45 miles an hour. The bus suddenly and without warning turned to the left and stopped. The truck crashed into the bus, overturned, and caught fire. Its driver was killed.

The court that tried the suit brought by the bus company decided in its favor. The owner of the truck appealed, because the question of negligence on the bus driver's part had not been submitted to the determination of the jury. Because it was shown that the bus driver had not signaled, the court reversed the judgment.

This court made a fundamental observation about cars traveling one behind the other. They must all observe the rules of the road, of course. However, the court said, "Just how close to a vehicle in the lead a following vehicle ought, in the exercise of ordinary care, to be driven; just what precautions the driver of such a vehicle must, in the exercise of ordinary care, take to avoid colliding with the leading vehicle which slows, stops, or swerves in front of him; just what signals or warnings the driver of the leading vehicle must, in the exercise of due care, give, before stopping or slowing up, of his intention to do so, may not be laid down in any hard-and-fast or general rule." Such issues are for a jury to decide after hearing all the evidence.

Reducing speed at crossings

A pedestrian at two o'clock on a winter morning was hit by an automobile while crossing intersecting streets and later died.

"I heard a crash like a thud," testified one witness. "I looked around and saw something flying around in the air that looked like a piece of cardboard. It hit the ground and it was a man."

The driver of the car appealed from the verdict against him. He claimed he had the right of way and that the man he had killed had been guilty of contributory negligence. He contended that when two or more persons traveling in different directions approach at a crossing, the one having the preference is entitled to the first use of the crossing—that it is the duty of others to give him a reasonable opportunity to use it.

The court refused to disturb the decision of the court below. "It was incumbent on the driver of the automobile to be continually watchful for the possible presence of persons on the crossing," declared the court, "and to have the speed of the car so reduced and controlled that it would be readily stopped or diverted in time to avoid collision with pedestrians who might be exposed to such danger."

Making a left turn

Many accidents arise from the making of left turns in the face of opposing traffic. One of the commonest hazards faced by the driver making such a turn is that he often cannot properly appraise the speed of the approaching car. At what distance can he make such a turn and be within the law?

Two automobiles were approaching each other when the driver of one of them made a left turn. They collided, and this driver was severely injured. The testimony of the injured man was that he had made the turn 300 yards from the approaching car. The testimony of the driver of the other car was that his turn had been made at less than 50 yards.

Here was a question of fact that a jury would have to determine. But the appellate court remarked that it was unwilling to hold, as a matter of law, that it is negligent to cross to the left in front of another car 300 yards away. On the other hand, said the court, if the approaching car was less than 50 yards from the one driven by the injured man when he turned to the left, he was clearly negligent. If the other driver was farther away than fifty yards, whether the driver making the turn could make it prudently would depend on the apparent speed of the oncoming car, and whether its driver saw and recognized a signal of the other driver that he wished to cross.

When you back on a highway

An automobile owner had parked his car parallel with the curb between two other parked cars. In maneuvering his car free, he backed into the pathway of an oncoming car. The cars collided. Before backing, the man in the parked car had looked and seen no approaching cars and, believing the road was clear, he had given no warning signal with his hand.

The court charged that this man's failure to give the hand signal as he was required to by law was negligence. Nevertheless, such a failure did not entitle the suing automobile owner to recover damages unless there had been no negligence on his own part.

Be careful when backing

A four-year-old child was playing in the yard of a Portland, Maine, tenement house used as a playground by the tenants' children. In the same yard Joe Balzamo was cleaning an automobile. When he finished his work, he started to back the car into the street and ran over the child, crushing his leg.

Damages were awarded for the injury. The court commented that since, in backing a closed car, a driver is greatly hampered because the lower edge of the rear window limits his field of vision, he must take further precautions or give a warning signal. Otherwise he is guilty of negligence.

When you drive a motorcycle

More than half of our states require motorcyclists to wear safety helmets, since many motorcycle accidents result in head injuries. Other states are likely to pass similar laws to protect cyclists. Check your state's driving code before adventuring out on a motorcycle as a driver or a passenger.

Parking

If you stop your car on a public highway just for a little while, to let passengers off, this is generally not considered parking. However, you are parking if you leave your car for a period longer than necessary, say, to load or unload passengers or freight, and there is no one in the car who can operate it.

Street lot owners and their rights

What are your rights if your city installs parking meters in front of your property?

The owner of property facing on a street brought an action to restrain the city from using the street as a parking-meter zone. He asserted the existence of the parking meters was an illegal interference with his right of access to his property.

The court held, however, that whatever right of access the owner pos-

sessed was subordinate to the rights of the public. He had no remedy or right to compensation, unless a special statute should be passed.

On this subject, all courts do not agree. In other instances it has been held that the owner's right of access to his property includes "passage, accessibility, and stopping briefly and reasonably in front of premises without unnecessarily inconveniencing the passage of the general public. The owner of property on the street has the right to have his family, guests, or customers come and go within reasonable limitations and, further, the owner has the right to park alongside his own property within reasonable limitations without the exaction of a parking tax."

Can an injured bus passenger always sue the carrier?

A Greyhound bus and a truck, each going in opposite directions, collided. The driver of the truck, traveling on the wrong side of the road, had refused to surrender a proper share of the highway. In a suit brought by a passenger of the bus for the injuries which she received, the court held the bus company was neither guilty of negligence nor liable for the injuries of its passenger. The driver of the bus, said the court, had the right to presume that the approaching vehicle, which was on the wrong side of the road, would go over to its proper side and the bus driver could not be expected to anticipate that it would not.

However, since the truck driver was definitely negligent, the injured passenger was entitled to bring suit against him.

Your duty toward children

A child running across a road was hit by an automobile and suffered substantial injuries. The verdict of the jury awarding damages to the child was reversed on appeal. The reason was that the jury had not been asked to determine whether the automobile horn was sounded by the driver of the car at a sufficient distance from the running child to be heard, since "it was the duty of the driver of the car to give a timely warning."

The specific facts are of great importance in all these cases. However, the courts of the different states have set various ages under which they hold a child is not capable of proper appreciation of dangers. But it is generally held that while age is a factor, and an important one, it is not the only factor. The capacity of a child to exercise care must be determined by a consideration, also, of his intelligence, experience, discretion, training, and other characteristics, as well as the nature of the danger itself. Nevertheless, unless a child is so young as to be incapable of using any care, he is responsible for a degree of care that can be determined only by the circumstances of each case.

The general rule is well summed up by one legal authority. "While it cannot be said as a general rule that all infants above the age of seven are required to exercise the same degree of care as an adult, such a one is required to exercise such degree of care as a person of like age, intelligence, experience, and capacity for understanding and avoiding the danger might reasonably be expected to exercise under similar circumstances and surroundings."

Parental responsibility

When an adult is accompanying a pedestrian child, then the duty of the driver to the child is changed. In a case in Alabama, a three-year-old child was killed by a postal truck. The accident occurred near a rural mailbox. The child's father was working on an automobile in the front yard when the mailtruck pulled up. Two older children went for the mail, which the driver handed to them. The tot had followed his older sisters and was in front of the truck when the driver started it up. Before moving the truck, the driver had looked around but the three-year-old was too small to be seen. The court found that, since older children were present and the child's father close by, and since all of them had a duty of care to the child, the mailman had no reason to expect that the child would be left in a position of danger. In any event, the father's contributory negligence in failing to take proper care of the child would prevent his recovery of any damages he suffered as a result of the loss of the child.

Nonresident motorist act

State statutes provide for what is called "constructive" or "substituted" service on a nonresident motorist. This is to be used when such motorist becomes involved in an accident while using the highways in the state where the statute has been enacted and leaves before any court action can be commenced.

Typically, the statute provides for serving a state official, such as the Secretary of the State or the Director of Motor Vehicles, with a copy of the process, and also for mailing to the nonresident motorist a copy of the same process and a notice of the service on the state official. The rationale behind the statutes allowing substituted service is that the motorist, when he drove into the state, consented to all the automobile laws of that state, including those governing the procedures for any action at law.

These statutes differ from state to state in the requirements they provide for mailing notices. Some states allow the notice simply to be sent by ordinary mail. Others require that it be sent by registered mail and that the return receipt be filed with the other papers in the case. It is important that the proper procedure be followed. Cases have been won or lost on points such as the notice being addressed to the wrong party or improperly addressed. Sometimes the party to whom the notice is sent refuses to accept the letter, which is why you need proof of registered mailing.

What if the accident occurs on private property?

Many of the nonresident motorist acts have been broadened to include accidents that occur "within the state" rather than just on the public highways. They may also include vehicles which are not in motion at the time of the accident.

If your state statute uses the word "highway," then, if the accident occurs in a parking lot, service station, or drive-in movie, you cannot sue the out-of-state driver by substituted service. The word "highway," however, can include the street, so a pedestrian area may be included within the terms of the statute.

What is a motor vehicle?

Of course, an automobile is such a vehicle, but what about a motorcycle? A nonresident motorcyclist who gets involved in an accident out of his state can be served under these statutes. However, a crane, tractor trailer, or semi-trailer is generally not considered a motor vehicle under these acts. It is obviously important to consult an attorney when you are involved in an accident with an out-of-state vehicle, or if you yourself are the out-of-state driver, so that all your rights will be fully protected.

Financial responsibility laws

These are statutes which most states have enacted to protect the public against the operation of motor vehicles by financially irresponsible persons. Usually the statutes provide that, within a stated period of time following the report of an auto accident to the Motor Vehicle Department, which accident involved significant property damage or serious personal injury, the operators or owners of all the vehicles must furnish reasonable security to satisfy any judgments and give proof of financial responsibility for the future. If security is not given, the driving licenses and registrations of those delinquent are suspended. If there is automobile insurance, then the statute does not apply.

In a recent case that went to the United States Supreme Court, a Georgia motor vehicle safety responsibility statute was found to be faulty. Under the statute, a motorist who did not have insurance and who was involved in an accident had to post security to cover the amount of damages claimed by the people injured, and failing to do so, his motor vehicle registration and driver's license were subject to suspension.

An uninsured motorist, who was a clergyman, was involved in an accident where a girl rode her bicycle into his automobile. He did not post the security required, and at the hearing held by the Georgia Director of Public Safety, the motorist's offer to prove he could not be liable for the accident was rejected, and he was told to post the security. The United States Supreme Court decided that before the license and registration could be suspended, due process of law required that there be a determination that there was a reasonable possibility of a judgment being rendered against the motorist as a result of the accident, because, if there was no such possibility of liability, it was unfair that he be required to post security.

On the other hand, in a similar situation in a Utah case that went to the United States Supreme Court, it was held that, even though the motorist was not granted a hearing on the question of reasonable possibility of fault, such a hearing had been given in the district court in Utah, and the suspension had been delayed pending the determination of that court. Accordingly, the Court ruled that the motorist had had a meaningful hearing and therefore the financial responsibility law could be applied.

Compulsory auto insurance

This is in effect in Massachusetts, New York, and North Carolina, and in Rhode Island for minors only. Under the New York law, no vehicle may be registered unless the application is accompanied by proof of financial responsibility such as liability insurance, a bond, or a deposit of a stated large sum of money. If a driver is involved in an accident while uninsured, the penalties are severe. The New York law applies to both resident and nonresident motorists. The Massachusetts law operates only as to cars registered in the state and to out-of-state vehicles operated in Massachusetts for more than 30 days. The Massachusetts statute does not apply when accidents occur on private property or to guest occupants of vehicles.

Drunk driving

Many states have enacted statutes on the subject of chemical tests to determine whether a driver is intoxicated. Alcohol in the brain causes intoxication, and the amount of alcohol in the brain is determined by the amount of alcohol in the blood. Opinions vary as to what percentage of alcohol must be in the blood for a determination of intoxication or being under the influence. Ten- or twelve-hundredths of 1 percent of alcohol in the blood is generally accepted as evidence of intoxication. However, the state statutes vary. Washington, D.C., stipulates twenty-one-hundredths of 1 percent must be found.

Must you take a drunk test?

Chemical tests may include the blood test, the breath test, the saliva test, or the urine test. Not all states are equipped to give a driver each test. The tests have been upheld as constitutional in that they do not involve an unreasonable search or violate a person's privilege against self-incrimination. This is because the operation of a motor vehicle on the roads of a state is not a right but a privilege. There have been challenges to all these tests as violations of the constitutional right against unreasonable search and seizure, but none of these have been successful.

New York was the first state to enact a law which says that any driver of a vehicle shall be deemed to have given his consent to a chemical test for alcohol content in the blood. If the driver does not consent, then he can lose his license. Other states that provide for revocation of the driver's license for refusal to be tested are Idaho, Iowa, Kansas, Nebraska,

North Dakota, and Utah. Certain prescribed procedures must be followed, however, before a license is revoked, including a hearing.

Can you get your own doctor to do the test?

Yes, at your own expense, of course. However, if your doctor cannot come, his absence is not sufficient reason to refuse to take the test.

Do you have a choice of tests?

The type of sobriety test to be given a driver is determined by the arresting officer. In Kansas, a driver said he was diabetic and wanted to choose the type of test. When he refused to take the test proposed, his license was revoked. The court later said he had no right to refuse since there was no proof he was a diabetic. The same results were reached in a case involving a man who claimed he had a heart condition, and in a situation where the driver refused to take the test claiming he had a rare blood disease. You should let police officers know if you prefer a particular test, or if you think the first one they gave you was not accurate. The officers are not obliged to comply with your wishes, but in several cases they have agreed to this expressed preference.

In many states, such as Georgia, Maine, Minnesota, New Jersey, Oklahoma, Oregon, Rhode Island, Texas, Washington, and the District of Columbia, refusal to take a sobriety test is not admissible in criminal proceedings. In New York, if you refuse to be tested for blood alcohol content, you cannot be required to submit to a test, and a refusal is not admissible as evidence in criminal proceedings. However, you can lose your driver's license.

In a New York case, a defendant was charged with driving while his ability was impaired. He refused to take a test, and at his trial he pleaded not guilty. The charge was dismissed, as there was insufficient evidence for conviction. The defendant then tried to use the criminal dismissal to block the revocation of his license, but since he had refused to take a test, he could not block the revocation.

Aviation accidents

These days, with highjacking of airplanes almost as common an occurrence as the highjacking of contraband liquor by rum-runners, one from another, during the days of prohibition*, we should consider claims involving accidents on airplanes.

*For those who do not remember, the 18th Amendment to the United States Constitution, passed in 1919, prohibiting the sale of liquor. It was repealed by the 21st Amendment in 1933.

Unlike the other usual accident cases, problems with air travel can be worldwide. First, you have the problem of venue, or where should you sue? Possible choices include the place of the accident, or where the plaintiff lives, or where the defendant corporation is incorporated or has its home office, or, possibly, if your lawyer thinks it is the fault of the manufacturer of the plane or the maintenance company, as well as of the operating airline, where those others are located. Naturally, your lawyer will try to select the place where the law and the damage claim can be most favorable. For example, we have heretofore considered for the automobile the problem of "guest statutes," where approximately 17 states prohibit recovery against the host for ordinary negligence. Suppose you are a guest in a private airplane taking off from a state with such a statute, and the accident occurs in another state. These are all complicated situations that require expert legal analysis.

In a case that went to the highest court of the State of New York, a New York resident took off from a New York airport as a passenger of a well-known airline. The plane crashed in Nantucket, Massachusetts. The suit was brought in New York. If the law of Massachusetts, where the accident occurred, was applied, the amount that could be recovered for negligently causing a passenger's death would be limited, as the Massachusetts law then provided, to no more than $15,000. The New York Court refused to apply the Massachusetts limitation in this action for wrongful death against a common carrier. If the suit had been brought in Massachusetts, the result would have been different.

Back in 1929, an international diplomatic conference was held in Warsaw, Poland. The United States did not participate in this conference, but it did have observers. Out of this came the Warsaw Convention, to which the United States became a party in 1934. This Convention limited the liability of an airline to 125,000 French francs or the equivalent of $8,300 in American money. Regardless of whether the airline was negligent or not, you could collect up to $8,300 and no more, if your flight was an international flight. This means that if you, an American, leave Los Angeles on your way to London and have an accident over the United States, the Warsaw Convention will apply. Not all of the countries of the world are parties to this Convention, and therefore, if you are flying to one of those countries, the Convention does not apply. In order to avoid the $8,300 limitation, it is possible to show wilful misconduct by the airline. Let us say that an employee mechanic deliberately puts sand in the fuel pump, then the limitation would not apply. Today the $8,300 figure is no longer relevant because most of the airlines have accepted a $75,000 limitation. Because there was so much dissatisfaction

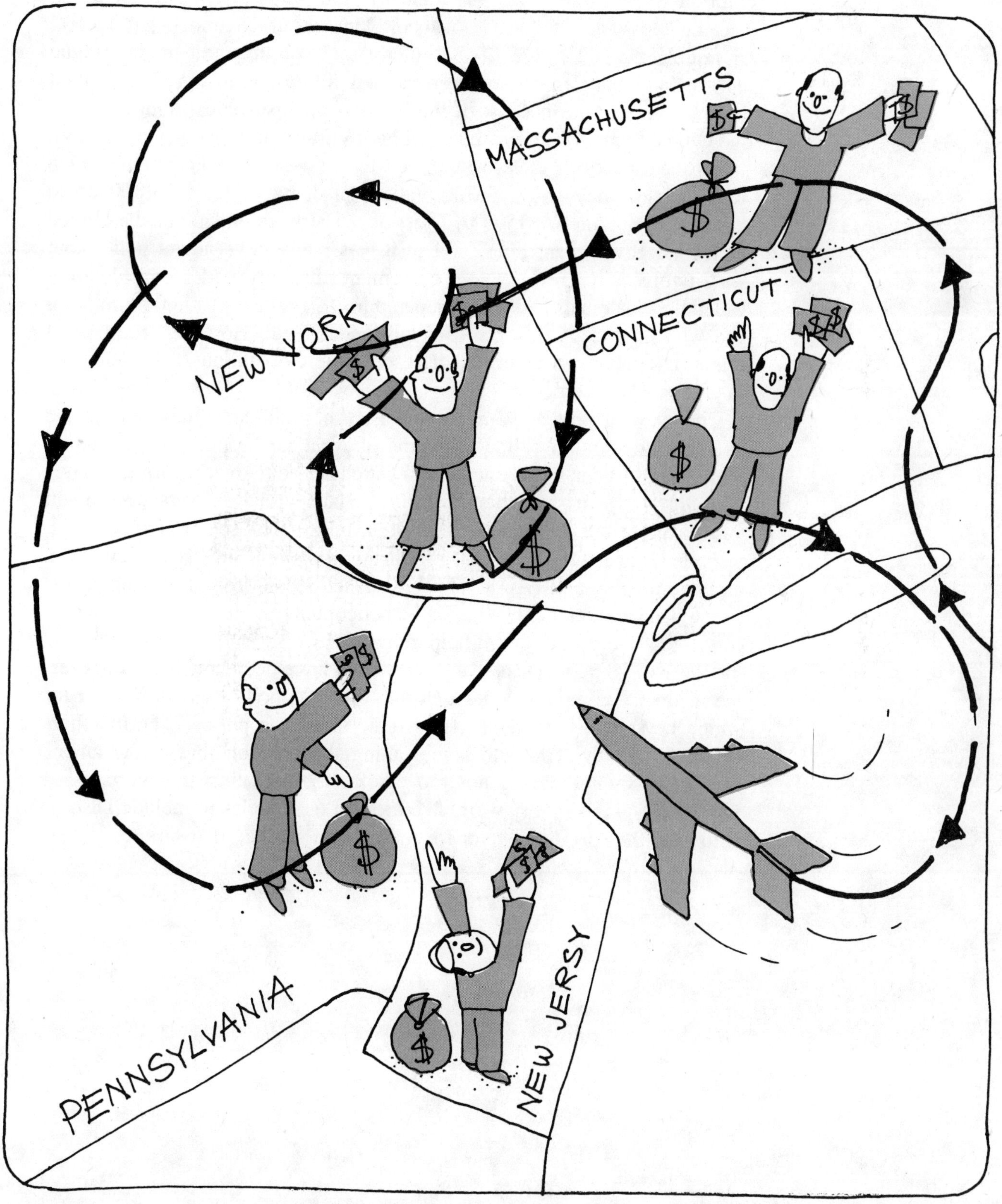
MASSACHUSETTS
CONNECTICUT
NEW YORK
PENNSYLVANIA
NEW JERSEY

with the $8,300 figure, in 1955 there was a meeting at The Hague, which became known as The Hague Protocol. This raised the amount to $16,600 or double the old figure. The United States participated in the Hague meeting and its delegates accepted the new figure, but it was never ratified by the U.S. Senate because it was clearly an insufficient sum. Finally, the United States was prepared to withdraw from the Warsaw Convention, when the airlines of the world agreed to the Montreal agreement, which required that they waive the limitation on damages from $8,300 up to the new limitation of $75,000. Most of the airlines outside of the United States are government lines, and so it was really government policy that was involved. There is a new agreement currently under consideration called the Guatemala Protocol, prepared in 1971 with a $100,000 limitation and with no exception for willful misconduct, etc. However, the United States has taken no action with respect thereto, although its delegates to Guatemala accepted it.

One way to protect yourself against the limitations imposed by the Warsaw Convention or the problems of what law applies in connection with your suit for negligence, is to purchase your own insurance. Then your only problem is whether the insurance you purchase covers the accident you have. In one case in New York, a man purchased insurance at the airport to cover his flight, as he indicated on the form, from New York to Los Angeles and return. He took a helicopter from Los Angeles to Disneyland and on the way back, the helicopter crashed. Did his insurance cover this sidetrip? If, when he purchased his insurance, he had indicated that he was going to Disneyland, he would have been covered. However, the insurance company contended that this was now a separate flight for which he should have purchased a new insurance policy. The members of the Court divided, with some taking the position that at the airline insurance counter one is not too careful in indicating the terminus of the flight and could very well have meant Los Angeles to include Disneyland. See the specific chapter for the general subject of Insurance.

CHAPTER 25

Criminal Law

One object of criminal law is to punish those guilty of crimes; a more important goal, however, under our system of justice, is to protect the innocent.

A civil action is based on an offense against an individual rather than against the community, and the plaintiff prosecutes the action himself, generally through a lawyer whom he retains. A criminal action is based on an offense against the state or the community and is conducted by the official prosecutor. To be guilty of a criminal act, one must either have intended to cause the action which occurred, or he must have acted in a manner that was so negligent or reckless that willfulness is implied by the law, which therefore recognizes no legal defense for committing the act.

Generally speaking, the word "crime" includes both felonies and misdemeanors. Felonies are offenses of a more serious nature which are defined by the statutes and constitutions of the states as offenses punishable by imprisonment in a penitentiary or state prison, or by death. Misdemeanors, on the other hand, are "faults and omissions" of less consequence, and are punished less severely.

For example, murder is a felony, while the violation of a traffic law or municipal ordinance is a misdemeanor; both are generally classified as crimes. A felony is sometimes defined as a crime which carries a punishment of imprisonment for one year or longer, and a misdemeanor is defined as a crime for which imprisonment is less than one year. A parking violation is not considered to be in the crime category. It is usually called an "offense."

In all felonies, the accused is entitled to trial by jury as a constitutional right. This is not true of all misdemeanors, which can be tried by a justice of the peace, a magistrate, or some special court composed only of judges, provided that the penalty is not more than six months imprisonment. If more, then the United States Supreme Court has ruled that a jury trial must be provided.

What is a warrant? A warrant is an order signed by a magistrate or a judge. It is made on a complaint by someone, and it charges that you committed a crime. The warrant must list the charge against you. It also must direct the policeman to make the arrest and to bring you before a magistrate or judge. If a policeman has a warrant for your arrest, he must tell you he has it. You have the right to ask to see it. If you ask, he must show the warrant to you.

A policeman can arrest a person without a warrant, however, if he sees that person commit a criminal offense. In nearly half of the states, a private person can make a citizen's arrest if he observes a criminal offense.

Recently, the United States Supreme Court ruled that a warrant is required for nonemergency inspection of your residence or place of business by city health or fire inspectors without your consent. However, in order to obtain a warrant, these officials need not prove that there is or may be a violation of the law as to your premises. A warrant will be issued based on their reasonable need to conduct periodic inspections for health and safety purposes.

Search and seizure

The Constitution has provided that any search of your person or your home must be reasonable. It is reasonable if it is conducted incidentally to a lawful arrest, if it is done with your consent, or if it is done pursuant to a legal search warrant. Even with a warrant, the officer normally has to give notice of his authority and the purpose of the search before entering. If a search is improper, then any evidence seized, however incriminating, cannot be used against you.

Recently, this constitutional rule was said by the Supreme Court to be enforceable against searches and seizures by state authorities.

In New York, an exceptional law provides that the officer need not give advance warning of his authority or purpose before entering your premises if his warrant provides that he does not have to do so. The court issuing the warrant must be convinced that an advance warning would serve to allow destruction of evidence, such as narcotics. This is known as the "no-knock" law.

"Stop and frisk" laws

Some states, including New York, Massachusetts, New Hampshire, Delaware, and Rhode Island, have laws which allow the authorities to question and/or temporarily detain and search persons, either at night or in public places, when there is reason to suspect them of having committed or being about to commit a crime.

Traffic violations

A mere traffic violation, such as parking too near a crosswalk, does not justify a search of the vehicle or the person. However, if the violation is the absence of license plates or obscured license plates, a search may be justified. Also, if you are arrested for driving while intoxicated, authorities are permitted to search you and your car for materials related to the offense, such as unconsumed liquor.

If an officer has reason to suspect a criminal violation—for example, if he sees that you have a weapon—he may search your car.

The hearing   The first step in the judicial process is normally a hearing at which witnesses are examined, and you have the right, but not the obligation, to testify. You can ask that this hearing be adjourned until your lawyer can be present. For certain misdemeanors, this hearing constitutes a trial; the presiding magistrate will dispose of the case directly and either dismiss the charge or find you guilty. In other cases, where he cannot try the charge himself, the magistrate decides only whether there is a reasonable basis for finding that you have committed the offense charged. In such case, you may waive the hearing. If you are charged with a misdemeanor, the magistrate will hold you for trial by another court. If a felony is involved, he will hold you for action by a grand jury.

Grand jury   A felony indictment can only be made by a grand jury, which is larger than a normal jury and hears evidence in secret session. You have the right to consult a lawyer at a grand jury, although he cannot be present in the jury room. You also have the right to ask to appear before the grand jury when it is considering your case, but you should not make this request without the advice of your lawyer. The trial itself is held before what is called a petit jury composed of 12 members. In many jurisdictions, a jury of six members is being used, and has been held constitutional by the United States Supreme Court.

Jury duty   As a citizen and resident of your community, you have the duty to answer the call to serve on the jury. Of course, when hardship is involved, the court will usually excuse your service. Sometimes you will not get to sit on a case because your presence may be challenged by the respective attorneys. There are two different types of challenges. You can be challenged with no reason given—this is called a peremptory challenge—or you can be challenged for cause, which means that there is something that would make your service unsuitable, such as your relationship to the defendant, your prior knowledge of the case, or your prejudgment of the issues.

Ignorance of the law   The presumption is that everyone knows the law, and from this springs the legal maxim that ignorance of the law is no excuse. If, for example, you do not know that your city has an ordinance forbidding you to litter the streets, you cannot, when charged with this misconduct, make your lack of knowledge a defense.

However, it is only to the law of your own country and state that this presumption relates.

When there are special circumstances in a case involving ignorance of the law, the court can at its discretion impose a lighter sentence.

When you are arrested

A policeman may arrest you without a warrant if he sees you commit or sees you try to commit a violation of the law. He can also arrest you without a warrant if a felony has been committed and he has reason to believe that you did it, even though he was not actually present at the time.

It is a crime to resist an officer who lawfully arrests you. If you believe you are not to blame, you can assert your rights through your attorney at the proper time. If you have been arrested without a legal basis, you have recourse through civil action. But if the arrest was proper, the fact that you are innocent will not give you the right to collect damages.

Your constitutional rights

In the last few years, the rights of the individual involved in a criminal action have been discussed at length by the United States Supreme Court, and landmark decisions have been handed down. You may have heard the names of many of the defendants—Gideon, Mallory, Escobedo, or Miranda. These decisions now directly bear upon the manner in which your case may be handled.

Mr. Gideon

Gideon was charged in Florida with having broken into a poolroom with the intent to commit a misdemeanor. He had no money, and when he appeared in court he asked that a lawyer be appointed to defend him. However, the Florida law permitted the court appointment of counsel for indigent defendants only in cases involving the death penalty. Gideon conducted his own defense and was convicted and sentenced to five years in prison. He appealed while in prison, and his case went to the United States Supreme Court. The Court held that the right of an indigent defendant in a criminal trial to have the assistance of counsel is a fundamental constitutional right, one essential to the conduct of a fair trial. The Sixth Amendment to the Constitution has provided that counsel must be appointed for poor defendants in criminal cases in the Federal courts, and now that right applies in state court criminal cases where the defendant is charged with a crime subject to a significant penalty of more than six months in jail.

Mr. Mallory

At about six o'clock one April evening in 1954 a woman was raped in the laundry room of her apartment house in Washington, D.C. Mallory was arrested the next day at about two o'clock in the afternoon. He was questioned and given a lie-detector test. He was the half-brother of the house janitor and had been helping in the laundry room. He was not told of his right to counsel or of his right to a preliminary hearing before a magistrate. He was not warned of his right to keep silent or that any statement he made could be used against him. At about 9 P.M. he confessed to the rape. He was taken before a magistrate the next morning and charged with the crime. After a trial, he was convicted and sentenced to death.

On appeal, Mallory claimed his confession should not have been admitted in evidence against him. The appellate court found that there had been an unnecessary delay between the time of his arrest and his being brought before the magistrate. An earlier arraignment would have meant he would have been advised of his right to remain silent. Therefore his confession was held to have been obtained illegally, and Mallory's conviction was reversed.

Mr. Escobedo   Danny Escobedo was 22 years old. He was arrested, along with his sister, in connection with the fatal shooting of his brother-in-law 11 days earlier. He had been arrested shortly after the shooting, but he obtained a lawyer and he was released. His second arrest came as a result of a statement by an alleged accomplice who implicated Escobedo. At the time of the second arrest, Escobedo asked to see his attorney, who was at the police station and asking to see his client. No meeting was permitted. During questioning, Escobedo made damaging statements connecting himself to the shooting and at the trial these were admitted in evidence, and he was convicted.

Escobedo's appeal went to the Supreme Court, and it held that it is unconstitutional to deny the right of counsel to an accused person who is no longer the object of a general inquiry but who has become a particular suspect. When the police are no longer investigating, but are accusing and are seeking to obtain a confession, the accused must be permitted to consult with his lawyer.

Mr. Miranda   Ernesto Miranda was a 23-year-old indigent Mexican with a ninth-grade education living in Phoenix, Arizona. A girl was raped and kidnaped, and Miranda was arrested. He was taken to the stationhouse and questioned for about two hours. He then wrote out a confession. He was later convicted and sentenced to 20 to 30 years in prison. He appealed, and his case went to the Supreme Court.

The Court stated that the rights of an accused in a criminal case must be protected, and it set out certain rules for the authorities to follow.

When a person has been taken into police custody, he must be given certain warnings concerning his rights. If these are not given, then any statements made during police questioning cannot be used in evidence at a trial. An accused must first be in custody or deprived of his freedom of action, but once he is, then he must be told he has the right to remain silent, that any statements he does make may be used as evidence against him, that he has the right to the advice of an attorney. The accused may voluntarily waive his rights, but, once he asks for a lawyer, he must have one before any further questions are put to him.

What about a spontaneous statement?

A man walked into a California police station and confessed to a crime he had committed in Oklahoma. This confession was allowed in evidence since the authorities were unaware of any crime until his confession. But remember, if you are under arrest or are placed under compulsion by the authorities, the Miranda warnings must be given. As soon as you are placed in custody, you are entitled to a lawyer.

In 1960, Mr. Killough strangled his wife and concealed her body in the city dump in Washington, D.C. She remained there undiscovered for two weeks until he took the police to the spot. He had been arrested on suspicion, since all anyone knew was that Mrs. Killough had disappeared and that blood was found in the Killough car. After being in custody for 34 hours, Killough confessed and was then taken before a United States Commissioner and charged.

After trial and conviction, Killough appealed. On appeal, Killough's confession was found to have been illegally obtained. However, Killough was retried and the government used another confession in evidence. This one had been made by Killough while in jail, to a graduate student who worked at the jail obtaining statistical information from the prisoners. Killough again appealed, and the second confession was also found to have been improper, since Killough had not been warned that his comments could not be kept confidential.

Another type of involuntary confession

In Oregon, a schoolteacher was induced by the school superintendent, the principal, and the parent of a child to confess to charges of contributing to the delinquency of a minor. The case was appealed, and the court said that the confession should have been excluded. Whether made to law enforcement officers or others, a confession induced by anyone in authority is not voluntary.

Store thefts

In California, a food store security agent saw a man steal some meat and go through the checkstand without paying. He arrested the man outside the store and took him to a room in the market where the man confessed. At his trial, the man claimed he had not been warned of his rights, but the court, unlike in the preceding Oregon case, said that the Supreme Court rules did not apply, since the store officer was a private person.

In New York, a department store security guard arrested a woman for shoplifting. She made statements which were later used in evidence against her. Here again the court would not apply the Supreme Court rules since no law enforcement officers were involved. But the New York court did emphasize that the confession had to be voluntary to be admissible. A confession need not be taken by an official to be considered coercive. The courts must make a judgment based on the facts of each situation.

Handwriting samples and fingerprints

You can be made to give your fingerprints, stand in a line-up, or give a sample of your blood for comparison purposes. These investigative actions are not considered violations of the rule against self-incrimination. However, the courts have compared the taking of handwriting samples to the giving of a confession. If the samples are not obtained voluntarily, they cannot be used in evidence. You are also entitled to counsel at the line-up.

The accessory to a crime

The accessory or accomplice to a felony is anyone who directly or indirectly assists in the commission of the offense.

An accessory before the fact is a person who uses his influence to have a crime committed, gets someone else to commit it, or participates in the crime before it happens, by planning it or in some other way. An accessory after the fact is a person who, with knowledge of a crime that has been committed, conceals it from the authorities and protects the one who is charged with committing the offense.

Solicitation to commit a crime

The law generally provides that anyone who solicits another person to commit a crime shall, if the crime is committed, be considered an accessory and punished severely. If the crime is not committed, the offense is generally punishable as a misdemeanor.

The publisher of a periodical which called for revolution and murder, naming poison and dynamite as the agencies to be used, was punished for the commission of a misdemeanor. On the other hand, had revolution and murder actually been accomplished in the way the periodical recommended, the publisher's crime would have been a felony.

When a child commits a crime

A child or an adult, to be guilty of a crime, must be capable of criminal intent. A boy of 14 was not guilty of a misdemeanor in shooting craps. Although he was capable of distinguishing generally between right and wrong, the normal standard for having the requisite intent, he did not classify gambling as unlawful or wrong. It is necessary, before a child can be held criminally guilty, that he know more than the difference between good and evil. He must realize the illegality of the particular act in question. This in turn depends not only on age but upon all the elements that enter into the mental equipment and attitudes of the child.

Abduction

This crime is the taking away of any child or woman by fraud, persuasion, or violence. Many of the statements speak of a taking for immoral purposes.

A woman persuaded her younger sister, a child under 14, to accompany her to a house of ill fame for the purpose of prostitution. For this offense she was convicted of abduction. Had she taken the child across a state line, she would have faced a charge under the Federal Mann Act, which we shall discuss later.

Is adultery a crime?

Whether or not adultery is a crime must be determined by the statutes of the state in which the adultery occurred. Adultery under the ancient common law was not an indictable offense but was punished only in the church courts. It is now an offense in rather more than half the states.

In some of the states, only the married person is guilty; if the other party is single, the offense of that person is not adultery but may be considered fornication. However, fornication is a crime in only about a third of the states.

Abortion

Abortion was at one time a serious offense. It had been defined as "the unlawful destruction or the bringing or causing to be brought forth prematurely of the unborn offspring of a pregnant woman at any time before birth according to the course of nature." Some states have recently legalized abortions performed under proper circumstances. This topic is covered in Chapter 6.

Arson

Arson, a felony, is the deliberate burning of another's building. However, in many states, criminal statutes include the burning of a building owned by the offender, although under the ancient law this did not constitute the crime of arson. If anyone is killed while in the fire, the crime is murder.

Assault and battery

Assault is the attempt made, within striking distance, to strike or injure another person—an attempt which, if not prevented, would result in a battery. Battery is the infliction of an unlawful beating or other physical violence on another without his consent.

Assault, then, is the threat to commit battery, and can be committed without actual physical contact. Battery requires some touching or contact.

Thus, if someone violently pushes you, he may be guilty of assault and battery. If he threatens to strike you, and you have good cause to believe he will carry out his threat, he may be guilty of assault.

Conspiracy

The Berrigan trial in Pennsylvania and the trial in Chicago (The Chicago 7) as an aftermath of the Democratic Convention of 1968, have revived interest in the crime of conspiracy. In general, an unlawful combination or agreement by two or more people to do an unlawful act or to do a lawful act by unlawful means, constitutes a conspiracy. Four elements are needed for the crime of conspiracy, being an agreement, specific intent, an unlawful object, and an overt act. The criminal act is the understanding or agreement itself. If a new party concurs in plans formed before he became a member of the conspiracy, and he comes in to aid in the execution of it, he becomes a fellow-conspirator, and each conspirator is liable for the acts of every other member done to carry out the conspiratorial plan. This is what makes the crime of conspiracy so all-encompassing, because once you are part of it, acts of the others become your problem as well. The reason for the requirement of an overt act is to have the dividing line between act and talk, so that the opportunity is provided to avoid liability by withdrawing before any action has been taken to further the arrangement.

Bigamy

A bigamist is a married person who, while his marriage partner is alive and undivorced, marries another person.

Bigamy is not always committed knowingly. A few months after the marriage of Lloyd C. and Sarah L., Sarah disappeared, eloping with another man. Five years later, Lloyd, hearing that Sarah was dead, married Frankie. After this second marriage he learned to his surprise that Sarah was still alive. He immediately obtained a divorce from her and again married Frankie.

Shortly after his first marriage to Frankie he was indicted for bigamy and convicted. The appellate court sustained the bigamy conviction but added that the good faith of the offender should be considered in mitigation of his punishment.

In a number of states, the law is that a person is not guilty of bigamy when, at the time of entering into the second marriage, he reasonably believed that the former marriage had been dissolved by divorce, annulment, or death. But in other states, this belief will not excuse the offense of bigamy.

Blackmail

In the law, "blackmail" has a wider meaning than popular usage gives it. The full range of the term was aptly shown by a New York court, which defined this felony as "equivalent to, and synonymous with, extortion—the exaction of money either for the performance of a duty, the prevention of an injury, or the exercise of an influence." It supposes the service to be unlawful and the payment unlawful.

"Not infrequently, it is extorted by threats or by operating upon the fears or the credulity, or by promises to conceal or offers to expose the weakness, the faults, or the crimes of the victim."

Bribery and extortion

A justice of the peace was convicted of accepting a dollar from a prisoner as consideration for dismissing and setting aside a warrant of arrest. The court that tried him supplied this definition of bribery:

"A voluntary giving or receiving of anything of value in corrupt payment for an official act done or to be done. The distinction between bribery and extortion seems to be that the former offense consists in offering a present or receiving one, the latter in demanding a fee or present by color of office."

"Color of office" means the pretense of acting in the capacity of a public official, and in a legal sense "extortion" is applied only to the acts of an officer.

One of the most publicized bribery cases of recent times involved Jimmy Hoffa, the former president of the Teamsters' Union. He was convicted of bribery because he attempted to have members of a jury vote for his acquittal in return for the payment of money. In this case, the jury members were performing an official act by making their decision.

Burglary–whether successful or not

This crime, under an ancient law, was "breaking and entering a dwelling house of another in the nighttime with intent to commit a felony therein, whether the felonious purpose be accomplished or not." This old definition is now generally modified by statute. A typical law now says, "A person is guilty of a burglary if he enters a nonabandoned building . . . or separately secured section therein, unless the premises are at the time open to the public or the actor is licensed or privileged to enter therein."

The factors of entry and intent are important here, and the crime is punishable even if nothing is stolen.

When worthless checks are passed

In most states, the giving of a worthless check with the knowledge that it is worthless is included as a crime in the broad category of obtaining money or property by false pretenses. In a few states, however, if a person merely gives a check without representing that there is money to cover it in the bank, it is not a criminal offense. Several jurisdictions are now beginning to pass legislation which also makes it a crime to use another's credit card if the rightful owner has not given his permission.

Disorderly conduct

Under the common law, these offenses were called breaches of the peace and were generally categorized as loud and unseemly noises, disturbing the peace and quiet of the neighborhood, collecting a noisy crowd, or disturbing a meeting or religious worship. Now the offenses are governed by local statutes and can include such actions as spitting on the sidewalk, public drunkenness, and begging without a license. One court said, "The gist of the crime of disorderly conduct is the doing, or saying, or both, of that which offends, disturbs, incites or tends to incite a number of people gathered in the same area.''

Some states have now also passed laws which make anyone who engages in, or solicits another to engage in, lewd public conduct, guilty of this crime.

Sometimes an arrest under such a statute can be considered a violation of a person's constitutional rights. In Connecticut, a member of Jehovah's Witnesses played a phonograph record attacking the Catholic Church. He was arrested and convicted for inciting a breach of the peace, but the conviction was reversed when the court found that his freedom of religion had been violated.

In Louisiana in 1965, over 2,000 college students went to the local courthouse to protest some convictions in cases with racial overtones. Many of the marchers were arrested and charged with disturbing the peace under a Louisiana statute which forbade pickets and parades near a courthouse with the intent of interfering with the administration of justice. The students appealed their fines, and the United States Appellate Court said that, although freedom of speech and assembly are basic rights, not everyone with opinions or beliefs to express may do so at any time and at any place. The court would not sanction even peaceful conduct which conflicted with statutes drawn to protect basic governmental functions.

With demonstrations becoming quite common, and at times causing disruption of traffic, business, and governmental affairs, the courts must answer the question in each case of which interest—the right to free expression or the threat to normal safety—will prevail. Much will depend on the extent to which the disturbance interferes with other activities. This should be kept in mind if you plan to engage in a demonstration. The right to free speech has its limits.

See Chapter 9 on Your Civil Rights for more on this subject.

Drunkenness   Most states and cities have laws against public drunkenness. Some statutes refer to the common drunkard as someone who offends peace and order. In Wisconsin and Virginia, one can be convicted of being a common drunkard regardless of where the arrest occurs. But other jurisdictions only punish, as disorderly conduct, public misconduct or acts done while in a state of intoxication which are deemed harmful to society.

Drunkenness is not always synonomous with intoxication. There is also the expression ''under the influence.'' Statutes which use this term do so in connection with driving. When someone is under the influence, he has decreased his driving ability so as to lose his normal control. Driving in this condition is a criminal offense in those states.

There are also particular laws involving drunkenness, such as the statute, which many states have passed, making it a misdemeanor for a physician to be intoxicated while acting in his professional capacity.

Embezzlement

A captain of the United States Army Field Artillery was in command of a Reserve Officers Training Corps unit. Among the stores in his custody were 4,221 blankets. These blankets were sold at public auction and, since the government had no depository in that vicinity, the captain deposited the proceeds of the sale in his personal bank account. Later, when he had failed either to account for this money or pay it over to the government, he was indicted for embezzlement.

The court, in deciding this case, gave a good basic definition of "embezzlement" and how it can be proved to the satisfaction of the law. It said that embezzlement is established by proof that property came lawfully into the embezzler's possession under circumstances which create a relation of trust between him and the owner, and that there was a breach of trust or unlawful appropriation of the property to the embezzler's use.

Since the blankets were sold, and since the captain received the proceeds and failed to pay over the money or account for it, he was guilty of embezzlement.

This crime can be committed by any employee or public official to whom money or property is entrusted during the course of his employment in office.

False weights and measures

False weights and measures are those that do not correspond to the standards set by the government. Often a merchant tampers with scales that originally conformed to the government standards, and in this way he manages to give the customer short weight. The intentional use of such weights and measures is punished generally by statutory provision. This crime is usually classed as a misdemeanor.

Compounding a felony

This means agreeing, for money or some other valuable consideration, to refrain from prosecuting a criminal, or to show some favor to him so that he may escape conviction. For example, a man was given a worthless check in a state where this is a statutory crime. Then a number of persons associated with the issuer of the check made an agreement with the defrauded man to pay him the amount of the check if he would conceal the offense from the county attorney and abstain from prosecution. They were found guilty of compounding the felony.

Forgery

Forgery is committed when someone, with the intent to defraud, makes or materially alters a writing which, if it were genuine, would have legal force. The offense is not limited to handwriting, but may also include printing, engraving, etc. Another definition is the fraudulent making or altering of a writing to the prejudice of another's right. It is not limited to the writing or altering of signatures, but applies to any part of a written instrument. For example, altering the sum of someone else's check is forgery.

Forgery can also be committed by using or negotiating a written instrument known to have been forged.

Homicide–with or without intent

"The unlawful killing of a human being with malice aforethought," was the phrase used in the indictment describing the offense for which a soldier named Myers was convicted in Texas for the murder of another soldier. Myers had been drinking heavily, and was irritable and quarrelsome. After a little altercation he went to his tent, loaded a pistol, and shot and killed the other man. He was convicted of murder in the first degree. His sentence was imprisonment for life.

Where the homicide, or killing, is done with prior deliberation or "malice aforethought," the legal term for a deliberate act, as in the Myers case, it may constitute murder in the first degree.

Where the homicide is committed with the intent to kill but the intent did not exist until the moment of the act, it is murder in the second degree. This applies to murder committed in a sudden fit of passion. For example, in the case just described, had the soldier, instead of going out and bringing back his gun, suddenly struck his victim down with a makeshift weapon, he would have been guilty of murder in the second degree. This crime never carries the death penalty.

Any killing that occurs during the commission of a felony—such as robbery, arson, or rape—is murder and is called felony-murder. Any person who was involved in the commission of the felony is deemed guilty of the murder, even if he did not do the actual killing.

To justify homicide in the defense of a home, it must appear that no greater force was used than was necessary. When, however, someone is seeking to break into a house at night, the owner may without penalty resort to the extremity of taking life.

Manslaughter, a still less serious crime, is different from both of these offenses. In general, manslaughter means killing without malice or intent, as in the heat of passion or by gross negligence.

Insanity Before any punishment may be exacted, it must be shown that the offender was to blame for the act. In a civilized and ordered society, people must assume responsibility for their deeds. However, what about the defendant who is insane? What is insanity? It used to mean wildness or possession by the devil. Now it can mean that someone is neurotic or psychotic.

In 1843, in England, a rule was set down by the court in a case involving a man called Daniel M'Naghten and ever since it has been called the M'Naghten Rule. It has been the basis for the finding of criminal insanity in most homicide cases to this day. What the court said then was that, if a defendant is found to be suffering from some mental disability or derangement of his mental processes of such severity as to render him incapable of knowing the nature and quality of his act, or from knowing that the act was wrong, he will be found not to be responsible for his crime. It has been called the "right and wrong" test.

Some courts in the United States felt that this test was not broad enough to explain the conduct of people with some mental difficulties. Modern-day psychiatry has come a long way since 1843. So another rule was developed called the "irresistible impulse" test. If, by reason of a mental disease, or abnormal mental state of passion, a defendant is unable to control his actions or impulses to commit the crime, he will be adjudged not responsible. A famous book, *Anatomy of a Murder*, later made into a popular motion picture, used this point of law as the basis for the plot. More than a dozen states recognize this test for insanity in homicide cases.

In 1954, the Durham Rule was developed, named after the defendant in a case in Washington, D.C. This rule requires the prosecution to prove that the crime was not a product of a mental disease or defect—that is, any abnormal condition of the mind which substantially impairs behavior control.

Many of our states have adopted still another test which provides that a person is not responsible for criminal conduct if, at the time of his act, as a result of a mental disease or defect, he lacked substantial capacity either to appreciate the criminality of his conduct or to conform his conduct to the requirements of the law.

In all cases, competent medical opinions must be obtained by both sides, no matter what rule the particular state follows.

Incest and related crimes

Incest is sexual intercourse, or in some states, merely a marriage, between blood relatives within the degrees where marriage is forbidden. It is a felony. Statutes provide the degree of blood relationship for incest. This may extend as far as uncle and niece. See Chapter 1.

Does incest require the consent of the female? In a case in California, a man was convicted of incest committed upon his young daughter. He based his appeal from this judgment on the assertion that the charge of the trial court to the jury was inaccurate. The trial court had charged that the accused was guilty of the crime of incest whether the intercourse was with or without the consent of the female. His lawyer asserted that the consent of both parties was essential to the crime of incest.

The appellate court held that the trial court's charge was a correct statement of the law and affirmed the conviction.

When incest is committed without consent, it necessarily becomes combined with another crime or crimes. A father, in a recent case, was convicted of incest, assault, and the rape of his own daughter, a child of 14.

Kidnapping as a Federal offense

While "kidnapping" means to abduct a person, it also involves the element of force or fraud in the seizure of the victim and connotes that he is carried off against his will.

This distinction was made in a decision affirming the conviction of Arthur Gooch for the kidnapping of two police officers. Gooch and another criminal named Nix were at a filling station in Texas, waiting for a tire of their automobile to be repaired. Two police officers in a patrol car passed the station, became suspicious of the car's owners, and stopped to search it. Inside they found a cache of food, money, automatic shotguns, rifles, and pistols.

They asked Gooch for papers showing his ownership of the car. Gooch, unable to produce them, reached for his gun. The criminals forced the two policemen into the rear seat of the automobile and, covering them with a gun, drove on to Oklahoma, where, after a ride of about 300 miles, they released them six hours later.

A month later, Nix was shot resisting arrest, and Gooch was tried and convicted of the crime of kidnapping. This was more than an offense against a state law (all the states provide severe penalties for kidnapping). Following the Lindbergh kidnapping, a Federal statute was enacted which makes any kidnapping a Federal offense where the person kidnapped has been taken from one state into another by the criminals. It was under this law, with its heavy penalties, that Gooch was convicted.

The Federal statute on kidnapping provides, in substance, that anyone who transports from one state to another anyone who has been unlawfully seized, inveigled, decoyed, kidnapped, abducted, or carried away and held for ransom or reward, shall be punished by death if the kidnapped person has not been liberated unharmed, and if the verdict of the jury recommends this punishment. If the death penalty is not imposed, the guilty person may be imprisoned for life or a term of years.

Anyone who receives or disposes of anything of value which has been delivered as a ransom and knows of that fact is subject to a fine and imprisonment under this statute.

Although in the Gooch case the abductors transported their prisoners a distance of 300 miles, the transporting of an unwilling person over any distance is technically considered kidnapping.

Robbery

Robbery is the felonious taking of personal property belonging to another from his person and against his will, by means of force or fear.

The force or fear is present when the robber is armed or threatens an assault, or does anything that would cause a reasonable person to fear harm if he did not give up his property. This element of compulsion is what distinguishes robbery from larceny, which by and large does not carry as heavy a penalty. The difference is clearly set forth in the following case:

Two men, Rito Ramirez and Jack Murray, were playing cards in an Arizona saloon. Later they left the saloon and were arrested. The police, in searching Ramirez, found a five-dollar gold piece, fifty cents in silver, and some other small coins. During the card game in the saloon, witnesses had seen Ramirez's hand in Murray's pocket. Ramirez was convicted of robbery and sentenced to five years in the penitentiary. When he appealed this conviction, the court set it aside, declaring, "While the evidence might be sufficient to sustain a charge of larceny, there is absolutely no evidence in the record showing, or tending to show, any force used by Ramirez, any fear on the part of Murray, or any intimidation by Ramirez calculated to place Murray in fear." In other words, Ramirez was guilty of picking pockets, which is larceny, whereas he had illegally been condemned for the more serious crime of robbery.

Two kinds of larceny

"Larceny" is the technical legal term for theft. A court decision defines "larceny" as "the felonious taking and carrying away, from any place, of the personal property of another without his consent, by a person not entitled to deprive the owner of the property, and to convert it to the use of the taker or of someone other than the owner." Picking pockets is an example. Some jurisdictions include embezzlement and the obtaining of property under false pretenses within the term "larceny."

The law recognizes two kinds of larceny—grand larceny, in varying degrees depending on the state, which is always a felony, and petit larceny. The punishment for grand larceny is more severe. The dividing line in terms of the value of the amount stolen varies from state to state.

In New York, at one time, there were two degrees of grand larceny: grand larceny in the first degree, bringing up to ten years in prison and covering a value of more than $500, or any value amount taken from a person at night, or taking more than $25 from a house at night; and grand larceny in the second degree, bringing up to five years in prison and covering value of more than $100 but not exceeding $500, or any value amount taken from the person of another. Petit larceny was a misdemeanor and involved property of the value of $100 or less.

Under the new New York penal law, grand larceny is divided into three degrees. When a person steals property, he is at least guilty of petit larceny. Petit larceny is a misdemeanor for which a sentence of up to one year can be imposed. All degrees of grand larceny are felonies. Grand larceny in the third degree occurs when property is stolen in a value exceeding $250, or when certain other property, such as a credit card, is stolen, or when the property was taken "from the person of another," regardless of its nature or value. Grand larceny in the third degree is a Class E felony, for which the penalty does not exceed four years in prison. Grand larceny in the second degree applies if the value of the property stolen exceeds $1,500. This is a Class D felony, for which the term of imprisonment would not exceed seven years. Grand larceny in the first degree applies, regardless of the nature and value of the property, when the property stolen is obtained by frightening the victim into thinking that resistance would result in physical injury to himself or in damage to that property. Grand larceny in the first degree is a Class C felony, for which the penalty could not exceed fifteen years.

It should be noted that the worst degree in crime is that of the first degree. It should also be noted that under the present New York system of classifying felonies, Class A, for which the term is life imprisonment, is the most serious, and as you proceed through the alphabet through Class E, the terms of imprisonment decrease in length. Misdemeanors are divided into Classes A and B. Petit larceny is a Class A misdemeanor.

Criminal and civil libel

To hurt a person's reputation by maliciously printing or writing harmful statements about him is libel. The law in many states punishes libel as a crime when the defamatory statement was published with a malicious intent. This does not necessarily mean that it was made with malice. Legally, the malicious-intent requirement is satisfied if the statement was made willfully and without legal justification. Some states find it a crime if the statement tends to cause a breach of the peace. If the statement is found to be privileged, criminal libel cannot occur. Statements made in judicial proceedings are always privileged. In addition, there is a "qualified privilege" in discussions between people, which depends upon the substance of the remark and the context in which it is made.

Discussions among family members about family matters, for example, enjoy this privilege. Remarks between members of a union about union matters also fall within this protected category. But a discussion between people who are unrelated to each other about the family of one of them is not privileged in this "qualified" manner. Defamation, of which civil libel is a part, is discussed further in another chapter.

Narcotics

"That humanity at large will ever be able to dispense with artificial paradises seems very unlikely."

This has become one of the major problems confronting our civilization. The incidence of drug use amongst people of all ages and social strata has reached alarming proportions. There are discussions at all levels of society concerning care, treatment, prevention, education, and punishment. Authorities disagree on all these aspects, as well as on what drugs should be considered harmful and therefore prohibited. Some courts have tried to develop theories which would apply equally to the use of alcohol and narcotics.

What is addiction?

Addiction has been defined by the World Health Organization of the United Nations as a state of periodic or chronic intoxication produced by repeated consumption of a drug, natural or synthetic. The characteristics include an overpowering need to continue taking the drug and to obtain it by any means, the tendency to increase the dose, psychological and general physical dependence on the effects of the drug, and an effect detrimental to the individual and to society.

What are narcotics?

The Uniform Narcotic Drug Act regulates and controls the manufacture, distribution, use, and possession of narcotics and has been adopted in most states. The Act designates narcotics as coca leaves, opium, cannabis, which is marijuana, and every other substance neither chemically nor physically distinguished from them. It also includes any other drugs to which Federal narcotics laws apply, and any drug found by any state, after reasonable notice and hearing, to have an addiction-forming or addiction-sustaining liability similar to morphine or cocaine. The laws in each state regarding penalties for possession of various drugs cover quite a broad range of severity. Penalties for possession of small amounts of marijuana, for example, have decreased during the last few years, but an Illinois man was recently sentenced to a 20-year prison term for possession of only a few ounces.

Barbiturates

There is a Federal Food, Drug and Cosmetic Act section which regulates barbiturates and amphetamines. Physicians have known that illness or death can be caused by the combined use of alcohol and barbiturates. However, only recently has that fact been brought home to the public, probably because several well-known personalities were found to have died as a result of such a lethal combination.

An interesting case

A defendant was on trial for murder. Before the trial, he had been nervous and emotional. However, on the day that he testified on his own behalf, he was cool and calculating. He was convicted and sentenced to death. He appealed and his conviction was reversed. It seems that on the morning he was to testify he had been given a sedative which altered his reactions. The court found that a drug-induced change was unfair to the defendant since the jury may have been influenced by his calm manner, thinking he was not sorry for the crime.

A witness who takes drugs

Can his credibility or truthfulness be questioned? The use of drugs is not sufficient for a court in determining a witness is incompetent. It must be shown the witness was under the influence of a drug at the time he witnessed the events in question, or that his habit was such that he could have been under their influence at the time, so that his testimony would probably not be reliable.

What about driving under the influence of drugs?

In California, a driver's license will be refused to anyone who has been convicted for the possession of narcotics. In Ohio, the law states that it is unlawful to operate a motor vehicle while under the influence of alcohol, narcotic drugs, or opiates. In Oklahoma, it is unlawful for an habitual user or anyone under the influence of drugs to a degree which renders him incapable of safely driving to operate a motor vehicle. Many other states have similar provisions.

The Supreme Court and addiction

A California statute made it a misdemeanor for any person to be addicted to the use of narcotics. It made the status of addiction a crime and the offender liable to prosecution at any time while in California. Robinson was picked up although he was not engaged in any antisocial behavior. After conviction under the statute, he appealed. The Supreme Court said, "It is unlikely that any state at this moment in history would attempt to make it a criminal offense for a person to be mentally ill, or a leper, or to be affected with a venereal disease." Therefore, since addiction is an illness, it is unconstitutional and cruel and unusual punishment to convict someone for being addicted. A defendant must commit some overt antisocial act before a crime can be said to have been committed.

What about addiction and insanity? Generally, addiction itself does not establish irresponsibility. But if a person becomes temporarily insane because of voluntary use of drugs he will still be considered responsible for his acts. There have been a few exceptions in trials for premeditated murder. The use of drugs is not considered voluntary if the drugs are taken because of medical need. Also, it may not be considered voluntary if the drug is taken due to a physiological dependence on it, even though the user takes the drug with awareness of the consequences.

L.S.D. and other chemicals The United States has an amendment to the Food and Drug Act that makes unlicensed L.S.D. manufacture and sale a felony. A number of states also have legislation on the subject. In New York, the law outlaws the possession of hallucinogenic substances by unauthorized persons and provides for a penalty of up to a year in jail. Recently the New York State legislature additionally provided for imprisonment up to four years for possession of hallucinogenics *with intent to sell* by making it a Class E felony.

Perjury Perjury is an assertion of fact or knowledge by a person under oath when that person knows, or is of the opinion, that what he is swearing to is false. The falsehood, however, must be a material one if it is to count as perjury.

An ordinary lie can become perjury, then, when it is spoken under oath. It is not likely to become perjury if it pertains to some small detail that does not affect the subject of the inquiry one way or the other.

The act of perjury is not necessarily oral. It may be committed in writing, too, as in signing income tax returns or other important papers requiring an oath.

Prostitution and the Mann Act

The offense of prostitution, according to an early decision, means "the act of permitting illicit intercourse for hire—an indiscriminate intercourse or what is deemed public prostitution." The definition still holds good today.

The punishment of prostitutes, like that of vagrants, is governed entirely by the statutes of the states or by municipal ordinances. These also provide punishment for keepers of bawdy houses. There is also on the Federal statute books a law called the Mann Act, also known as the White Slave Act, enacted by Congress to prevent commerce in prostitution. This Federal statute punishes anyone instrumental in persuading, inducing, enticing, or coercing any woman or girl to go from one place to another in interstate or foreign commerce for the purpose of prostitution or debauchery or for any other immoral purpose, whether with or without her consent. This crime is punishable by a maximum fine of $5,000 and five years' imprisonment.

A typical violation of the Mann Act began when a young girl met a man at a public festival in Virginia. He promised her that, if she would go to New York, he would obtain for her a place of employment with "easy work and plenty of money." After spending the night with her in Virginia, he gave her the money for her transportation to New York.

There she was met at the station by the man's wife and another woman. They told her that she could either lead a life of prostitution or starve. For two weeks she plied this age-old trade, then, with the aid of an elevator boy, she escaped from the hotel where she was confined and returned to Virginia.

She had been induced to cross a state line for an immoral purpose. That she did this of her own free will was not an extenuating circumstance under this Federal law, and the man and his accomplices responsible for this violation were punished.

Rape and attempt to rape

This crime consists of having sexual relations with a woman forcibly and against her will. The law specifies that the offense is complete when the woman is made to yield from fear, or the use of drugs, or does not consent voluntarily and consciously.

"Attempted rape" is also a crime, even though the rape is not completed.

One of the problems in obtaining a conviction for rape is the rule in many jurisdictions regarding corroboration, which means that someone besides the complainant, or something in the way of additional independent evidence, confirms that the rape was committed.

Even if there be proof beyond a reasonable doubt that there was penetration, forcibly and against the will of the woman, and that the defendant is the one who did it, unless there is independent corroboration, in many jurisdictions the defendant must go free. The reason for this is that experience has shown that a woman may accuse a man of rape when there was no actual force involved. Where the woman has not known the man previous to the time of the accusation of rape, this explanation has no validity, but corroboration may still be required. In the absence of a witness to the event, and there seldom is a witness, corroboration may consist of some independent evidence. In one case in New York, a rapist told the girl that his name was Frenchie. It turned out that the defendant did answer to the name of Frenchie and that his father had also been called Frenchie. This was sufficient corroboration.

"Statutory rape" is different. This consists of sexual intercourse with a girl who is younger than the age specified by the particular state statute. A crime is committed even though no force is used and the girl consents to the act of intercourse. The theory is that a very young girl should not be taken advantage of, even if she agrees. Each state decides on the age of consent, and the age varies among the states. In New York, 17 is the age of consent. In the majority of states it is 16. That a girl may look much older than her age is no defense; it is her actual age that counts.

No seduction without consent

Seduction is the use by a man of some artifice or promise (such as a promise to marry) or other means by which he induces an unmarried woman to submit to unlawful intercourse with him when she is, and has previously been for a reasonable time, a person of chaste conduct. The promise involved need not be false. If a man seduces a woman by honestly promising marriage, this does not legally excuse him from the crime. In those states where seduction is still considered a crime, the law is seldom enforced.

It should be noted that seduction cannot be committed by a woman against a man.

The woman's consent is essential to this offense. Failing that consent, the case is likely to come under the heading of rape. It does not matter how old the woman is—it is seduction as long as she is able to distinguish between right and wrong and has the capacity to consent. For example, if a man drugs a woman, she loses the capacity to consent, and the court will probably hold that the man who had sexual relations with her when she was in this condition was raping her, not seducing her.

A commonplace case of seduction is one in which a chaste woman agrees to have sexual intercourse with a man because he promises to make her his wife afterward. He then fails to live up to his promise. Her consent has been won—by a promise, in this instance—and so the conditions specified by the statutes exist. Of course, if the man could establish that the woman had habitually had relations with other men, there could be no charge of seduction.

Receiving stolen goods

The offense of receiving property from another, knowing that it has been stolen, is punishable as a crime. This factor of knowledge is an important one. If you buy something that is represented as the lawful property of the seller, and have no reason to think it is stolen property, although that is its actual status, you cannot be charged with a crime.

Threatening the life of the President

At common law, a mere threat was not a criminal offense unless it put a reasonable man in fear and unless there was the ability and intent to carry out the threat.

In 1964, after the assassination of President Kennedy, a Federal statute was passed making it a crime to threaten the life of the President. The crime exists even though the President may not even know about the threat, or if the party involved claims he was only joking. "Whoever knowingly and willfully deposits for conveyance in the mail or for delivery from any post office or by any letter carrier any letter, paper, writing, print, missive, or document containing any threat to take the life of or to inflict bodily harm upon the President or knowingly and willfully otherwise makes any such threat against the President shall be fined not more than $1,000 or imprisoned not more than five years or both."

Pierce was a Navy seaman who went AWOL. While in Kansas he got into trouble and was put in jail. He received permission to write to a relative, but instead he wrote to Lyndon Johnson that he would kill the President the first chance he got. He gave the note to a guard. He was tried and convicted under the 1964 statute. He claimed that he was only joking and that the threat was only idle talk, but this carried no weight with the court. The serious thing about such a threat, even when made in an offhand way, is that it may plant the seed of crime in the mind of another who may not take it as a joke.

Extradition

The United States Constitution provides that any person charged in any state with treason, felony, or other crime (and this can include misdemeanors) who shall flee from justice and be found in another state shall, on demand of the executive authority of the state from which he fled, be delivered up to be removed to the state having jurisdiction of the crime. The object of interstate extradition is to prevent the escape of persons accused of a crime and to secure their return to the state from which they fled.

The Uniform Criminal Extradition Act has been adopted in most states, the Virgin Islands and the Panama Canal Zone. Thus far Louisiana, Mississippi, Nevada, North Dakota, South Carolina, and Washington have not adopted the Act. The Act sets up the procedural rules governing the extradition of fugitives and gives the accused certain rights. He may see the legal papers used as the basis for the extradition proceedings. Sometimes innocence of the charge can be of importance in creating public pressure to block the return to the demanding state. Other factors which also may be influential are that the punishment in the demanding state does not fit the crime or that the accused has been rehabilitated.

The Fugitive Felon Act covers the authority of the Federal courts over those fleeing to avoid prosecution for certain crimes. Extradition is not needed in these situations.

International extradition is governed by Federal treaties with foreign nations. You no doubt have read about criminals fleeing to certain countries, such as Brazil, because the United States has no treaty which can assure their return. Sometimes diplomacy will achieve the result.

Compensation for victims of violence

California and New York are the only states in the United States that have, thus far, enacted legislation to assure some compensation to those who have suffered at the hands of criminals. Proposals have been considered in Oregon, Wisconsin, and Maryland. Among all the rest of the countries of the world, only Great Britain and New Zealand have such compensatory laws.

In New York, the state legislature has provided for a Crime Victims' Compensation Board to administer the program of awards to victims and their dependents who may suffer disability, incur financial hardship, or become dependent on public assistance because of crimes. No act involving the operation of a motor vehicle will be considered a crime unless the injury inflicted was done intentionally.

Those eligible for compensatory awards include the victim of the crime, the surviving spouse or children of a dead victim, or any other person dependent upon a dead victim for his principal support. Anyone responsible for the crime, an accomplice, or members of the families of such persons are excluded. Also, no victim who, by his conduct, contributed to the infliction of his own injury may recover.

Because of the importance of this whole process and because the claim form must comply with the board's rules, if you are eligible for an award you should seek counsel at your earliest opportunity. Claims generally must be filed within 90 days after the commission of the crime or 90 days after the death of the victim, although the board may extend the time up to one year. There is a minimum allowable dollar amount for each claim, and the maximum allowance for each award is $15,000.

Each claim is reviewed and investigated, and a hearing is held. Findings must be made that a crime was committed, that personal physical injury or death resulted, that the police records show the crime was reported promptly after it occurred, and that the claimant would suffer serious financial hardship if an award were not made. The decision is sent to the claimant. If he is dissatisfied, he has 30 days to request, in writing, consideration by the full board. Their action is final. The claimant has no right to a review by the courts since all awards are made as a matter of grace by the state.

The awards are not subject to attachment except for expenses resulting from the injury. Awards may be reduced if insurance proceeds or other monies are forthcoming.

The New York law also provides for compensation to persons who have suffered a financial loss because of an attempt, whether or not successful, to prevent a crime or apprehend a criminal. The California law distinguishes between those who are the objects of crime and those who aid in prevention or apprehension of the criminal. Those in the former category must show need before being compensated, but those who assist are indemnified for expenses regardless of financial hardship. The California law also provides that before a victim may be compensated the criminal must be convicted. In New York it does not matter what happens to the criminal. He may even be found not guilty by reason of insanity. The claimant may still be given an award.

Do you have to take the stand?

A person accused of a crime need not take the stand to offer testimony. However, can an inference be drawn from his silence? In 1965, the United States Supreme Court said that the Constitution gives every accused the right to remain silent and no inference of guilt can be raised by the prosecutor because of this silence. At the time this decision was made, five states allowed the prosecutor to comment on the defendant's silence: California, Connecticut, Iowa, Ohio, and New Mexico.

Sometimes, however, a prosecutor can use words which are not a direct comment but are an implied reference. In Florida, a defendant was charged with breaking and entering. He did not testify at his trial. While summing up the case for the state, the prosecutor said that it was uncontroverted that the defendant told a police officer he had committed the crime. This was considered to be an improper reference to the accused's failure to testify. Since the defendant had not testified, it should not have been said that the fact was "uncontroverted."

Beyond a reasonable doubt

In an ordinary civil suit, the person who establishes a preponderance of the evidence wins the case. In a criminal case, for the defendant to be convicted, guilt must be established beyond a reasonable doubt. The presumption of a defendant's innocence in a criminal trial is one of the basic tenets of our law.

Reasonable doubt

In the usual criminal case, the court will charge the jury at the conclusion, after the summation by the defense and the prosecution, that the defendant is presumed to be innocent, and that the presumption of innocence remains unless and until the defendant is proven guilty beyond a reasonable doubt.

The judge will go on to say: "The burden is on the government to prove the defendant guilty beyond a reasonable doubt. This burden of proof never shifts throughout the trial. The law does not require a defendant to prove his innocence or to produce any evidence. Unless the government proves beyond a reasonable doubt that the defendant has committed every element of the offense with which he is charged, you must find him not guilty. Reasonable doubt, as the name implies, is a doubt based on reason, a doubt for which you can give a reason. It is such a doubt as would cause a juror, after careful and candid and impartial consideration of all the evidence, to be so undecided that he cannot say that he has an abiding conviction of the defendant's guilt. However, it is not a fanciful doubt, nor a whimsical doubt, nor a doubt based on conjecture. It is a doubt which is based on reason. The government is not required to establish guilt beyond all doubt, or to a mathematical certainty or a scientific certainty. Its burden is to establish guilt beyond a reasonable doubt."

CHAPTER 26

Sports Law

The issue of baseball's exemption from the operation of the Federal antitrust laws, and the various restrictions in the contracts of professional players, have made the subject of law as applied to sports one of more than general interest.

The Sherman Antitrust Act passed by the Congress in 1890 provided that there can be no contract in restraint of trade affecting interstate commerce. When the question of the restrictive contracts covering baseball players first reached the United States Supreme Court in 1922, it was held that "the business of professional baseball was not within the scope of the Federal antitrust laws because the exhibitions were purely state affairs, were not trade or commerce in the ordinary accepted use of the words, and the interstate transportation of players was merely incidental. . . ." Of course, in this era of broadcasting and the big business of sports, there is no doubt in anybody's mind that interstate commerce is involved. However, the problem has been that the United States Supreme Court felt that if the rule was to be changed for the business of baseball, it would be up to Congress to make the change. This situation was not the case for various other sports, which were held subject to the Sherman Antitrust Act, and so boxing, football, and other sports are not free from the requirements of competition.

Participants in sports and athletic events

A person of sufficient age and understanding who participates in any sport, game, or athletic event, accepts whatever obvious and necessary dangers there are in such an activity. This certainly applies to those who voluntarily participate, such as umpires, referees, and managers. Nonetheless, you do not assume risks which come solely from the negligence of others.

Assault at a sports event

If you are assaulted while at a sports event, you may not be able to recover from the proprieter or promoter for the injury. A woman in Kansas was hurt by an unknown man while she was on her way to the ladies' room after seeing a wrestling match. She claimed she had not been provided with safe premises. The court agreed that one who gathers together a large number of people for profit must be vigilant to protect them, but the care required is what is ordinary or reasonable; and the proprietor could not, therefore, be liable for this irresponsible and unforeseeable act. In another case, in New York, a fight broke out in Yankee Stadium and a fan was hurt. The court said that ordinary rudeness and jostling is characteristic of crowds at sporting events, and you need something more than that to cause a liability.

Even an umpire may not be successful in his suit for assault. In North Carolina, an umpire was on his way to the lockers when he was hit by a fan. It had been a wild game. One team's manager kept going out to shout at the umpire, and the manager was finally ejected from the game. After the game, the fans came onto the field and cursed the umpire, but no one hit him at that time. He was escorted out by a policeman, and then he was injured. He claimed that the manager was responsible, as well as the fan who hit him. He felt the manager had incited the crowd. The court said the manager did not sow the seeds of the disorder, and that he could not be responsible for the actions of unstable people at games.

A decision like that, when brought to his attention, must have made Leo Durocher feel good after all the years he went storming out to take on the umpires!

We have been discussing the question of the liability of the proprietor or promoter or manager. However, of course, the person who actually did the assault would be liable for such action.

Golf One court has said that a golf ball is a dangerous missile and can be more dangerous than firing a gun. But danger notwithstanding, more than 8 million people play this game, which has been around in some form since about A.D. 1400. Golfers, as other sportsmen, must assume the ordinary risks of the game, but they do not assume the risk of another's negligent conduct. One of the rules of golf etiquette is that no player should play until a party in front is out of range. Shouting ''fore,'' however, will not save a golfer from the consequences of his other careless acts.

In a New York case, an 11-year-old was found to have been negligent

when he hit the player ahead with his driven ball. This young man had taken lessons, played regularly, and in fact was playing in adult company at the time of the accident. The court held him to an adult standard of reasonable care. They compared cases involving juveniles driving motorboats, riding watercycles, and operating airplanes. Golf requires skill and involves danger, and infants do not usually partake in such activity, but when one does, he must conform to a level of care.

In another case involving a 14-year-old who was himself injured on a golf driving range, an Iowa court felt the child was not entitled to recover damages. He and a friend had been to the range before. On this day, they were side by side. When some balls spilled over, the 14-year-old bent to get them and was struck by his companion's club. No dangerous condition existed on the range. The accident was caused by a sudden movement and the range management was not held liable.

In a case that went to the highest court in New York, the plaintiff was struck in the eye by the golf ball hit by one of the members of his threesome. The plaintiff had helped the defendant find his ball in the rough to the left of the fairway. He then was walking on the rough between the defendant and the green when the defendant hit the ball without warning and it struck the plaintiff. It was contended that the plaintiff assumed the ordinary risks of the game, including an accident like this. However, the court said the jury was free to find the plaintiff had left a place of safety with the defendant's knowledge in order to help defendant find his ball, and after it was found, was struck without warning when defendant played the recovered ball. The court was in effect sustaining the jury's finding that defendant was negligent and that the plaintiff was not guilty of contributory negligence and had not assumed the risk in this situation.

Wrestling   Like to watch wrestling on TV? It is probably safer than seeing it in person. In Vermont a spectator at ringside was injured when one wrestler threw the other out of the ring into the spectator's lap. The court in that case held that it was not to be expected that a wrestler would throw his opponent out of the ring, and held for the patron. A court in Georgia, however, came to a different conclusion in a somewhat similar situation. In that case the injury was caused by a wrestler diving through the ropes to get away from his opponent. He hurt the timekeeper, whose job required him to be close to the ring. The Georgia court felt that the experienced timekeeper should have known that wrestlers are thrown, pushed, or fall from the ring, and that being within three feet could be dangerous, and he had assumed the risk. He did not recover for his injury.

Softball What happens when you play on a company softball team and you are injured? Are you entitled to collect workmen's compensation for a job-related accident? The general rule seems to be that a) if the injury occurred on your employer's premises, and b) you were on your lunch hour or regular recreation period, and c) your employer either expressly or by implication required participation or attendance at the function; or he derives a substantial benefit from your participation; or it is part of your contract of employment, you will probably get compensation. The recreation cannot be only for your own health or morale, but must be work-related.

In a New Jersey case, a jeweler played softball on his lunch break with other employees on grounds behind his employer's building. When he was injured during a game, the court decided that the accident was work-related. The intershop softball competition was helpful in labor-management relations and was encouraged by the employer, who provided all the sports equipment. In a case in Colorado, however, a member of a gas and electric club recreation association was not given compensation when he was injured during a softball game. The games were held on public grounds after work, and although the company furnished the equipment and uniforms, the court felt the employer did not benefit except indirectly through the good morale of the employees.

Bowling

If you like bowling, you will be interested in two cases which deal with bowling accidents. A woman in Louisiana was acting as a scorekeeper at a bowling tournament for women. She took a coffee break and went to a snack table, which was near a rack where there were spare balls. Just as she was getting up from the table, one of the bowlers came to the rack to test a ball, and as she swung it in her arm, she hit the scorekeeper, who sued the owner claiming that the premises were unsafe. The court said that since there was nothing hidden about the rack, and the plaintiff was familiar with the area and with the fact that bowlers test balls, she had assumed the normal, obvious and ordinary risks of use of the alleys. On the other hand, in Illinois, a male bowler, while attempting to deliver his ball, found his foot stuck to the alley and he was injured. He had been to the men's room and there got some liquid on the bottom of his shoes. The court said that because of the added dangers to bowling patrons from foreign matter on the floors, the alley management should have taken more care to see that the restrooms were kept dry so that liquid would not be brought into the play area.

Roller Rink

These cases show that sometimes an owner or occupier of the premises will be held to a slightly higher standard of care for providing safety in the non-game portions of the play area.

If you are a roller-rink user, you are entitled to have the premises and equipment maintained with care, consistent with the purposes for use. For instance, if you rent skates they should be able to be used safely. In a case in Massachusetts, a 12-year-old girl, the first customer of the day at the rink, rented some skates. They were dirty and the laces had knots from having been broken and retied. She skated around in them for a few hours and then one lace broke, the shoe came loose, and she fell. The court said the condition of the shoes should have been noted by the person in charge, and that the skater was not herself negligent in accepting the skates. In another case, however, a Louisiana court said that the rink was not responsible when a 14-year-old skated out of the skating area. She went toward a tier of seats where her skate caught on a part of the platform and she fell into a plate-glass window behind the seats. The accident was not a foreseeable one. The court said hazards must be reasonably expected or else the owner would be an insurer of everyone's safety.

Tennis and Ping-Pong

In cases involving participants in Ping-Pong and tennis, the courts have relied heavily on two criteria: 1) had an accident occurred before the one in the suit? 2) had the participant been observant? In a New York case, a tennis player was injured when he bumped into a stone wall behind a wire fence on the side of his court. No one had done that in 30 years of playing there. A hotel guest playing in a Ping-Pong tournament had his arm go through a window in the wall behind him. He had played other games, and the court believed he should have been aware of the space limitations despite his concentration on the game.

Basketball

Basketball is considered the sort of game in which bodily contact is expected. It is not intrinsically dangerous, as has been said of soccer, but accidents can happen. A student at Brooklyn College in New York was playing when he and his opponent knocked heads during a jumpshot. It caused his death, but the New York court held that no one could be blamed. The plaintiff's father alleged that the accident was caused by lack of supervision, but the court reasoned that no referee could have prevented the jumpshot, which is part of the game.

Ski lift

In a case in New York, a plaintiff fell from a ski lift while attempting to dismount, breaking her leg. She contended the ski lift was a common carrier, and that she was accordingly owed the duty of highest care. (On the duty of a common carrier generally, see Chapter 24 on automobiles and other vehicles.) She contended that the failure to have an attendant to assist her in getting down from the chair was negligence. The court noted that the chairlift would carry anyone presenting a ticket, and therefore, it could be considered a common carrier. However, the court went on to say that skiing is a dangerous sport, so that if you ride the ski lift up the hill, you should have the same degree of skill for the ride as you propose to employ in skiing down the hill. This means that getting someone to assist you off the chair would make things more difficult, because you would need a clear area in which to land when alighting. Under the circumstances, the carrier was held not liable.

Floodlights

Does your town have night ballgames? One community in New York tried to prevent the use of floodlights on the local ballfield for Little League night games. They claimed it would bring noise and traffic to the local neighborhoods, the glare would attract insects, and the serenity of the area would be lost. The courts did not agree and would not enjoin the use as a public nuisance. The lights would be used only on weeknights during the summer till 9:30 P.M. Games had been held in the park regularly and the lights would only be on for an hour or so after dusk. Night Little League games would not change the character of the neighborhood.

Acceptance. Receiving, with the intention of retaining, something offered by another; the act of accepting an offer which results in a binding contract.

Accessory. One who, though not present at the commission of a crime, becomes guilty as a participant.

Acknowledgment. The declaration by a person of the execution of a written instrument as his voluntary act, made to a public officer, such as a notary public, commissioner of deeds, etc.

Action. A proceeding in a court of justice for the enforcement or protection of a right, the redress or prevention of a wrong, or the punishment of a public offense; a case at law.

Actionable. A term used to describe incidents or circumstances that are grounds for instituting a legal action or lawsuit.

Adjudge. To pass on judicially; to decide, settle, or decree, by court decision; to sentence or condemn.

Administration of estates. The management and settlement of the estate of a deceased person.

Administrator. A person appointed by a probate court to administer the estate of a deceased person.

Adoption. The taking of another's child into one's own family and giving that child all the rights and duties of one's own children.

Adult. One who has attained the age of majority, or full responsibility.

Adultery. Voluntary sexual intercourse of a married person with one other than his or her spouse.

Agent. One authorized to represent and act for another in the transaction or management of some business or affair of his.

Alibi. The fact or statement that one was not at the scene of a crime or other happening when it occurred.

Alien. A person who resides in one country and owes allegiance to another; a person born outside the jurisdiction of the United States who has not been naturalized under the Constitution and laws of this country.

Alimony. Allowance made by order of the court to a woman for her support, out of her husband's property, in an action for divorce, separation, or annulment, payable in periodic installments or a lump sum.

Allegiance. The obligation of fidelity and obedience owed by an individual to the country in which he lives or of which he is a citizen.

Amortization. The payment of an indebtedness by installments, at stated intervals, for a definite time. The term is usually applied to the payment of bonds, stocks, or mortgages.

Annuity. A specific yearly sum paid to a person for life or for a fixed period.

Annulment action. An action to have a marriage declared void or nonexistent; to be distinguished from a divorce action, which is brought to dissolve an existing marriage.

Appeal. The review of a case by a court of superior jurisdiction.

Appellate court. A court having jurisdiction of appeals and reviews.

Apprehension. The seizure, taking, or arrest of a person on a criminal charge. The term is applied exclusively to criminal cases, whereas "arrest" is applied to both criminal and civil proceedings or actions.

Appurtenance. That which belongs to, or is a part of, something else; a barn, for example, is an appurtenance of land.

Arbitration. The investigation and settlement of a matter of contention between opposing parties, by persons or organizations chosen by the parties; government boards also perform this function when the public interest is concerned. The American Arbitration Association is available to act as an impartial administrator for the arbitration of disputes.

Arson. The intentional and malicious burning of a dwelling house or other building, or causing one to be burned.

Assault. An attempt or threat to beat another without touching him; an unlawful offer or attempt with force or violence to commit a bodily hurt upon another.

Assessment. To set a valuation on; the listing and valuation of property and establishment of a rate for the purpose of taxation.

Assets. All the property one possesses that may be made available for the payment of debts.

Assign, Assignee. He who receives property from another by assignment, conveyance, devise, descent, or act of law.

Assignment. The transfer to another of real or personal property.

Assignor. He who makes an assignment to another.

Assured. A person indemnified by an insurance company against the loss described in the policy; the insured.

Attachment. The seizure of property by virtue of judicial order or other process.

Attestation. The act of witnessing the signature of an instrument and subscribing it as a witness at the request of the party executing the instrument.

Award. A judgment, sentence, or final decision.

Bail. The surety or sureties who become responsible for the appearance in court of a person under arrest in return for the release of the prisoner; money pledged for such an appearance.

Bail bond. An obligation signed by the accused with sureties for the performance by the accused of certain acts, generally for his appearance at court at a required time.

Bailment. The delivery of goods by one person to another for an agreed purpose and to be ultimately redelivered to the owner.

Bankruptcy. Proceedings taken under the bankruptcy statute to have the assets of the bankrupt divided among his creditors.

Bastard. A child born of unlawful intercourse before the lawful marriage of its parents; a child born out of wedlock.

Battery. Any unlawful physical injury inflicted on a person without his consent.

Bench warrant. Process issued by the court or "from the bench" for the arrest of the person named in the warrant.

Beneficiary. One receiving or to receive the benefits, profits, advantages or enjoyments of property by inheritance or under a trust; the person to whom the proceeds of insurance are payable.

Bequeath. To give personal property to another by will; distinguished from *devise,* which relates to real property.

Bequest. A gift of personal property by will.

Bigamy. The criminal offense of contracting and going through the form of a second marriage while the first marriage still exists.

Blue ribbon jury. A jury chosen for its outstanding qualifications, and used to consider cases of special importance.

Bona fide. Honestly, openly and sincerely; without deceit or fraud.

Bona fide holder for value. One who takes a negotiable instrument in good faith for a valuable consideration in the ordinary course of business before it is due.

Bona fide purchaser. One who buys for a valuable consideration with the belief that the seller has a right to sell and with no knowledge of any impediments to the transfer.

Bookmaking. The recording or registering of bets or wagers.

Bottomry. The contract under which a ship owner borrows money for the use or repair of a vessel.

Breach of promise. Chiefly used to indicate "breach of promise of marriage," or failing to keep one's promise to marry someone.

Breach of the peace. The breaking or disturbing of the public peace by riot or other unlawful action.

Bribery. A payment made to a person to influence his behavior and incline him to act contrary to his duty.

Broker. One whose business is to negotiate purchases and sales.

Capital. The money and other property owned by a person or corporation, used in business.

Capital stock. The sum of money raised by the subscriptions of stockholders and divided into shares.

Carrier. A person or corporation that undertakes to transport persons or property from one place to another by means of a conveyance.

Case. A general term for actions or suits at law or in equity.

Casualty. Accident.

Cause of action. The ground on which a lawsuit can be sustained.

Caveat emptor. Literally, "Let the buyer beware"; a Latin phrase used in the law to indicate that it is the buyer's responsibility to examine, judge, test, and otherwise inspect the article by himself—he is buying at his own risk.

Cestui que trust. He who has a right to and a beneficial interest in an estate of which the legal title is in another.

Chattel mortgage. An instrument giving a lien on personal property as security for a debt or the performance of an obligation.

Chattels. Articles of personal property; property that is not land; goods.

Circumstantial evidence. Facts that establish a condition, or circumstances from which the principal fact is a possible conclusion. Proof of the motive for murder by the accused, with the additional proof of his ownership of the weapon and a failure to account for his whereabouts at the time of the crime, is circumstantial evidence of guilt.

Citation. A writ commanding a person to appear before a named judicial tribunal or officer on a day named.

Citizen. One who under the Constitution and laws of the United States by virtue of birth or naturalization owes allegiance to this country and is entitled to the enjoyment of full civil rights in the United States.

Civil rights. Rights of a nonpolitical kind, secured to citizens by the Thirteenth and Fourteenth amendments to the Constitution of the United States or by various state or Federal statutes.

Cohabitation. Living together in the relationship of husband and wife; sexual intercourse.

Collusion. A secret combination, conspiracy, or concerted action between two or more persons for fraudulent, deceitful, or unlawful purposes.

Color of office. The claim or assumption of the right to do an act by virtue of an office.

Co-maker. A person who signs or endorses the promissory note of another before delivery of the note to the payee.

Committee of incompetent. Person or persons invested by order of court with the guardianship of the person or estate of one adjudged an incompetent or lunatic.

Common law. The principles of law derived from the ancient law of England embodied in court decisions; distinguished from statutory law (enacted by the Congress or the state legislatures) and civil law (the law of countries following the Roman or Napoleonic codes, such as we have in the State of Louisiana).

Common-law marriage. A marriage without ceremony created by an agreement between the parties and followed by cohabitation.

Community property. Property owned in common by husband and wife. In community-property-law states, property so owned because acquired by either spouse during marriage.

Complainant. One who applies to the courts for legal redress.

Compromise. An arrangement made either in or out of court for the settlement of a dispute.

Concubinage. The act or practice of cohabiting without the sanction of the law or of a legal marriage.

Consanguinity. The relation of persons descended from a common ancestor; blood relationship; kinship.

Constructive. That which is inferred by legal interpretation; that which has not in its own nature the character assigned to it, but acquires such character as a consequence of the way it is regarded in the law.

Contempt. A willful disregard of the authority of a court of justice or legislative body, or disobedience to its lawful orders.

Contract. A promissory agreement between two or more persons that creates, modifies, or ends a legal relation; an agreement creating legal rights enforceable by action.

Contributory negligence. The negligent act of a person claiming damages for injury from negligence of another; this negligent act must also be a genuine contributory cause without which the injury would not have occurred; negligence contributing to cause the accident.

Conversion. An unauthorized assumption and exercise of the right of ownership over another's goods.

Convert. To assume or exercise the right of ownership over another's goods without authorization.

Conveyance. The transfer of title to land; a deed.

Conviction. The verdict by a jury of guilty or the final judgment of a court of the criminal guilt of the accused.

Covenant. An agreement by deed, in writing, by which either party pledges himself to the other that something is or will be done, or not done, or stipulates the truth of certain facts.

Coverture. The legal condition or state of a married woman at common law.

Creditor. A person to whom a debt is owed by another person, who is called a debtor.

Crime. An act violating the sanctions of the criminal law, for which the law provides the offender shall make satisfaction to the state by undergoing punishment.

Curtesy. Under common law the life interest a man has at the death of his wife in her real property, when children of the marriage inherit the fee title.

Damages. The money compensation which is recovered in the courts by a person who has suffered a loss, detriment, or injury through the unlawful act of another.

Debtor. A person who owes money.

Decision. The judgment or decree of a court.

Deed. A written instrument by which one person conveys land to another.

Deed poll. A deed which is made by only one person.

Defamation. The offense of injuring a person's character or reputation by false statements.

Defendant. The person against whom an action is brought.

Deportation. The sending back of an alien to the country from which he came.

Descendant. One who is descended from another; a child, grandchild, etc.

Descent. Succession to the ownership of property by inheritance.

Devise. A disposition of land by will. See *bequeath*.

Disability. The lack of legal capacity to perform an act.

Discharge in bankruptcy. The release of the bankrupt from the obligations of his debts which were, or might have been, proved in the bankruptcy proceedings.

Disorderly conduct. Any behavior contrary to law, but, more particularly, conduct that tends to disturb the peace or shock the public sense of morality.

Domicile. The true, fixed, and permanent home or residence of a person.

Donee. One to whom property is given.

Donor. The giver of property.

Double indemnity. The provision in an insurance policy that under certain conditions the insurance company will pay to the beneficiary under the policy twice the face amount of the policy.

Dower. The widow's life interest in land her husband owned when he died.

Due process of law. The law in its regular course of administration through the courts of justice.

Easement. A liberty, right to use, or privilege of access which one person may acquire in relation to the land of another.

Eminent domain. The power of the state to take private property for public use, providing a reasonable compensation.

Encumbrance. A claim or lien attached to and binding on real or personal property.

Endorse (also *indorse*). To write your name on the back of a paper or document; the act of a payee, drawee, or holder of a bill, note, check, or other negotiable instrument in writing his name on the back whereby the property in such instrument is assigned and transferred to another.

Equity. The system of legal rules and principles used in certain areas of jurisdiction not adequately covered by statute and common law; derived from ecclesiastical law to have a fair rather than technical approach to legal matters. "Equity" can also refer to a share or interest in property.

Escrow. Money, property, or a document held by a third person for delivery to the grantee upon the occurrence or performance of certain conditions; title does not pass until the conditions are fulfilled, but the grantor no longer controls the escrow.

Evict. To dispossess or turn out of possession of land or home by process of law.

Execution. A writ issued to a sheriff or other law enforcement officer requiring the execution of a judgment of the court.

Executor. A person appointed by a will to administer the will of a deceased person.

Exemplary damages. Damages increased by reason of the aggravation of a wrong by violence, fraud, or malice; punitive damages not limited to actual damages suffered.

Expatriation. The voluntary act of abandoning one's country.

Extradition. The surrender of a criminal, by a foreign state to which he has fled, to the state in which the crime was committed, on the demand of the latter state; legal proceedings to obtain this surrender.

False imprisonment. The unlawful arrest or detention of a person whereby he is deprived of his liberty.

False pretenses. False representations and statements made with the design of obtaining something of value, with intent to cheat.

False representation. An untrue representation willfully made to deceive another to his loss.

Family purpose. The doctrine that the owner of an automobile is liable for damages resulting from the negligent operation of his automobile by members of his family whom he has permitted to use it.

Fee simple. The absolute ownership of land with the unrestricted power of sale or other disposition.

Felony. A crime of a graver nature than a misdemeanor, and more seriously punished.

Fiduciary. A person invested with rights and powers to be used for the benefit of another.

Fixtures. Chattels or goods that, by being annexed to land or attached to a building, become in law a part of it and belong to the owner of the land.

Foreclosure. The court proceedings for the sale of mortgaged land or personal property for the payment of the mortgage, and the disposal of the mortgagor's right to redeem.

Forgery. Falsely making or materially altering any writing with intent to defraud.

Fornication. Sexual intercourse by persons unmarried to each other.

Fourteenth Amendment. An amendment to the Constitution of the United States that became law July 28, 1868. It forbids the making or enforcement by any state of any law abridging the privileges and immunities of citizens of the United States. It secures all persons against any state action by which they may be deprived of life, liberty, or property without due process of law or a denial of the equal protection of the law. This is also known as the "due process" amendment.

Fraud. The deceitful practice or device used to deprive another of his rights or to effect an injury.

Frauds, Statute of. An ancient statute, still in current use, that, among other features, provides that no suit can be maintained on certain contracts unless a note or memorandum in writing has been made and signed by the person sought to be held to the agreement.

Garnishment. A notice to a person holding another's property (for example, a bank account) to give the court an accounting of it and not to yield it to the one who holds title to it; a notice to present oneself in court.

Grantee. The person to whom a grant is made.

Grantor. The person by whom a grant is made.

Guaranty. A warranty, given by a third party, of the payment of a debt or other obligation or of the performance of some act.

Guardian. A person invested with the power to, and charged with the duty of, taking care of the person and property of another, usually a minor.

Habeas corpus. A writ or order commanding the person detaining another (generally an officer of the law) to produce him and submit to a decision on the legality of the detention by the court or judge granting the writ of habeas corpus.

Heir. One who inherits property, either real or personal.

Hereditaments. Things capable of being inherited.

Hold over. To retain possession as tenant of leased property after the expiration of the lease.

Holographic will. A will written by its maker (the testator) entirely in his own handwriting.

Homestead. The home, the house, and adjacent land where the head of the family dwells.

Homicide. The killing of one person by another.

Hypothecate. To pledge a thing, generally as security for a loan, without delivering possession to the pledgee or maker of the loan.

Illegitimate. That which is contrary to law, usually applied to bastards or children born out of lawful wedlock.

Impounded. To shut up stray animals or distrain goods in a pound; to seize and hold a fund of money or goods by legal process.

Incompetency. The legal status of a person unable or unfitted to manage his own affairs by reason of insanity, imbecility, or feeblemindedness.

Indemnify. To secure against loss or damage; to make reimbursement to one for a loss already suffered.

Indenture. A deed to which two or more persons are parties, entering into mutual grants and obligations.

Indictment. An accusation in writing, based on the findings of a grand jury, charging that the person named has been guilty of a punishable crime.

Infancy. The state of a person under the age of legal majority; minority.

Indorse (see endorse).

Infancy. The state of a person under the age of legal majority; minority.

Injunction. A writ or order requiring a person to refrain from, or to do, a particular act.

Instrument. A written document; a formal or legal document in writing.

Insurable interest. An interest in property or a person's life or health that the beneficiary must have if an insurance policy is to be issued. An insurable interest exists, by and large, if the beneficiary has a serious stake in the life of the person or the safety of the property insured.

Interstate commerce. Traffic, trade, or transportation of persons or property between the states of the United States.

Intestate. Said of one who dies without leaving a will.

Judgment. The decision of a court of justice.

Jurisdiction. The power and authority of a judge or magistrate to determine legal causes and carry his determinations into execution; the extent of a court's, state's, country's, or other governmental unit's authority.

Larceny. The wrongful taking and carrying away of the personal goods of another; theft, stealing.

Lawsuit. A suit, action, proceeding, or controversy between two or more persons in a court of law.

Legacy. A gift of personal property by a will.

Levy. The seizure of property by a sheriff, marshal, or other court officer under an execution or attachment.

Libel. Published written or printed matter, or signs, pictures, or other representations calculated to injure the character or reputation of a person by bringing him into ridicule, hatred or contempt. Civil libel is a libel for which damage may be collected. Criminal libel—libel punishable as a crime—is that which tends to excite a breach of peace.

License. Permission to do some act that without such authority or permission would be illegal.

Lien. The claim of one person on the property of another as security for a sum due.

L.S. The abbreviation for the Latin *locus sigilli,* the place occupied by the seal on a written instrument, as the seal of a public officer, such as a notary. Private persons seldom use a seal nowadays, though legal documents often provide a place for one.

Mandatory. Said of a court order or statute which must be obeyed.

Material. Having bearing on the subject at issue; important, as in the phrase "a material witness."

Mechanic's lien. A lien created by statute in most states in favor of persons who have performed work or furnished material used in the construction of a house or other construction work.

Minority. Infancy; under legal age.

Misdemeanor. A crime that is of a less degree than a felony and distinguished from one by not being punishable by death or imprisonment in a penitentiary.

Mortgage. A pledge of particular property to secure the payment of a debt or the performance of an obligation.

Mortgagee. A person who lends money on a property and receives a mortgage on it in exchange.

Mortgagor. He who gives a mortgage; the owner of mortgaged property.

Naturalization. The act of adopting an alien into a nation as a citizen and giving him the rights of a natural-born citizen.

Negotiable Instrument. A bill of exchange, promissory note, check, or other security, which may be transferred by endorsement and delivery, or only by delivery, so as to give to the endorsee or recipient a legal title and thus enable him to collect pursuant to the terms of the written instrument, or to sue thereon in his own name. A negotiable instrument carries its legal title to the next person by endorsement or delivery, and when transferred before maturity, the transferee has the right to demand the full amount which the face of the instrument calls for. Under the Uniform Negotiable Instruments Act, an instrument to be negotiable must be in writing and signed and contain an unconditional provision or order to pay a certain sum of money on demand or at a fixed or determinable future time; it must be payable to the bearer or to the order of someone.

Nuncupative will. An oral will or will made by a word-of-mouth declaration.

Pawn. Goods entrusted to a creditor as security for a loan, a pledge, or hypothecation.

Pawnbroker. A person whose business is the loaning of money on the security of personal property deposited in pawn with him.

Pawnee. A person to whom goods are delivered by another in exchange for a loan.

Pawnor. A person who pawns goods.

Per capita. By heads, that is, by individuals. Persons taking equal shares each in his own right in the distribution of decedent's estate, in contradistinction to a share for an entire class, which is termed *per stirpes.*

Per stirpes. Taking property by right of representation is called "succession per stirpes," in opposition to taking in one's own right or as a principal, which is termed *per capita*; distribution of shares by classes of kindred relations.

Plaintiff. A person who brings an action.

Pledge. The deposit of goods with a creditor as security for a debt or obligation; hypothecation.

Posthumous. After death; a term used to describe a child born after the death of his father or (by means of a cesarian operation) after the death of the mother.

Power of attorney. An instrument authorizing another to act as one's agent or attorney.

Presumption. A particular inference that is drawn from particular evidence or a state of facts unless and until the contrary of such an inference is proved—for example, a man is presumed to be innocent until proved guilty.

Primogeniture. In ancient law, the supreme or exclusive right possessed by the eldest son to succeed to the entire land of his father to the exclusion of the younger sons.

Principal. The person who constitutes and gives authority to an agent to do some act for him; the person for whom an agent acts.

Probate. The judicial determination which establishes the validity of a will.

Proceeding. Any application to a court for aid in the enforcement of rights, the redress of injuries or other remedial relief; a litigation.

Process. The writ by which a court compels compliance with its demands.

Prosecution. A criminal proceeding for the purpose of determining the guilt or innocence of the person charged with a crime.

Proxy. A person acting as the deputy or agent of another, generally at some meeting; also the instrument by which the person is appointed to act as the deputy for another.

Punitive damages. Damages intended to punish a wrongdoer for violence, fraud, or malice, rather than simply to compensate the victim.

Purchase money mortgage. A mortgage given to secure the unpaid balance of the purchase price on the conveyance of land.

Putative father. The alleged or reputed father of an illegitimate child.

Quiet enjoyment. A covenant or agreement contained in deeds or leases that the grantee or tenant will be permitted to enjoy the premises in peace and without disturbance by the grantor or landlord.

Quitclaim deed. A deed that passes any title, interest, or claim which the grantor has in the property, but contains no warranty of title or representation that the title is valid.

Realty. Land, as distinguished from personal property.

Rebuttable presumption. A legal presumption that may be disproved by evidence.

Remise. To remit or give up.

Representation. The principle by which the descendants of a deceased person inherit the share of an estate which he would have inherited if living; the taking or inheritance *per stirpes*.

Res ipsa loquitur. It literally means "the thing speaks for itself." In law, it means that the accident is one that would not have happened in the normal course unless there were negligence, and so the reasonable inference can be made that there was negligence, that the negligence caused the accident, and that it was the defendant's fault. Of course, this inference can only be made where the instrumentality causing the accident was in the exclusive control of the defendant.

Residence. A fixed or permanent home or dwelling place.

Revocation. A recall of some power, authority, or thing granted.

Right of action. The right to bring suit.

Right of redemption. The right to free property from a claim or lien by payment of what is due with interest, etc.

Search warrant. An order issued by a judge directed to a sheriff or other peace officer to search specific premises.

Second mortgage. The second lien on property.

Slander. Oral defamation within the hearing of a third party; speaking false words about another person in public, by which his reputation is or may be injured.

Statute. An enactment of the legislature.

Stipulaton. A material provision in an agreement; an agreement between attorneys in the conduct of litigation.

Sublease. A lease by a tenant to another person.

Subpoena. A writ requiring one's attendance as a witness.

Subpoena duces tecum. A subpoena requiring a witness to bring with him books or documents in his possession.

Subtenant. An undertenant; one who leases premises from a tenant.

Sufferance. Negative permission by not forbidding; passive consent; a license implied from the omission or neglect to enforce an adverse right.

Summation. In a jury trial, counsel for both sides summarize the evidence already presented to the jury in order to draw its attention to the outstanding points in favor of the side summing up.

Summons. A notice to a person that an action has been commenced in court against him.

Surety. A person who binds himself for the payment of a sum of money or for the performance of some act by another.

Surrender. A yielding up of an estate by which the lesser estate is merged in the greater by mutual consent; for example, the surrender of a lease to a landlord.

Tenancy at will. The occupation of realty by a person without a lease or after the termination of a lease with neither the agreement nor disagreement of the person in whom is the right of possession; a tenancy ended at the will of either landlord or tenant.

Testamentary. Pertaining to a will.

Testator. One who makes a will.

Things in action. Claims with a money value; judicial proceedings to recover money or personal property.

Title. Ownership; the grounds by which the owner of property has a just possession; a person's right to property.

Tort. A legal wrong committed on a person or property.

Treasure trove. Money, gold, silver, or bullion found hidden, and the owner of which is unknown.

Trespass. An entry on the ground of another without lawful authority.

True bill. The endorsement made by a grand jury on a bill of indictment when it is satisfied with the truth of the accusations.

Trust. A holding of another person's property subject to a duty of employing it according to directions of the person from whom it was derived.

Trustee. A person appointed to execute a trust.

Usury. Interest paid for borrowing of money beyond the maximum rate permitted by law.

Verdict. The decision of a jury after the trial of a case.

Visa. An endorsement on a passport by proper authorities permitting the person who bears it to enter a particular country.

Void. Having no legal force or binding effect.

Waiver. Relinquishment of a known right.

Ward. A person placed by authority of law under the care of a guardian.

Warranty. A representation or promise in a contract.

Will. A legal declaration or testament of a person's wishes for the disposition of his property after death.

Index

ALICE K. HELM, L.L.B. and J.D., was born on December 24, 1927, in New York City. She was educated in the New York City public school system and went on to graduate *cum laude* from the School of Business at the City College of New York, receiving the degree Bachelor of Business Administration.

Mrs. Helm received her law degree from Columbia University in 1950. At Columbia she received the Burkhan Copyright Award and was an editor of the Columbia Law School Yearbook. She also attended the American University, Washington, D.C., taking graduate courses in the School of Education.

For over 17 years she has been in the federal legal service, serving with the Departments of Justice, and Health, Education and Welfare, and as a Deputy Assistant General Counsel with the Department of Commerce. She served as chairman of the Juvenile Delinquency Committee of the Federal Bar Association, and through that association has engaged in volunteer legal work.

Mrs. Helm is a member of both the Bar of the State of New York and the Bar of the District of Columbia. She has been admitted to practice before the United States Supreme Court.

KENNETH BIRNBAUM is a native of New York City. He received his law degree from Columbia University, where he served as an editor of the Law School's Journal of Transnational Law. He has also received the degree of Master of Business Administration from Columbia University.

Mr. Birnbaum has served as a researcher for the Walker Commission, which investigated the demonstrations at the 1968 Chicago Democratic Convention, and has been a member of the legal staff of the Office of Economic Opportunity. He has served as a volunteer attorney for the American Civil Liberties Union and has worked with the New York City Addiction Services Agency.

ALLEN H. BRILL is a practicing attorney associated with the New York City law firm of Marshall, Bratter, Greene, Allison & Tucker. He received his law degree in 1968 from Columbia University Law School and a master's degree in business administration from Columbia in 1969.

At Columbia Law School, Mr. Brill was Chairman of the Moot Court Committee and a researcher for a book on business law, *Law in a Business Environment*.